United States Law and Policy
on Transitional Justice

"Why does the United States not consistently embrace prosecution for mass atrocities committed abroad? Dr. Zachary Kaufman has made a seminal contribution to this topic with this superbly well-documented and argued book. He improves our understanding of transitional justice, international governance, and U.S. foreign policy. The 2010 and 2015 U.S. National Security Strategies state that preventing mass atrocities is a responsibility that all nations share. Following in Kaufman's footsteps, we should seek to understand the transitional justice policies of China, India, Russia, and the one hundred liberal states parties to the International Criminal Court."
The Honorable Luis Moreno-Ocampo, first Chief Prosecutor, International Criminal Court; Senior Fellow, Jackson Institute for Global Affairs, Yale University

"Dr. Zachary Kaufman is at the forefront of the transitional justice movement in the international sphere. His scholarship, his work experience with the U.S. government and three war crimes tribunals, and his personal philanthropy in Rwanda and elsewhere inform his new book, taking it out of the ivory tower and into the human and institutional wreckage left by crimes against humanity."
Peter H. Schuck, Simeon E. Baldwin Professor Emeritus of Law, Yale Law School

"*United States Law and Policy on Transitional Justice* is a thought provoking study of postwar U.S. foreign policy concerning transitional justice, useful for students of diplomatic history, international law, and international relations alike. Dr. Zachary Kaufman examines U.S. support for international criminal tribunals and other transitional justice options to address atrocities abroad in the aftermath of World War II and the Cold War, arguing that U.S. policy is best explained by 'prudential factors' that mix law, pragmatism, and politics."
Dr. David W. Kennedy, Manley O. Hudson Professor of Law and Faculty Director, Institute for Global Law and Policy, Harvard Law School

"Dr. Zachary Kaufman's book makes an important contribution to our understanding of the how's and why's of America's transitional justice policies. His 'prudentialism' account of the making of U.S. transitional justice policies is deftly executed, backed up by substantial primary sources, and, ultimately, persuasive. A superb achievement."
Dr. Yuen Foong Khong, Li Ka Shing Professor of Political Science, Lee Kuan Yew School of Public Policy, National University of Singapore; former Professor of International Relations and Professorial Fellow of Nuffield College, University of Oxford

"In *United States Law and Policy on Transitional Justice*, Dr. Zachary Kaufman offers a historically-rich and nuanced account of how the U.S. government has addressed perpetrators of the most serious international crimes from 1945 up to the present day. He reminds us that the prosecution of alleged perpetrators has not always been the first or only preference of the U.S., and that its behavior has been shaped less by a principled commitment to the rule of law, and more by a case-specific balancing of normative beliefs on the one hand, and pragmatic and political considerations on the other. The result has been an inconsistent pattern of transitional justice responses that combines prosecution with amnesty, and unilateral with multilateral action. At a time when both international organizations and national governments are trying to bring perpetrators of atrocity crimes to justice, and when the project of international criminal justice itself is under scrutiny, this book is an important resource for understanding the motivations and track record of U.S. law and policy."
Dr. Jennifer M. Welsh, Professor and Chair in International Relations, European University Institute; Senior Research Fellow, Somerville College, University of Oxford; Special Adviser to the UN Secretary-General on the Responsibility to Protect

"Illuminating and trenchant, Dr. Zachary Kaufman's book takes us behind the scenes and sheds needed light on the high stakes policymaking guiding the U.S. role in transitional justice and humanitarian intervention."
Ruti G. Teitel, Ernst C. Stiefel Chair of Comparative Law, New York Law School; author, *Transitional Justice* and *Globalizing Transitional Justice*

"Dr. Zachary Kaufman's original research and first-rate analysis deepen our understanding of the role played by the United States in establishing international criminal tribunals. His book casts new light on the interplay of politics, pragmatism, and the declared support for international norms in making the policy decisions to submit alleged perpetrators 'to the judgment of the law.'"
The Honorable Stephen J. Rapp, former Chief of Prosecutions, UN International Criminal Tribunal for Rwanda; former Chief Prosecutor, Special Court for Sierra Leone; former U.S. Ambassador-at-Large for Global Criminal Justice

"This important, original, and unique contribution to the literature on transitional justice examines one of its foremost practitioners, the United States, starting with the post-Second World War context in Germany and Japan to the challenges of Yugoslavia, Rwanda, and the modern day. Profound new insights, of relevance to many parts of the world, emerge from such a compelling comparative approach."
Dr. William A. Schabas, Professor of Human Rights and International Criminal Law, University of Leiden; author, *The International Criminal Court: A Commentary on the Rome Statute* and *Unimaginable Atrocities: Justice, Politics, and Rights at the War Crimes Tribunals*; former Commissioner, Sierra Leone Truth and Reconciliation Commission

"In a world of recurrent barbarism, should perpetrators of atrocities be held accountable and, if so, how should they be brought to justice? In this thoughtful and impressively researched volume, Dr. Zachary Kaufman explores how American policymakers have sought to grapple with this vexing question. Kaufman provides a comprehensive analysis of transitional justice options and detailed analysis of six major cases, showing how politics and practical factors have shaped the impact of normative and legal considerations in American policy on transitional justice. This is an important argument, well made."
Dr. Steven E. Miller, Director, International Security Program, Belfer Center for Science and International Affairs, John F. Kennedy School of Government, Harvard University; Editor-in-Chief, *International Security*

"In a world that has accepted international criminal justice as law's predominant response to mass atrocity, Dr. Zachary Kaufman presents a valuable realist perspective on the factors, political and pragmatic, that influence state choices to pursue justice, via prosecutions, for the gravest episodes of abuse. Through succinct but well-documented and revealing accounts of U.S. decisions to support the key specialized international tribunals since World War II, this book analyzes considerations that affected those decisions and their inconsistencies and contradictions."
James J. Silk, Clinical Professor of Law and Director, Orville H. Schell, Jr. Center for International Human Rights, Yale Law School

"*United States Law and Policy on Transitional Justice: Principles, Politics, and Pragmatics* offers a magnificent and detailed examination of the domestic and international politics of international criminal tribunals, from Nuremberg and Tokyo to Arusha and The Hague. Dr. Zachary Kaufman shows that not only does the study of such tribunals and other transitional justice mechanisms belong in the realm of international relations, but it can also inform international relations theory itself."
Dr. David J. Simon, Director, Genocide Studies Program, and Lecturer, Department of Political Science, Yale University

"An important contribution to our understanding of the politics of international criminal justice. Dr. Zachary Kaufman emphasizes the calculations that American leaders made about the costs and benefits of backing war crime tribunals in the aftermath of the Second World War. These same cost-benefit calculations have continued to shape America's choices in this increasingly prominent foreign policy domain."
Dr. Leslie Vinjamuri, Co-Director, Centre for the International Politics of Conflict, Rights and Justice, and Associate Professor in International Relations, School of Oriental and African Studies, University of London

"Dr. Zachary Kaufman has provided an intricate examination of attempts to restore the rule of law after war and regime collapse. Selectivity of prosecutions, the loss of interest by sponsoring states, and the stubbornness of regime habits are all part of the problem that Dr. Kaufman tackles, in the hope of doing it better next time around."
Ruth Wedgwood, Edward B. Burling Professor of International Law and Diplomacy, School of Advanced International Studies, Johns Hopkins University; President, International Law Association; former U.S. member, United Nations Human Rights Committee

"Dr. Zachary Kaufman's excellent book highlights the United States' complicated role in legal approaches to transitional justice since the Second World War. While the United States has refused to sign the Rome Statute of the International Criminal Court, it has consistently supported—and often catalyzed—international justice efforts across the globe. The six cases in this book draw on unprecedented interviews with elite actors and documents unearthed through Freedom of Information Act requests. These materials highlight not only the profound influence of the United States in prosecuting atrocity perpetrators but also the impact of international justice on U.S. policymaking and practice. This book is a must-read for anyone who wants to understand why international criminal law persists today as a central component of transitional justice, despite major setbacks since Nuremberg and Tokyo, and the key role of the United States in encouraging international trials."
Dr. Phil Clark, Reader in Comparative and International Politics, School of Oriental and African Studies, University of London; co-founder, Oxford Transitional Justice Research, University of Oxford

"Dr. Zachary Kaufman pierces the legalist bubble that has dominated our understanding of U.S involvement in transitional justice globally. Highlighting the extensive deliberations about other options, like extrajudicial killings, and emphasizing the undeniably political factors driving pragmatic policymakers, Kaufman challenges those who would suggest that a normative commitment to justice was the defining factor in the American response to atrocities."
Akshaya Kumar, Deputy United Nations Director, Human Rights Watch

United States Law and Policy on Transitional Justice

PRINCIPLES, POLITICS, AND PRAGMATICS

Zachary D. Kaufman

OXFORD
UNIVERSITY PRESS

OXFORD
UNIVERSITY PRESS

Oxford University Press is a department of the University of Oxford. It furthers the University's objective of excellence in research, scholarship, and education by publishing worldwide.

Oxford   New York

Auckland   Cape Town   Dar es Salaam   Hong Kong   Karachi   Kuala Lumpur   Madrid
Melbourne   Mexico City   Nairobi   New Delhi   Shanghai   Taipei   Toronto

With offices in

Argentina   Austria   Brazil   Chile   Czech Republic   France   Greece   Guatemala   Hungary
Italy   Japan   Poland   Portugal   Singapore   South Korea   Switzerland   Thailand
Turkey   Ukraine   Vietnam

Oxford is a registered trademark of Oxford University Press in the UK and certain other countries.

Published in the United States of America by
Oxford University Press
198 Madison Avenue, New York, NY 10016

© Oxford University Press 2016

Library of Congress Cataloging-in-Publication Data
Names: Kaufman, Zachary D. (Zachary Daniel), 1979- author.
Title: United States law and policy on transitional justice : principles, politics, and pragmatics / Zachary D. Kaufman.
Description: New York : Oxford University Press, 2016. | Includes bibliographical references and index.
Identifiers: LCCN 2015032004 | ISBN 9780190243494 ((hardback) : alk. paper)
Subjects: LCSH: Transitional justice—Government policy—United States. | International criminal courts. | Transitional justice. | War crime trials. | Transitional justice—United States. | United States—Foreign relations.
Classification: LCC KF9390 .K38 2016 | DDC 345.73/0231—dc23 LC record available at http://lccn.loc.gov/2015032004

1 3 5 7 9 8 6 4 2

Printed in the United States of America on acid-free paper

Note to Readers

This publication is designed to provide accurate and authoritative information in regard to the subject matter covered. It is based upon sources believed to be accurate and reliable and is intended to be current as of the time it was written. It is sold with the understanding that the publisher is not engaged in rendering legal, accounting, or other professional services. If legal advice or other expert assistance is required, the services of a competent professional person should be sought. Also, to confirm that the information has not been affected or changed by recent developments, traditional legal research techniques should be used, including checking primary sources where appropriate.

(Based on the Declaration of Principles jointly adopted by a Committee of the American Bar Association and a Committee of Publishers and Associations.)

This book is dedicated to the victims of atrocities (including my relatives) committed by Nazi Germany and Imperial Japan during World War II; in the Balkans, Rwanda, Iraq, and Kuwait in the 1990s; and in numerous other places before and since. We will always remember you. This book is also dedicated to survivors of atrocities, who inspire us with your strength, courage, and hope. Finally, this book is dedicated to my brilliant and wonderful wife, Elizabeth, who also provides me with strength, courage, and hope.

{ CONTENTS }

{ LIST OF FIGURES AND TABLES }

{ ACKNOWLEDGMENTS }

This book is adapted from my dissertation in the DPhil (PhD) program in International Relations at the University of Oxford. An earlier version of Chapter II was published by invitation in the inaugural issue (2005) of the *St. Antony's International Review*, the University of Oxford's journal of international relations; an earlier version of Chapter V was published by invitation in volume 27 (2013) of the *Emory International Law Review*; and an earlier version of Chapter VII appeared in *After Genocide: Transitional Justice, Post-conflict Reconstruction, and Reconciliation in Rwanda and Beyond*, which was originally co-published in 2009 by Columbia University Press and C. Hurst & Co. and was republished in 2013 by Oxford University Press. Professor Phil Clark—my graduate school classmate, friend, and frequent collaborator—and I co-edited that book. I have greatly valued and benefited from our regular conversations about and work together on transitional justice issues. This book undoubtedly has been shaped by those long talks, often while drinking Mutzig while looking out at banana trees atop the verdant hills of bucolic Rwanda.

The research and reflection represented in this book began before I even started graduate school in 2002 and involved many more people and experiences than I could enumerate. I will endeavor here to note some of the most important, and I apologize in advance for any omissions, which are unintentional. Given that my preparation of this book spanned more than a decade (during which I took many detours, including to attend law school and practice law), the number of individuals and institutions I am compelled to thank is quite large.

First and foremost, I thank my primary academic supervisor at Oxford, Professor Jennifer Welsh (Professor in International Relations at the University of Oxford, currently on leave to serve as the Special Adviser to the UN Secretary General on the Responsibility to Protect; Professor and Chair in International Relations at the European University Institute; and Senior Research Fellow at Somerville College, University of Oxford), who guided me through all phases of the research and writing of the dissertation I adapted into this book. Professor Welsh provided extensive oral and written comments on earlier drafts of that dissertation. I am greatly indebted to her for her patience, kindness, encouragement, and brilliance, and for inspiring me as a role model in my academic, professional, and personal growth.

I also wish to thank my other, temporary academic supervisor at Oxford, Professor Henry Shue. Professor Shue provided critical advice and guided my literature review on the history of the Rwandan genocide, a tragedy upon which he has reflected greatly and from which he has drawn valuable lessons about ethics in international relations.

Thank you to the examiners of my dissertation. My examiner from within Oxford was Professor Yuen Foong Khong, and my examiner from outside Oxford was Professor William Schabas. Thank you to both Professor Khong and Professor Schabas for all of the time and thought they invested into reviewing the written dissertation, conducting my oral examination of it, and providing extensive feedback.

In addition to Professors Khong, Shue, and Welsh, other Oxford faculty members have also been very supportive and helpful. In particular I thank the leaders of my section of the MPhil thesis seminar, Professor Kalypso Nicolaïdis and Professor Ulrich Krotz, who led a critical discussion of my thesis research at an early stage; Professor Khong, who taught the MPhil optional course on "The United States in International Relations since 1945," which provided the foundation for my analysis of U.S. foreign policy; Professor Vaughan Lowe and Professor David Fidler, who taught the MPhil optional course on "The Function of Law in the International Community," which provided the basis for my analysis of international law; Professor Martin Caedal and Professor Melvyn Leffler, who taught my section of the MPhil core course, "The Development of the International System pre-1950," which provided background on World War II and the birth of the United Nations; Professor Alexandra Gheciu and Professor David Williams, who taught my section of the MPhil core course, "Contemporary Debates in International Relations Theory," which provided my early exposure to international relations theories; Professor Nicolaïdis and Professor James Piscatori, who taught my section of the MPhil core course, "The Development of the International System post-1950," which provided background on the Cold War and post–Cold War eras; Professor Rosemary Foot, who conducted my Confirmation of DPhil Status; the anonymous reviewers of my Research Design Essay; the anonymous reviewers of my MPhil thesis; Professor Sir Adam Roberts, for his assistance during the process of submitting Freedom of Information Act (FOIA) requests to the U.S. government; and Professor Giovanni Capoccia, my (Magdalen) college supervisor from 2002 to 2004, who helped me acclimate to Oxford and encouraged my academic life there, and for whom I served as a research assistant.

Thank you to each of the individuals who generously granted me their time and reflections in the interviews I conducted with them for this book. These individuals are listed in the bibliography. I am especially grateful to Professor (and former U.S. Ambassador-at-Large for War Crimes Issues) David Scheffer, who not only granted me multiple interviews but who also has been an invaluable mentor to me.

I wish to thank my classmates in the MPhil in International Relations program—David Arulanantham, Dr. Ingrid Barnsley, Dr. Matthew Baugh, Dr. Alia Brahimi, Paul Brione, Dr. Julia de Clerck-Sachsse, Professor Matthew

Eagleton-Pierce, David Graham, Dr. Tarun Gupta, Hideaki Konagaya, Vivek Krishnamurthy, the late John Kuhn, Sherry-Lee Singh, Stephanie Leung, Marshall Mattera, Mitsue Morita, Professor Vipin Narang, Sarah Robinson, Dr. Patrick Travers, Taiye Tuakli-Wosornu, Marisa Van Saanen, Krishanti Vignarajah, and Ilya Zaslavsky—for providing such helpful feedback and warm companionship during and outside of class. Other peers from Oxford who provided the most helpful and frequent feedback and encouragement are my dear friends Fahim Ahmed, Dr. Samuel Charap, Mauro De Lorenzo, Scott Grinsell, Sarah Martin, Dr. Tanusri Prasanna, and Dr. Yong Suh.

For the research for this book, I thank the many librarians who helpfully provided assistance, including Emily Howie from the Library of Congress; Christine Ferdinand, Sally Speirs, and Hilary Pattison from Magdalen College, Oxford; Maureen Andersen and Marleen Buelinckx from the UN libraries and archives system; and Ryan Harrington, Professor S. Blair Kauffman, Evelyn Ma, Teresa Miguel-Stearns, John Nann, Barbara Olszowa, Dr. Sarah Ryan, Daniel Wade, and Cesar Zapata from Yale Law School. Others who formally assisted me with research and to whom I am grateful are Jim Hogan, FOIA Office, U.S. Department of Defense, and Margaret Roman and Richard Devine, FOIA Office, U.S. Department of State. I also wish to thank those who informally assisted me with research, including the late Dr. Alison Des Forges; Linda Melvern; Jim Silverwood, former Regional Director for Africa & the Middle East, Office of Overseas Prosecutorial Development, Assistance, and Training, U.S. Department of Justice; Pierre St. Hilaire, former U.S. Resident Legal Advisor to Rwanda; Don DeGabrielle, former U.S. Attorney (Houston, Texas) and former U.S. Resident Legal Advisor to South Africa; Cynthia DeGabrielle, former U.S. Resident Legal Advisor to South Africa; Michael Johnson, former Chief of Prosecutions, ICTY; Mayee Warren, former Chief of Information and Evidence Section, ICTR Office of the Prosecutor, former Chef de Cabinet, ICC Office of the Prosecutor, and former Chief of Legal Operations, SCSL Office of the Prosecutor; Professor Victor Peskin, Arizona State University; Rosalyn S. Park, Staff Attorney, Minnesota Advocates for Human Rights; John Washburn, Wasana Punyasena, and Simge Kocabayoglu of the American Non-Governmental Organizations Coalition for the International Criminal Court; Barbara Elias, Freedom of Information Coordinator, The National Security Archive; Dr. Mark Selden, Cornell University's East Asia Program; Professor Alan J. Kuperman, University of Texas at Austin's Lyndon B. Johnson School of Public Affairs; and three of my former students from George Washington University's Elliott School of International Affairs: Christina Beasley, Alex Treuber, and, most of all, Jana Everett.

I also wish to express my enormous gratitude to the Marshall Aid Commemoration Commission for awarding me a 2002–2005 Marshall Scholarship to pursue the MPhil and DPhil in International Relations at Oxford. Furthermore, I wish to express my tremendous thanks to the Center on Democracy, Development, and the Rule of Law, Freeman Spogli Institute for

International Studies, Stanford University for awarding me a 2005–2006 fellowship to complete a substantial portion of the writing of the dissertation. I wish to thank the following individuals for their support, friendship, and feedback during my time at Stanford and since: Professor David Backer, Professor Larry Diamond, Professor Julia Gray, Professor Terry Karl, Professor Moonhawk Kim, Professor Amichai Magen, Professor Mike McFaul, Professor Helen Stacy, Professor Kathryn Stoner-Weiss, and Professor Allen Weiner. Thank you, as well, to my many professors and mentors during my time (2006–2009) as a student at Yale Law School, in particular Professor Amy Chua, Professor Mirjan Damaška, Professor Oona Hathaway, Professor Harold Koh, Professor Yair Listokin, Professor Peter Schuck, Professor Jim Silk, and Professor Kate Stith.

While adapting my doctoral dissertation into this book, I split time between Yale and Harvard. Thank you to my colleagues in the Yale Law School Orville H. Schell, Jr. Center for International Human Rights (especially Professor Paul Kahn, Soo-Ryun Kwon, Katherine Lawder, Barbara Mianzo, and Professor Jim Silk), the Yale University Genocide Studies Program (particularly Professor Ben Kiernan and Professor David Simon), the Harvard Law School Institute for Global Law & Policy (specifically Professor David Kennedy), the Harvard University John F. Kennedy School of Government Carr Center for Human Rights Policy (particularly Professor Charlie Clements, Federica D'Alessandra, Professor Doug Johnson, Christopher Kintzing, Sarah Peck, Professor Sushma Raman, and Professor Kathryn Sikkink), and the Harvard University John F. Kennedy School of Government Belfer Center for Science and International Affairs (especially Dr. Steven Miller, Susan Lynch, Sean Lynn-Jones, and Professor Stephen Walt).

While finalizing the manuscript for this book, I served as a 2014–2015 U.S. Supreme Court Fellow. I thank the following individuals for their encouragement and support during that time: Regina Andrews, Melissa Aubin, Cara Gale, LaNay George, Michel Ishakian, Lauren Jeffords, Margarita Kofalt, Jeff Minear, Laura Minor, Emmanuel "Manny" Moore, Michele Reed, Wanda Rubianes, David Sime, Shelly Snook, and my fellow Fellows: Dr. Matthew Axtell, Dr. Isra Bhatty, and Dr. Derek Webb.

I want to express my gratitude to the International Studies Committee, Gilbert Murray Trust; Magdalen College, University of Oxford; the Marshall Aid Commemoration Commission; the Center on Democracy, Development, and the Rule of Law, Freeman Spogli Institute for International Studies, Stanford University; and Yale Law School for awarding me grants for expenses relating to my travel for this research, particularly to Arusha, Tanzania; Kigali, Rwanda; Washington, DC; New York City; Stanford, California; The Hague, The Netherlands; and Oxford. Thank you to my friends, Dr. Samuel Charap and Prateek Tandon, for accompanying me on a trip to Nuremberg, Germany, to visit Courtroom 600, the former site of the International Military Tribunal.

I also wish to express enormous appreciation to Dr. Judith Goldstein, Executive Director, Humanity in Action, and Professor Peter Schuck, Simeon E. Baldwin

Professor Emeritus of Law, Yale Law School, for their kindness, encouragement, friendship, mentorship, and the many wonderful opportunities they have provided me since I met them in 1999.

I am honored by and grateful for the privilege to have served at the U.S. Department of State's Bureau of Democracy, Human Rights, and Labor; the U.S. Department of Justice's Office of Overseas Prosecutorial Development, Assistance, and Training; the ICTY; the ICTR; and the ICC, where I had the opportunity to work on some of the transitional justice issues explored in this book. I thank my supervisors and colleagues at those institutions, including Carl Alexandre, Professor Rosa Ehrenreich Brooks, Professor Laura Dickinson, Faye Ehrenstamm, Professor Harold Koh, William "Bill" Lantz, Barbara Mulvaney, Luis Moreno-Ocampo, Tom Perriello, Jim Silverwood, Pierre St. Hilaire, and Mayee Warren.

Thank you to Yale University's Department of Political Science, George Washington University's Elliott School of International Affairs, and the University of Puerto Rico Law School, where I taught courses in 2014, 2011–2012, and 2010, respectively, on transitional justice and related international issues. I thank these three institutions for providing me with the opportunity to further develop my thoughts on and to teach these subjects. And I am grateful to my students from these courses for their enthusiasm, which has motivated me to continue teaching, and for their feedback, which has undoubtedly helped shape my own thoughts.

I am also grateful to the members of the audiences who provided valuable feedback at the related talks I delivered in the course of researching this book. Over the years I was working on this book, I was honored to have delivered almost 200 such talks at the law schools, political science departments, international affairs schools, public policy schools, and/or business schools of the following universities in the United States—American, Bard, the College of William & Mary, Columbia, Dartmouth, Emory, Fordham, George Washington, Georgetown, Harvard, John Marshall, Johns Hopkins, Kean, NYU, Stanford, Tufts, the U.S. Naval Academy, Yale, and the universities of Connecticut, Maryland, Miami, Michigan, Puerto Rico, San Diego, and Southern California—and abroad—Hebrew University of Jerusalem (Israel), Kigali Institute of Education (Rwanda), Kigali Institute of Management (Rwanda), Kigali Institute of Science & Technology (Rwanda), London School of Economics & Politics Science (United Kingdom), Melbourne (Australia), the National University of Rwanda, Nottingham (United Kingdom), and Oxford (United Kingdom). I also thank the following U.S. governmental institutions for hosting related talks: the Central Intelligence Agency, U.S. Africa Command, the U.S. Department of State's Bureau of Intelligence and Research, and the U.S. Judicial Conference's International Judicial Relations Committee. In addition, I am grateful for the feedback I received during talks I delivered at the following institutions: the Aspen Institute, the Council on Foreign Relations, Humanity in Action, the Institute for International Mediation and Conflict Resolution, the New York City Bar Association's Committee on African Affairs, and the British and Rwandan embassies in Washington, DC.

Thank you to my family, which has been an extraordinarily valuable source of support and encouragement. Specifically, I am grateful to my father, Dr. Howard H. Kaufman; my mother, Romaine H.M. Kaufman; my brother, Ezekiel "Zeke" A. Kaufman; my sister-in-law, Chan Joo "CJ" Park; my niece, Stella Anne Kaufman; my nephew, Julian Alexander Kaufman; my grandfather, Rabbi Dr. Shalom Coleman; my late grandmother, Stella Lande Kaufman; my uncle, Martin "Marty" Coleman; my aunt, Heidi Zajd; my cousins, Alexandra "Lexie" Coleman, Andrea and Dr. Deborah Meizlish, Ruth and Pete Salinger, and Adrienne, Dr. Mark, Amy, Talia, and Mica Bernhard; my parents-in-law, Cheryl Dater and Dr. Mark and Dr. Jodi Katz; my sisters-in-law, Shoshana and Dr. Alexis Katz; and my future brother-in-law, Shaun Tarzy. A special thank you to my wife, Elizabeth Katz, who provided immense support and feedback on this book and everything else.

Thank you, as well, to my friends not already listed above, including Mike Buchwald, Phil Carter, Jared Cohen, Yochi Dreazen, Pierre Gemson, Josh Goldman, Dr. Brendon Graeber, Professor Christopher L. Griffin, Jr., Arvind Grover, Fawzi Jumean, Tisana "O" Kunjara Na Ayudhya, Jason Levine, Dianne Liu, Brendan and Lacey Lupetin, Ligia Markman, Jim Mitre, Jackson Muneza Mvunganyi, Professor Jennifer Nou, Joel Phillips, Ilya Podolyako, Bev Prosser, Albert "Al" Robinson, Eve Semins, Dr. Michelle Jo Semins, Vance Serchuk, Katherine Southwick, Anthony Triolo, Dr. Tamara "Tammy" Vanderwal, Lauren Vestewig, Dr. Sunil Wadhwa, Subo Wijeyeratne, and Dr. Jared Williamson. I am deeply indebted to all of my wonderful and generous friends and relatives for spending so much time with me, including many late nights, discussing transitional justice, international law, international relations, and U.S. foreign policy. These conversations and experiences influenced and inspired me immeasurably, and bits and pieces of them have inevitably found their way into this book.

I have spent a significant amount of time in Rwanda over the years, and I thank all of my friends and colleagues there, particularly my partners in building Rwanda's first public library, the Kigali Public Library (also now known as Rwanda Library Services), including Karin Alexander, Lauren Baer, Caroline Batambuze, Beth Bensman, Page Brannon, Urmi de Baghel, Michelle Drucker, Jill Fenton, Neil Fenton, Rose Gahire, Benjamin Heineike, Amanda Hektor, Neil Helfand, Jonathan Home, Sarah Ingabire, Diana Kakoma, Sarah Kakoma, Vivek Krishnamurthy, Janet Labuda, Gwenn Laviolette, Beth Haines Levitt, Dr. Martin Levitt, Professor Abbie Liel, Binu Malajil, Paul Masterjerb, Jolly Mazimhaka, Jennifer McCard, Edson Mpyisi, Gerald Mpyisi, Ambassador Zephyr Mutanguha, Grace Nkubana, Dr. Andrew Park, Beth Payne, Michael Rakower, Raj Rajendran, Professor Geoffrey Rugege, Sheba Rugege-Hakiza, Duhirwe Rushemeza, Liliane Rushemeza, Joan Rwanyonga, Jelena Šljivić Mishina, Janepher Turatsinze, Dudu Thabede, Violette Uwamutara, Priya Vallabhbhai, Viresh Vallabhbhai, Claudia Veritas, Gitau Wamukui, and Nils Zirimwabagabo.

Finally, I wish to thank Oxford University Press (OUP) for all of its encouragement and assistance on the publication of this book. In particular, I want to express my enormous appreciation to Blake Ratcliff, OUP's Acquisitions Editor for International Law, for supporting this book from inception to fruition and for providing such helpful guidance on substance, style, and structure. Thank you, as well, to Alden Domizio for his masterful editorial oversight, Arun Kumar Vasu for his efficient project management, and Brooke Smith for her skillful copyediting.

Acknowledging such inspiration, wonderful and critical guidance, and generous institutional and individual support, I further acknowledge that any errors and views stated in this book are mine alone, and that the latter do not necessarily represent any of the organizations with which I have been or am affiliated.

Zachary D. Kaufman
July 26, 2015

{ ABBREVIATIONS }

ACJ	Allied Council for Japan
ASP	Assembly of States Parties (to the Rome Statute of the International Criminal Court)
CAR	Central African Republic
CIC	Counter Intelligence Corps, U.S. Army
CoE	Commission of Experts. Also known as: 780 Commission or UN War Crimes Commission.
CSCE	Commission on Security and Cooperation in Europe. Also known as: Helsinki Commission.
Daesh	"al-Dawla al-Islamiya fi al-Iraq wa al-Sham" (meaning Islamic State of Iraq and the Levant). Also known as: ISIL, ISIS.
DRC	Democratic Republic of the Congo
ECCC	Extraordinary Chambers in the Courts of Cambodia for the Prosecution of Crimes Committed During the Period of Democratic Kampuchea
FEAC	Far Eastern Advisory Commission
FEC	Far Eastern Commission
FDR	Franklin Delano Roosevelt
FOIA	Freedom of Information Act
FRY	Former Yugoslavia
Geneva Conventions	Series of conventions adopted by the international community in Geneva in 1949 and expanded in 1977.
Genocide Convention	Convention on the Prevention and Punishment of the Crime of Genocide
GoR	Government of the Republic of Rwanda
ICC	International Criminal Court
ICJ	International Court of Justice
ICT	International criminal tribunal
ICTJ	International Center on Transitional Justice
ICTR	International Criminal Tribunal for the Prosecution of Persons Responsible for Genocide and Other Serious Violations of International Humanitarian Law Committed in the Territory of Rwanda and Rwandan Citizens responsible for genocide and other such violations committed in the territory of neighboring States, between 1 January 1994 and 31 December 1994.

	Also known as: United Nations International Criminal Tribunal for Rwanda.
ICTY	International Tribunal for the Prosecution of Persons Responsible for Serious Violations of International Humanitarian Law Committed in the Territory of the Former Yugoslavia since 1991. Also known as: United Nations International Criminal Tribunal for the Former Yugoslavia.
ILC	International Law Commission
IMT	International Military Tribunal. Also known as: Nuremberg Tribunal.
IMTFE	International Military Tribunal for the Far East. Also known as: Tokyo Tribunal.
IPS	International Prosecution Section (of the IMTFE)
ISIL	Islamic State of Iraq and the Levant
ISIS	Islamic State of Iraq and Syria
IST	Iraqi Special Tribunal
JNA	Jugoslavenska narodna armija (Yugoslav national army)
Nazi Party	National Socialist German Workers Party
NGO	Nongovernmental organization
NLI	Neoliberal institutionalism
NMT	Nuremberg Military Tribunal
Nuremberg Tribunal	International Military Tribunal for Germany at Nuremberg
OTP	Office of the Prosecutor
POWs	Prisoners of war
RPF	Rwandan Patriotic Front
SCAP	Supreme Commander of the Allied Powers
SCSL	Special Court for Sierra Leone
STL	Special Tribunal for Lebanon
Tokyo Tribunal	International Military Tribunal for the Far East at Tokyo
TRC	Truth and Reconciliation Commission
U.K.	United Kingdom
UN	United Nations
UN/CHR	UN Commission on Human Rights
UN/HCHR	UN High Commissioner for Human Rights
UN/ICEfY	UN Independent Commission of Experts on the former Yugoslavia
UN/ICER	UN Independent Commission of Experts on Rwanda
UN/PR	UN Permanent Representative
UNAMIR	UN Assistance Mission to Rwanda
UNGA	UN General Assembly
UNGAR	UN General Assembly Resolution

UNPROFOR	UN Protection Force in Bosnia and Herzegovina
UNSC	UN Security Council
UNSCR	UN Security Council Resolution
UNSC/P	UN Security Council President
UNSC/P5	Permanent five member states of the UN Security Council
UNSG	UN Secretary-General
UNWCC	UN War Crimes Commission. Also known as: United Nations Commission for the Investigation of War Crimes, United Nations Allied War Crimes Commission, 1943 War Crimes Commission, 1943 Commission.
U.S.	United States
U.S./DoD	U.S. Department of Defense
U.S./DoJ	U.S. Department of Justice
U.S./DoJ/OPDAT	U.S. Department of Justice Office of Overseas Prosecutorial Development, Assistance, and Training
U.S./DoS	U.S. Department of State
U.S./DoS/DRL	U.S. Department of State Bureau of Democracy, Human Rights, and Labor
U.S./DoS/IO	U.S. Department of State Bureau of International Organization Affairs
U.S./DoS/L	U.S. Department of State Office of the Legal Adviser
U.S./DoS/US-UN	U.S. Mission to the United Nations
U.S./DoS/WCI	U.S. Department of State Office of War Crimes Issues
U.S./HCIR	U.S. House of Representatives Committee on International Relations
U.S./IWCWG	U.S. Interagency War Crimes Working Group
U.S./NSC	U.S. National Security Council
U.S./SCFR	U.S. Senate Committee on Foreign Relations
USG	U.S. Government
USSR	Union of Soviet Socialist Republics (or Soviet Union)
WWI	World War One
WWII	World War Two

Options Abbreviations

ICT-Separate	Completely separate UN ad hoc ICT.
ICT-Tied	Separate UN ad hoc ICT sharing bureaucracy with existing ICT.
ICTY-Expanded	Expansion of existing ICT's (e.g., ICTY's) jurisdiction to include another atrocity (e.g., 1994 Rwandan genocide).

{ CITATIONS }

Citations are formatted in conformity with: THE BLUEBOOK: A UNIFORM SYSTEM OF CITATION (Columbia Law Review Ass'n et al. eds., 20th ed. 2015). Where *The Bluebook* does not provide clear guidance for the formatting of a particular source, or where a deviation from *The Bluebook* would be more efficient, the author has sought to consistently and thoroughly include all relevant information in the citation. The bibliography contains additional information on sources cited in and consulted for the book.

Personal interviews and declassified documents are listed in shorthand in the citations. Charts containing full information for each appear in the bibliography.

{ GLOSSARY }

Denazification	Lustration specifically relating to Nazis.
Épuration	French word for lustration.
Gacaca	Literally meaning "the grass" or "the lawn" in Kinyarwanda, *gacaca* is Rwanda's traditional form of community justice and refers to the fact that its proceedings occurred outside while participants and observers sat or stood on the ground.
Génocidaires	French word for perpetrators of the 1994 Rwandan genocide.
Interahamwe	Literally meaning "those who fight together" in Kinyarwanda, the *Interahamwe* were Hutu paramilitary groups.
Lustration	Process of purging political officials.
Pastoralization	Process of changing a region from industrial to agricultural.
SS	Abbreviation for *Schutzstaffel*, meaning "defense squadron" in German. The SS was an elite paramilitary organization of the Nazi party.
Zaibatsu	Japanese term for a pre-WWII Japanese financial or industrial conglomerate.

{ ACTORS }

Key Actors and Their Mid-1940s Positions/Affiliations

Australian Officials

Sir William Webb	Chief Justice, Supreme Court of Queensland (1940–1946); Australian judge and chief judge / president, IMTFE (1946–1948).

French Officials

Yves Beigbeder	Legal Secretary to the IMT's French Judge (1946).
Henri Bernard	French judge, IMTFE (1946–1948).
Charles de Gaulle	President, Provisional Government (1944–1946).
Maurice Papon	Senior Official, Vichy Government (during WWII).

German Officials

Klaus Barbie	Senior official, Nazi Party, SS, and Gestapo; Head of Gestapo in Lyon, France.
Wernher von Braun	Member, Nazi Party and SS; German scientist.
Adolf Eichmann	Senior official, Nazi Party and SS.
Hans Globke	Official, Federal Republic of Germany.
Joseph Goebbels	Senior official, Nazi Party; Minister of Propaganda and National Enlightenment (1933–1945); Chancellor (1945).
Hermann Wilhelm Goering	Senior official, Nazi Party; Founder, Gestapo; Reich Marshal (1940–1946).
Alfons Goetzfried	Member, Gestapo.
Karl Hass	Member, SS.
Heinrich Himmler	Commander, SS (1929–1945).

Adolf Hitler	Leader, Nazi Party (1921–1945); Chancellor (1933–1945); *Führer* (1934–1945).
Rudolf Hoess	Senior official, Nazi Party and SS; Commander, Auschwitz concentration camp (1940–1943).
Josef Mengele	Nazi physician.
Franz von Papen	Chancellor (1932); Vice Chancellor (1933–1934).
Erich Priebke	Senior official, SS.
Josef Schwammberger	Senior official, SS.

Italian Officials

| Benito Mussolini | Prime Minister (1922–1943). |

Japanese Officials

Hirohito	124th Emperor (1926–1989).
Shiro Ishii	Lieutenant General, Unit 731, Japanese Imperial Army (during WWII).
Nobusuke Kishi	Minister, Commerce and Industry (1941–1945); 56th Prime Minister (1957–1960).
Mamoru Shigemitsu	Foreign Minister (1943–1945).
Hideki Tōjō	40th Prime Minister (1941–1944).
Tomoyuki Yamashita	Commanding General, Fourteenth Army Group, Imperial Japanese Army (1944–1945).

U.K. Officials

Winston Churchill	Prime Minister (1940–1945).
Anthony Eden	Foreign Secretary (1940–1945); Leader, House of Commons (1942–1945).
John Simon	Lord Chancellor (1940–1945).

U.S. Officials

Murray C. Bernays	Staff member, Personnel Division, Army General Staff (1943–1945).
Francis Biddle	58th U.S. Attorney General (1941–1945); U.S. judge, IMT (1945–1946).
James F. Byrnes	81st Justice, U.S. Supreme Court (1941–1942); 49th U.S. Secretary of State (1945–1947).

Myron C. Cramer	Judge Advocate General, U.S. Army (1941–1945); 2nd U.S. judge, IMTFE (1946–1948).
Ammi Cutter	Colonel, Assistant Executive Officer, Office of the Assistant Secretary of War, U.S. Department of War (1944–1946).
William O. Douglas	79th Justice, U.S. Supreme Court (1939–1975).
Dwight D. Eisenhower	1st Supreme Allied Commander Europe (1951–1952); 34th U.S. President (1953–1961).
Benjamin Ferencz	Prosecutor, NMT (1945–1948).
Felix Frankfurter	78th Justice, U.S. Supreme Court (1939–1962).
Whitney Harris	Staff member, Prosecution, IMT (1945–1948); Author of *Tyranny on Trial: The Trial of the Major German War Criminals at the End of the World War II at Nuremberg Germany 1945-1946*.
Harry Hopkins	8th U.S. Secretary of Commerce (1938–1940); Personal Aide to President Franklin Delano Roosevelt (1940–1945).
Solis Horwitz	Staff member, Prosecution, IMTFE (1945–1948); Author of "The Tokyo Trial."
Cordell Hull	47th U.S. Secretary of State (1933–1944).
Robert H. Jackson	82nd Justice, U.S. Supreme Court (1941–1954); U.S. Chief Prosecutor, IMT (1945–1946).
Joseph Berry Keenan	Chief of Counsel (Chief Prosecutor), IMTFE (1946–1948).
George F. Kennan	1st Director, Bureau of Policy Planning, US/DoS (1947–1949).
William Langer	U.S. Senator, North Dakota (1941–1959).
Douglas MacArthur	Supreme Commander of the Allied Powers (1945–1951).
George C. Marshall	U.S. Army Chief of Staff (1939–1945); 50th U.S. Secretary of State (1947–1949).
Joseph R. McCarthy	U.S. Senator, Wisconsin (1947–1957).
John J. McCloy	Assistant Secretary of War, U.S. Department of War (1941–1945); 2nd President, World Bank (1947–1949).
Henry J. Morgenthau, Jr.	52nd U.S. Secretary of the Treasury (1934–1945).
Herbert C. Pell, Jr.	U.S. representative, UNWCC (1943–1945).
John E. Rankin	Member from Mississippi, U.S. House of Representatives (1921–1953).
Franklin Delano Roosevelt	32nd U.S. President (1933–1945).

Samuel Rosenman	White House Counsel (1943–1946).
Edward R. Stettinius, Jr.	48th U.S. Secretary of State (1944–1945).
Henry L. Stimson	46th U.S. Secretary of State (1929–1933);
	46th U.S. Secretary of War (1940–1945).
Harlan Fiske Stone	73rd Justice, U.S. Supreme Court (1925–1946);
	12th Chief Justice, U.S. Supreme Court (1941–1946).
Robert A. Taft	U.S. Senator, Ohio (1939–1953).
Telford Taylor	U.S. Chief of Counsel for War Crimes, NMT (1946–1949);
	Author of *Nuremberg and Vietnam: An America Tragedy* and *The Anatomy of the Nuremberg Trials: A Personal Memoir.*
Harry S Truman	34th U.S. Vice President (1945);
	33rd U.S. President (1945–1953).
Henry Wallace	33rd U.S. Vice President (1941–1945).
Charles F. Wennerstrum	Justice, Iowa Supreme Court (1941–1958);
	Presiding judge, "Hostages Case," NMT (1947–1948).

USSR Officials

Ivan Maisky	Soviet Ambassador to the U.K. (1932–1943).
Iona T. Nikitchenko	Judge, Soviet purge trials (1936–1938);
	Vice President, USSR Supreme Court (1938–1949);
	Soviet judge, IMT (1945–1946).
Joseph Stalin	General Secretary, Central Committee, Russian Communist Party (1922–1953);
	Premier, USSR (1929–1953).

Key Actors and Their 1980s—2000s Positions/Affiliations

Rwandan Officials

Théoneste Bagasora	Colonel, Military (during genocide);
	Cabinet Director, Ministry of Defense (during genocide).
Manzi Bakuramutsa	UN/PR (post-genocide).
Jacques Bihozagara	Minister of Rehabilitation and Social Integration (post-genocide).
Augustin Bizimungu	Chief-of-Staff, Military (during genocide).
Pasteur Bizimungu	President (post-genocide until 2000).
Claude Dusaidi	RPF Representative to the UN (during genocide);
	Political Adviser to Vice President Kagame (post-genocide).

Paul Kagame	Commander, Rwandan Patriotic Army, and Vice President, RPF (during genocide); Vice President and Minister of Defense (1994–2000); President (2000–present).
Alphonse-Marie Nkubito	Minister of Justice (post-genocide).
Léonard Nkundiye	Lieutenant Colonel, Military (during genocide).
Pascal Simbikangwa	Captain, Military (during genocide).
Faustin Twagiramungu	RPF Prime Minister-designate (during genocide).

U.S. Officials

Morris Berthold Abram	U.S. Permanent Representative to the UN in Geneva (1989–1993).
Madeleine Albright	UN/PR (1993–1997); 64th U.S. Secretary of State (1997–2001).
Douglas Bennet	Assistant U.S. Secretary of State for International Organization Affairs (1993–1995).
Alan Blinken	U.S. Ambassador to Belgium (1993–1997).
George H.W. Bush (Bush, Sr.)	41st U.S. President (1989–1993).
George W. Bush (Bush, Jr.)	43rd U.S. President (2001–2009).
Prudence Bushnell	Principal Deputy Assistant U.S. Secretary of State for African Affairs (1993–1996).
Warren Christopher	63rd U.S. Secretary of State (1993–1997).
William Jefferson Clinton	42nd U.S. President (1993–2001).
Joan Donoghue	Assistant U.S. Legal Adviser for African Affairs, US/DoS (1993–1994).
Lawrence Eagleburger	Acting U.S. Secretary of State (1992); 62nd U.S. Secretary of State (1992–1993).
Toby Gati	Assistant U.S. Secretary of State for Intelligence and Research (1993–1997).
Edward Gnehm, Jr.	Deputy Permanent Representative of the U.S. to the UN (1994–1997).
Tony Hall	Member from Ohio, U.S. House of Representatives (1979–2002).
Conrad Harper	Legal Adviser, U.S./DoS (1993–1996).

Richard C. Holbrooke	Ambassador to Germany (1993–1994); Assistant Secretary of State for European and Canadian Affairs (1994–1996); Ambassador to the UN (1999–2001).
Melinda Kimble	Deputy Assistant Secretary of State for International Organization Affairs (1991–1997).
Anthony Lake	National Security Adviser (1993–1997).
Michael Matheson	Acting or Principal Deputy Legal Advisor, US/DoS (1990–2000).
George Moose	Assistant Secretary of State for African Affairs (1993–1997).
Barack Obama	44th U.S. President (2009–present).
David Rawson	Ambassador to Rwanda (1993–1996).
Michael P. Scharf	Attorney-Adviser for United Nations Affairs, U.S./DoS (1991–1993).
David J. Scheffer	Senior Advisor and Counsel to Ambassador Albright, U.S./DoS/US-UN (1993–1997); 1st Ambassador-at-Large for War Crimes Issues (1997–2001).
Richard Schifter	Ambassador to the UN Human Rights Commission (1983–1985); Assistant Secretary of State for Human Rights and Humanitarian Affairs (1985–1992).
John Shalikashvili	Chairman, Joint Chiefs of Staff (1993–1997).
John Shattuck	Assistant Secretary of State for Democracy, Human Rights, and Labor (1993–1998).
Christine Shelly	Deputy Spokesperson, U.S./DoS (1993); Acting Spokesperson, U.S./DoS (1993–1995).
Gregory Stanton	Political Officer, Office for United Nations Political Affairs, U.S./DoS/IO (1992–1999).
Donald Steinberg	U.S./NSC Senior Director for African Affairs and Special Assistant to the President for African Affairs (1994–1995).
Stephen Walker	Croatia Desk Officer, U.S./DoS (1993).
Maxine Waters	Member from California, U.S. House of Representatives (1991–present).
Edwin D. Williamson	Legal Adviser, U.S./DoS (1990–1993).
Timothy Wirth	Undersecretary for Global Affairs, U.S./DoS (1993–1997).
Warren Zimmerman	Ambassador to Yugoslavia (1989–1992).

UN Officials

Atsu-Koffi Amega	Chairman, UN/ICER (1994).
M. Cherif Bassiouni	Member and then Chairman, CoE (1992–1994).
Boutros Boutros-Ghali	6th UNSG (1992–1997).
Hans Correll	Under-Secretary-General for Legal Affairs and Legal Counsel (1994–2004).
René Degni-Ségui	Special Rapporteur on the situation of human rights in Rwanda, UN/CHR (1994–1997).
Ramón Escovar-Salom	Chief Prosecutor, ICTY (1993).
Richard Goldstone	Chief Prosecutor, ICTY and ICTR (1994–1996).
Frits Kalshoven	Chairman, CoE (1992–1993).
José Ayala Lasso	High Commissioner for Human Rights (1994–1998).
Theodor Meron	Judge, ICTY (2001–present); President (Chief Judge), ICTY (2003–2005; 2011–present).
Bacre Waly Ndiaye	Special Rapporteur on extrajudicial, summary, or arbitrary executions, UN/CHR (1992–1998).
Raymond Ranjeva	Judge, ICJ (1991–2009).
Nigel Rodley	Special Rapporteur on the question of torture, UN/CHR (1993–2001).
Daphna Shraga	Staff member, Legal Affairs Office, UN (1989–2012).
Cyrus Vance	UNSG Special Envoy to the FRY (1991–1995).
Ralph Zacklin	Member, Office of Legal Affairs, UN (1973–2005); Assistant Secretary-General for Legal Affairs, UN (1998–2005).

Yugoslavia Officials

Radovan Karadžić	1st President, Republika Srpska (1992–1996).
Milan Kučan	1st President, Slovenia (1991–2002).
Slobodan Milošević	1st President, Serbia (1989–1997); 3rd President, Federal Republic of Yugoslavia (1997–2000).
Ratko Mladić	Chief of Staff, Army of Republika Srpska (1992–1995).
Josip Tito	1st President, Yugoslavia (1953–1980).
Franjo Tudjman	1st President, Croatia (1990–1999).

Others

Muammar Gaddafi	Leader, Libya (1969–2011).
Saddam Hussein	5th President, Iraq (1979–2003).
Colin Keating	UNSC/P (April 1994).
Sergey Lavrov	Deputy Foreign Minister, Russia (1992–1994).
Nelson Mandela	President, South Africa (1994–1999).
Alfred Nzo	Foreign Minister, South Africa (1994–1999).
Jerome Shestack	Chairman, International League for Human Rights (1972–1979; 1980–1991).

{ 1 }

Introduction

On November 21, 1945, in his opening address to the International Military Tribunal for Germany (IMT) at Nuremberg, chief U.S. prosecutor Robert Jackson declared: "What makes this inquest significant is that these prisoners represent sinister influences that will lurk in the world long after their bodies have returned to dust."[1] Indeed, during the twentieth century, often referred to as "the bloodiest century,"[2] some scholars estimate that between 60 and 150 million people were killed through atrocities (including genocides) and other mass murders.[3] These horrific events claimed more lives than all wars during the century combined,[4] and this "problem from hell" continues in the twenty-first century.[5]

I. Terms and Parameters

Some terms used in this book—such as "atrocities" and "transitional justice"— are contested. According to former U.S. Ambassador-at-Large for War Crimes Issues and current international law scholar David Scheffer, the following criteria characterize "atrocity crimes": "high-impact crimes of severe gravity that are of an orchestrated character, result in a significant number of victims or large-scale property damage, and merit an international response to hold at least the top war criminals accountable under the law."[6] Sarah Sewall—current U.S. Under Secretary of State for Civilian Security, Democracy, and Human Rights, and previous director of the Harvard University John F. Kennedy School of Government's Carr Center for Human Rights Policy as well as the Carr Center's Mass Atrocity Response Operations Project—defines "mass atrocities" using numerical and temporal thresholds and focusing on noncombatants: "violence directed against civilians that is somewhere in the range of above 500 people over a sustained period of time."[7]

Typically, in both international relations and international law, the term "atrocities" has referred to genocide, war crimes, and crimes against humanity.[8] Along with the crime of aggression,[9] these offenses constitute the subject-matter jurisdiction of the world's first permanent international criminal tribunal (ICT), the International Criminal Court (ICC).[10] Increasingly, as conceptions of heinous crimes have broadened, the United States and other countries have also recognized terrorism[11] and non-genocidal ethnic cleansing[12] as atrocities. Scheffer has coined the term "atrocity law" to describe the intersection of four disciplines of international law—international criminal law, international humanitarian law, international human rights law, and the laws and customs of war—that comprise the ICTs' evolving law.[13]

The extent and persistence of atrocities as well as questions about the most effective means of addressing their perpetrators, victims, and survivors demonstrate how important and timely it is to study the origins, operations, and outcomes of "transitional justice." Transitional justice refers to both the process and objectives of societies addressing past or ongoing atrocities and other serious human rights violations through judicial and nonjudicial mechanisms.[14] The tools available to those seeking and implementing transitional justice are numerous and varied, including, for example, prosecution, amnesty, lustration, truth commissions, exile, indefinite detention, and lethal force.

Just as certain terms used in this book are contested, so too are the parameters of transitional justice. Some scholars seek to distinguish "international criminal justice"[15] (often pursued through ICTs[16]) and transitional justice.[17] However, international criminal justice is a crucial component of transitional justice, as transitional justice mechanisms can be international (as opposed to domestic or hybrid) and often involve criminal justice (instead of or in addition to other objectives and processes).[18] Rather than separate fields, the two subjects overlap and are inextricably linked because ICTs may be the primary or exclusive mechanisms through which suspected atrocity perpetrators are addressed in a particular context. As such, a holistic view of transitional justice necessarily includes ICTs. Other academics and practitioners agree. For example, Ruti Teitel—who, in 1991, coined the phrase "transitional justice"[19]—focuses in part on ICTs in her analysis of the field.[20] Other leading scholars of transitional justice, including Kathryn Sikkink and Naomi Roht-Arriaza, similarly include ICTs in their work on transitional justice.[21] Cambridge University Press's three-volume *Encyclopedia of Transitional Justice* features entries on ICTs,[22] one of which is my own contribution on the United Nations (UN) International Criminal Tribunal for Rwanda (ICTR).[23] The leading periodical and civil society organization in the field of transitional justice, *The International Journal of Transitional Justice*[24] and the International Center for Transitional Justice,[25] both regularly publish materials on the establishment, operation, and impact of ICTs. Even scholarship that treats international criminal justice and transitional justice as distinct fields acknowledges that their goals and mechanisms often overlap and can be mutually supportive.[26]

I acknowledge that I am unusual in including lethal force among transitional justice options. But, as will be discussed throughout this book, just as with ICTs, a full consideration of transitional justice options necessarily includes extrajudicial killing because such a tool is—and has been—seriously considered and actually used as a means of addressing alleged atrocity perpetrators.

The tense and shifting international landscape—especially the rise of violent extremism and enduring conflict in the Middle East, Near East, and sub-Saharan Africa—has at once promoted and impaired international cooperation regarding transitional justice. Specifically, many members of the international community have agreed in principle that they must individually and collectively do more to prevent and stop atrocities,[27] but they have disagreed about how to accomplish those goals in practice. This book focuses on the particular role of the U.S. government (USG) in transitional justice. I have chosen to focus on America's reaction to international crises because it often significantly shapes the larger global response due to its role as a superpower and its preponderance of resources since the end of World War II (WWII).

The immediate aftermaths of WWII and the Cold War were seminal periods for transitional justice. At the conclusion of WWII, the Allies defeated a German dictatorship and its partners in Japan, Italy, and elsewhere bent on fascist world domination. The Allies also liberated states in Europe and East Asia that had endured atrocities, the scale of which had never before been witnessed in the history of mankind. At the end of WWII, the victorious Allies—and the USG in particular, under the presidencies of Franklin Delano Roosevelt (FDR) and then Harry Truman—faced questions of whether, how, when, and where to bring to justice suspected atrocity perpetrators (particularly from Nazi Germany and Imperial Japan), and who among them.

Despite promises made after the Holocaust by the international community to "Never Again" allow genocide and other atrocities to be committed, these crimes against humanity have been perpetrated again and again. The Cold War, which pitted the world's two nuclear superpowers—the United States and the Union of Soviet Socialist Republics (USSR or Soviet Union)—against each other, and the concurrent process of decolonization, led the rival nations to engage in proxy clashes, resulting in, for example, the Korean War of the early-1950s and the Vietnam War from the late-1950s to the mid-1970s. At the same time, the Cold War's structure and norms privileged political sovereignty and territorial integrity above all else, providing a perverse carte blanche for states to perpetrate some of the world's most horrific crimes against peoples within their own borders, such as the Cambodian genocide of the mid- to late-1970s, in which Pol

Pot's Khmer Rouge regime caused the deaths of approximately 1.7 million people (roughly one-fifth of the country's population).[28]

In the immediate post–Cold War era, the world no longer faced potential nuclear war between two superpowers, as one had collapsed. But the end of the Cold War did not signal a complete Pax Americana; rather, instead of indirect or direct war *among* states, conflict occurred more often *within* states and involved massive human rights violations perpetrated against specific ethnic, racial, gender, religious, and political groups.[29] The 1994 Rwandan genocide (also known as the genocide against the Tutsi in Rwanda)—during which Hutu extremists slaughtered approximately 1 million Tutsi and moderate Hutu[30]—featured a daily killing rate that was three to five times faster than during the Holocaust.[31] Just a year later, in July 1995, the Srebrenica massacre—in which an estimated 7,000 Muslim men and boys were summarily executed during the war in the former Yugoslavia (FRY)[32]—represented the largest single mass atrocity in Europe since WWII.[33]

During the immediate post–Cold War period, states were more willing and able to confront atrocity perpetrators in foreign societies, partly because the superpower rivalry that had previously fomented international gridlock had dissolved. Like the FDR and Truman administrations, the presidencies of George H.W. Bush (Bush, Sr.) and Bill Clinton faced difficult questions about addressing suspected atrocity perpetrators, but this time from Libya, Iraq, the FRY, and Rwanda.

II. Central Research Questions

This book features two central research questions. First, I analyze USG policy on transitional justice in certain cases. The aim is to understand why the USG supported particular transitional justice options in the immediate aftermaths of WWII and the Cold War. (The purpose is not to argue whether the USG *should have* supported or *should* support particular transitional justice options, such as ICTs.[34] As such, this inquiry is more descriptive than prescriptive.)

In particular, this book analyzes USG support for various transitional justice options, including the establishment of four ICTs: the IMT (also known as the "Nuremberg Tribunal"), the International Military Tribunal for the Far East (the IMTFE, also known as the "Tokyo Tribunal"), the UN International Criminal Tribunal for the FRY (the ICTY, also known as the "Yugoslavia Tribunal"), and the ICTR (also known as the "Rwanda Tribunal"). In doing so, I determine why and how the USG backed ICTs and other particular solutions to the problem of transitional justice for suspected perpetrators of atrocities in Europe and East Asia during WWII as well as the FRY and Rwanda in the 1990s. I also examine why and how the USG chose *not* to support ICTs for some of the alleged atrocity perpetrators in the first three situations as well as individuals suspected of committing heinous crimes in some contemporaneous contexts, particularly the 1988 bombing of Pan Am flight 103 over Lockerbie, Scotland, and the 1990–1991 Iraqi offenses against Kuwaitis.

This book's second research objective is to posit a theoretical framework to explain USG policy on transitional justice. I contrast my theory, "prudentialism,"[35] with the most established theory on the subject, "legalism," a term political scientist Gary Bass repurposed[36] in his canonical book on transitional justice.[37]

As will be discussed further in Chapter III, legalism derives from the international relations theory of liberalism whereas prudentialism derives from the international relations theory of realism. A legalist approach emphasizes normative beliefs about transitional justice. By "normative beliefs," I do not mean "norms" as constructivists do; for example, international relations scholars Michael Barnett and Kathryn Sikkink define "norms" as intersubjective "standards of appropriate behavior."[38] Rather, I mean certain beliefs held by individual decision-makers that may be embraced by a state as part of its collective national identity, ideology, and foreign policy.[39] Legalism analyzes liberal states' transitional justice behavior by explaining their commitment to the normative belief that suspected atrocity perpetrators should be prosecuted.[40] Legalism is thus a parsimonious theory that, if accurate, is quite favorable to U.S. policy on transitional justice for taking such a principled approach to addressing individuals who allegedly commit atrocities.

Whereas legalism emphasizes this single, consistent factor, prudentialism focuses on three interrelated factors that are often in tension. In addition to normative beliefs about transitional justice, prudentialism considers the role politics and pragmatics play. Prudentialism theorizes that individual decision-makers may hold conflicting normative beliefs about transitional justice and therefore that states, whether liberal or illiberal, may not embrace a consistent policy preference about transitional justice.[41] Prudentialism's political factors concentrate on the dynamics of different bureaucratic relationships, both within and outside the state. Internally, these political factors focus on the relationship among government officials and agencies as well as the relationship between government officials and the citizenry. Externally, these political factors concern the relationship between a state's government and its key allies and adversaries. This external political factor includes the attention a state's government pays to its position of power within international institutions and the international system as a whole. Prudentialism's pragmatic features concentrate on the logistics of transitional justice. Such factors concern the efficiency, effectiveness, and expense of transitional justice options. Prudentialism thus explains liberal and illiberal states' policies on transitional justice as a function of a case-specific balancing of politics, pragmatics, and normative beliefs. Whether the two theories consider the security interests of states is thus a main difference of them; legalism does not, whereas prudentialism does. Prudentialism is thus less parsimonious than legalism and offers both a more complex as well as a more critical view of U.S. policy on transitional justice.

The following table, Table 1.1, provides an overview of these differences between prudentialism and legalism:

TABLE 1.1 Legalism Versus Prudentialism: Overview

	Legalism	Prudentialism
Derivative of?	Liberalism	Realism
Factors?	Normative beliefs	Case-specific balancing of: (1) Normative beliefs, (2) Politics, and (3) Pragmatics.
Parsimonious theory?	Yes	Less
Considers security interests of United States?	No	Yes
View of U.S. policy on transitional justice?	Complimentary	More complex/critical

There are a number of ways in which this research is valuable and salient to both the scholarly and policy-related worlds.

A. SCHOLARLY RELEVANCE

Examining USG policy on transitional justice is important for several theoretical reasons. First, a conspicuous disparity exists between the analytical emphasis regarding, on the one hand, U.S. policy with respect to military intervention and, on the other hand, whether and how the United States is involved post-conflict.[42] However, the baseline question of what U.S. foreign policy *is* with respect to post-conflict reconstruction and reconciliation in general, and to transitional justice in particular, is a crucial and recurring one.

Second, the nature of U.S. foreign policy differs across the six transitional justice cases (Germany and Japan in the immediate aftermath of WWII as well as Libya, Iraq, the FRY, and Rwanda in the immediate aftermath of the Cold War) and therefore requires explanation. A precise form of transitional justice the USG supported in each of the four primary case studies (Germany, Japan, the FRY, and Rwanda)—an ICT—shared some characteristics, given that each (1) used prosecution instead of—or in addition to—other transitional justice options; (2) was multilateral rather than unilateral;[43] (3) focused on only a few dozen of the suspected atrocity leaders; (4) commenced within a few years after the relevant atrocities occurred; and (5) operated on or near the site of the relevant atrocities. But the two contemporary pairs of ICTs (the IMT and the

IMTFE, and the ICTY and the ICTR) also differed crucially. For example, in the case of the first pair, the USG supported separate, ad hoc, narrowly multi-lateral (limited to just the victors of WWII rather than a broader international consortium), military tribunals, which could institute capital punishment, and which operated outside the auspices of the nascent UN. Judicial decisions of the IMT (in which only four states supplied judges and prosecutors) could not be appealed, while those of the IMTFE (in which eleven states were repre-sented as judicial and prosecutorial officials) could be. The ICTs of the imme-diate post–Cold War period broke with the design precedent established by the IMT and IMTFE by involving the UN Security Council (UNSC) as the overall administrator of the transitional justice mechanism. The ICTY and the ICTR also deviated from the IMT and the IMTFE by foreclosing a particular punish-ment, the death penalty, which the USG employs domestically. Furthermore, unlike the IMT and the IMTFE, the ICTY and the ICTR were not completely separate. After the ICTR was established, the two ad hoc UN tribunals over-lapped bureaucratically, although the degree changed over time (as discussed in Chapters II and VII). The question is why, even though each of these four ICTs was established as a transitional justice response to a mass atrocity, the USG supported design mechanisms that were similar across certain dimensions but different across others.

Furthermore, in exploring the nature of USG policy on transitional justice, it is crucial to understand certain "puzzles," that is, counterintuitive, inconsistent, or surprising developments in the design and establishment of these ICTs. For example, why did the USG withdraw its initial support for extrajudicial execu-tion in favor of prosecution as the method for handling the principal suspected atrocity perpetrators from Nazi Germany? Why did the USG provide amnesty to thousands of Japanese suspected of committing atrocities, including against Americans, during WWII? Why did the USG support the establishment of an ICT to address atrocities in the FRY but not contemporaneous atrocities alleg-edly involving Libya and Iraq? And why did the USG support an ICT for Rwanda that would be tied to the ICTY despite genuine concerns about the ICTY's prec-edent and operations?

Third, studying the reasons the USG supported particular transitional jus-tice options is critical to understanding the development of international law during and immediately after the Cold War as well as relations among states both outside and inside the UNSC. The four ICTs are particularly significant in this respect in two ways. First, the tribunals specifically addressed atrocities in Central Europe, East Asia, and sub-Saharan Africa. Second, the tribunals generally influenced post-atrocity activities in those regions. These four ICTs also have established important legal, political, and moral precedents: they have served as models for the design of subsequent war crimes tribunals, such as the Special Court for Sierra Leone (SCSL), the ICC, the Iraqi Special Tribunal

(IST), the Special Tribunal for Lebanon (STL), and the Extraordinary Chambers in the Courts of Cambodia for the Prosecution of Crimes Committed During the Period of Democratic Kampuchea (ECCC). The IMT, the IMTFE, the ICTY, and the ICTR—on which vast resources were or have been expended—also have contributed significantly to the development of international criminal jurisprudence.

Finally, my analysis of competing explanations for USG behavior toward transitional justice carries implications for theoretical debates in international relations and international law. Transitional justice is an important subject for both disciplines.[44] More specifically, this project provides an opportunity to explore how both international relations theories focused on institutional design as well as foreign policy analysis apply to the cases of the IMT, the IMTFE, the ICTY, and the ICTR. A rich literature exists on why states, particularly powerful states, create international institutions. That literature focuses primarily on traditional economic and security concerns.[45] This book explores states' creation of a comparatively new category of institutions: those concerning transitional justice. Furthermore, holding individuals, in addition to states, accountable for atrocities is a relatively recent phenomenon in international relations. The International Court of Justice (ICJ), the principal judicial organ of the UN established in 1946 to succeed the Permanent Court of International Justice, can only hear cases between states,[46] whereas the IMT (1945), the IMTFE (1946), the ICTY (1993), the ICTR (1994), the ICC (1998), the SCSL (2000), the ECCC (2001), the IST (2003), and the STL (2007) were established to prosecute individuals.[47] As a result, this study constitutes one of the few efforts to explain state behavior with respect to this trend.[48] Unlike some of the existing literature,[49] however, this book focuses on more than merely a single transitional justice institution or context. And unlike some other existing literature,[50] this book concentrates on the particular role of the USG in transitional justice. The only other book to date focusing specifically on U.S. foreign policy on transitional justice centers on different case studies and reaches other conclusions.[51]

As my research deepens our understanding of how the USG has addressed suspected atrocity perpetrators from Europe, East Asia, the Middle East, and Rwanda, students of the history of the United States and each of those regions also will benefit from this analysis. The transitional justice institution(s) implemented in each case impacted post-conflict reconstruction and reconciliation, which have been critical historical drivers in each region. Better understanding of those dynamics is especially crucial in the case of the IMTFE. Considering that the IMTFE comprised eleven states representing more than half of the world's population, and also given that institution's role in addressing some of the most egregious atrocities perpetrated during WWII, this ICT showcased, according to one of its prosecution staff members, "one of the most important trials in world history."[52] And yet there is a relative dearth of scholarly analysis about this particular institution.[53]

Recent events have reinforced the salience and impact of transitional justice, and the more specific issue of what drives USG policy in that domain. Which transitional justice option is chosen to address a particular atrocity matters both to the states and societies directly involved as well as to the international community as a whole. For example, in response to the Rwandan genocide, the international community (through the UNSC acting under Chapter VII of the UN Charter) established the ICTR, which claimed primary jurisdiction,[54] or the right to decide which cases it would prosecute. Consequently, the international community could prosecute whomever it chose, and, regardless of its own preferences, the Government of Rwanda (GoR) was required to defer to and abide by the international community's preferences over the number and identity of defendants as well as the logistical features of the trials and any punishment.

To be sure, the importance and consequences of the varying transitional justice options remains a controversial topic. For example, when debating which transitional justice option to pursue in response to a recent atrocity (in Darfur), some suggested that what mattered was merely "doing something." Others argued that the transitional justice option chosen was crucial because it effectively determined otherwise sovereign decisions, namely when, where, how, which, and by whom suspected atrocity perpetrators would be brought to justice.[55]

The ICC, which was established by the Rome Statute in 1998 and which officially launched in 2002,[56] is currently investigating atrocities allegedly committed in eight countries—the Central African Republic (CAR), Côte d'Ivoire, the Democratic Republic of Congo (DRC), Kenya, Libya, Mali, Sudan, and Uganda[57]—and is currently conducting preliminary investigations in nine other situations—Afghanistan, Colombia, Georgia, Guinea, Honduras, Iraq, Nigeria, Palestine, and Ukraine.[58] In each case, as well as in some others, the international community has considered whether, how, and when to address the suspected perpetrators of these atrocities. This book's analysis of why the United States supported the establishment of past transitional justice institutions therefore may illuminate how and why decision-makers reach their transitional justice policies in the present day.

Transitional justice has also caught the attention of current U.S. foreign policymakers. The USG's priorities and distribution of resources with respect to conflicts and post-conflict situations help determine decision-making on transitional justice. Particularly since the events of September 11, 2001, the USG has contemplated how to address suspected terrorists, foreign government (e.g., Iraqi Ba'ath Party) leaders, and suspected atrocity perpetrators in its own military and civilian command. The U.S.-led campaign to combat terrorism (formerly known as the "Global War on Terror") has focused on efforts to prevent, mitigate, and stop terrorism, including through attempts to capture or kill members of al-Qaeda and other transnational terrorist groups. Though some are unlikely, Scheffer theorizes that there are at least nine judicial fora that the USG could use to prosecute suspected terrorists (some of whom are being detained indefinitely in a U.S. military facility in Guantánamo Bay, Cuba). These options include civilian and military courts within the United States or abroad, ad hoc ICTs established by the UNSC or the UN General Assembly (UNGA), a coalition treaty-based criminal tribunal, and a special Islamic court.[59] Before settling in December 2003 on an Iraqi-led war crimes tribunal (as opposed to a hybrid or international tribunal), the USG considered various options for handling captured Iraqis (including Saddam Hussein), such as exile, assassination, a war crimes tribunal that was either unilateral or multilateral, and a domestic truth commission.[60]

Finally, the USG has become embroiled in a controversy over whether and how to handle cases involving Americans accused of committing atrocities (particularly war crimes, crimes against humanity, and torture). Such cases have included suspected abuses against civilians in Haditha, Iraq, as well as against inmates at the Abu Ghraib prison in Iraq, the Bagram Air Base in Afghanistan, and the U.S. military detention facility at Guantánamo.[61] This controversy stems from the fact that no institution outside the USG, including the ICC and the ICJ, has clear jurisdiction, leaving the USG complete latitude to make its own decisions. Such discretion has been criticized for being too lenient on American citizens and too harsh on foreigners.

The contemporary debate within the United States about whether and how to bring suspected terrorists and other alleged atrocity perpetrators to justice has sparked controversy over military tribunals/commissions, with commentators debating whether they are—or are even perceived to be—legal and/or just, and, regardless, what the consequences of using them might entail.[62] This debate also occurs against the backdrop of the USG's decision not to ratify the treaty that established the ICC, the international community's only permanent transitional justice institution and the one with the greatest territorial jurisdiction.[63] With these issues not fully resolved, in 2008, the administration of President George W. Bush (Bush, Jr.) opened the first war crimes trial since WWII, against Salim Hamdan,[64] who was subsequently transferred to his home country of Yemen and released.[65]

At least two U.S. Supreme Court rulings relevant to the case studies explored in this book directly concern and are often cited in these matters. In the 1942 case of *Ex parte Quirin*, the Court held that the USG could lawfully constitute and use military commissions to try alleged war criminals.[66] Six years later, in his concurring opinion in *Hirota v. MacArthur*, Associate Justice William O. Douglas offered a prescient warning, one crucially relevant to current events. Justice Douglas argued that the Court's denial of motions by those convicted by the IMTFE for leave to file petitions for writs of habeas corpus

> would have grave and alarming consequences . . . . Tomorrow or next year an American citizen may stand condemned in . . . a military court or commission. If no United States court can inquire into the lawfulness of his detention, the military have acquired, contrary to our traditions . . . a new and alarming hold on us . . . . It leaves practically no room for judicial scrutiny of this new type of military tribunal which is evolving. It leaves the power of those tribunals absolute. Prisoners held under its mandates may have appeal to the conscience or mercy of an executive; but they apparently have no appeal to law.[67]

Justice Douglas, while agreeing with the majority that the Court has "no authority to review the judgment of an international tribunal," nonetheless foreshadowed the USG's reluctance to embrace the ICC, noting his concerns with allowing U.S. citizens to be tried and convicted by an international tribunal without the right to challenge in domestic courts that tribunal's legality, jurisdiction, procedures, verdict, or sentencing.[68]

But contemporary interest in policymaking concerning transitional justice is not limited to foreign affairs. In 2014, the deans of Yale and Harvard law schools jointly cited transitional justice institutions abroad in suggesting reforms to the American legal system.[69]

The central contribution of this book is to understand how and why the USG has developed its transitional justice policy. I document the history of and key issues in the USG's preference for or opposition to various transitional justice options, including the USG role in establishing four ICTs—the IMT, the IMTFE, the ICTY, and the ICTR. In so doing, I demonstrate that, although many options for addressing transitional justice have theoretically been available to the USG, it has considered and ultimately supported only a fraction of these alternatives. This book explains what dynamics made some options more attractive than others and how larger issues (e.g., the nature of crimes) factor into the formulation of USG responses to certain atrocities. In addition to explaining past U.S. foreign policymaking, my research helps illuminate paths that the USG might take in the aftermath of future atrocities, and what the USG's preferences are likely to be regarding various transitional justice options.

III. Focus of Analysis

The scope of this book's analysis is narrowed in two ways. First, I focus on ICTs (as opposed to other types of transitional justice institutions, such as truth commissions) for two reasons. ICTs were the first and have been the longest-running attempts to promote and pursue transitional justice on the international stage. Consequently, ICTs have been instituted in response to many of the worst atrocities in the twentieth and twenty-first centuries. ICTs are therefore perhaps the most significant type of transitional justice institution demanding critical study.

As I discuss in Chapter II, ICTs also vary widely in form and function. While this book focuses on state-sponsored ICTs, whether through or outside the UN, several international "tribunals" have been established, staffed, and operated by NGOs and/or independent individuals. These bodies have tried to hold accountable, even if only symbolically, USG officials and others accused of committing atrocities.[70] Such "courts" are outside the scope of this book.

Second, this book examines the behavior of one state, the United States, toward transitional justice. There are three main reasons for this focus. First, as one of the world's two superpowers after WWII and as the world's sole superpower since the Cold War, the United States has been enormously influential in shaping international responses to atrocities. U.S. policy is thus critical to understanding the development and nature of transitional justice institutions. Second, the USG has arguably been the strongest backer of ad hoc ICTs, especially the IMT, the IMTFE, the ICTY, and the ICTR. The USG has favored their establishment, financed much of their operational costs, and provided technical expertise and staff.[71] Third, the United States historically has been one of the most actively involved states leading international support for—or opposition to—particular transitional justice options and institutions. Although much scholarly attention focuses on the USG's opposition to the ICC,[72] academic discourse often neglects the USG's leading role in establishing and supporting other transitional justice institutions, including the IMT, the IMTFE, the ICTY, and the ICTR. Studying these latter cases provides better understanding of why the USG is at once the strongest opponent of some ICTs and the most active supporter and funder of others.

Although this book focuses on USG policy on certain transitional justice options, the USG pursued additional initiatives following each related atrocity. For example, after WWII, U.S. Secretary of State George Marshall devised and implemented his eponymous Plan, an aid package to help European states, including former antagonists, recover from the war and to combat the potential spread of communism.[73] As another example, after the Rwandan genocide the USG instituted Operation Support Hope, a humanitarian relief project that assisted refugees.[74] An analysis of these post-conflict development assistance efforts, however, is beyond this book's scope. Furthermore, this project does not examine transitional justice plans targeting individuals or groups besides suspected atrocity perpetrators. Such options include providing compensation or reparations to victims; delivering physical and psychological therapy to survivors; constructing, rebuilding, and reforming public education, social programs, and civic institutions; and commemorating victims through museums, memorials, artistic representations, and other practical or symbolic initiatives.[75]

IV. Methodology

This book's central research aim is to determine how and why the USG formulated particular transitional justice policies in the immediate aftermaths of WWII and the Cold War. In doing so, I identify the most significant political factors, pragmatic features, and normative beliefs shaping U.S. foreign policy in this issue area. Using these findings, this book offers prudentialism as an alternative to legalism, the dominant theoretical framework on this topic. The final part of this Introduction describes the key methodologies employed in the analysis: case study, as opposed to other research paradigms; the selection system for the case studies; and the sources upon which the analysis draws.[76] By way of conclusion, I outline the core elements of the argument to follow.

A. CASE STUDY APPROACH

This book employs the "case study" method,[77] which political scientists Alexander George and Andrew Bennett define as "the detailed examination of an aspect of a historical episode to develop or test historical explanations that may be generalizable to other events."[78] Case study research is often conducted on two dimensions: the number of cases investigated and the amount of information collected per case. Rather than collect a small amount of data on a large number of cases, as often occurs with survey research, this book examines a large amount of data on a small number of cases. And unlike the process of generating cases to be studied, as accomplished through experimental research, this book uses preexisting data. As is common in case study research, this book employs a qualitative, rather than quantitative, analysis of and a narrative approach to the data concerning the cases investigated.

There are several purposes behind this book's "small-N" approach. First, this book uses "process tracing"—what George and political scientist Timothy McKeown define as "the decision process by which various initial conditions are translated into outcomes"[79]— to understand the cases studied for their own sake: to document and comprehend the USG role in these transitional justice situations, with their unique features and in their particular circumstances. Each of the six case studies serves as an instance of a type of USG approach to transitional justice. Second, I examine the decision points preceding each transitional justice option selected to determine whether the reasoning behind each decision comports more with legalism or prudentialism. Third, although not all case study research must do so, this book aims to draw theoretical inferences about which framework—legalism or prudentialism—better explains USG policy on transitional justice generally.[80] As a result, this book's objectives are to employ within-case examination as well as cross-case comparisons.

B. CASE STUDY SELECTION

I have deliberately selected six cases (Germany and Japan in the immediate aftermath of WWII as well as Libya, Iraq, the FRY, and Rwanda in the immediate aftermath of the Cold War), consistent with case study selection theory,[81] based on seven criteria. First, the number of case studies—six—is large and varied enough to take into account certain trends in USG policy on transitional justice while being sufficiently manageable for rigorous analysis within this book's space constraints. Such a "small-N" study therefore allows me "to introduce nuance and complexity into the understanding" of transitional justice.[82] The set permits comparative analysis and avoids the pitfalls of single case study research, such as misinterpreting multivariate causation.[83]

Second, I have chosen the IMT, the IMTFE, the ICTY, and the ICTR for their historical innovation (they were the first ICTs), their precedential value (as both legal and political institutions), and the challenges accompanying their creation. Furthermore, any analysis of the ICTY and the ICTR necessarily requires a corresponding study of the objectives and institutional design relating to the establishment of the IMT and the IMTFE, as I argue that the ICTY and the ICTR are modeled primarily on them. As these four tribunals are not entirely isolated developments, they should be considered together, as I do in this book.

Third, my research also reveals that USG policy objectives on transitional justice issues in the immediate aftermaths of WWII and the Cold War were similar and interrelated. For example, USG officials pursued many of the same transitional justice objectives in each case and justified doing so by referring to the government's precedent. Consequently, studying these transitional justice situations collectively provides a more complete picture of the motivations driving the USG role in designing and establishing such institutions.

Fourth, I have chosen the six cases in part for the overlapping historical eras in which they were created. For example, each contemporary pair of tribunals (the IMT and the IMTFE, and the ICTY and the ICTR) was established in a separate two-year time frame (1945–1946 and 1993–1994), corresponding with the administrations of Presidents FDR and Truman, on the one hand, and President Clinton, on the other. When comparing contemporary pairs of ICTs, it is possible to analyze transitional justice during periods when much of the political, social, and economic landscapes (particularly domestically in the United States) remained the same. Thus, it is feasible to hold some variables during those eras relatively constant in order to better determine key factors influencing USG policymaking on transitional justice. In other words, because the two pairs of ICTs were created almost simultaneously and under similar conditions, I can isolate more credibly the elements leading to certain ICTs.

Fifth, these transitional justice situations occurred during great upheavals in global affairs. For example, each coterminous pair of tribunals was fashioned as a radical shift in the international structure emerged—the IMT and the IMTFE were created as the international system evolved from multipolarity to bipolarity, and the ICTY and the ICTR were established as the international system changed from bipolarity to unipolarity.[84] As such, it is possible to explore how, if at all, such revolutionary changes in world politics influenced U.S. policy on transitional justice in these cases.

Sixth, the particular forms of the four ICTs investigated were unprecedented and conceptually different from prior transitional justice institutions, even within overlapping pairs. This variance (including why the USG supported it) needs explanation. The IMT and the IMTFE were the first and only ad hoc multilateral military war crimes tribunals yet were different from each other in important ways (as explored in Chapters IV and V).[85] The ICTY and the ICTR are the first and only purely international ad hoc war crimes tribunals (as opposed to, for example, hybrid UN/successor state war crimes tribunals, such as the SCSL and the ECCC, or the world's first permanent ICT, the ICC) to have been established through the UNSC acting under Chapter VII of the UN Charter. However, the ICTY and the ICTR certainly differ along several dimensions (as discussed in Chapters VI and VII).

Finally, because of the requisite passage of time, relevant primary documents from each of the six case studies could be declassified. In addition, USG policymaking on Libya, Iraq, the FRY, and Rwanda occurred recently enough (in the 1990s) that it was also possible to conduct interviews with key decision-makers and observers.

Some suggest that deliberately selecting cases based on the dependent variable undermines the quality of the analysis.[86] In each of this book's four primary cases (Germany and Japan in the immediate aftermath of WWII and the FRY and Rwanda in the immediate aftermath of the Cold War), an ICT, with a limited range of variation, was established following an atrocity; thus there is little variation in these outcomes. However, as the goal of this book is to analyze actual instances of the outcome studied (including variation across outcomes in which an ICT emerged), it is necessary to study these types of cases.[87] In addition, because instances in which such outcomes did not occur can provide additional insight into policy choices and underlying motivations, the book also explores such occurrences both within and outside the four primary cases. Chapters II and III consider state motivations about whether to confront suspected atrocity perpetrators, whereas Chapters IV, V, and VI discuss Nazis, Imperial Japanese, and Serbs who were not addressed immediately or at all through ICTs. Moreover, Chapter VI investigates why an ICT was not established following atrocities concerning Libya and Iraq.

Though I have chosen the six case studies because they are representative of responses to atrocities in many ways, they are *unrepresentative* in one crucial way. The atrocities examined in this book were state-sponsored or, in the case of Libya,[88] were suspected of being such. Considering the impact of al-Qaeda, Daesh (also known as the Islamic State of Iraq and the Levant (ISIL) and the Islamic State of Iraq and Syria (ISIS)), associated or copycat groups, and other nonstate actors, future research should also explore U.S. policy on transitional justice as responses to atrocities, such as terrorist attacks, that are not state-sponsored.

C. SOURCES

This book investigates and draws conclusions about each of the six case studies by examining primary documents and secondary sources relating to USG decision-making on transitional justice; by consulting further primary and secondary sources in the fields of political science, law, history, and area studies; by considering additional facts and the logic and persuasiveness of arguments put forth in interviews with U.S. officials involved in, and others familiar with, these cases; and by analyzing events before, during, and after the six case studies.

1. Source Sets—Types

My research therefore draws upon three main sets of sources. First, I researched primary sources, including published and unpublished USG documents, UNSC resolutions and reports, statements by U.S. and other state and intergovernmental officials reported in the press, and documents from European, East Asian, and the Rwandan governments. As part of this process, I filed Freedom of Information Act (FOIA) requests with the U.S. Departments of State (U.S./DoS), Defense (U.S./DoD), and Justice (U.S./DoJ), and I sent similar requests to the UN Libraries and Office of the UN Secretary General (UNSG) to declassify and make available primary documents (e.g., cables, intra- and interagency memorandums) relevant to transitional justice policymaking in the six case studies. These primary sources provided critical and unfiltered insight into the evolution of the USG decision-making process, including the perspectives and motivations of key individuals.

Second, I consulted secondary sources to review the literature on the USG role in transitional justice issues and to facilitate my assessment of the application of related international relations theories to particular challenges inherent in understanding international cooperation and coordination on transitional justice issues. I drew these secondary sources from the fields of international relations (including international cooperation and institution creation), international law (especially international criminal law), history (including the history of conflict, diplomatic history, legal history, and the history of the UN), human rights, transitional justice, U.S. foreign policy, conflict prevention and management, and regional studies. These materials provided useful information on the background of and theoretical framework through which USG policy on transitional justice can be analyzed.

Finally, in order to supplement written primary and secondary sources, and to gain further insight into the reasons for and motivations behind certain transitional justice policy choices, I conducted personal interviews with current and former USG officials involved in or familiar with U.S. foreign policy regarding suspected perpetrators of the atrocities I investigated. I also interviewed other individuals who are knowledgeable about USG policymaking in this issue area, including from NGOs (human rights organizations, think tanks, etc.), academia, other state governments, and the ICTs themselves.[89]

I sought declassified documents and personal interviews not only for the additional insights they would provide but also to confirm or refute arguments proffered in secondary sources or through other primary sources.

2. Source Sets—Potential Pitfalls and Mitigations

Each of the primary sources features potential pitfalls. These problems concern possible bias due to the inaccessibility and censorship of certain material.

I was unable to access some primary documents, in whole or in part. Although I did receive a large number of relevant documents after submitting declassification requests to the USG and the UN,[90] I was not provided with all of the materials I sought. Because the USG partially or completely withheld some documents,[91] I obtained only a selective portrait of USG internal discussions and decision-making. Moreover, it is possible that the authors of these documents or their sources anticipated that these materials would be declassified and released to the public, so these materials might reflect self-censorship. Owing to the passage of time and the evolution of more precise documentation and declassification practices within the USG, I obtained more primary documents concerning Libya, Iraq, the FRY, and Rwanda than I did relating to Germany and Japan.

Similarly, I also conducted more personal interviews concerning Libya, Iraq, the FRY, and Rwanda than about Germany and Japan. Therefore, a great deal of my primary research on the former four case studies benefits from "elite interviewing," or interviewing individuals involved in the decision-making process.[92] Elite interviewing, like researching declassified documents, is potentially hazardous. One possible problem is bias related to accessibility: most of the individuals involved in establishing or who otherwise had first-hand knowledge about Germany and Japan died before I could request an interview.[93] Even though their contexts were much more recent, some key individuals relating to the four later cases studied had also passed away or did not grant me an interview.

A second pitfall of elite interviewing is that the data must be understood for what they are—personal interviews, with all of their possible, inevitable human flaws. Intentionally or not, a decade or longer after certain events, USG officials might not tell the whole truth or be completely thorough. Involvement in a decision may inherently prevent impartiality. Additionally, there may be incentives to exaggerate or lie, such as the desire to self-aggrandize or to avoid criticism.[94]

Moreover, these individuals may not remember or know why they supported or opposed a particular decision.[95]

Although availability and censorship of documents and interviewees may bias the data I collected, I have mitigated the potential problems that exist with these sources. I used "triangulation," or the process of collecting and cross-checking data from multiple sources to corroborate events or explanations,[96] whether through other interviews or by surveying the documents declassified to me or the secondary literature on this topic. In the cases of the FRY and Rwanda, the potential for bias from self-selection or availability of primary sources was slight because, as I determined, the decision-making process concerning transitional justice was conducted primarily by mid-level U.S./DoS officials, many of whom I interviewed. On the one hand, these officials could state their own rationales, which were most crucial, and also could reveal their assessment of the objectives of and influences on higher-level officials whom they consulted. On the other hand, the ultimate decisions implicitly reveal information about the preferences of more senior officials, as the decisions to support certain transitional justice options—such as the creation of the IMT, the IMTFE, the ICTY, and the ICTR— would not have been made without their approval.

Triangulation notwithstanding, there is also reason to believe that officials may be accurate sources of information even years after events in which they participated, possibly more so than documents they or others created at the time. As political scientist Yuen Foong Khong argues, "[t]o be sure, former policymakers may forget or prevaricate, but one supposes that the passage of time may also allow them a sense of detachment that makes them more forthcoming about what they do remember."[97]

D. OUTLINE OF ARGUMENT

This book is divided into seven additional chapters. Chapter II provides background and context for my arguments about prudentialism by presenting transitional justice options and the USG's experience with them. Chapter III explores the particular problems and challenges transitional justice represents for international relations. This chapter considers the particular explanatory frameworks—legalism and prudentialism—evaluated in this book and uses them to generate hypotheses about U.S. policy on transitional justice that are tested in later chapters.

The subsequent four chapters focus on the case studies: they document and analyze the U.S. role in transitional justice for Germany and Japan in the immediate aftermath of WWII, and Libya, Iraq, the FRY, and Rwanda in the immediate aftermath of the Cold War. These chapters first determine which transitional justice options were considered and instituted and then analyze the most important factors driving the USG's support for or opposition to these options. Three of these four case study chapters contain four parts, whereas one of the chapters contains five parts. The chapters on Germany; the FRY, Libya, and Iraq; and Rwanda each contain four parts. Part I provides historical background, including negotiations leading to the creation of the IMT, the ICTY, and the ICTR, respectively. Part II enumerates the transitional justice options seriously considered and actually implemented alongside each of these ICTs, including those options ultimately rejected for handling the suspected criminals behind the most egregious atrocities. In doing so, this Part compiles thematically the transitional justice decision-making that was presented chronologically in Part I—while adding discussion of some other decisions. Throughout the negotiations leading to the establishment of each ICT, several events occurred that were surprising or counterintuitive and thus demand additional scrutiny. So, Part III elucidates critical developments in the decision-making process, resolving some key puzzles involving the USG to understand further the process leading to the creation of the ICT and implementation of other transitional justice mechanisms. (This part of Chapter VI investigates the bombing of Pan Am flight 103 and Iraqi offenses against Kuwaitis.) Each of these three case study chapters ends with Part IV, which draws conclusions about U.S. policymaking based on these important episodes in transitional justice.

The case study on Japan, Chapter V, features each of the aforementioned parts found in the other case studies but this case study also contains an additional part in the middle of the chapter. Given the relative dearth of research on the IMTFE and the fact that the U.S. role in establishing this ICT was perhaps the most significant of the four primary case studies, this chapter contains an extended section on the U.S. role in the overall transitional justice system in postwar Japan.

Finally, Chapter VIII summarizes the case studies' key findings and revisits the explanatory framework for this book. This chapter begins by reviewing the factors influencing USG behavior in each case study. The chapter then assesses the strengths of legalism and prudentialism in accounting for USG behavior, concluding that U.S. policy on transitional justice is ultimately, as prudentialism theorizes, a product of politics, pragmatics, and normative beliefs.

Overview of Transitional Justice Options and the United States Role in Transitional Justice

I. Introduction

This chapter provides background and context for U.S. policy on transitional justice by presenting the panoply of options for addressing suspected atrocity perpetrators and the U.S. experience with them.[1] There are numerous and widely differing (in terms of purpose and design) transitional justice options that have been or could be created, and the USG has employed many of them. Transitional justice issues can be complicated and controversial because of the number, attractiveness, precedence, and pitfalls of the alternatives. This chapter therefore enumerates and describes various transitional justice options and explores their benefits and drawbacks. As Bass notes, states have contemplated or used a wide array of methods to deal with suspected atrocity perpetrators, including prosecutions through an ICT, executions on sight, en masse executions later, show trials followed by executions, exile, concentration camps, and amnesty. FDR and British prime minister Winston Churchill even suggested castrating suspected atrocity perpetrators in WWII.[2] A more complete list includes the general options of and specific variations on inaction, lustration, amnesty, exile, indefinite detention, lethal force, and prosecution. Figure 2.1 displays these general transitional justice options, their various permutations (except for prosecution), and how they interrelate. Figure 2.2 displays specific prosecutorial transitional justice options, their various permutations, and how they interrelate.

As this book documents, the political and pragmatic context, as well as U.S. officials' normative beliefs, make some transitional justice options more appealing to the USG than others, including those options the USG has previously supported. Indeed, as displayed in Figure 2.3, especially since September 11, 2001, the USG has favored four general transitional justice options—inaction, indefinite detention (primarily in Guantánamo Bay, Cuba), lethal force (especially

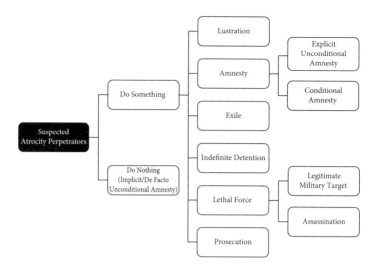

FIGURE 2.1 *Transitional Justice Options Tree for Suspected Atrocity Perpetrators—General.*

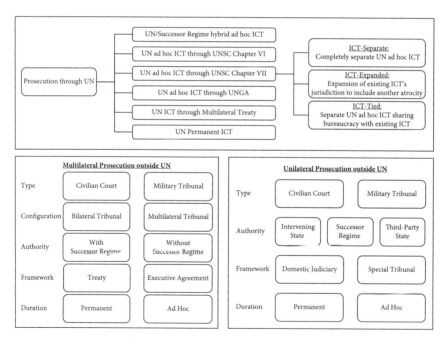

FIGURE 2.2 *Transitional Justice Options Tree and Table for Suspected Atrocity Perpetrators—Prosecution.*

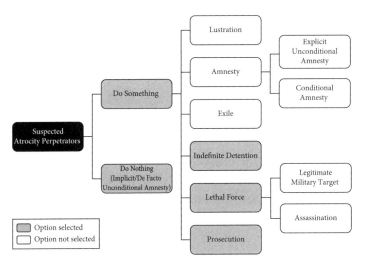

FIGURE 2.3 *U.S. Government Transitional Justice Options Tree for Suspected Atrocity Perpetrators—Since 9/11.*

through drone strikes), and prosecution (through military commissions and civilian courts)—as methods of responding to suspected atrocity perpetrators.

The IMT and the IMTFE represent the only U.S. experience with prosecution through multilateral military war crimes tribunals. The American role in other transitional justice institutions and processes is noted and explored in this chapter, although these experiences are much less important than the IMT and the IMTFE for establishing precedent and serving as models for the ICTY and the ICTR. Investigating the factors that drove the USG to back the IMT, the IMTFE, the ICTY, and the ICTR is all the more interesting, considering that those options were somewhat unprecedented and conceptually distinct from other past, contemporaneous, and future USG decision-making regarding transitional justice, including USG consideration of and support for a variety of prosecutorial and non-prosecutorial options.

II. Transitional Justice Options

Transitional justice options, like many other policy choices, can be mutually supportive, mutually exclusive, or conflicting. For example, killing an individual likely precludes resort to any other methods for dealing with that person.[3] From a logistical standpoint, choosing one option also may preclude others because of limited resources or time. Choices pertaining to a transitional justice situation as a whole may not be mutually exclusive, however, as the same or related suspected atrocity perpetrators may be concurrently or sequentially addressed through alternative options.[4] As Scheffer has argued, "[t]here may well be occasion to prosecute different terrorist suspects in different courts in different jurisdictions simultaneously."[5] The transitional justice options listed below begin with the decision surrounding whether to pursue some version of transitional justice at all. The options then are listed in no particular order.

A. ACTION VERSUS INACTION

In confronting suspected atrocity perpetrators, the first decision is whether to do anything at all.[6] For example, in the immediate aftermaths of the Armenian and Cambodian genocides, the USG chose not to pursue the individuals allegedly responsible for these heinous crimes.

Some government officials may not want to help foreign states or societies address suspected atrocity perpetrators. Doing nothing may serve both humanitarian and political ends by encouraging combatants to stop fighting, surrender themselves, or testify without fear of punishment. However, inaction (which, as discussed below, could also be referred to as implicit or de facto unconditional amnesty) carries serious moral implications because it may result in allowing suspected atrocity perpetrators to evade accountability. Furthermore, inaction can be considered illicit when states are legally obligated to proactively bring suspected atrocity perpetrators to justice. For example, signatories to the 1948 Genocide Convention, including the United States, "confirm that . . . they undertake to prevent and to punish" genocide.[7]

The grounds for declining to pursue transitional justice may be legal, normative, practical, or some combination, and often echo arguments against humanitarian intervention.[8] The normative reasons frequently emphasize pessimistic warnings against paternalistic, imperialistic, or even well-intentioned efforts that may be counterproductive. Transitional justice efforts may promote justice at the expense of peace, in the sense that such efforts could spur further conflict between and among victims and their victimizers, a potential tension explored further in Chapter III.[9]

Alternatively, states may decide not to pursue transitional justice elsewhere because of the normative and legal commitment to nonintervention—the notion that states should refrain from interfering in the affairs of other states. This principle, dating back to the 1648 Treaty of Westphalia and enshrined in the UN Charter, holds that states are generally proscribed from violating the political sovereignty or territorial integrity of other states.[10] Such legal arguments against foreign involvement in transitional justice usually stress that the post-atrocity society or state has jurisdiction, and it would therefore be an illegal usurpation of that society or state's rights to impose options, procedures, and/or staff that the local population would not choose voluntarily. A related normative concern focuses on the notion of self-determination.[11] Under this principle, foreign powers should allow or perhaps even enable a post-atrocity society to select and then implement the society's preferred transitional justice institution. The reasoning is that, as the people of victimized societies emerge from their horrific experiences, it should be their prerogative to enjoy final discretion over how to move forward. As international relations scholar Jennifer Welsh observes, citing philosopher John Stuart Mill, this objection to intervention "is based on the belief that our highest moral duty is to respect the right of self-determination . . . . It is through the act of self-government that political communities—and by extension, individuals—realize freedom and virtue."[12]

Several practical concerns relate to whether a foreign state becomes involved in a post-atrocity society. In some instances, participation by a post-atrocity society in its own transitional justice process may be crucial for reconstruction and reconciliation. Unwanted interference from foreign powers might make matters worse in the short term, perhaps by further traumatizing survivors by forcing them to undergo the ordeal of reliving the past. Finally, involvement in addressing suspected atrocity perpetrators might be too costly (both in terms of resources and time) for foreign states, especially in a post-atrocity society or state that has suffered devastation to its infrastructure and professional ranks.

One justification for "doing nothing" that often lacks credibility is that state leaders did not know of the atrocities. Given worldwide media accounts, reports by NGOs, and global intelligence collection, especially by the USG in the modern era, it is unrealistic today to believe that many if not all states could possibly remain unaware of atrocities, wherever they occur. In that case, a state's decision to "do nothing" is likely made in conscious neglect of realities on the ground. Advances in journalism, technology, and advocacy make ignorance of atrocities less plausible over time.

Some pragmatists argue that a deliberate or de facto strategy of inaction, either due to insufficient demand for justice and accountability or because efforts to pursue these goals were effectively deterred, need not constitute failed policy. For example, as these commentators argue, remaining passive toward suspected atrocity perpetrators has been a strategy in Namibia and Afghanistan, which may have contributed to peace-building and post-conflict reconstruction in both states. No attempt to apprehend and hold individuals accountable was pursued in either case, thus insulating peace settlements from the often politically fraught transitional justice process.[13]

On the other hand, there are several, either discrete or mutually reinforcing, reasons that state leaders may wish to confront suspected atrocity perpetrators. These reasons may be normative, political, or some combination.

First, foreign leaders may accord significant weight to humanitarian ideals, namely that all human beings should be treated equally and uniformly protected from harm. The humanitarian leader may choose to intervene, trumping competing concerns about state sovereignty and self-determination as well as risking unintended negative consequences.

Another possible normative motivation is backward-looking and remedial but also includes a political aim. Foreign leaders may conclude that they should take proactive, public steps to compensate for previous unwillingness or inability to prevent or mitigate an atrocity through more effective and timely (e.g., military) action. Such leaders may seek to offset recent inaction or failures in the region through a singular foreign policy success: bringing suspected perpetrators of the atrocity to justice. A successful effort could resuscitate a foreign leader's credibility and reputation by demonstrating that the state can operate successfully in that region. One risk inherent in this context is that observers may interpret the foreign leader's decision-making as motivated by feelings of guilt.

A third possible normative reason is forward-looking and rehabilitative: foreign leaders may realize belatedly the particularly egregious nature and scope of crimes and only then feel compelled to become involved as a logical, appropriate, and necessary response. These leaders may conclude that they should aid victims, stop victimizers, and deter potential atrocity perpetrators, regardless—or even because—of how many individuals have already suffered.

Yet a fourth normative motive concerns the moral obligations of power, particularly as such conceptions impact national identity. A foreign leader may feel a sense of duty in addressing suspected atrocity perpetrators, stemming from the leader's conception of his or her home state's role in the world as a peacemaker and strong pro-democratic force. As Scheffer, an American, argues:

> We must, indeed, do something [about atrocities]. That is my view of what America, as the dominant power in the world, is all about. Otherwise, our understanding of dominance becomes so insular and self-protective that it is no longer dominance, no longer leadership, and no longer the moral high ground. It is just plain lethargic power, intimidated by the challenges of the world. The issue, when confronted with atrocities, is what must be done, not whether something should be done.[14]

Politics also factor into many of the reasons state leaders may decide to "do something" to confront suspected atrocity perpetrators. First, public demand for action—especially from survivors of atrocities, citizens of intervening states, and other domestic or foreign special interest groups—may be so strong as to make inaction a politically risky option.

A second possible political explanation is backward-looking: intervening state leaders may invoke a foreign regime's past behavior as justification for the intervention. A state may seek to expose or publicize the atrocities of a foreign regime in order to validate how harshly the state treated that foreign regime after the latter planned or perpetrated those offenses. For example, after the USG invaded Iraq in 2003 and failed to uncover the weapons of mass destruction the Bush, Jr. administration had claimed justified the intervention, the USG shifted the impetus for its action to confronting Saddam Hussein's human rights violations.[15] Some commentators argue that the subsequent trial of Saddam himself provided the opportunity for the USG to achieve its political objective of bolstering its supposed humanitarian motivations for intervening in Iraq.[16]

A third conceivable political motivation is forward-looking: leaders of an intervening state may want to become involved in a current transitional justice solution because of its perceived impact on future transitional justice initiatives. Especially if the intervening state views a transitional justice solution as inevitable and not necessarily against its own interests, the intervening state may support that transitional justice option because it wants to ensure the most favorable design of that institution relative to its interests. When institutions potentially serve as important precedents and models for subsequent transitional justice institutions, the intervening state has a clear stake in their design. For example, if U.S. hegemony were in decline (or at least perceived to be), then the USG might have an incentive to inject its own preferences into transitional justice negotiations either to reassert its hegemony or to benefit from the structure it helped erect if U.S. hegemony expires.

A fourth political reason that state officials may address suspected atrocity perpetrators is that government leaders are concerned with the act or perception of applying consistent transitional justice solutions. In other words, leaders may wish to frame their state's participation in transitional justice as fairly constant over time and across victimized communities. Inaction might be considered tantamount to racism and regionalism in prioritizing the tragedy of, for example, a European country and its white inhabitants over that of an African country and its black inhabitants, especially if the latter had arguably suffered even more. If the leaders of a state choose not to "do something" about suspected atrocity perpetrators, particularly after having taken bold action against other suspected atrocity perpetrators, they may be politically and morally obligated to justify their inaction, and their reputation may suffer at home and abroad unless and until they do so. Such motivations played a role in the USG response to the Rwandan genocide, as discussed in Chapter VII.

When state leaders decide to take action against suspected atrocity perpetrators, they face six general transitional justice options: (1) amnesty, (2) lustration, (3) exile, (4) lethal force, (5) prosecution, and (6) indefinite detention.

B. AMNESTY

Amnesty is a mechanism whereby an authorized entity grants a pardon for alleged past offenses, thus restoring any previously curtailed rights and privileges or preserving those that might have otherwise been restricted. The authority may be motivated by outright compassion, a desire to use clemency powers to be seen as merciful, a determination in light of new evidence that the accused was not actually guilty, or some strategic calculation that the benefits of granting amnesty outweigh the costs.

Like inaction, this transitional justice option may be morally and legally problematic because providing amnesty to suspected atrocity perpetrators prevents any official punitive accounting for their actions. However, the authority may grant amnesty only after a period of public humiliation and shaming, perhaps by forcing the accused to admit their alleged crimes in detail. Such tactics can serve as an alternative punishment for suspected atrocity perpetrators. This penalty, however, may not meet the moral or legal threshold of what constitutes appropriate punishment for particular crimes.[17] Amnesty may be granted posthumously, even though the subject is obviously unaware of the official exoneration for crimes he was accused or even convicted of committing.

There are two general amnesty options: conditional and unconditional. The former combines carrots and sticks; an official pardon is granted in exchange for truthful testimony. In this case, the transitional justice authority reserves the right to prosecute and, therefore, punish the suspected atrocity perpetrator if his testimony is judged to be incomplete or inaccurate.[18] This option could have the benefit of holding accountable uncooperative suspected atrocity perpetrators or enhancing their cooperation by threatening prosecution. Conditional amnesty is somewhat less morally problematic than the unconditional version, because, through the former, at least suspected atrocity perpetrators may be prosecuted and then punished if they resist requests for information about their alleged crimes. Such a system was most famously established in South Africa in 1995 as the Truth and Reconciliation Commission.[19]

Unconditional amnesty is a general exoneration granted to suspected atrocity perpetrators not based on any requirements, such as the breadth or accuracy of testimony. (Some have equated doing nothing about suspected atrocity perpetrators with unconditional amnesty. Political scientists Jack Snyder and Leslie Vinjamuri have deemed inaction a "de facto amnesty."[20] Doing nothing can also be understood as an "implicit unconditional amnesty," as distinguished from an explicit official grant of amnesty.) El Salvador established an explicit unconditional amnesty with its 1991 Commission on the Truth, and the USG was the most generous financial contributor (supplying 40 percent of its total budget). Another example of explicit unconditional amnesty occurred after World War I, when the Allied Powers, including the United States, signed the 1923 Treaty of Lausanne with Turkey, which contained a "Declaration of Amnesty" for crimes committed between 1914 and 1922, including the Turkish massacre (often characterized as a "genocide"[21]) of Armenians.[22] More recently, the Algerian government has pursued an official policy of forgetting (although, crucially, not necessarily forgiving), rather than confronting, the past.[23]

Some states beyond South Africa and El Salvador have instituted truth commissions domestically. For example, at least three such commissions have been established in the United States. A truth and reconciliation commission operated from 2004 to 2006 in Greensboro, North Carolina, to address the events of November 3, 1979, when a group of extremists murdered and injured civilians in a racially mixed gathering of political activists and labor organizers. The State of Illinois established the Torture Inquiry and Relief Commission in 2009 to investigate allegations of police torture. Most recently, the governor of Maine and the state's five tribal chiefs jointly authorized what became known as the Maine Wabanaki-State Child Welfare Truth and Reconciliation Commission, which, from 2013 to 2015, investigated the removal of Wabanaki children from their communities and then published a report that included findings and recommendations.[24]

Other truth commissions have been suggested, including within the United States. In 2009, the then-chairman of the U.S. Senate Committee on the Judiciary, Patrick Leahy, proposed the creation of a truth commission to investigate various controversial measures taken by the Bush, Jr. administration, including its treatment and torture of terrorism suspects.[25] Five years later, the deans of Yale and Harvard law schools jointly advocated drawing lessons from the use of foreign truth commissions in addressing police violence in the United States.[26] Even more recently, a *New York Times* columnist suggested that an "American Truth and Reconciliation" commission would be the ideal forum for a "national conversation on race."[27] Since the mid-1990s, a proposal to create a permanent international truth commission to supplement the ICC has also materialized.[28]

C. LUSTRATION

A second option for state leaders taking action to address atrocities is lustration. Transitional justice expert Neil Kritz defines lustration, or *épuration*, as the non-criminal sanction of "purging from the public sector those who served the repressive regime."[29] Lustration was employed in post-WWII France and Germany, and, after the fall of the USSR, in Germany, the Czech Republic, Bulgaria, Latvia, and Estonia. More recently, the USG implemented lustration to purge members and associates of the Ba'ath Party from the Iraqi government and other domestic institutions.[30] Essentially a collective, extrajudicial punishment of excluding certain individuals from government service because they are presumed guilty of atrocities by political association, lustration is often viewed by proponents as a quick and relatively easy method of dealing with a large number of suspected atrocity perpetrators and their accomplices. Besides punishment, lustration may be motivated by a desire to eliminate supposed impediments to the post-atrocity transition. The effect of lustration is to remove individuals from, or block them from obtaining, political office.[31] The same outcome may also follow at least four other transitional justice options—exile, lethal force, prosecution, and indefinite detention—by effectively eliminating exiled, targeted, convicted, or otherwise imprisoned individuals from government service.

Some argue, however, that lustration violates laws prohibiting discrimination based on political association. Specifically, lustration may run afoul of international law (e.g., the Fourth Geneva Convention and the International Covenant on Civil and Political Rights) and domestic law (e.g., the First Amendment to the U.S. Constitution). Like inaction and amnesty, lustration is also morally and legally problematic, because elimination from government may not be considered a sufficient punishment for heinous crimes.

Lustration also can be counterproductive. The process may not be narrowly tailored enough to effectively target those individuals (1) who committed atrocities or who were truly loyal to suspected atrocity perpetrators, and (2) who remained a threat to an intervening force and the process of (re) building a peaceful, just, democratic, and stable post-atrocity society. Instead, administrators of the lustration may be grossly indiscriminate in their purging of individuals from positions of authority, excluding from civil service and possibly leaving jobless many well-trained and experienced professionals who are vital to post-conflict reconstruction and management. The purged may include teachers, engineers, doctors, police officers, judges, soldiers, and bureaucrats. Because purged individuals may be left unemployed and feeling stung from unfair discrimination, lustration may generate resentment among citizens toward the intervening authority. Thus, lustration may convert many potential allies into fervent enemies of the intervening force. Those who might have contributed to a peaceful, efficient post-conflict transitional period may become dedicated, perhaps violently so, to thwarting the intervening force's efforts, even if those efforts are in the best interests of their compatriots. Lustration may ultimately generate ill will that foments insurgency and crime in the post-atrocity society.

Part of the problem is that lustration implicitly assumes much about the targeted group. By hastily and, therefore, inadequately screening a large number of people for their past affiliations and actions, lustration may elide the subtleties of those people's circumstances. The truth is that many individuals join political parties that ultimately become responsible for atrocities (e.g., the Nazi Party, the Ba'ath Party) not for ideological but for instrumental reasons: they wanted to obtain or keep a job; to receive other social, political, or economic benefits flowing from membership; or simply to help guarantee survival for themselves, their families, and their friends. A quick and broad lustration may be efficiently designed but flawed in implementation, and it runs the risk of creating a security vacuum, removing professionals with manpower and skills necessary to facilitate the post-atrocity transition, forcing some groups (e.g., ethnic or religious communities) to shoulder a disproportionate amount of hardship, and enraging large segments of the post-atrocity population.

D. EXILE

Exile as a transitional justice option can facilitate a transition to peace by physically removing an individual or group from the region.[32] Two former presidents of Haiti went into exile. In 1986, Jean-Claude "Baby Doc" Duvalier fled to France but then returned to Haiti in 2011, where he died in 2014.[33] And, in 2004,

Jean-Bertrand Aristide either voluntarily absconded to or was kidnapped by the United States and transported to the Central African Republic, after which he fled to Jamaica and then to South Africa, and then, like Duvalier, returned in 2011 to Haiti, where he allegedly remains.[34] Other famous cases of exile include Idi Amin, the former dictator of Uganda, who in 1979 went into exile in Libya and eventually Saudi Arabia, where he died in 2003,[35] and Mengistu Haile Mariam, the former dictator of Ethiopia, who in 1991 went into exile in Zimbabwe, where he allegedly remains.[36] Charles Taylor, the former president of Liberia, went into exile in 2003 in Calabar, Nigeria.[37] On March 25, 2006, Nigerian president Olusegun Obasanjo announced that he would renege on his promise to provide Taylor with asylum,[38] thus prompting Taylor to disappear from Calabar two days later.[39] After receiving pressure from the USG, Nigeria arrested Taylor the following day and then transferred him to Liberia to face prosecution at the SCSL.[40] He was ultimately convicted of war crimes and crimes against humanity and sentenced to fifty years imprisonment.[41]

Exile may be voluntary, as when an individual or group elects to yield power and position and move to another state, or involuntary, as when other entities oust leaders and banish them to a foreign land. Some argue that exile is a reasonable option for deposing leaders in certain cases, at least in the short term. Exile may represent a compromise of sorts, whereby removed leaders escape other transitional justice options in exchange for not causing further conflict or continuing to pilfer from the state's treasury. Political scientists Edward Mansfield and Snyder argue that potential spoilers should be exiled and offered a "golden parachute," or a generous departing provision, to foster democratization by reducing incentives to retain or regain power.[42] Even where there is little likelihood of their wielding authority, suspected atrocity perpetrators may still be induced to move. For example, in a practice that pejoratively became known in some circles as "Nazi dumping," the USG reportedly allowed alleged Nazis who had become U.S. citizens to keep accruing millions of dollars in Social Security benefits if they agreed to leave the United States voluntarily.[43]

Yet the long-term effects of exiling an accused atrocity perpetrator could be disastrous, far outweighing any short-term benefits. First, exile is morally problematic. Although it punishes alleged atrocity perpetrators through banishment from their homeland or a third-party state (thereby constraining freedom of movement), exile may be considered too lenient, as it does not hold these suspects accountable in a court of justice and forgoes possible punishment through traditional means, such as imprisonment. Golden parachutes, under this interpretation, are perverse rewards for committing heinous crimes.

Second, exile is strategically problematic, as it may undermine the international community's ability to deter atrocities. The relatively mild nature of the punishment of exile may embolden other potential warlords and human rights violators and fail to deter them from continuing or commencing horrific acts.

Third, exile is legally problematic. If suspects are not arrested and prosecuted, any jurisdiction that has indicted them—such as an ICT—would be excluded from the transition process, and domestic and/or international law may be violated. States providing asylum may face doubts about their reliability in the international system, complicating their role and relations in world politics.

Finally, exile can result in problematic consequences for victims. The emotional and psychological reconciliation process for persecuted individuals may suffer setbacks without a formal prosecution (or other mechanism for holding perpetrators accountable), as victims might continue to feel unsafe and unable to lead productive lives. Victims may also feel that their suffering has not been validated or vindicated, making it more difficult for them to establish or re-establish relationships with those with whom they have experienced conflict in the past.

Furthermore, even if in exile, a despot might continue to foment conflict in his home state through his loyalists in that region, causing further violence and hampering post-conflict reconstruction. If the accused leaves his place of exile and returns to his home state or seeks asylum elsewhere, he may be able to operate with even fewer constraints. Taylor's temporary escape, for example, calls into question the ability to confine an exiled individual to a region or to track that person's movements.

Other potential practical problems include situations in which home states renege on grants of exile, adopting states break promises of asylum, and other authorities (such as ICTs) ignore exile arrangements altogether—any of which threatens the credibility of exile deals. Nigeria's arrest and transfer of Taylor first to Liberia and then to the SCSL's authority implies that other suspected atrocity perpetrators may be less likely to accept such offers by resigning and leaving a state voluntarily.

Opponents of an alleged atrocity perpetrator may decide to pursue alternative, perhaps forcible methods to transfer power to new leadership. Instead of the peaceful process of exile, such violent means could, in the short term, cause more conflict if targeted individuals fight to retain power and freedom. On the other hand, if the new leadership's violent response were successful, it could, in the long run, help combat impunity, support reconciliation efforts, bolster efforts to deter atrocity perpetrators, stem regional conflict, and uphold international law.

E. LETHAL FORCE

The use of lethal force—employing perhaps a gun, grenade, or guided missile instead of a gavel—involves an attempted act of state-sponsored, premeditated, deliberate, extrajudicial, targeted killing.[44] This option is arguably the most extreme, retributive, and legally problematic of all transitional justice alternatives because it does not provide for due process, exacts the death penalty without observing a right to a fair trial or appeal, and violates the principles of respect for human life and presumption of innocence. As a result, critics often characterize such measures as simpleminded vengeance or vigilantism. Killing may also be counterproductive because it can eliminate individuals critical to negotiations,[45] create martyrs from whom the killer's enemies can draw inspiration and grievance, forgo the possibility of interrogating someone with crucial knowledge of past and incipient offenses, or leave a power vacuum that enables an equally or even more potent enemy to assume leadership. Such killings may also result in the death or injury of secondary, untargeted individuals (e.g., innocent civilians), euphemistically deemed "inevitable collateral damage" by the killers. Killing also carries with it the risk that the target himself is not actually responsible for the alleged offenses or he is mistakenly identified, resulting in the further shedding of innocent blood. A 2011 book on the history of high-priority manhunts concludes: "killing or capturing an individual seldom correlates to strategic success."[46]

For transitional justice and other purposes, governments have pursued targeted killings throughout history because extrajudicial executions have been viewed as relatively quick, inexpensive, simple, and permanent solutions for dealing with enemies, including individuals suspected of heinous crimes. Owing to the development, destructive force, mobility, and accessibility of certain technologies (e.g., weapons of mass destruction), and to the increasing role of nonstate actors in perpetrating global threats, incapacitating such suspects is a growing concern and strategy of some states. Also in part because of advanced technologies (such as unmanned aerial vehicles (also known as "drones") and precision-guided munitions), identifying and targeting individuals to be killed has become increasingly more feasible. Precisely because international criminal law and its concepts such as "command responsibility" individualize culpability for atrocities, killing suspected criminals is a means of dispatching a "flesh-and-blood villain."[47] Through decapitation strikes that degrade or destroy an adversary's command and control capabilities, these lethal actions may actually or effectively dispose of an enemy group's leadership, precipitating a turning point in a conflict. In the process, less collateral damage may occur than if a full-blown war had emerged. Such killings can also be dramatic spectacles, which may raise morale (perhaps unintentionally) among the killer's supporters and demoralize—and deter—his enemies. Furthermore, deceased individuals cannot use an amnesty hearing, trial, or other public forum as a bully pulpit from which to further their cause, perhaps inciting even more atrocities. Killing an individual also precludes the decedent retaining or regaining power and position if otherwise subject to a different transitional justice option, such as prosecution or exile, from which he escapes or is deliberately released.

Finally, targeted killing helps avoid some of the political, legal, and practical challenges (discussed elsewhere in this book) associated with detaining a suspect. For example, how could or should a suspect be apprehended? What level of resources—including soldiers' lives—should be expended in the process? An intervening state may calculate, for example, that targeting a suspect through an air strike as opposed to a mission by ground troops would incur less safety risks for both military personnel and equipment. Also, which of the other transitional justice options could or should be used to address the individual once captured, including questions about whether the captor or the suspect's home state will take custody? Indeed, the lack of such a coherent policy—and the deliberate avoidance of the thorny problems of due process—have sometimes been cited for the USG's preference for killing over capturing an atrocity suspect.[48]

There are essentially two practices constituting the use of lethal force: legitimate military targeting, which is legal, and assassination, which is illegal. The former applies force—often predictable, overt, and with a lethal objective—to non-civilian targets during a military conflict. The Geneva Conventions define legitimate military targets as "those objects which by their nature, location, purpose[,] or use make an effective contribution to military action and whose total or partial destruction, capture[,] or neutralization, in the circumstances ruling at the time, offers a definite military advantage."[49] Proponents argue that this use of lethal force is a justifiable, legal exercise of state power and does not constitute assassination. These individuals contend that such killing is consistent with both international and domestic laws, as it occurs in the context of self-defense or armed conflict. In these scenarios, targets are generally not afforded due process, and targeting these combatants, facilitated by modern advanced technologies, abides by ethical and legal principles of precision and proportionality.[50]

Assassination is the second type of lethal force. It is the targeted killing of an individual (including civilians), usually by surprise, often in secret, not necessarily in the context of a military conflict, and possibly in furtherance of political rather than military objectives. Though often suspected, the identity of the assassin is not always known. If the assassin is discovered, however, he and the state for which he works may suffer significant backlash from adversaries and allies alike. Because the legitimacy of a military target may be controversial, the line between legitimate military targeting and assassination may not always be clear.

Using military personnel to target individuals has always been a weapon in the USG's foreign policy arsenal. Over the past decade, such targeted killings have been particularly prominent. In 2006, the USG conducted a successful targeted killing of Abu Musab al-Zarqawi, the Jordanian leader of al-Qaeda in Iraq.[51] Bush, Jr. referred to the killing as a mechanism that "delivered justice."[52] More recently, the administration of President Barack Obama has fatally targeted suspected terrorists and other alleged atrocity perpetrators.[53] In 2011, after USG forces had been hunting al-Qaeda leader Osama bin Laden for years with the intent to kill him,[54] American soldiers mortally shot him. The USG strike team was reportedly explicitly ordered to kill, not capture, bin Laden.[55] Bush, Jr. and Obama both characterized this targeted killing as "justice" being "done."[56] The same year, the USG also used a drone attack in Yemen to kill Anwar al-Awlaki, an American-born Muslim cleric and al-Qaeda propagandist, and Samir Khan, an American citizen of Pakistani origin who was an editor of al-Qaeda's English-language online magazine.[57] The U.S./DoJ wrote a secret memorandum authorizing the targeting of al-Awlaki, justifying the legality of this lethal attack.[58] By April 2013, the Obama administration had killed approximately 3,000 individuals in counterterrorist strikes overseas, mostly by using drones.[59] Since then, the USG has continued killing or injuring individuals through such means.[60]

Members of the Obama administration, however, have not always agreed on the morality, legality, or utility of its potential targets or tactics.[61] Some of these targets, such as bin Laden, were unarmed and foreigners.[62] Others, such as al-Awlaki and Khan, were American citizens, who some commentators argue are, or at least should be, entitled to due process under the U.S. Constitution and thus protected from extrajudicial executions.[63] Contrary to the Obama administration's repeated claims, the targeted killings have not been limited only to officials, members, and affiliates of al-Qaeda who pose an imminent threat to the United States.[64] Sometimes these missions have resulted in unintended deaths, fatalities that the USG has, on occasion, belatedly admitted after attempting to cover up.[65] The USG has also participated in military targeting indirectly by providing support to non-USG groups that use force against suspected atrocity perpetrators.[66]

Like legitimate military targeting, assassination has historically been a part of the USG's foreign policy toolbox. The USG has attempted or carried out assassinations (or has acquiesced to or supported assassinations attempted or carried out by its allies) in which transitional justice may have been a motivating factor. As discussed in Chapter IV, U.S. officials considered summarily executing Nazis after WWII. More recently, as revealed by a 1975 U.S. congressional report, the USG has either attempted or completed the assassination of several foreign leaders (who may or may not have been involved in atrocities), including Congolese prime minister Patrice Lumumba in 1961, Dominican president Rafael Trujillo in 1961, Cuban president Fidel Castro from 1961 to 1963, South Vietnamese president Ngo Dinh Diem in 1963, and Chilean president Salvador Allende in 1970 to 1973.[67] Commentators suggest that the USG was involved in other assassinations, including that of Ernesto "Che" Guevara in 1967.[68] Even after President Gerald Ford signed a 1976 Executive Order prohibiting political assassinations,[69] which was refined by President Jimmy Carter in 1978,[70] the USG has allegedly in some cases and admittedly in others continued to plan assassinations, including on Guyanan opposition leader Walter Rodney in 1980.[71] Furthermore, even after President Ronald Reagan's 1981 Executive Order, which expanded the prohibition on political assassination to include all types,[72] the USG, without issuing any superseding directives, has attempted several assassinations, including on former Iraqi president Saddam Hussein and former Libyan leader Muammar Gaddafi.[73] One American commentator noted that al-Alwaki "appears to be the first United States citizen that our government has publicly targeted for assassination."[74]

F. PROSECUTION

A fifth proactive general transitional justice option reviewed in this chapter is prosecution, which its proponents argue promotes stability, the rule of law, and accountability, as well as contributes to deterring future atrocities.[75] Prosecution advocates also contend that due process resulting in legitimate convictions and stern sentences appropriately punish atrocity perpetrators. Yet this option may be relatively expensive and slow, as well as legally and politically risky. It may also be counterproductive, by facilitating martyrdom and perpetuating a cycle of vengeance if a defendant's supporters sense injustice. Furthermore, prosecution may involve politicized or frivolous charges, and it may result in the release of genuine atrocity perpetrators through acquittals, which can lead to embarrassment and, more critically, recidivism.[76]

Prosecution can further objectives beyond the most obvious: achieving justice by trying, convicting, and punishing suspected criminals. For example, states may use prosecution to establish an accurate record of an atrocity, which can contribute to full and truthful documentation of history. However, some commentators believe that these secondary purposes may dilute the main focus of prosecution: trial and punishment. As political philosopher Hannah Arendt said in her reflections on Israel's unilateral prosecution of Nazi Adolf Eichmann:

> The purpose of a trial is to render justice, and nothing else; even the noblest of ulterior purposes—"the making of a record of the Hitler regime which would withstand the test of history," as Robert G. Storey, executive trial counsel at Nuremberg, formulated the supposed higher aims of the Nuremberg Trials—can only detract from law's main business: to weigh the charges brought against the accused, to render judgment, and to mete out due punishment.[77]

Prosecution of suspected atrocity perpetrators, which vary in form and function, can be conducted by the UN or other entities. Prosecution not administered under the UN aegis can be conducted either unilaterally or multilaterally. In either case, prosecution may follow from the controversial assertion of "universal jurisdiction," in which a prosecuting entity claims that some crimes are so heinous that they are considered *hostis humani generis* (an enemy of all mankind) and therefore fall within the jurisdiction of any state or institution. Under universal jurisdiction, suspected atrocity perpetrators can be prosecuted anytime, anywhere in the world.[78] Some scholars argue that the USG has invoked universal jurisdiction in certain unilateral military commissions.[79]

If prosecutions are unilateral, they may occur under the auspices of an intervening state, the successor regime, or a third-party state. Such unilateral prosecution can be administered either by a civilian court or a military tribunal.[80] In turn, a unilateral prosecution may be conducted through either the domestic judiciary or a special tribunal, which may be permanent or ad hoc.[81] A famous example of a unilateral prosecution of atrocities was the post–World War I (WWI) German trials held at Leipzig, at which only 6 suspects were convicted out of the 896 accused.[82] Another notable unilateral prosecution was the court-martial of only one U.S. soldier, Lieutenant William Calley, Jr., for the American massacre of civilians in the village of My Lai, Vietnam, in 1968.[83] The USG has chosen to prosecute suspected terrorists either in U.S. federal courts or military tribunals. The first such case before a U.S. military tribunal since the end of WWII commenced in 2004 against a Yemeni, Salim Ahmed Hamdan, who was accused of conspiring to commit acts of terrorism.[84]

Yet another prominent unilateral prosecution of suspected atrocity perpetrators concerns Iraq. In 2003, the Iraqi Coalition Provisional Authority (ICPA), the transitional government of Iraq created and led by the USG from April 2003 to June 2004, established the IST. The following year, the ICPA transferred power to an interim domestic government, which, in 2005, converted the IST into the Supreme Iraqi Criminal Tribunal (SICT).[85] This tribunal is dedicated to trying any Iraqi national or resident accused of committing genocide, crimes against humanity, or war crimes, or of violating certain stipulated Iraqi laws, including those that proscribe "manipulat[ing] the judiciary," "the wastage of national resources," "the squandering of public assets and funds," "the abuse of position," and "the pursuit of policies that may lead to the threat of war or the use of the armed forces against an Arab country."[86] The temporal jurisdiction of the tribunal was established to run from July 17, 1968, when the Ba'ath Party seized power, until May 1, 2003, when the war against Iraq officially ended.[87] The tribunal, which tried, convicted, and executed Saddam and also prosecuted and punished other members of his Ba'ath Party, was therefore designed as a unilateral prosecution conducted outside the aegis of the UN through an ad hoc special tribunal established by the successor regime as a civilian court. Consequently, it serves as an example of a purely domestic criminal tribunal—albeit one with significant international involvement and assistance (especially from the USG).

Unilateral prosecution also occurs through civil proceedings in the United States. The Alien Tort Statute (ATS) of 1789 states that "[t]he district courts shall have original jurisdiction of any civil action by an alien for a tort only, committed in violation of the law of nations or a treaty of the United States."[88] The Torture Victim Protection Act (TVPA) of 1991 permits U.S. courts to hold liable "[a]n individual who, under actual or apparent authority, or color of law, of any foreign nation subjects an individual to" torture or extrajudicial killing.[89] Perhaps the most famous and influential case brought under the ATS or TVPA against a suspected atrocity perpetrator concerned crimes allegedly committed by the Bosnian-Serb leader Radovan Karadžić in the Balkans.[90]

If non-UN prosecutions are multilateral, either a civilian court or a military tribunal may preside over the trial. Either option may be bilateral or multilateral (perhaps involving the successor regime as one of the administering parties), may be established by treaty or executive agreement, and may be either ad hoc or permanent. Multilateral courts date back to at least 1474, when an ad hoc tribunal comprised of judges from four neighboring jurisdictions tried Peter von Hagenbach for crimes he allegedly committed during his occupation of Breisach.[91] Although a commission of inquiry recommended after WWI the establishment of an ad hoc ICT to prosecute war crimes and crimes against humanity allegedly committed during the war, the Allies deferred to Germany, allowing it to conduct the aforementioned sham trials at Leipzig.[92] Two examples of ad hoc multilateral military tribunals established by executive agreement are the IMT and the IMTFE. The ICC is the first permanent multilateral court established outside the UN through a treaty,[93] which occurred in 1998, although calls for the creation of a permanent ICT date back to at least the 1872 proposal by Gustav Moynier, a founder of the International Committee of the Red Cross.[94]

If prosecutions are conducted through the UN, there are at least six venue options: (1) a permanent international criminal court,[95] (2) a hybrid UN/successor regime ad hoc tribunal, (3) an ad hoc ICT established through multilateral treaty, (4) an ad hoc ICT established through the UNGA, (5) an ad hoc ICT established through the Chapter VI powers of the UNSC, and (6) an ad hoc ICT established through the Chapter VII powers of the UNSC. Although all of these options have been considered, only the second and sixth have been implemented.[96] Five examples of the second option are the SCSL, the ECCC, the Serious Crimes Panels of the District Court of Dili in East Timor, the "Regulation 64" Panels in the Courts of Kosovo, and the STL.[97]

Examples of options six are the ICTY and the ICTR. This option manifests in three variations. A prosecution pursuant to the UNSC's Chapter VII powers could occur through: (1) a UN ad hoc ICT completely separate from any existing UN ad hoc ICT (what I call the "ICT-Separate" option, as in the case of the ICTY when it was established in 1993[98]), (2) the expansion of an existing UN ad hoc ICT to include jurisdiction over another atrocity (what I call the "ICT-Expanded" option), or (3) a UN ad hoc ICT that shares some bureaucracy, such as an appeals chamber and/or chief prosecutor, with an existing UN ad hoc ICT (what I call the "ICT-Tied" option, as in the cases of the ICTR[99] and the ICTY after the ICTR was established in 1994).

G. INDEFINITE DETENTION

Some commentators have argued that, instead of dealing with suspected atrocity perpetrators through, for example, prosecution, the United States should detain alleged criminals indefinitely. Such a mechanism involves incarceration for an unspecified period of time without trial or even a formal charge. Proponents of this extrajudicial practice argue that such detentions serve as well as, if not better than, prosecutions when incapacitating suspects is a key objective. Indefinite detention advocates further argue that the capability of a trial to provide additional objectives—including the possibility of capital punishment, greater legitimacy in certain circles, and the cathartic and historical benefits a criminal verdict can bring—may be exaggerated.[100]

Because indefinite detention is not necessarily infinite detention, detainees could be released or escape. Consequently, some of the risks of this transitional justice option mirror those for other non-lethal tools. For example, a released or escaped detainee may seek to regain power and engage in criminal activity.

Since September 11, 2001, the USG has detained numerous suspected terrorists indefinitely, most notably at a military facility in Guantánamo Bay, Cuba. More than a decade later, President Obama has not followed through on his 2008 campaign promise to close the facility,[101] which has held a total of 779 individuals since 2001, 149 of whom remain there as of July 2015.[102]

The U.S. president's authority to impose indefinite detention, including on U.S. citizens, is grounded in two pieces of legislation: the Authorization for Use of Military Force Against Terrorists[103] and the National Defense Authorization Act.[104] Proponents of this practice can thus claim some basis in law for their position. Advocates also contend that indefinite detention is critical for confronting the real and growing threat of certain atrocity perpetrators, particularly terrorists, who use strategies and tools not effectively addressed through conventional legal systems.

Critics of indefinite detention claim that it violates the most basic American legal principles concerning due process enshrined in the U.S. Constitution (particularly the Bill of Rights), including the presumption of innocence and the rights to habeas corpus, a speedy trial, a jury of peers, and confrontation of witnesses. These opponents further argue that the practice is unnecessary, as the traditional American system of investigations and prosecutions has, since September 11, 2001, successfully punished criminals and prevented terrorist attacks on U.S. soil. In addition, opponents contend that the USG's approval of the practice for U.S. citizens erodes American civil liberties and therefore indicates that terrorists are indeed succeeding in their plans to undermine freedom in the United States and abroad. Opponents further suggest that indefinite detention is counterproductive because it damages the nation's reputation for promoting liberal democratic values, it discourages suspects held by the military from cooperating with investigations, and it serves as a recruiting symbol for anti-American groups.[105]

III. Conclusion

This chapter makes three points clear. First, there are numerous ways suspected atrocity perpetrators have been or could be handled after identification or capture; legalistic options—such as prosecution through an ICT—are only a subset of such means.

Second, the USG has used a wide array of these transitional justice instruments, including each of the general transitional justice options: inaction, amnesty, lustration, exile, lethal force, prosecution, and indefinite detention. Despite centuries of exalting the principles of due process and the presumption of innocent until proven guilty, the USG's use of non-legalistic alternatives—including inaction, lustration, amnesty, exile, indefinite detention, and lethal force—is an accepted, if not preferred, means of addressing many of the government's worst enemies, including some of its own citizens. What sort of "justice" is "done" in these cases is unclear, but that justice surely does not include indicting, prosecuting, convicting, and sentencing a suspected atrocity perpetrator based on legally admissible evidence.

Third, the wisdom and effectiveness of many of these options are dubious. Not only are these mechanisms politically, legally, and morally problematic, but they almost all risk backfiring or generating other unintended consequences—one of which may be, ironically, the commission of more atrocities. Naturally, context matters; an option that works well in one situation may be disastrous in another.

Having sketched this overview of transitional justice options and the USG experience with them, I proceed to consider the two frameworks—legalism and prudentialism—through which I then evaluate six case studies. These cases include four instances in which the USG chose to support the establishment of ICTs—twice in each of the immediate aftermaths of WWII and the Cold War—and two situations in which the USG did not.

{ 3 }

Competing Theories of United States Policy on Transitional Justice

LEGALISM VERSUS PRUDENTIALISM

I. Introduction

In this chapter, I develop a conceptual framework to explain U.S. policy on transitional justice. Specifically, I consider two theories—the dominant theory of "legalism" and what I call "prudentialism"—about what motivated USG support for, or opposition to, various transitional justice options described in the previous chapter for each of this book's four primary case studies (Germany and Japan after WWII, as well as the former Yugoslavia and Rwanda after the Cold War) and two secondary case studies (the 1988 bombing of Pan Am flight 103 over Lockerbie, Scotland, and the 1990–1991 Iraqi offenses against Kuwaitis). Later in this book, I assess these two theories' relative strengths in explaining U.S. policy in each case.

Part II of this chapter discusses the particular problems and concerns transitional justice represents for international relations, focusing on security and cooperation. Part III then reviews what two prominent international relations theories, realism and liberalism, would posit about transitional justice issues. I then set out, in Part IV, two transitional justice theories: legalism and prudentialism (which are subsets of liberalism and realism, respectively). Part V concludes the chapter by discussing the application of these transitional justice theories to this book's case studies. Much of the analysis in this chapter concentrates on ICTs, one of the many transitional justice options discussed in the previous chapter, because ICTs are the focus of legalism and are also central to the case studies of this book.

II. Transitional Justice as
an International Relations Phenomenon

This Part explores challenges transitional justice represents for international relations, with a particular focus on issues related to security and cooperation.

A. TRANSITIONAL JUSTICE AND INTERNATIONAL SECURITY

The first lens through which transitional justice can be considered is that of international security. International security traditionally has been defined in international relations as "state security." This conception of international security, based on state sovereignty and survival, was embodied in the 1648 Treaty of Westphalia and reinforced by threats to and breaches of state sovereignty during the two World Wars and the Cold War. The primary concern of this type of international security is interstate warfare, and the principles expounded to promote security are the sovereign equality of states, the nonintervention of states in each other's internal affairs, and the right of states to respond militarily to existential threats.[1]

Especially since the end of the Cold War, the dominant view of international security has expanded to include or even prioritize "human security." Political scientists S. Neil MacFarlane and Khong define human security as "freedom from threat to the core values of human beings, including physical survival, welfare, and identity."[2] MacFarlane and Khong observe that

> [t]he notion of human security is based on the premise that the individual human being is the only irreducible focus for discourse on security . . . . [H]uman security is distinct in its focus on the human individual as the principal referent of security. Many proponents of human security would go further to argue that it is also distinct in its recognition that the security needs of individuals go beyond physical survival in the face of violence to access to the basic necessities of life and to the establishment of the basic rights that permit people to lead lives in dignity.[3]

This alternative conception of international security was a liberal response to the failure of states to ensure the safety and basic needs of their citizens. This view recognizes that international and civil conflict directly caused human rights violations and exacerbated underlying humanitarian crises, such as poverty, famine, and disease. In many cases, a state either deliberately caused these problems or was unable or unwilling to address them. Moreover, this perspective identifies nonmilitary threats,[4] such as environmental disasters or degradation,[5] as hazards to human life and liberties beyond the desire or capacity of states to address. Proponents of human security, such as the UN Secretary-General's High-Level Panel on Threats, Challenges, and Change and the International Commission on Intervention and State Sovereignty, have therefore declared that there is a "Responsibility to Protect" individuals that can politically, legally, and morally justify violating a state's political sovereignty and territorial integrity.[6]

Transitional justice relates to both state and human security. On the one hand, the pursuit of transitional justice—at least through the potential of retributive transitional justice options (e.g., exile, prosecution, lustration, lethal force) to prevent or respond to atrocities by deterring or punishing atrocity perpetrators—can promote the maintenance of international security. Atrocities threaten state security by upsetting regional stability and balances of power. Atrocities may engulf an entire state or extend to neighboring states, causing refugee flows and, as a result, possible health and financial crises. Atrocities also can jeopardize access to valuable resources, such as oil, if those resources are located in areas that are rendered perilous from the violence.[7] Atrocities threaten human security by violating individual rights and endangering entire communities. Atrocities thus imperil the stability and survival of regions, states, groups (e.g., ethnic, racial, religious), and individuals regardless of whether they are contained within a state or spill over borders.

Transitional justice can promote state and human security by building or rebuilding domestic and international infrastructure that prevents or stops atrocities. In addition, transitional justice institutions, especially those that are retributive (e.g., ICTs), may deter the commission of future atrocities by promoting accountability and punishment for perpetrators, thus reducing threats to human, domestic, and international security.[8] Furthermore, transitional justice activities may be designed, among other purposes, to identify, apprehend, and incapacitate atrocity perpetrators; to render a full, accurate history of atrocities; and to promote reconciliation among former antagonists.

On the other hand, the pursuit of transitional justice may and often does compromise the maintenance of international security. Attempting to hold individuals or groups accountable may hamper peace processes and otherwise foment conflict. Classifying and punishing individuals and groups as suspected atrocity perpetrators (by the issuance of arrest warrants or through less formal actions, such as "naming and shaming" campaigns) may lead them or their interlocutors to resist or cease negotiations as well as precipitate further violence. Suspected individuals and groups may resent the perpetrator label or may commit more atrocities in the process of attempting to flee justice.[9] Furthermore, the process of apprehending, investigating, prosecuting, and punishing individuals may require authorities to cross boundaries or to try individuals without the permission of their home governments. Such efforts may violate territorial integrity and political sovereignty—critical components of international order as defined by the UN Charter and recognized as fundamental principles of international law.[10]

In these situations, the pursuit of justice can present a fundament tension with international security.[11] Part of the challenge of transitional justice is to reconcile potentially conflicting goals (e.g., trade-offs between short- and long-term justice and security) when possible and to prioritize them when not. Whether transitional justice fosters or hampers international security depends on the particular transitional justice option pursued, its location, its scope, and its pace.

In promoting security, the objectives of transitional justice matter and might include achieving durable peace, individual or group accountability, general or specific deterrence, or some other goal. For example, although transitional justice often focuses on punishing individuals suspected of committing atrocities, even successful imposition of individual accountability may not halt ongoing or prevent future atrocities. Disciples or imitators may assume the mantle of the defanged. The current U.S.-led campaign to combat terrorism (formerly known as the "Global War on Terror") is a case in point. Incapacitating the planners and perpetrators of the atrocities of September 11, 2001, certainly will not avert future terrorism. The National Commission on Terrorist Attacks Upon the United States reported:

> al Qaeda represents an ideological movement, not a finite group of people. It initiates and inspires, even if it no longer directs. In this way it has transformed itself into a decentralized force. Bin Laden may be limited in his ability to organize major attacks from his hideouts. Yet killing or capturing him, while extremely important, would not end terror. His message of inspiration to a new generation of terrorists would continue.[12]

This report recognizes that addressing individual suspected atrocity perpetrators, even if they are leaders of a group responsible for atrocities, is a necessary but sometimes insufficient tactic to prevent, mitigate, or stop atrocities.

Transitional justice, for whatever type of atrocity, is inextricably linked to international security. The pursuit of transitional justice may either help or hinder international security; thus, policymakers must pay particular attention to the method, form, location, and timing of transitional justice. The theories explored below help us understand why countries, particularly the United States, make such decisions.

B. TRANSITIONAL JUSTICE AND INTERNATIONAL COOPERATION

Beyond its role in promoting or jeopardizing international security, transitional justice also presents particular challenges for international cooperation. Some international relations scholars view cooperation as requiring total synchronization of interests and actions. Others, such as political scientists Robert Axelrod and Robert Keohane, believe cooperation "is not equivalent to harmony. Harmony requires complete identity of interests, but cooperation can only take place in situations that contain a mixture of conflicting and complementary interests. In such situations, cooperation occurs when actors adjust their behavior to the actual or anticipated preferences of others."[13] These competing perspectives on cooperation, in turn, inform different views on noncooperation. Some view noncooperative actors as unable to alter their beliefs and behavior, whereas others believe these actors are simply unwilling to do so.

A wide range of actors in the international system may cooperate to pursue transitional justice, including the USG, U.S. allies and adversaries, other member states of relevant international institutions (e.g., UNSC), and states that are targets of transitional justice. Transitional justice may also involve nonstate actors, including NGOs such as stakeholder (e.g., survivor, perpetrator, and resistance) groups and humanitarian organizations (e.g., Human Rights Watch, Amnesty International, International Center for Transitional Justice), which may advocate particular policy positions or provide crucial resources such as evidence and expert testimony. Intergovernmental organizations (IGOs), like the UNGA, the UNSC, and ICTs themselves, also play important roles, either because they are the fora in which relevant decisions are made or because they are consulted for recommendations. Individuals, such as politicians, celebrities, and business leaders, may exert their influence for a variety of motives, including out of concern for the stability of the region or the involvement of a particular group of people, or because they care (or want to be seen to care) about humanitarian causes generally. Transitional justice requires a careful consideration of the interplay within and among all of these actors.

1. Transitional Justice as a Special Case of International Cooperation

Transitional justice represents a unique collective action manifestation of international cooperation. As discussed above, many actors with myriad motives—states, NGOs, IGOs, and individuals—can be involved in transitional justice. However, as this book focuses on the U.S. role in transitional justice, the following discussion concentrates on state actors.

A. DILEMMA OF COMMON INTEREST OR INDIFFERENCE

Many international actors (e.g., IGOs, states, NGOs, peoples, individuals) involved in transitional justice agree (or purport to agree) that the goals of transitional justice (e.g., accountability of and punishment for atrocity perpetrators, post-conflict reconstruction and reconciliation) are desirable and that the international community should, if possible, cooperate to achieve them. Those who disagree unsurprisingly are often the potential targets of transitional justice. Opponents of transitional justice may also be strict realists who deprioritize or delegitimate such goals relative to order, security, or competing demands in other regions. Instead of the transitional justice objectives themselves, then, it is the application of those goals (i.e., the kind of transitional justice institution that should be established and the amount of resources that should be invested) that generally causes disagreement in the international community. Transitional justice is thus largely a "dilemma of common interest" or a "dilemma of common indifference," not a "dilemma of common aversions."[14]

This facet of transitional justice—that it is often either a "dilemma of common interest" or a "dilemma of common indifference"—yields important consequences. Unlike with some other issue-areas, such as climate change,[15] the international community does not need to expend valuable time, especially as an atrocity is rapidly occurring, debating the merits of transitional justice principles. Instead, the international community usually can proceed to a discussion of whether and how to pursue such transitional justice. This more advanced starting point does not necessarily mean that transitional justice will be pursued; it only suggests that the debate about its pursuit begins further ahead of some other issue-areas.

Despite favoring transitional justice generally, some states may have principled or practical objections to, or preferences for, particular types of transitional justice. For instance, although each option arguably promotes the overarching transitional justice goal of accountability, some states may prefer to address suspected atrocity perpetrators through formal legal means, such as prosecution, whereas other states may prefer expedient political methods, such as exile, lustration, indefinite detention, or lethal force. (Some options, such as amnesty, may be legal, political, or both.) A state's particular transitional justice option preference may depend on, among other considerations, whether the state is ideologically committed to a retributive or reconciliatory method of justice or a process that is strictly domestic versus one that involves the international community.

B. NO ZERO-SUM GAME

A second attribute of transitional justice is that it is not necessarily zero-sum (unlike some other issues, such as security,[16] are often considered to be). In other words, "more" transitional justice for one individual or group of suspected atrocity perpetrators does not theoretically mean "less" for another; there is no necessary scarcity of transitional justice arising from its consumption/application, at least in theory. That said, transitional justice can be a zero-sum game in the practical sense that transitional justice for one individual or group may mean little or no transitional justice for another. For example, where there are numerous alleged perpetrators of a particular atrocity (such as in the Rwandan genocide), limited time and/or resources may prevent the often costly and lengthy process of apprehension, investigation, prosecution, and punishment of all suspects. In such cases, the primary transitional justice authority (in the case of the Rwandan genocide, the ICTR) must prioritize the individuals it seeks to hold accountable and then defer to other transitional justice authorities (in the case of the Rwandan genocide, the Rwandan ordinary domestic judicial system, *gacaca*, and foreign justice systems) to try those individuals, or to allow those individuals to escape justice completely.[17]

C. RELATIVE VERSUS ABSOLUTE GAINS

A third feature of transitional justice is that it does not necessarily motivate states to jockey over relative gains, a point that relates in part to whether zero-sum games affect transitional justice decision-making. One of the central cleavages in the "neo-neo debate"[18] involves relative versus absolute gains. In considering states' opportunities to cooperate for shared gain, neorealists claim that states are concerned primarily with relative gains and thus will not cooperate if gains are uneven, while neoliberal institutionalists believe that states focus on absolute gains and thus will cooperate even if gains are uneven.[19] Unlike institutions that promote security or economic development, where the possibility of relative gains is more obvious, there are few tangible profits or other gains to be distributed among the member states of a transitional justice institution. On the other hand, suspected atrocity perpetrators may be concerned about relative gains. A transitional justice system in which some accused atrocity perpetrators enter into plea agreements may help convict other alleged atrocity perpetrators, leaving the latter group worse off. As such, neither neorealists nor neoliberal institutionalists would necessarily be skeptical of cooperation in this issue-area, as long as the operation of the transitional justice process did not depend upon suspected atrocity perpetrators. Even then, though, states would not necessarily incur, and thus would not necessarily be concerned with, their relative or absolute gains merely because suspected atrocity perpetrators' gains may be uneven.

D. CHEATING = nonicsue

A fourth special trait of transitional justice with respect to international cooperation is that cheating is not an intrinsic problem, which also relates to the notion that transitional justice is not necessarily a zero-sum game. That said, it is possible that supposedly cooperative actors could sabotage transitional justice efforts by facilitating the escape of, destroying incriminating evidence about, or bribing a judge presiding over the trial of an alleged atrocity perpetrator because, for example, that suspect had been a former ally. But both the frequency of these activities and the extent to which they endanger the survival or vital interests of other actors are rare. There is no "special peril of defection" due to cheating within transitional justice institutions that could "inflict a decisive defeat on the victim state."[20] This phenomenon contrasts markedly with the security realm, including issues such as weapons proliferation, where the possibility and consequences of breaking agreements are real and significant. Given the absence of a cheating problem and few concerns over relative gains, neorealists are less likely to be skeptical of cooperation in this issue-area.

E. LOW POLITICS = *not very impt, politically* [handwritten] [*TJ*]

A fifth quality of transitional justice is that many consider it a "low politics" issue, like social matters. The fact that transitional justice does not rank as a vital interest to most states means that other issues, such as the protection of national security, often assume higher priority.[21] As a result, when resources and time are limited, a government will pursue transitional justice after other state goals, and so transitional justice may not be pursued at all.

F. FREE RIDERS

A sixth characteristic of transitional justice is that it can present a problem of free riders. Transitional justice involves costs: evidence collection, suspect apprehension, case development, staff salaries, and infrastructure building, among others. States or societies emerging from an atrocity may receive assistance along the path from conflict to peace, including through addressing suspected atrocity perpetrators. Furthermore, the entire international community may receive benefits when transitional justice bolsters the rule of law and, especially if accountability and punishment are involved, future atrocities are deterred. Good-faith actors operating in the international community thus have an interest in promoting transitional justice, yet relatively few actors actually contribute to its achievement. As a result, some actors in the international system accrue positive externalities of transitional justice without shouldering any of the expenditures, whether because they are unwilling or unable. These actors free-ride within the system. *PRoblems w/ Free Riding* [handwritten]

As transitional justice can generate free-riding, this quality, like that of creating a "dilemma of common interest" or a "dilemma of common indifference," is highly consequential. First, the free-rider problem can overburden those actors willing and able to shoulder the costs of transitional justice. Second, free-riding can breed resentment among those actors who incur the expenses against those actors who do not. Third, free riders may criticize a transitional justice process as illegitimate. Without all relevant and capable actors in the international community contributing to transitional justice efforts, the transitional justice process may be severely undermined. Some states may withdraw from the process, perhaps leaving a transitional justice institution stillborn. Observers may criticize the process for not garnering broader or even universal support. As a result, transitional justice may lack sufficient backing or credibility, which may in turn require the process to be amended or even abandoned.

[handwritten margin note: *consequences of free riding* with circled ① ② ③]

G. RETURNS = *immeasurable + evaluating "success" = impossible* [handwritten]

A seventh attribute of transitional justice is that its returns are not necessarily tangible. In other issue-areas, such as economic policy or national security, many state efforts are obvious and concrete (e.g., arms control agreements to reduce the amount and type of weapons of mass destruction held by participating states).

Although some aspects of transitional justice are certainly measurable, such as the number of suspected atrocity perpetrators prosecuted or convicted, more general goals of promoting reconciliation are not necessarily quantifiable. As a result, gauging the respective contributions of participating states or evaluating the success of a particular transitional justice can be difficult, if not impossible.

H. COST

A final trait of transitional justice that makes it a special problem for international cooperation is that its pursuit is relatively inexpensive for dominant actors. As compared to, for example, the more "high politics" activities of waging and winning large-scale wars,[22] transitional justice is much less costly in monetary terms. Even at the expense of $100 million per year that the ICTY and the ICTR each roughly cost,[23] an individual, wealthy state could single-handedly establish and maintain one or more transitional justice institutions.

The fact that transitional justice is relatively inexpensive means that the USG has possessed sufficient resources to propose, as it occasionally has, that it unilaterally or disproportionately fund certain transitional justice institutions.[24] As these institutions are relatively inexpensive, the USG retains flexibility in lobbying for or unilaterally pursuing its optimal outcome. The USG is not necessarily reliant, at least not for financial support, on other actors in the international community to establish and maintain these institutions. Especially since—and as a direct result of—the establishment of the ICTY and the ICTR, whose budgets are significant, the international community has prioritized the expense of an ICT's design—whether it is completely international or a hybrid tribunal involving local staff, structures, and laws—when ad hoc ICTs have been created.[25] If that trend continues, the USG may enjoy even wider latitude to pursue its preferences, despite the opposition of other states, because of its peculiar willingness and ability to support such transitional justice institutions financially. A powerful state actor, such as the USG, may have an incentive and the capability to eschew joint in favor of independent decision-making because it believes the former could produce suboptimal, inefficient, or counterproductive results.[26] One example is the IST, established in 2005. Despite criticisms by humanitarian organizations and legal experts that the IST would lack impartiality and competence and that it suffered other design and operational shortcomings,[27] the USG supported an Iraqi-led tribunal to prosecute Saddam and his Ba'ath Party cohorts instead of an ICT because the USG believed the former method would be more effective and efficient.[28]

Transitional justice is a relatively inexpensive, popular, but not necessarily zero-sum game of "low politics," the outcomes of which are not necessarily tangible. Furthermore, it is a cooperative enterprise that is comparatively unconstrained by concerns over relative gains or cheating, which exert little impact on this issue-area. Transitional justice also seems not to be inhibited by concerns

over the problem of free riders. As such, one would expect neorealists not to be
overly skeptical about cooperation in this issue-area.

2. Potential Benefits and Drawbacks of International Cooperation on Transitional Justice

Although transitional justice presents unique challenges as a collective action
problem, benefits certainly exist, as suggested by NLI,[29] for states to cooperate on transitional justice. International cooperation through ICTs illustrates
such potential benefits. States can use ICTs to facilitate reciprocity by demonstrating that the international community would help successor regimes
in atrocity locations render justice if the successor regime, in turn, supports
the international community by providing witnesses, documents, and other
evidence crucial to investigations and prosecutions. States can also use ICTs
to promote the sharing of information and expertise across the participating governments by creating an institution that investigates and centralizes
data about the atrocity. As unique institutions that specialize in investigation and prosecution using dedicated and expert staff, ICTs also can help
lower transaction costs. Similarly, as particular organizations with identifiable staff in a specific location sharing data and otherwise collaborating,
ICTs can serve as focal points for interstate coordination. This construct is
likely to be more efficient than any single state acting or multiple entities
separately (whether simultaneously or sequentially) pursuing transitional
justice, especially if those actors work at cross purposes. ICTs can facilitate
burden-sharing among states by distributing the costs and responsibilities
of identifying, apprehending, trying, and, where appropriate, punishing suspected atrocity perpetrators through collective participation in an international criminal justice system. ICTs can make commitments more credible
by having all participating states ratify the statute that creates the tribunal,
dedicate resources and staff, or affirm minimum budgetary contributions.
These actions would convey that signatories are invested in the ICT and
legally devoted to helping the ICT fulfill its mandate. Finally, states can use
ICTs to create issue linkages in several ways. The investigation and prosecution of suspected atrocity perpetrators can be connected to stability and
reconstruction in the post-atrocity location and its surrounding region by
removing individuals who foment conflict. Yet another way in which states
may use ICTs to promote issue linkage is in the great game of power politics. States may understand war crimes trials as opportunities through which
international law and institutions can neutralize the military and economic
superiority of opponents by employing legal tools that favor their interests
and undermine their enemies' power.

When considering the United States in particular, additional benefits—
beyond those suggested by NLI—may exist for transitional justice cooperation.
Applying notions from economist Charles Kindelberger's hegemonic stability

theory,[30] the United States, as a dominant power, can provide crucial capital toward and foster coordination during the process of identifying, investigating, apprehending, prosecuting, and punishing suspected atrocity perpetrators. That said, Kindelberger's theory is not wholly relevant, as ICTs can be established and maintained by states less powerful than hegemons,[31] and because transitional justice institutions (such as ICTs) often require much less financial backing than the economic institutions about which Kindelberger was concerned (such as the International Monetary Fund, the World Bank, and the World Trade Organization).

The composition of states involved in the transitional justice process may matter significantly for the process's credibility and effectiveness. Only a subset of states has the ability to provide financial support, competent staff, witnesses, evidence, and other resources that help ensure a successful transitional justice process. Furthermore, the international community generally or specific stakeholders, such as survivors and perpetrators, may feel that a transitional justice process is legitimate only if certain states are involved or excluded.

In sum, establishing an ICT can be a mutually beneficial, strategic endeavor among members of the international community. States cooperating through the ICT framework could reduce the probability of creating a potentially more costly, practically and legally chaotic, ineffective, and illegitimate transitional justice solution. The benefits that transitional justice presents for international cooperation are clear; it is difficult or nearly impossible for any state, even a hegemon, to secure its transitional justice interests unilaterally.

However, as with the potential benefits, the potential drawbacks of international cooperation on transitional justice are also significant. One possible downside of pursuing cooperation through international institutions is that those institutions may unexpectedly prevent necessary or desirable action. For example, UNSC vetoes can and have paralyzed important international action.[32] The international community's joint decision *not* to intervene in atrocities, including genocide, has been an excuse for inaction. In such cases, it may be both necessary and desirable for states *not* to cooperate, by pursuing unauthorized interventions. The defense of human rights and the bolstering of deterrence against future atrocities may compensate for what is lost in terms of the violation of international law. In such instances, there is a double standard at work: often only the United States has the capabilities to respond, yet it is criticized whether or not it acts.

There are multiple reasons the USG sometimes does not cooperate in global affairs. The USG and other actors in the international system periodically face principled disagreements based on domestic ideas and values. These fundamental differences of opinion inform their decisions to pursue conflicting paths, which sometimes lead to noncooperation. One point on which the USG and other actors may disagree is the physical threat a particular state or group poses and what the most effective and ethical response would be. Another example involves the proper status of international law in domestic jurisprudence.[33] The USG may in such contentious situations be accused of caring too little (or not at all) about issues of concern to other actors, as well as being unwilling to cooperate.

Noncooperation in the international community may also manifest when the USG prioritizes some issues above those deemed important by other actors and pursues those priorities even if they are at odds with other actors' preferences. This situation can occur when the USG perceives threats to its vital interests, such as terrorism, and is willing to pursue what it considers necessary and appropriate acts of self-defense (such as torture, rendition, and extrajudicial incarceration), even if other actors disagree.[34] Another example of interstate disagreement stemming from varying preference orderings arises in the climate change debate. The USG reportedly did not ratify the Kyoto Protocol because the USG valued its own economic well-being above the global environment.[35]

Yet another rationale for U.S. noncooperation in global affairs is that the USG deliberately pursues policies to assert its primacy in the international system. Through these acts, the USG seeks to maintain American hegemony and, in turn, to ensure other actors' relative powerlessness. There is some basis in this claim: the 2000 report of the Commission on America's National Interests declared one of the "six cardinal challenges for the next US president," and the means through which its vital interests would be enhanced and promoted, to "maintain the United States' singular leadership, military, and intelligence capabilities . . . ."[36] The same report also listed preventing "the emergence of a regional hegemon in important regions, especially the Persian Gulf" as one of its "extremely important" interests.[37] Similarly, fifteen years later, the United States's National Security Strategy stated: "America must lead. Strong and sustained American leadership is essential to a rules-based international order that promotes global security and prosperity as well as the dignity and human rights of all peoples."[38]

Countries, including the United States, often confront the aforementioned benefits and drawbacks to international cooperation on transitional justice. Attempts to explain how states resolve these situations are presented through the theories discussed in this chapter's following two Parts.

III. Traditional International Relations Theories

This Part considers what the traditional international relations theories of realism and liberalism would posit about transitional justice issues.[39] Neither theory, as originally formulated, specifically discusses transitional justice, nor does either theory specify conditions under which a state would support particular types of transitional justice options. However, each theory does speak to related issues. Part IV then discusses prudentialist and legalist variants of these two theories.

A. REALISM

The international relations theory of realism is, according to political scientist William Wohlforth, a "centuries-old foundational school of thought."[40] With its stated focus on how international relations *actually* operates, rather than how it *should*, realism posits a state-centric worldview in which the anarchic international system compels states, as rational unitary actors, to seek power and security. Realism is deeply skeptical of the role that international law plays in influencing state behavior; realists view international rules and norms as epiphenomenal. There are several variants of realism, such as classical realism[41] and neorealism.[42] Classical realists assert that states seek power, whereas neorealists argue that states seek security—with power as only a means to that end.[43]

Realism has enjoyed a long and prominent place in U.S. policymaking, especially on foreign affairs. Modern realist foreign policymakers include George Kennan and Henry Kissinger. Kennan, the architect of the USG's Cold War containment policy, cautioned against U.S. policymaking that was grounded in what he called "the legalistic-moralistic approach to international relations."[44] As Bass points out, Kissinger, in his epic review of diplomacy (published in 1994, but before the Rwandan genocide), never once mentions the IMT (nor, would I add, does Kissinger mention the IMTFE or the ICTY).[45] Apparently, Kissinger—a skeptic about the significance and utility of international law and institutions—did not think that ICTs merited mention in even a voluminous tome on international relations.

Realists should be presumptively skeptical of ICTs' value. Citing philosopher and political scientist Raymond Aron and other realist theorists and practitioners, Bass notes that realism levies two significant criticisms against war crimes trials: "such efforts will perpetuate a war, or destabilize postwar efforts to build a secure peace."[46] Recognizing that the pursuit of transitional justice may and often does compromise the maintenance of international security, realists argue for what they believe to be more productive methods of dealing with suspected atrocity perpetrators than, say, ICT-convened trials. Such a prosecutorial strategy, according to Snyder and Vinjamuri, "risks causing more atrocities than it would prevent, because it pays insufficient attention to political realities."[47] Because convictions cannot be guaranteed, realists would question the wisdom of risking scenarios in which international criminals are freed. Also, as trials can be expensive, complicated, and lengthy, realists would doubt that they are the most efficient use of resources. This concern is especially compelling when a state that would otherwise cooperate in establishing and operating an ICT already shoulders the burdens of halting the atrocity in which the accused criminal was involved and providing aid for post-conflict reconstruction. Because international criminals also might be useful in some way, such as in promoting post-conflict peace and order, realists also would hesitate to punish them immediately or automatically and therefore foreclose

the possibility of having those individuals serve as potentially helpful interlocutors and collaborators.

Realism, of course, allows for the possibility that states, especially hegemons,
will support the establishment of ICTs if doing so would further state interests.
More specifically, supporting the creation of ICTs could, as discussed above, promote international security and cooperation in a region of importance to that state,
or it could enable countries such as the United States to solidify their hegemonic
positions. Alternatively, realists might concede that cooperating to create an ICT
would occur as long as such a move does not threaten a state's material interests.
If, for example, the creation of an ICT did not upset the distribution of power in
the international system, which it would be unlikely to do, or if the ICT's financial
and staffing requirements were not too great, then U.S. willingness to cooperate on
such transitional justice, according to realists, should not necessarily be inhibited.

B. LIBERALISM

Liberalism shares realism's beliefs that the international system is anarchical and
that states pursue their interests. However, liberalism rejects the realist assumption that states are unitary rational actors. Rather, liberalism argues that state
interests can be more expansively defined (beyond just power and security to
include, for example, values), and that states also are driven by domestic factors,
such as societal identity (e.g., who belongs to the society, political ideology) and
institutions (e.g., the nature of domestic political representation) that shape state
preferences. Liberalism stresses that these preferences can vary among states,
leading to conflict. Like realism, liberalism has several variants, such as ideational liberalism, commercial liberalism, and republican liberalism.[48]

Political scientist Stanley Hoffmann defines liberalism in international relations as "the doctrine whose central concern is the liberty of the individual: both
his or her freedom from restraints and contraints [sic] imposed by other human
beings ... and his or her freedom to participate in a self-governing polity."[49]
Hoffmann cites "self-restraint, moderation, compromise, and peace" as ideas
that comprise "the essence of liberalism."[50] His work has set out a "liberal trans-
formist strategy" that seeks to promote the principles of what he calls "transpar-
ence," "accountability," "responsibility," "solidarity," and "nonviolence," in part
to defend human rights, including by combating genocide.[51] Liberals thus focus
on the "second image," or second of three levels of analysis in international relations that Waltz laid out.[52] Philosopher Immanuel Kant is one of the earliest liberals;[53] more modern liberals include political scientists Michael Doyle,[54] Bruce
Russett,[55] Andrew Moravcsik,[56] and Anne-Marie Slaughter.[57]

One of the primary claims of liberalism is that liberal states do not engage
each other in war. Rooted in Kant's *Perpetual Peace*, and later developed and pop-
ularized by Doyle and Russett, this view is termed Democratic Peace Theory.[58]
A variation of Democratic Peace Theory makes a similar claim based on shared

markets instead of shared polities. The "Golden Arches Theory" of conflict prevention, coined by commentator Thomas Friedman, claims that "no two countries that both have McDonald's have ever fought a war against each other since they each got their McDonald's."[59]

Like realism, liberalism proponents have been well-represented within the U.S. foreign policy establishment, perhaps most famously President Woodrow Wilson. Although they have not always practiced what they preached, Reagan and every subsequent U.S. president have espoused the need to promote democracy throughout the world, in part to make the world safer, including for the United States itself.[60]

Liberalism adherents are more optimistic than realists about the likelihood and desirability of interstate cooperation, including on justice issues.[61] Moreover, liberalism theory would predict that the United States would export its liberal values,[62] and would do so through the creation and operation of ICTs if such institutions were viewed as facilitating that goal. Bass claims that liberalism does indeed view ICTs as buttressing those values. He summarizes "the liberal case" as being

> broken down into a series of five major arguments. Liberals argue that international war crimes tribunals build up a sturdy peace by, first, purging threatening enemy leaders; second, deterring war criminals; third, rehabilitating former enemy countries; fourth, placing the blame for atrocities on individuals rather than on whole ethnic groups; and, fifth, establishing the truth about wartime atrocities.[63]

As Bass argues, although liberals might acknowledge the risks inherent in this transitional justice option, they "still argue that the benefits of war crimes tribunals outweigh them."[64]

IV. Frameworks for Explaining State Behavior on Transitional Justice

The traditional international relations theories of realism and liberalism do not speak directly to the theoretical underpinnings of transitional justice, so their insights must be extrapolated into more specific explanations of state behavior in this issue-area. In his *Stay the Hand of Vengeance: The Politics of War Crimes Tribunals*, Bass developed the theory of "legalism" to describe what the liberal tradition would proffer about state behavior with respect to supporting ICTs. I respond here by developing a derivative of realism, what I term "prudentialism," to serve as a competing theory to legalism. Each of these transitional justice theories lays out a different framework for why states participate in establishing ICTs. This Part describes those frameworks and generates corresponding hypotheses that are tested in later chapters through this book's case studies. I begin with legalism.

A. LEGALISM

Bass states that government leaders sometimes accept the risks inherent in prosecuting alleged atrocity perpetrators "because they, and their countries, are in the grip of a principled *idea*."[65] Bass employs the term "legalism" to describe this idea: a belief in the rule of law that leads one to think it is correct[66] and necessary[67] for suspected atrocity perpetrators to be prosecuted. Legalism thus derives from a normative belief about *whether* and *how* to confront suspected atrocity perpetrators. Legalism predicts that certain states will consistently pursue transitional justice and will do so in the form of trials.

Legalism, as Bass has articulated it, contends that particular liberal ideals matter to states' foreign policymaking. Bass's overall argument is that "liberal ideals make liberal states take up the cause of international justice, treating their humbled foes in a way utterly divorced from the methods practiced by illiberal states .... Liberal states are legalist: they put war criminals on trial in rough accordance with their domestic norms."[68] He also argues that "legalism is a concept that seems only to spring from a particular kind of liberal domestic polity. After all, a war crimes tribunal is an extension of the rule of law from the domestic sphere to the international sphere."[69] He further contends that "[l]egalists remain devoted to the idea that a *trial* is the proper way of dispensing justice .... The accusation may be murder, rape, or theft—or genocide, or aggression—but the case will wind up in a court."[70] Bass goes on to claim that a commitment to legalism explains the decision by the USG, as well as other liberal states, to establish war crimes tribunals.

Bass offers two pieces of evidence to support legalism: "First, *every* international war crimes tribunal that I am aware of—Leipzig, Constantinople, Nuremberg [(the IMT)], Tokyo [(the IMTFE)], The Hague [(the ICTY)], and Arusha [(the ICTR)]—has rested on the support of liberal states. Second, conversely, when illiberal states have fought each other, they have *never* established a bona fide war crimes tribunal."[71]

In order to present his work as accurately as possible, I have deliberately quoted Bass's articulation of legalism at length in this chapter and elsewhere in the book instead of paraphrasing it in my own words. Although he never explicitly characterizes legalism as a theory and does not use the term "transitional justice" in his book, a fair reading of *Stay the Hand of Vengeance* indicates that legalism is indeed a theory concerning the transitional justice policymaking of states, including the United States. In explicitly asking "[s]o why not adopt a realist approach?"[72] Bass presents legalism as an alternative to the theory of realism (including its modern variant of neorealism), at least with respect to states' foreign policymaking when confronting suspected atrocity perpetrators.[73] Then, citing such theorists as Kant, David Lumsdaine, and Moravcsik, all of whom Bass says subscribe to "a long tradition of seeing domestic politics as critically important for foreign policy,"[74] Bass situates legalism within the broader theory of liberalism.[75] Bass acknowledges that his "argument is related to" Democratic Peace Theory,[76] the subset of liberalism described in the previous Part. Tipping his hat to legalism's subject-matter origins, Bass explains that his book "owes its greatest debt to a work of political theory, not international relations, which emphasizes moral questions over political ones."[77]

Although not specifically referring to "transitional justice," legalism does fit squarely within that field. The term "transitional justice" has become much more popular today than when Bass published his book, in 2000. Perhaps for that reason, and because *Stay the Hand of Vengeance* narrowly focuses (to a fault, as I will discuss later) on war crimes tribunals, Bass uses the term "international justice"—a phrase occasionally used as a synonym for transitional justice on the international level—throughout his book.[78] In asking "Why support a war crimes tribunal?"[79] Bass's book explicitly and implicitly questions states' preferences in certain situations for this particular prosecutorial mechanism over (and, as I will discuss later and to Bass's neglect, alongside) other transitional justice options discussed in the previous chapter. The appropriateness of situating Bass's book in the field of transitional justice is further demonstrated by its frequent inclusion in the syllabi of courses on the subject.[80] Some scholars also explicitly locate *Stay the Hand of Vengeance* within the field of transitional justice.[81]

B. PRUDENTIALISM

Bass argues that totalitarian show trials (of the sort conducted by the Nazis and Stalinist Soviets) represent the antithesis of legalism. He notes that bona fide trials, subscribed to by legalists, include "an independent judiciary, the possibility of acquittals, some kind of civil procedure, and some kind of proportionality in sentencing."[82] In contrast, Bass contends, a show trial "has no chance of returning an acquittal, keeps the judges in thrall to the prosecution and behind that the state, cares little for procedure or standards of evidence, and has a propensity toward the quick execution."[83] Such show trials, Bass suggests, represent "the complete subversion of legal norms" by involving, inter alia, a judiciary that is not independent and "arbitrary terror."[84] I offer another interpretation: the true antithesis of legalism is a theory that explains why states support transitional justice options—even legalistic ones—for reasons other than fidelity to the rule of law.

Call this approach "prudentialism." Prudentialism follows from the concept of "prudence," already well established in international relations.[85] Such prudence, according to political theorist Alberto Coll, is a sort of "practical wisdom" that addresses ethical dilemmas in the theory and practice of statecraft.[86] Coll identifies two main types of prudence, the first of which is "normative prudence," as represented by philosophers Aristotle, Thomas Aquinas, Edmund Burke, and Reinhold Niebuhr. This school of thought argues that prudence "is not value-free; it remains under the guidance, however ambiguous or indirect, of moral principles."[87] International relations scholar Martin Wight, in an examination of Western values in diplomacy, argues that prudence, which he declares is a "moral virtue," reflects the desirable intertwining of political expedience with moral value to create a particular kind of "political morality."[88] Coll's second strand of prudence appears in the writings of secular realists, such as Thucydides, Niccolò Machiavelli, and Thomas Hobbes, who "define prudence as the skill of discerning that course of action which best serves one's self-interest and, therefore, as unconnected to morality, which is supposedly the pure or unencumbered search for the truly good."[89] Some modern realists adopt this latter conception of prudence, which is pragmatically focused on achieving certain desired ends rather than adhering to particular principles or employing particular means. Hans J. Morgenthau, for example, conceives of prudence as "the weighing of the consequences of alternative political actions—[what realism considers] to be the supreme virtue in politics."[90] Relatedly, in his discussion of a "prudentialist approach to order and justice," Hurrell argues that a "strong account" of philosopher Max Weber's ethic of responsibility[91] dictates that "there are no overarching global principles of justice that apply to foreign policy."[92] Similarly, international relations scholar Chris Brown describes the role of prudentialism in realism thusly:

> Some realists dismiss the role of morals in politics at all levels, others are amoralist only in international relations. The characteristic position is that to be concerned with morals is likely to lead to a "moralizing" attitude to international affairs and this in turn is likely to lead to disaster. Prudence is the only virtue of the statesman. The important point here is the assumption that the alternative to the prudentialism of the realist is a universalist code in which principles of conduct appropriate to private life are applied inappropriately to international affairs.[93]

It is this latter type of prudence—represented by secular realists—that I draw upon in formulating my own theoretical framework articulated in this book. My explanatory approach suggests that creating an ICT may be the best outcome after a state conducts a case-specific balancing of relevant politics, pragmatics, and normative beliefs. Prudentialism allows for the possibility that a state, even one that is liberal, *will not* support the establishment of an ICT if that state's balancing dictates otherwise.

Prudentialism deviates from legalism, which is based on a principled commitment to the rule of law, by positing that states are not necessarily committed to normative beliefs in transitional justice. In other words, even liberal states do not necessarily adhere to the view that putting suspected atrocity perpetrators on trial is (morally and legally) "right." According to my version of prudentialism, addressing suspected atrocity perpetrators through trials may be the best transitional justice option in some cases after considering a combination of relevant politics, pragmatics, and normative beliefs. Unlike legalism, prudentialism contends that it is neither correct nor essential in all circumstances for war criminals to be prosecuted.

Accordingly, despite the nature or severity of an atrocity, supposedly liberal states may decide to address the case outside of a courtroom, if at all. Where politics and pragmatics conflict with principles, prudentialism contends that the former two factors will prevail. For example, prudentialism takes into account states' security interests, whereas legalism does not. Consequently, contrary to legalism, prudentialism predicts no necessary consistency in whether and how states pursue transitional justice. And where consistency does appear, the reason, prudentialism suggests, may relate less to principle and more to "path dependence."[94]

Prudentialism, then, resembles realism; it emphasizes underlying rational-actor motivations to address suspected atrocity perpetrators through particular transitional justice institutions—including judicial institutions. As realism does not explicitly determine what would drive a state to support the establishment of ICTs, the remainder of this chapter is dedicated to formulating such an explanation.

C. COMPARATIVE HYPOTHESES

One can use both legalism and prudentialism to generate hypotheses about when and why a state would support the establishment of a war crimes tribunal for trying alleged atrocity perpetrators. Some of these hypotheses are at odds, whereas others overlap.

1. Legalism

Bass offers five propositions rooted in legalism concerning the origins of war crimes tribunals. The first and most significant, for purposes of this study, is the empirical claim that "it is only liberal states, with legalist beliefs, that support bona fide war crimes tribunals."[95] As discussed above, this claim is based on the legalist belief Bass ascribes to liberal states that "war criminals must be put on trial."[96] As applied to the case studies in this book, legalism thus would predict that, if the USG were to address suspected atrocity perpetrators from Germany, Japan, Libya, Iraq, the FRY, and Rwanda, its position as a liberal state would compel the use of a genuine judicial process. Moreover, the USG would have been motivated primarily to pursue legal methods out of a principled commitment to the rule of law. Legalism would also predict that no illiberal states would support authentic and valid prosecutorial responses to these—or other—conflicts.

Legalism makes other claims, as well, about states' motivations to deal with suspected atrocity perpetrators. The theory's second proposition is that "liberal states tend not to push for a war crimes tribunal if so doing would put their own soldiers at risk."[97] Third, legalism posits that "liberal states are more likely to be outraged by war crimes against their own citizens than war crimes against foreigners. The more a state has suffered, the more likely it is to be outraged."[98] Legalism's fourth assertion is that "liberal states are more likely to support a war crimes tribunal if public opinion is outraged by the war crimes in question. And they are less likely to support a war crimes tribunal if only elites are outraged."[99] Finally, legalism claims that "nonstate pressure groups can be effective in pushing for a tribunal, by shaming liberal states into action and providing expertise."[100]

2. Prudentialism

Prudentialism does not dispute the second, third, fourth, or fifth propositions of legalism. Concerning the second proposition, both theories would suggest that if apprehending and then trying suspected atrocity perpetrators from Germany, Japan, Libya, Iraq, the FRY, or Rwanda would have imperiled American soldiers, then the USG likely would not have supported the establishment of corresponding ICTs. Relating to the third proposition, both theories agree that the USG would have been more motivated to establish tribunals to prosecute Germans, Japanese, and Libyans than Iraqis, Yugoslavs, and Rwandans. After all, Americans fought in WWII and suffered casualties at the hands of Germans and particularly the Japanese (e.g., Pearl Harbor, Bataan Death March) and Americans flew on Pan Am flight 103. On the contrary, Americans were not the target of atrocities committed in Kuwait, the Balkans, or Rwanda. With respect to legalism's fourth and fifth claims, legalism and prudentialism would again find agreement. Both theories allow for the possibility that the USG would be more inclined to support the establishment of an ICT for those conflicts concerning WWII, Libya, Iraq, the FRY, and Rwanda about which public opinion expressed outrage. Moreover, both theories allow for the possibility that the USG would be more inclined to support the establishment of an ICT where NGOs lobbied for the establishment of some sort of transitional justice institution and provided expertise. Within the prudentialist framework, this possibility would arise when supporting the establishment of the ICT is consistent with the USG's independent balancing of relevant politics, pragmatics, and normative beliefs. As discussed above, states could use ICTs to share information and expertise. Thus, prudentialism would intimate USG support for such a transitional justice institution if it provided this pragmatic benefit, so long as other relevant political dynamics and normative beliefs were not impaired.

According to prudentialism, however, any state—liberal or illiberal—may support bona fide war crimes tribunals, and would do so *not* out of a principled commitment to pursuing justice through the rule of law, but as a result of a case-specific balancing of politics, pragmatics, and normative beliefs. This hypothesis directly contrasts with legalism's first proposition. The following table, Table 3.1, compares the empirical claims and causal logics of legalism and prudentialism.

When prudentialism's empirical claim and causal logic is applied to this book's case studies, the USG would have supported or led the establishment of the IMT, the IMTFE, the ICTY, and the ICTR if it believed that, in each case, the benefits to the United States of the relevant politics, pragmatics, and normative

TABLE 3.1 Legalism Versus Prudentialism: Empirical Claims and Causal Logics

	Legalism	Prudentialism
Empirical claim: Type of state that supports bona fide war crimes tribunals?	Only liberal states, never illiberal states.	Any state—liberal or illiberal.
Empirical claim: Consistency in whether and how liberal states pursue transitional justice?	Yes.	No.
Causal logic?	Leaders of liberal states have legalistic beliefs: it is correct and necessary for suspected atrocity perpetrators to be prosecuted.	Case-specific balancing: (1) Normative beliefs, (2) Politics, and (3) Pragmatics.

beliefs outweighed their costs. The relevant explanations would thus find no or only partial purchase in the profound moral convictions that legalism claims drive liberal states to act in such contexts. Conversely, prudentialism holds, the USG would support alternative transitional justice options for Germany, Japan, Libya, Iraq, the FRY, and Rwanda (e.g., inaction) if the benefits of supporting such options outweighed their costs. For example, the USG may have calculated such a significant strategic benefit in working with alleged atrocity perpetrators from those conflicts that prosecution would prove too costly. Prudentialism also allows for the possibility that illiberal states would support the IMT, the IMTFE, the ICTY, and the ICTR, because this transitional justice option emerged as the most preferable after a case-specific balancing of political factors, pragmatic features, and normative beliefs. Moreover, prudentialism predicts that this case-specific balancing would lead the USG to support different forms of prosecution, as described in the previous chapter, whereas legalism contains no such insight.

Unlike legalism, prudentialism does not generate a hypothesis about whether a specific type of state would support ICTs. If a state did not believe that an ICT would serve as a useful precedent or that its establishment was not inevitable, that state would be less compelled to play a role in its creation. More important, if a state believed that an ICT would negatively affect its economic or political interests, the state might resist supporting the ICT's creation. One potential negative consequence to a state of contributing to the formation of an ICT would be if the tribunal's jurisdiction extended to the supporting state's citizens and actions. If jurisdiction were that broad, the state might decide not to become involved in— or might actively work to undermine—the establishment of that ICT. In doing so, the state may seek to protect its sovereignty or to preserve its ability to decide unilaterally how, if at all, to address atrocities allegedly committed by its citizens and/or within its borders. Overall, when states—liberal or not—abjure from supporting a given tribunal, prudentialism asserts that promoting the rule of law takes a back seat to a cost-benefit analysis in which the state's interests are assigned primary weight.

3. Comparative Hypotheses

The following table, Table 3.2, summarizes the comparative hypotheses of legalism and prudentialism.

As this book focuses on a lone liberal country, the United States, this book will not be able to fully test these hypotheses. Conclusions drawn from the case studies in the next four chapters will necessarily be limited to the United States.

TABLE 3.2 Legalism Versus Prudentialism: Comparative Hypotheses

	Legalism	Prudentialism
(1) Whether and how states pursue transitional justice?	States will consistently pursue transitional justice and will do so in the form of trials.	States will not necessarily formulate consistent policies on whether or how to pursue transitional justice.
(2) What types of states support bona fide war crimes tribunals?	"[I]t is only liberal states, with legalist beliefs, that support bona fide war crimes tribunals."	Any state—liberal or illiberal—may support bona fide war crimes tribunals and would do so not out of a principled commitment to pursuing justice through the rule of law, but as a result of a case-specific balancing of politics, pragmatics, and normative beliefs.
(3) Types of transitional justice options states would support?	Liberal states would not support non-legalistic transitional justice options.	Any state—liberal or illiberal—may support non-legalistic transitional justice options.
(4) Types of legalistic transitional justice options states would support?	No prediction.	Any state—whether liberal or illiberal—may support variation in forms of prosecution.
(5) Impact of own soldiers at risk?	"[L]iberal states tend not to push for a war crimes tribunal if so doing would put their own soldiers at risk."	No difference.
(6) Impact of own citizens suffering?	"[L]iberal states are more likely to be outraged by war crimes against their own citizens than war crimes against foreigners. The more a state has suffered, the more likely it is to be outraged."	No difference.
(7) Impact of public opinion?	"[L]iberal states are more likely to support a war crimes tribunal if public opinion is outraged by the war crimes in question. And they are less likely to support a war crimes tribunal if only elites are outraged."	No difference.
(8) Impact of nonstate pressure groups?	"[N]onstate pressure groups can be effective in pushing for a tribunal, by shaming liberal states into action and providing expertise."	No difference.

V. Conclusion

As discussed in this chapter, transitional justice creates particular challenges for international security and international cooperation, especially when the United States is involved. That transitional justice implicates both security and cooperation raises questions that are addressed throughout this book. For example, why, given the drawbacks to security and cooperation that establishing ICTs may present, did the USG decide to collaborate with other states to create the IMT, the IMTFE, the ICTY, and the ICTR? Given those same concerns, what explains the variation in form among each of these USG-backed ICTs? What factors have driven USG decision-making in this issue-area?

Extrapolating from two of the dominant international relations theories—realism and liberalism—the following analysis provides answers to these vexing questions by exploring why the United States favored ICTs instead of—or in addition to—alternative transitional justice options in this book's four primary case studies and opposed ICTs in this book's two secondary case studies. Legalism claims that the USG was primarily driven by a principled commitment to the rule of law, whereas prudentialism asserts that the USG was motivated by a case-specific balancing of politics, pragmatics, and normative beliefs.

The following four chapters present a history and analysis of the USG role in transitional justice concerning (1) Germany; (2) Japan; (3) Libya, Iraq, and the FRY; and (4) Rwanda. These chapters—and then the Conclusion—consider whether legalism or prudentialism provides a more compelling explanation for why and how the USG was involved in the creation of groundbreaking ICTs as well as other transitional justice mechanisms. Which theory is more persuasive will depend on their respective abilities to explain the factors that animate and constrain U.S. action. Specifically, the stronger theory would explicate more than just the United States' support for a legalistic transitional justice option, given its liberal status. First, taking into account the array of transitional justice options outlined in Chapter II, what explains the USG's preference for a particular option? Second, why might the USG support a non-legalistic transitional justice option over a legalistic one? Third, why might the USG support both legalistic and non-legalistic transitional justice options for the same atrocity? Fourth, why might the particular transitional justice options the USG supports vary across time and space? I begin these considerations with the first and perhaps most famous ICT in history, the IMT.

The United States Role in
Transitional Justice for Germany

I. Background

What is commonly referred to as "Nuremberg" is actually a series of thirteen trials that occurred in Nuremberg, Germany, from 1945 to 1949. These proceedings can be divided into two sets. The first was the Trial of the Major War Crimes Before the International Military Tribunal (IMT) between 1945 and 1946 (what is popularly known as the "Nuremberg Tribunal"). The second set was the twelve subsequent Trials of War Criminals Before the Nuremberg Military Tribunals (NMT). As will be discussed, the IMT and the NMT were two of only several transitional justice options the USG supported for addressing Nazis suspected of committing atrocities during WWII.

A. NEGOTIATIONS LEADING TO "NUREMBERG"

It was not preordained that at least some prominent Nazis would be prosecuted after WWII. In fact, at various points during the conflict, the Allies, including the USG, considered alternative transitional justice options for addressing Nazi crimes. Six major diplomatic steps led to holding accountable almost two dozen of the principal Nazis suspected of committing atrocities during WWII.

1. January 1942: Declaration of St. James's

The first critical diplomatic step occurred on January 13, 1942, at approximately the same time the USG began interning Japanese-Americans and exactly one week before the Nazi leadership formulated its so-called Wannsee Protocol, which detailed the "final solution of the European Jewish question."[1] That day,

the Inter-Allied Commission on the Punishment of War Crimes, comprising representatives of the nine governments-in-exile in London (Belgium,
Czechoslovakia, France, Greece, Luxembourg, The Netherlands, Norway,
Poland, and Yugoslavia), issued its Declaration of St. James's, in which the signatories stated that they would

> Place amongst their principal war aims punishment through the chan-
> nel of organized justice of those guilty of or responsible for these crimes,
> whether they have ordered them, perpetrated them[,] or in any way partici-
> pated in them;
>   Determine in the spirit of international solidarity to see to it that
> (A) those guilty and responsible, whatever their nationality, are sought for,
> handed over to justice[,] and judged; (B) that sentences pronounced are
> carried out.[2]

In July 1942, the United States, the United Kingdom, and the Soviet Union
approved the Declaration of St. James's;[3] FDR and Churchill declared that suspected Nazi war criminals would stand trial; and the Soviet leader, Joseph Stalin,
specifically mentioned that these trials would occur through "a special international tribunal."[4] A month later, the USG used even more explicit language, calling for trials of suspected atrocity perpetrators. FDR declared on August 21, 1942:

> When victory has been achieved, it is the purpose of the Government of the
> United States, as I know it is the purpose of each of the United Nations, to
> make appropriate use of the information and evidence in respect to these
> barbaric crimes of the invaders in Europe and in Asia. It seems only fair
> that they should have this warning that the time will come when they shall
> have to stand in courts of law in the very countries which they are now
> oppressing and answer for their acts.[5]

Consequently, by the summer of 1942, the Allies had publicly committed to a
collaborative scheme for addressing Nazi atrocities during WWII.[6] The specific transitional justice option they would jointly implement remained vague
and undecided, but, at least according to FDR, included prosecution (and corresponding punishment).

At the same time, a crucial development occurred within the United States.
From July 29 to 30, 1942, the U.S. Supreme Court heard oral arguments on
whether it was legal, according to the U.S. Constitution and other American
laws, for the USG to detain German spies for trial by military commissions that
FDR had established. The Court rendered its decision on July 31, 1942, holding
that the USG lawfully detained the petitioners and lawfully constituted military
commissions. The decision also stated that the U.S. president possessed authority to order the petitioners' trial by the commissions for their alleged offenses.[7]
The path was thus cleared for the USG to lawfully exercise the option of using

military tribunals to hold accountable individuals suspected of committing atrocities during WWII and beyond.

2. October 1942: Establishment of the United Nations War Crimes Commission

The second major diplomatic step toward Nazi accountability occurred a few months later. On October 7, 1942, the United States and the United Kingdom jointly proposed the establishment of the United Nations Commission for the Investigation of War Crimes (also known as the United Nations War Crimes Commission, or UNWCC),[8] which would identify suspected war criminals and collect evidence about their alleged atrocities.[9] Specifically, FDR declared that day: "It is our intention that just and sure punishment shall be meted out to the ringleaders responsible for the organized murder of thousands of innocent persons in the commission of atrocities which have violated every tenet of the Christian faith."[10] FDR's vice president, Henry Wallace, publicly and dutifully echoed FDR's sentiment. On December 28, 1942, Wallace declared:

> A special problem that will face the United Nations immediately upon the attainment of victory over either Germany or Japan will be what to do with the defeated nation. Revenge for the sake of revenge would be a sign of barbarism—but this time we must make absolutely sure that the guilty leaders are punished, that the defeated nation realizes its defeat and is not permitted to rearm.[11]

The U.S. Congress later announced its support for FDR and Wallace's position, declaring in a March 9, 1943 U.S. Senate resolution, with which the House of Representatives concurred, that "it is the sense of this Congress that those guilty, directly or indirectly, of these criminal acts shall be held accountable and punished in a manner commensurate with the offenses for which they are responsible."[12] Although the specific transitional justice option the USG would pursue remained vague, the legislative branch at this point affirmed its commitment to punishing suspected atrocity perpetrators and ruled out the possibility of inaction or other alternatives that would bar accountability, such as unconditional amnesty and exile.

As the major Allied powers (the United States, the United Kingdom, the Soviet Union, and France) sought to retain control over addressing Nazis suspected of perpetrating the most egregious atrocities, the UNWCC's mandate was narrow. To that end, the UNWCC's activities were limited as soon as it was established in London on October 20, 1943, and held its first meeting six days later. An internal U.S./DoS document provides the following description of the UNWCC:

> The [UNWCC], which started its work in 1943, developed and maintained individual case files concerning alleged war criminals. Fifteen

nations participated in the [UNWCC]. The [UNWCC] served primarily as a clearinghouse for information provided by countries concerned; it also made recommendations concerning the tribunals to be established, procedures for the tribunals, and the definition of war crimes. It concluded operations in 1945, having submitted its files and recommendations to the participating governments, which had decisionmaking authority.[13]

The Soviet Union never participated in the UNWCC's activities, opting instead to establish, on November 2, 1942, its own agency with a similar mandate: the Soviet Extraordinary State Commission to Investigate War Crimes.[14]

Despite statements by the Big Three (the United States, the United Kingdom, and the Soviet Union) in support of the Declaration of St. James's apparent prosecutorial approach, the United Kingdom harbored a desire to address major Nazi war criminals through an alternative transitional justice option. On November 12, 1942, a month after the UNWCC proposal and just before the Naval Battle at Guadalcanal between the United States and the Japanese, Ivan Maisky, the Soviet ambassador to the United Kingdom, sent British foreign secretary Anthony Eden a memo suggesting that an ICT be established to try the "major war criminals."[15] But Churchill, Eden, and other senior British officials opposed the Soviet proposal, instead favoring lethal force through extrajudicial execution for addressing major Nazi war criminals. The reason, Eden argued, was that "[t]he guilt of such individuals is so black that they fall outside and go beyond the scope of any judicial process."[16] The British were also concerned about repeating the failure of bringing suspected war criminals from WWI to justice.[17]

3. October 1943: Moscow Declaration

This lack of consensus among the Allies led to the third major diplomatic step, which occurred a year later in the Soviet Union. On October 30, 1943, the Big Three and China signed the Moscow Declaration, in which the Big Three issued a "Statement on Atrocities." According to the statement, after the end of hostilities, the three Allied powers would send Nazis accused of atrocities "back to the countries in which their abominable deeds were done in order that they may be judged and punished according to the laws of these liberated countries and of free government which will be erected therein." The signatories made one important qualification, however, writing that "[t]he above declaration is without prejudice to the case of German criminals whose offenses have no particular geographical localization and who will be punished by joint decision of the government of the Allies."[18] As a result, this declaration raised the possibility of both domestic trials and the establishment of an ICT. By Churchill's design, this declaration also allowed the Allies to adopt other transitional justice options jointly, such as the U.K.-favored option, extrajudicial execution.

4. 1943–1945: The Allies' Deliberations

Signatories to the Moscow Declaration continued issuing warnings to suspected WWII atrocity perpetrators. For example, on March 24, 1944, FDR threatened: "none who participate in these acts of savagery shall go unpunished . . . . All who share in the guilt shall share the punishment."[19]

Although Soviet leaders had supported the establishment of an ICT, they may have changed their minds temporarily in favor of the British preference for lethal force through extrajudicial execution. During the Tehran Conference, from November 28 to December 1, 1943,[20] Stalin stated that between 50,000 and 100,000 German military officers should be summarily executed, though it is unclear whether he meant this comment seriously.[21] Whether or not the Soviet Union sincerely took this position, though, no doubt exists that certain U.S. officials momentarily sided with the British preference for lethal force.

FDR consulted in early-September 1944 with two of his senior advisors. Secretary of the Treasury Henry Morgenthau, Jr. advocated, in addition to harsh economic penalties on Germany, that "arch-criminals of this war whose *obvious guilt* has generally been recognized by the United Nations . . . shall be *put to death forthwith by firing squads* made up of soldiers of the United Nations."[22] Morgenthau further suggested that other war criminals be tried by military commissions and, if convicted, sentenced to death. In extenuating circumstances, he recommended, the USG could pursue alternative punishments, such as exile through "deportation to a penal colony outside of Germany."[23] Morgenthau also advocated the exile of all SS members and their families.[24] His proposal received support from Secretary of State Cordell Hull and FDR's personal aide, Harry Hopkins.[25] In contrast, Secretary of War Henry Stimson, who initially (though privately) also considered supporting summary judgment (through execution),[26] later argued explicitly against such punishment without due process. Instead he proposed that "at least as to the chief Nazi officials, we should participate in an international tribunal constituted to try them," and that other war criminals "should be returned in accordance with the Moscow Declaration to those territories for trial by national military commissions . . . ."[27]

Contrary to U.S. Supreme Court Justice Jackson's later claim that "President Roosevelt had steadily and insistently favored a speedy but fair trial for these men, fearful that if they were punished without public proof of their crimes and opportunity to defend themselves there would always remain a doubt of their guilt that might raise a myth of martyrdom,"[28] and despite FDR's own declaration of August 21, 1942, supporting trials, the president temporarily sided with Morgenthau's summary execution proposal. Morgenthau accompanied FDR to a September 1944 meeting with Churchill in Quebec at which Churchill submitted to the American delegation a document authored by British lord chancellor Sir John Simon. The document argued that "trial, conviction, and judicial sentence is quite inappropriate for notorious ringleaders" and that, instead, these individuals—whose atrocities had no geographical location—should be dealt with through a political decision of "execution."[29] On September 15, 1944, while still in Quebec, FDR and Churchill agreed that they would present the Lord Simon memorandum (which echoed Morgenthau's summary execution proposal) to Stalin and invite his concurrence.[30]

British advocacy—and American and possibly also Soviet support— for summarily executing major Nazi war criminals proved fleeting. When Churchill met with Stalin in Moscow in October 1944, Stalin rejected the summary execution proposal memorialized in the Lord Simon memorandum and Morgenthau Plan, arguing that its implementation would convey to the world the Allies' fear of prosecuting the major Nazi war criminals.[31] As a result, Churchill withdrew his proposal shortly thereafter.[32] And, by that time, FDR had independently changed his mind. On September 24, the *New York Times* ran a front-page article that described the economic proposals of the Morgenthau Plan for effectively turning Germany into an agrarian state through a process called "pastoralization," but the article did not mention his proposals for addressing war criminals.[33] Through opinion polls and newspaper editorials, the American public, focusing on economic policy rather than transitional justice options, expressed its outrage over treating the entire German nation so severely. In response, on October 3, 1944, FDR voiced his regret to Stimson for approving the Morgenthau Plan. Notably, this event occurred *before* Churchill recounted his meeting with Stalin to FDR in which Stalin rejected the Lord Simon memorandum.[34]

While FDR reconsidered his position, a political vacuum emerged in Washington regarding war crimes issues; bureaucratic infighting resulted in the War Department seizing leadership on this policy matter. As a result, Stimson's preference for trials over mass extrajudicial execution dominated the discourse and gained the support of other senior U.S. officials, including the Army Chief of Staff, General George Marshall; the Judge Advocate General and future U.S. judge on the IMTFE, Major General Myron Cramer; and U.S. Supreme Court Justice Felix Frankfurter.[35]

In mid-September 1944, just after Allied troops entered Germany, a memorandum authored by Lieutenant Colonel Murray Bernays, who worked in the Personnel Division of the Army General Staff, was circulated within the War Department. This document explicitly argued against the transitional justice options of prosecution through domestic courts and lethal force through summary execution, and instead advocated prosecution through an "appropriately constituted international court." The "Bernays Plan" also articulated many of the core concepts that would be included in the IMT's subject-matter jurisdiction, such as conspiracy and organizational guilt.[36] On October 1, 1944, Colonel Ammi Cutter, Assistant Executive Officer in the Office of the Assistant Secretary of War, sent a memorandum to his direct superior, Assistant Secretary of War (and future World Bank president) John McCloy, positively evaluating the Bernays Plan.[37] By the end of the month, Stimson felt that the Bernays Plan merited circulation outside the War Department; on October 27, 1944, he wrote a memorandum to Hull favorably citing the plan.[38]

By November 11, 1944, the War, State, and Navy departments had developed a draft memorandum (written largely by Bernays) on prosecuting European war criminals.[39] Disagreements within the USG persisted during the following month, however, with senior USG officials criticizing the most basic aspects of the Bernays Plan. Then, on December 17, 1944, during the Battle of the Bulge, the 1st SS Panzer Division Leibstandarte Adolf Hitler, which was commanded by Joachim Peiper, slaughtered dozens of American prisoners of war in Malmédy, Belgium.[40] This German atrocity committed against Americans stifled much of the opposition within the USG to the Bernays Plan.[41] Shortly thereafter, on January 22, 1945, Stimson and the new Secretary of State, Edward Stettinius, Jr., joined by Attorney General (and future U.S. judge on the IMT) Francis Biddle, presented a memorandum to FDR. The document, based on the Bernays Plan, explicitly argued against extrajudicial executions and instead called for the establishment of an "international military commission or [military] court" to prosecute the most senior Nazi officials and implicated Nazi organizations. It also featured proposals for prosecution charges to include conspiracy ("joint participation in a broad criminal enterprise"), individual guilt for organizational membership, and, as an element of the criminal enterprise, crimes against peace ("the waging of an illegal war of aggression"). The memorandum further proposed that "subsequent trials" would be held in "occupation courts," civil or military courts of "the country concerned," or "international military courts."[42] Notably, whereas the Bernays Plan called for the establishment of a treaty-based international court, the new memorandum backed the establishment of a tribunal by "Executive Agreement of the heads of State of the interested United Nations," which "would require no enabling legislation [or treaty]" or, if it were preferred, "by action of the Supreme Authority [(Control Council for Germany)]."[43]

The following month, during the Yalta Conference held from February 4 to 11, 1945,[44] the British once again argued for extrajudicially executing the major Nazi war criminals, although they allowed for lesser Nazi offenders to be prosecuted.[45] No final decisions were made at the conference.[46] Two months later, the Allies still could not reach agreement. In April 1945, French leader Charles de Gaulle stated a preference for prosecution over the extrajudicial execution of major Nazi war criminals, while the British War Cabinet declared its absolute opposition to trials for those individuals.[47]

5. 1945: The U.S. Government Reaches Internal Consensus and Agreement with Allies

When FDR died on April 12, 1945, Truman was sworn into office as the 33rd U.S. president. Soon thereafter, Truman (who had served as a judge on Mississippi's Jackson County Court) declared his opposition to extrajudicial executions and his preference for establishing a court to try major Nazi war criminals.[48] Following suit, on April 20, 1945, McCloy's office in the War Department produced a memorandum arguing for "judicial trial" over "political disposition," such as summary execution,[49] and Cutter drafted a similar memorandum for the Department.[50]

On May 2, 1945—four days after Benito Mussolini was killed, two days after Adolf Hitler committed suicide, and one day after Nazi propagandist Joseph Goebbels and his family also ended their own lives—Truman took another step toward using judicial trials to prosecute senior Nazi war criminals by naming Jackson to be

> the Representative of the United States and its Chief of Counsel in preparing and prosecuting charges of atrocities and war crimes against such of the leaders of the European Axis powers and their principal agents and accessories as the United States may agree with any of the United Nations to bring to trial before an international military tribunal.[51]

Jackson would thus serve as the chief U.S. representative in negotiations leading to the IMT's creation, and then the chief U.S. prosecutor before that tribunal.

The following day, the British War Cabinet officially revised its position on how major Nazi war criminals should be addressed. In a message to Eden, the British War Cabinet stated:

> The position as regards the major war criminals has greatly changed since this matter was last considered. Many of these have already been killed, and the same fate may well overtake others before the fighting is over.
>
> The War Cabinet still see objections to having formal state trials for the most notorious war criminals whose crimes have no geographical location. But if our two major allies remain convinced that this is necessary, we are willing to accept their views on principle.[52]

That same day, during a meeting of the Big Three at the UN conference in San Francisco, Eden declared his government's willingness to work with the United States and the Soviet Union to prosecute the major criminals through an ICT.[53] Over the following months, the British "rapidly adjusted themselves to the American vision" of a thorough, potentially lengthy trial that would draw upon new principles and procedures in international law.[54] On June 6, 1945, Jackson submitted a report to Truman describing his progress in the investigation and prosecution of the foremost Axis war criminals. Truman approved the report, which was published throughout the United States and Europe.[55]

Although the major Allied powers (the United States, the United Kingdom, the Soviet Union, and France) had agreed by mid-1945 to prosecute the principal Nazi war criminals through an ICT, negotiations over this transitional justice option did not cease. On procedural issues, the participating countries' divided adherence to the common law (the adversarial, Anglo-American system) and civil law systems (the inquisitorial, Continental system, which was followed by France and the Soviet Union) created some tension that ultimately resulted in compromise.[56] Furthermore, the Soviet Union and the United States disagreed emphatically and repeatedly about the nature of the trials on three major points. First, the Soviet Union argued that the Nazis' guilt already had been determined and that the tribunal should be mandated only with adjudicating the degree of culpability and accompanying punishment. The United States, by contrast, argued that the trials should not presume guilt.[57] A second point of contention concerned the Soviets' belief (supported by both the United Kingdom and France) that waging an aggressive war should not be considered illegal per se, probably out of concern for its own actions during WWII, particularly against Poland, Finland, Latvia, Estonia, and Lithuania. The opposing American view held that a political-legal argument condemning aggressive militarism was the cornerstone of the future prosecution case against the major Nazi war criminals.[58] A third point of controversy was that the Soviet Union (joined by France) did not favor the trial of organizations, whereas "the concept of a conspiracy or common plan involving not only individuals but organizations was at the heart of the American proposal . . . ."[59]

Throughout these contentious discussions, Jackson occasionally suggested that a lack of coordination might be desirable and pragmatic: "the idea of separate trials for each nation for the trial of its separate groups of prisoners may be the easiest and most satisfactory way of reconciling" these different positions.[60] The Soviet Union responded, citing previous agreements, that such separate national prosecutions "would be directly opposed to the Moscow declaration, which laid down that the trial of the war criminals should be a common task of the United Nations."[61] This prompted Jackson to declare:

> there are some things worse for me than failing to reach an agreement, and one of them is reaching an agreement that would stultify the position which the United States has taken throughout . . . . I think there are four possible courses here: one is to set up the international Four Power trials we have been considering; another is to refer the war crimes matter back to the Potsdam Conference for a political decision as to what they will do with these prisoners; another is for the United States, whose interests and views in the matter do not seem to be in accordance with those of the European

Allies, to turn over its prisoners to those Allies and permit the trial or disposition by such method as you three agree upon; and the fourth course
would be for each of us, by separate trials, to proceed to try those we have
as criminals.[62]

Jackson privately proposed yet a fifth option to other senior USG officials: that
the United States, the United Kingdom, and France conduct a joint trial without the Soviet Union.[63] Comparing the fourth and fifth options, Judge Samuel
Rosenman, a U.S. presidential advisor, stated that the former was preferable
because the latter "would be quite a slap at the Russians, leading to recrimina-
tions, where it would not be quite so bad if it was decided that each nation would
try its own war criminal prisoners."[64] Brigadier General Telford Taylor, who, on
October 17, 1946, was appointed by Truman to succeed Jackson (who by then had
returned to his seat on the U.S. Supreme Court) as the U.S. Chief of Counsel for
War Crimes, concurred. As Taylor argued: "Given the history of the relations
between Russia and the other three [major Allies], it would have been the height
of political folly to proceed with an international trial of war criminals without
the participation of the Soviet Union."[65]

In part because of skilled British mediation between the United States and
the Soviet Union, the latter eventually yielded to the American plan on all three
points: the ICT would not presume the defendants' guilt, and its mandate would
include considering both crimes against peace and the common plan or conspiracy. The involvement of the United Kingdom in brokering these negotiations was
an ironic development given the British opposition to a tribunal only a couple of
months earlier. Yet their about-face was somewhat understandable in light of the
U.K. government's change from Conservative to Labour leadership during the
interim election.[66] At the same time as the Kremlin caved to the USG preferences,
the British also yielded to the American plan on a separate point. Although the
United Kingdom originally had preferred a trial that would "last at most two
weeks," the Americans favored a lengthier and thus more thorough proceeding.[67]

6. August 1945: London Agreement

The final major diplomatic step toward establishing a transitional justice system for addressing the principal Nazis' atrocities occurred on August 8, 1945.
Exactly three months after Germany formally surrendered and two days after
the U.S. atomic bombing of Hiroshima, the four major Allied powers signed
the London Agreement, which provided for the "prosecution and punishment
of the major war criminals of the European Axis."[68] On behalf of the USG,
Jackson signed the Agreement, which established the IMT, the charter of
which was annexed to the Agreement. Articles 4 and 6 of the Agreement stated
important qualifications. Article 4 declared: "Nothing in this Agreement
shall prejudice the provisions established by the Moscow Declaration concerning the return of war criminals to the countries where they committed

their crimes."[69] Article 6 stated: "Nothing in this Agreement shall prejudice the jurisdiction or the powers of any national or occupation court established or to be established in any allied territory or in Germany for the trial of war criminals."[70] The creation of the IMT thus left open the possibility of other simultaneous or sequential transitional justice options, including additional prosecutorial mechanisms.

B. THE INTERNATIONAL MILITARY TRIBUNAL'S TRIALS

The IMT exercised subject-matter jurisdiction over "crimes against peace," "war crimes," and "crimes against humanity."[71] The tribunal could impose the death penalty, or any other punishment considered "just," on convicted individuals.[72]

On October 6, 1945, the four prosecuting powers—the United States, the United Kingdom, the Soviet Union, and France—issued a joint indictment, charging twenty-four men and six organizations with four counts: crimes against peace, war crimes, crimes against humanity, and the common plan or conspiracy.[73] Rather than base their selection of defendants on explicit legal criteria, the quadripartite Allied powers chose individuals for a combination of political and pragmatic reasons. The Allied powers jointly made the following decisions: (1) the Allied powers would each have at least one of its prisoners in the dock, (2) they would try at least one representative of each indicted organization in order to establish that organization's role and therefore pave the way for subsequent trials of the organization's members, (3) they would try at least one representative of each of the critical components of the alleged Nazi conspiracy,[74] and (4) they agreed on the pointlessness of prosecuting the deceased, such as Hitler, Goebbels, and SS commander Heinrich Himmler.[75]

Opening statements were delivered to the IMT on November 20, 1945,[76] and the IMT's verdicts were handed down from between September 30 to October 1, 1946.[77] The IMT ultimately sentenced twelve defendants to death by hanging, three to life imprisonment, two to twenty years imprisonment, one to fifteen years imprisonment, one to ten years imprisonment, and acquitted three other indictees. Those serving prison terms did so at Spandau prison in Berlin. Two individuals were not sentenced: one had committed suicide before the verdict and one had been judged unfit for trial.[78]

II. Transitional Justice Options Seriously Considered and Actually Implemented for Alleged Nazi Atrocity Perpetrators

The IMT was one of only several transitional justice options seriously considered and actually implemented for addressing Nazis suspected of committing atrocities during WWII. In the immediate aftermath of the war, the USG and its allies also applied three other transitional justice options to Nazis: unilateral prosecution through ad hoc Allied military tribunals, conditional amnesty, and lustration. Such amnesty violated the USG's stated preference for punitive transitional justice mechanisms, as articulated, for example, in the Declaration of St. James's, the Moscow Declaration, and FDR's threat on March 24, 1944. And such lustration similarly violated USG rhetoric favoring prosecution. Figure 4.1 shows the general transitional justice options the USG supported for addressing Nazis, whereas Figure 4.2 displays the specific prosecutorial transitional justice options the USG supported in this case.

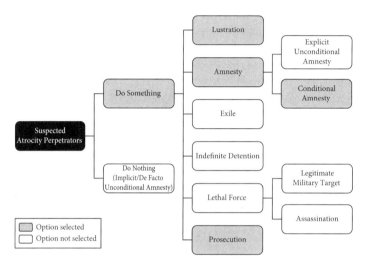

FIGURE 4.1 *U.S. Government Transitional Justice Options Tree for Suspected Nazi Atrocity Perpetrators—General.*

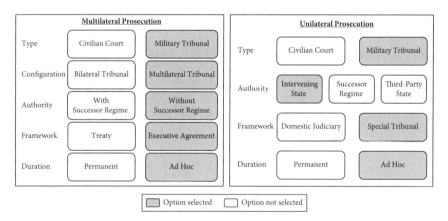

FIGURE 4.2 *U.S. Government Transitional Justice Options Table for Suspected Nazi Atrocity Perpetrators—Prosecution.*

Part II.A summarizes what transitional justice options the Allied Powers collectively and the USG individually seriously considered for addressing suspected Nazi atrocity perpetrators. Part II.B discusses the transitional justice options the Allied powers—in particular, the USG—actually implemented. Part II.C explores the transitional justice options the Allied powers—again, in particular the USG—did *not* seriously consider implementing.

A. TRANSITIONAL JUSTICE OPTIONS SERIOUSLY CONSIDERED

1. Transitional Justice Options
the Allied Powers Seriously Considered

Throughout the negotiations leading to the IMT's establishment, the quadripartite Allied powers seriously considered two general transitional justice options for handling Nazis suspected of committing the most egregious atrocities: lethal force and prosecution. Within the general transitional justice option of prosecution, the Allied powers weighed both unilateral and multilateral approaches. Under the unilateral prosecution plan, some or all of the Allied powers would separately prosecute suspected atrocity perpetrators from Nazi Germany. The multilateral prosecution option combined some or all of the Allied powers in collaborative prosecution of alleged atrocity perpetrators.

In fact, the development of the negotiations reveals just how close some or all of the Allies came to pursuing a transitional justice option other than the establishment of the IMT. Before FDR died, the United Kingdom, the United States, and perhaps the Soviet Union nearly agreed on lethal force through extrajudicial executions. Moreover, negotiations, especially between the American and Soviet delegations, demonstrate how close the Allies came to pursuing a prosecutorial transitional justice option either unilaterally or among a smaller number of countries rather than through a broader multilateral scheme, as ultimately chosen.

2. Transitional Justice Options
the U.S. Government Seriously Considered

The USG seriously considered at least five transitional justice options in addressing the principal suspected Nazi war criminals: (1) lethal force through extrajudicial execution, (2) prosecution in an ICT established through a treaty, (3) prosecution in an ICT established through an executive agreement, (4) unilateral prosecution, and, as discussed below, (5) de facto conditional amnesty. For addressing other suspected Nazi war criminals, the USG also considered at least five transitional justice options: (1) prosecution in occupation courts, (2) prosecution in civil courts established by third-party states, (3) prosecution in military courts established by third-party states, (4) prosecution in an international military tribunal, and, as discussed below, (5) lustration.

B. TRANSITIONAL JUSTICE OPTIONS
ACTUALLY IMPLEMENTED

1. Multilateral Prosecution Through
an Ad Hoc International Military Tribunal

In the end, the quadripartite Allied powers chose to prosecute the principal suspected atrocity perpetrators multilaterally through an ad hoc international military tribunal. Because Jackson led diplomatic negotiations about the IMT on
behalf of the USG, his explanations for the USG's positions on transitional justice
can be considered representative and well informed. Jackson explained that this
decision ultimately strengthened the USG's position, stating that the best course
of action "is to determine the innocence or guilt of the accused after a hearing as
dispassionate as the times and horrors we deal with will permit, and upon a record that will leave our reasons and motives clear."[79] According to Taylor, Jackson
also stated that the purpose of prosecution would be to provide

> a well-documented history of what we are convinced was a grand, con-
> certed pattern to incite and coerce the aggressions and barbarities which
> have shocked the world . . . . Unless we write the record of this movement
> with clarity and precision, we cannot blame the future if in days of peace
> it finds incredible the accusatory generalities uttered during the war. We
> must establish incredible events by credible evidence.[80]

Jackson further contended on June 30, 1945, that the USG, in particular,
favored prosecutions to establish Nazi atrocities because it afforded the due
process familiar to most Americans, lest U.S. citizens become as suspicious of
these offenses' accuracy as Americans had been of alleged German atrocities
from WWI.[81] Jackson further explained why the USG favored a single, prominent international trial of the principal suspected atrocity perpetrators from
Nazi Germany. Jackson advocated this method on the basis that, even though the
USG intended to participate in holding other alleged Nazi atrocity perpetrators
accountable, principal and representative suspected Nazi atrocity perpetrators
should be tried jointly and prominently to demonstrate the conspiracy underpinning their heinous crimes.[82] Jackson also noted that such prosecutions would
occur through a military commission rather than a civilian court, to accommodate the necessary compromises reached among the legal systems of the participating states and also because of the special circumstances of the case.[83]

The specific method of prosecution on which the Allies settled would be a
newly established ad hoc ICT that would exist outside the UN,[84] created through
an executive agreement among the four states. The tribunal would be a military
commission with limited subject-matter (crimes against peace, war crimes, and
crimes against humanity), temporal (crimes committed during WWII), and personal (major war criminals of the European Axis) jurisdiction.

2. Unilateral Prosecution Through
Ad Hoc Allied Military Tribunals

Although the Allies decided to prosecute many of the most senior Nazis before an international military tribunal, other Nazis were prosecuted through alternative systems. On December 20, 1945, a month after the IMT trial began, the Allied Control Council issued Control Council Law No. 10, which provided that each occupying authority, within its Zone of Occupation, could arrest, prosecute, and, if convicted, punish suspected atrocity perpetrators located within its respective Zone. The only exception arose if individuals were transferred to another tribunal, such as the IMT.[85] Ten months later, on October 18, 1946, the USG established unilateral American military tribunals with the power to try and punish these suspected atrocity perpetrators.[86] The U.S. Military Governor retained the option to enter into agreements with other Zone commanders of the member states of the Allied Control Authority to establish joint trial of any cases.[87]

After the IMT trials ended in October 1946, the quadripartite Allied powers disagreed over whether and how to proceed with subsequent trials of the remaining suspected atrocity perpetrators, who numbered in the thousands. One plan, offered by Taylor, was that each of the four Allied powers would divide Nazi prisoners into groups of 200 to 400 and then prosecute them in unilateral tribunals in their respective Zones of Occupation. However, the Allied powers disagreed over the plan; for example, some USG officials cited the unacceptable expense, and some Soviets opposed any trials not held in Berlin.[88] Ultimately, the United States, the United Kingdom, and France would organize trials under the authority of Control Council Law No. 10, whereas the Soviet Union would not.[89]

The USG pursued unilateral trials in its Zone of Occupation in addition to military commissions and lustration (called "denazification"). Two months after the IMT proceedings concluded, the USG organized twelve subsequent war crimes trials, which they also held in Nuremberg. In his position as Jackson's successor, Taylor, who had tried the case against the German High Command before the IMT, served as chief prosecutor at these trials of the NMT. The first of these twelve subsequent trials began on December 9, 1946, and the final proceeding concluded on April 13, 1949.[90] Of those convicted through the NMT trials, 13 were executed, 8 received life sentences in prison, and 111 others received either light sentences or early parole (due in large part to a commutation of sentences issued by the High Commissioner for Germany on January 31, 1951).[91] By 1963, including unilateral trials beyond the NMT, the USG had tried 1184 Germans in its Zone of Occupation, sentencing 450 of them to capital punishment.[92] Other Allied states produced comparable or, in the case of the Soviet Union, much greater numbers. In total, the British convicted 1085, sentencing 240 to death; the French convicted 2107, sentencing 104 to death; and the Soviets independently tried approximately 10,000 Germans, sentencing an unknown (but presumably large) number of them to death.[93]

Despite the efforts of Jackson, Taylor, and others, the Allied powers failed to hold accountable many of the worst suspected atrocity perpetrators from WWII. One reason was that some of the Allied powers either declined to prosecute these suspects themselves or refused to hand them over to one of the Allied powers that was willing and able to do so. For example, despite U.S. efforts, the Soviets chose not to hold accountable some of the staff from the Nazi concentration and death camps that they held in their Zone of Occupation.[94]

The debate within the USG about the utility, legality, and morality of these subsequent trials did not cease once the decision to pursue them was made, however. Several members of the U.S. Congress, including Senators Joseph McCarthy, William Langer, Robert Taft,[95] and Congressman John Rankin; some members of the judicial branch, including U.S. Supreme Court Chief Justice Harlan Stone, his colleague William Douglas, and Iowa Supreme Court Justice Charles Wennerstrum, who also served as a presiding judge in one of the NMT cases; various academics, including political realist Hans J. Morgenthau; and the editorial boards of several newspapers (including "liberal" media outlets), such as the *Chicago Tribune* and the *Nation*, denounced the Nuremberg trials for assorted reasons, including that they were part of a Communist plot.[96] General political will to support the Nuremberg trials also diminished over time as a result of other pressing international affairs of the era. As scholar Robert Conot reports: "By 1949 the Cold War had undermined any further inclination for prosecution, and the next year the start of the Korean War completed the process of diverting the world's attention."[97] Although these developments would signal the NMT's end, unilateral domestic prosecutions by willing states would continue on an ad hoc basis against Nazis and their collaborators, including Klaus Barbie, John Demjanjuk, Eichmann, Alfons Goetzfried, Karl Hass, Rudolf Hoess, Maurice Papon, Erich Priebke, Dinko Sakic, Anthony Sawoniuk, and Josef Schwammberger.[98]

3. Conditional Amnesty

After WWII, in a joint military and intelligence action codenamed "Operation Paperclip," the USG located, imported, and hired more than 1600 German scientists formerly associated with the Nazi Party who, before and during WWII, had developed expertise and conducted research of interest and deemed valuable to the USG. The USG sought out these Germans not only to improve American research in the fields of weapons development, nuclear physics, and rocket science, but also to prevent the Soviet Union from doing so.[99] The U.S. military so prized these Germans' experience and expertise that it deliberately altered background investigations on at least 130 of them to whitewash their pasts as ardent Nazis and potential security threats so that the U.S./DoS and the U.S./DoJ would not block their immigration to the United States.[100] Because the USG would presumably have revoked their immunity in the face of intransigence, the USG effectively provided these German scientists de facto conditional amnesty.

Perhaps the most famous German recruited to the United States through Operation Paperclip was Dr. Wernher von Braun. Von Braun, who is widely regarded as the father of the U.S. space program, was an admitted member of the Nazi Party and the SS who developed the V-2 rocket that Nazi Germany showered on the United Kingdom during WWII. Von Braun allegedly also committed atrocities during WWII by using slave labor from concentration camps for his research, leading some commentators to characterize him as a war criminal.[101] A second famous German scientist brought to the United States through Operation Paperclip was Arthur Rudolph, who eventually designed the Saturn V shuttle that put American astronaunts on the moon. Like Von Braun, Rudolph allegedly committed atrocities during WWII while developing V-2 rockets. Von Braun and Rudolph were among the German scientists whose pasts the U.S. military deliberately obfuscated.[102]

Some Nazi scientists whom the U.S. military employed through Operation Paperclip, such as Major General Walter Schreiber, Siegfried Ruff, Konrad Schaefer, and Kurt Blome, were accused of experimenting on humans during WWII. These gruesome tests allegedly included locking concentration camp inmates in low-pressure chambers that simulated high altitudes as well as depriving other inmates of food and giving them only chemically processed seawater to drink. Once again, the U.S. military covered up evidence of these Germans' atrocities in order to harness their knowledge and skills, including in furtherance of the USG's biological weapons program.[103]

But Nazi scientists were not the only suspected atrocity perpetrators from Germany with whom the USG made deals. The USG also offered de facto conditional amnesty to at least 1000—and possibly as many as 10,000—former Nazi officials who boasted expertise in counterintelligence.[104] The most notorious of these individuals was Barbie. During WWII, Barbie was known as "The Butcher of Lyon" for his notorious leadership of the local Gestapo and his alleged responsibility for the deportation and murder of hundreds, if not thousands, of Jews and other Nazi victims.

Despite knowledge of his work as a senior Nazi official, USG officials recruited, employed, and used Barbie for counterintelligence work during most of the period between 1947 and 1951. During these four years in which Barbie maintained a relationship with the USG, he agreed to sever ties with certain Nazis and act as an informant on German communist activities, to report on French and Soviet intelligence operations in the United States, and sometimes to provide intelligence about French zones of occupation in Germany. In exchange, USG officials promised not to arrest Barbie for his suspected crimes during WWII even though he was sought by American allies, particularly France and the United Kingdom. Barbie's supervisors in the Counter Intelligence Corps (CIC) of the U.S. Army even lied about their knowledge of his whereabouts and whether they had contact with Barbie, to protect him from other parts of the USG, particularly the U.S. High Commission for Germany, which sought to arrest him and possibly extradite him to France. As a U.S./DoJ investigation later concluded: "Barbie's background as an SS and Gestapo officer appears to have been distinctly subordinate to [CIC] Region IV's interest in using him as an informant and [CIC] HQ's interest in extracting from him information about other SS officers involved in postwar 'subversive activities.' "[105]

Despite the USG's promise of immunity, after using him for six months the USG did arrest and interrogate Barbie from December 1947 to May 1948. He later was released and then reinstated and re-employed as an informant for the USG until 1951. The USG continued to employ Barbie, even after more of his sordid past was uncovered, in part to prevent Barbie from seeking employment with the British or the French. USG officials were concerned that Barbie might otherwise reveal the nature (including the use of former Nazis such as Barbie) and extent (including against the USG's wartime allies) of the USG's postwar counterintelligence activities, which would embarrass the USG and potentially strain relations with its allies. After finishing using him for counterintelligence, USG officials assisted Barbie in escaping through the "rat line" out of Europe to Bolivia. He then lived in Bolivia until 1983, when he was expelled to and tried, convicted, and sentenced to life imprisonment in France, where he died in 1991.[106]

In an unusual act of humility and self-criticism as well as acknowledgment of its dark, unprincipled past, the USG officially apologized to France in August 1983 for deliberately and actively obstructing its efforts to locate and bring Barbie to justice. Allan Ryan, Jr., a U.S./DoJ official commissioned in March 1983 to investigate the relationship between Barbie and the USG, concluded from his research that:

> It is a principle of democracy and the rule of law that justice delayed is justice denied. If we are to be faithful to that principle—and we should be faithful to it—we cannot pretend that it applied only within our borders and nowhere else. We have delayed justice in Lyon.[107]

In June 2006, the declassification of relevant USG intelligence documents revealed that West German officials informed the USG in 1958 of the location and alias of Eichmann, who oversaw the mass deportation and execution of Jews and others in Nazi-occupied Eastern Europe during WWII. The USG apparently had colluded with West Germany to keep this information private in order to protect Hans Globke, the West German national security adviser. West Germans assumed Eichmanm would denounce Globke for his involvement in anti-Semitic activity during WWII if Eichmann were captured. Meanwhile, both West German officials and the USG wanted to safeguard Globke, who was an anti-communist asset during the Cold War.[108] In choosing to keep this intelligence secret, the USG effectively cloaked Eichmann in de facto conditional amnesty (presumably because, had Eichmann revealed Globke's Nazi past or if Globke became less valuable, the USG would have been less inclined to keep Eichmann's whereabouts and identity secret). Ultimately, Israel's Mossad agency apprehended Eichmann in 1960 and Israel's government prosecuted and sentenced him to capital punishment in 1962.[109]

4. Lustration

In addition to prosecuting many Nazis (through the multilateral IMT and unilateral military tribunals) and providing de facto conditional amnesty to others, the Allies implemented lustration in post-WWII Germany. The basis of this official purge was the Potsdam Agreement of August 1, 1945. Through this agreement, which concluded a conference held in Potsdam, Germany, from July 17 to August 2, 1945, the leaders of the United States, the United Kingdom, and the Soviet Union agreed in part that:

> All members of the Nazi Party who have been more than nominal participants in its activities and all other persons hostile to Allied purposes shall be removed from public and semi-public office, and from positions of responsibility in important private undertakings. Such persons shall be replaced by persons who, by their political and moral qualities, are deemed capable of assisting in developing genuine democratic institutions in Germany.[110]

Denazification was a widespread policy enacted by the United States and its allies, though pursued to different degrees by each of the quadripartite Allied powers.[111]

The IMT trials thus occured simultaneously with or before other transitional justice options: unilateral prosecution through military commissions (e.g., NMT); domestic unilateral prosecution through civilian courts, either by trying individuals under a state's established jurisdiction (e.g., Barbie and Papon in France) or under a claim of universal jurisdiction (e.g., Eichmann in Israel); conditional amnesty; and lustration (denazification).

C. TRANSITIONAL JUSTICE OPTIONS
NOT SERIOUSLY CONSIDERED

Four transitional justice options the United States and other Allied powers never seriously considered for addressing the principal Nazis were: (1) inaction (implicit or de facto unconditional amnesty), (2) explicit unconditional amnesty, (3) unilateral prosecution by German courts, and (4) unilateral prosecution by a third-party state, such as one that remained neutral during WWII.

Jackson reported that public opinion within the United States and abroad compelled the USG to bring suspected Nazi atrocity perpetrators to justice *proactively*: "we might have refused all responsibility for either their safety or their [Nazi war criminals'] punishment and turned them out scot free. But in 1945 what we had to fight against was an insistent and world-wide demand for immediate, unhesitating, and undiscriminating vengeance."[112] Taylor also recounts that Jackson cited the "inescapable responsibility" stemming from the similarly inescapable fact that the United States maintained custody over many of the principal Nazi officials: "What shall we do with them? We could, of course, set them at large without a hearing. But it has cost unmeasured thousands of American lives to beat and bind these men. To free them without a trial would mock the dead and make cynics of the living."[113] Thus, neither implicit nor explicit unconditional amnesty was seriously considered.

Jackson also explained that parties to the negotiations ruled out domestic prosecution within Germany itself, which some critics of the IMT would have preferred as an alternative transitional justice institution.[114] These objections followed from the failed efforts at Leipzig to try suspected atrocity perpetrators from WWI and the widespread belief that the post-WWII German domestic judiciary was incapable or highly suspect. As Jackson argued:

> To expect the Germans to bring these Germans [(the Nazi war criminals)] to justice was out of the question. That was proved by the farcical experiment after World War I. But after World War II, organized society in Germany was in a state of collapse. There was no authoritative judicial system except remnants of the violently partisan judiciary set up by Hitler. And German law had been perverted to be a mere expression of the Nazi will.
>
> To have turned the men over to the anti-Nazi factions in Germany would have been a doubtful benevolence. Even a year and a half later when [Hjalmar] Schacht, Von Papen, and [Hans] Fritzsche were acquitted by the Tribunal, they begged to remain within the protection of the American jail lest they be mobbed by the angry and disillusioned elements of the German population. They knew the fate of Mussolini.[115]

Whitney Harris, who served on the U.S. prosecution staff at the IMT, adds that the ruling of a German judge would have introduced thorny sociopolitical questions, such as the public's concern about whether a particular German judge was biased or treasonous, which might have adversely affected the trial.[116] Others suggest that Germans would have been unwilling or unable to prosecute the Nazi leadership, considering (1) that the two Allied doctrines imposed on Germany—unconditional surrender and collective guilt—would act as constraints, (2) that the overwhelming majority of Nazi judges remained in office after the war, and (3) that given the opportunity for trying some of the Nazis after the war, the German judiciary proved to be lenient.[117]

Jackson further recalls that third-party (i.e., neutral) state prosecution, as suggested by Arendt,[118] also was not seriously considered because such states, even if officially neutral during WWII, were no less biased in reality:

> Where in the world were neutrals to take up the task of investigation and judging? Does one suggest Spain? Sweden? Switzerland? True, these states as such were not engaged in the war, but powerful elements of their society and most leading individuals were reputed not to be impartial but to be

either for or against the Nazi order. Only the naïve or those forgetful of conditions in 1945 would contend that we could have induced "neutral" states to assume the duty of doing justice to the Nazis.[119]

III. Explaining the United States Role in Transitional Justice for Germany

A. THE EVOLUTION OF THE U.S. GOVERNMENT'S GENERAL TRANSITIONAL JUSTICE PREFERENCES

One of the major issues inviting further reflection is why the USG withdrew its support of lethal force in favor of prosecution as the method of addressing the principal suspected atrocity perpetrators from Nazi Germany. Although during the FDR administration the USG initially considered the use of lethal force through extrajudicial execution, Jackson explained why the government swiftly abandoned that position. Regarding show trials, Jackson argued at a lecture to the American Society of International Law on April 13, 1945, that "the world yields no respect to courts that are merely organized to convict."[120] Regarding summary judgment without even show trials, Jackson argued, "we could execute or otherwise punish them without a hearing. But undiscriminating executions of punishments without definite findings of guilt, fairly arrived at, would violate pledges repeatedly given, and would not set easily on the American conscience or be remembered by our children with pride."[121]

Jackson's arguments about why the USG did not ultimately select lethal force are dubious. His contention is that the USG's adherence to the rule of law led it to support the prosecution of suspected atrocity perpetrators from Nazi Germany. But Jackson's conclusion ignores the facts. FDR did not abandon his support for extrajudicial executions until *after* and *because* economic aspects of the Morgenthau Plan (those concerning the "pastoralization" of Germany) were leaked to the press. When the American public expressed its outrage at treating Germany so harshly through a form of economic sanctions, FDR extrapolated this sentiment to the perception that his fellow countrymen were unsupportive of severe treatment for the Germans through summary execution. As Bass acknowledges, "[i]t was only after a bruising cabinet fight, and a timely leak that undermined Morgenthau . . . that the Roosevelt administration chose a legalistic policy that led to the great trials at Nuremberg."[122]

And it was not until after FDR died that the USG fully embraced the general transitional justice option of prosecution. FDR's death and the consequent ascendancy of the pro-trials Truman to the White House was therefore one of the most significant events that led, first, to the solidification of U.S. policy and then to a unified Allied policy on addressing major Nazi war criminals through prosecution. Almost immediately after assuming the presidency, Truman unambiguously declared his transitional justice preference: he opposed extrajudicial

execution and, instead, favored the establishment of a tribunal for legally trying suspected atrocity perpetrators from Nazi Germany. Truman's preference
for the rule of law reflected his considerable experience as a judge. This strong
and clear presidential direction, which had been absent under FDR, galvanized
the pro-prosecution lobby within the USG (specifically at the War Department),
by adding public presidential support for its internal memoranda, such as those
authored by McCloy and Cutter in April 1945, and culminating in the appointment of a distinguished jurist, Jackson, to be the USG's chief negotiator on and
prosecutor before the IMT.

Whereas legalism argues that liberal states follow principled commitments to
the rule of law in trying suspected war criminals, the USG's decision to support
trials in this case actually resembles a prudentialist narrative. The policy choice
depended on two factors: (1) misperceived public outrage over the Morgenthau
Plan, and (2) FDR's death, which permitted Truman's preferences to assume priority. This point is supported further through a counterfactual illustration. If the
Morgenthau Plan had not leaked to the press, or if it had been made clear that the
economic proposals were only part of that Plan, then the public might not have
responded with such hostility. Referring to polling data collected by Gallup on
the American public's preferences for addressing the principal Nazis suspected
of perpetrating atrocities (which demonstrates that the American public overwhelmingly favored summary execution for Hitler, Hermann Wilhelm Goering,
and other Nazi leaders), Bass himself acknowledges: "The whole Morgenthau Plan
was destroyed by American public opinion, but not because of its summary execution plan. Had Americans evaluated the Morgenthau Plan on war criminals, they
would probably have sided with Morgenthau."[123] In that case, FDR would not have
felt compelled to abandon his support for summary executions. However, FDR
likely would have felt at least some pressure to change his initial position after
Churchill made Stalin's preferences (against summary execution) clear to him.
At that point, FDR may have decided to support prosecution. Under all of these
assumptions, Jackson's implicit and Bass's explicit legalistic theory would not
explain why the USG supported trials over summary execution. Rather, a prudentialist account, emphasizing the USG's desire to accommodate its erstwhile ally
(the Soviet Union), indicates that political expediency mattered more. Logistical
factors also played a role. If FDR had not died, the USG might have joined with
the United Kingdom to pursue Anglo-American extrajudicial execution of the
principal Nazis.

Similarly, Jackson seems to have overstated the role American pledges, conscience, and pride played in the USG decision to oppose summary executions.
If these factors had been so compelling, presumably they would have motivated
related USG policymaking on transitional justice in this case. However, consistency in rhetoric and potential shame for the nation and posterity were implicitly neglected when the USG implemented de facto conditional amnesties for
certain Nazis.

B. JACKSON'S THREATS TO PURSUE
A UNILATERAL TRANSITIONAL JUSTICE INSTITUTION

A second issue worthy of additional exploration relates to why Jackson threatened that the USG might—and that other Allies therefore would have to—pursue either unilateral or less multilateral (i.e., excluding the Soviet Union) transitional justice institutions given the Allies' earlier joint statements that they would collaborate in whatever transitional justice institution was established. Different theories exist to explain why Jackson publicly and repeatedly suggested that the Allied powers consider establishing separate national tribunals as an alternative to an ICT. One rationale is that Jackson viewed the Americans' and Soviets' diametrically opposed positions regarding the nature of multilateral trials as fundamental and insurmountable; thus he either honestly believed that an ICT would be superior or that his threat for supporting a different process would persuade his interlocutors to adopt the U.S. position. An alternative explanation could be that he did not actually want to work with the Russians, after hearing reports of their own atrocities (for example, in the Katyn Forest[124]), and concluding through his own experience that they were difficult, untrustworthy, and unreliable colleagues. Jackson probably also was disturbed by the fact that the Soviet Union was once allied with Nazi Germany, had committed its own aggression during WWII (especially against Finland, Poland, Latvia, Estonia, and Lithuania), and had notoriously conducted show trials against its own people.

Whether Jackson issued his repeated threat merely to persuade his interlocutors to agree with the American position, or because he genuinely wished for the negotiations to fail in order to pursue an alternative transitional justice option without Soviet involvement, has not been definitively determined. According to Taylor, though, it is more likely that Jackson was only using the threat to try to influence the Soviets. Had the negotiations failed, Jackson probably would not have attained his goals of multilaterally prosecuting the principal Nazis suspects, having the trial include the crime of aggression, and locating the trial within the American Zone of Occupation's city of Nuremberg.[125]

There is yet another factor that helps explain both of the preceding two puzzles. Each of the Allies likely held reservations about contradicting the public commitment offered early in their negotiations, namely, to address suspected Nazi atrocity perpetrators through multilateral prosecution. As Lord Simon reminded Jackson and the Soviet representative, General Iona Nikitchenko (who was then vice president of the Soviet Union's Supreme Court and who would become the Soviet judge on the IMT), during their negotiations after the Potsdam Conference: "it would be a bad thing before the world, after having declared we should have a joint trial, if we should now declare we are not going to have it."[126] Again, as prudentialism would suggest, politics mattered.

C. THE U.S. GOVERNMENT'S PREFERENCE
FOR EXECUTIVE AGREEMENT

Why did the USG, given its initial support for a treaty-based creation of the IMT, ultimately choose (along with the other Allies) to sign an executive agreement instead? Recall that the Bernays Plan proposed that the ICT be established through a treaty among the collaborating states, whereas the memorandum signed on January 22, 1945, by Stimson, Stettinius, and Biddle called for the tribunal to be created by executive agreement among the leaders of the participating states, which is what occurred.

The most compelling explanation for the USG's preference for executive agreement over treaty involves a broader consideration of the politics of the mid-1940s, especially the power struggle between the USG's executive and legislative branches. The U.S. Congress, reflecting a growing belief that American involvement in WWI may have been a mistake and concerned that FDR might risk starting another major war over Italy's October 1935 invasion of Abyssinia (now Ethiopia), passed the Neutrality Act of 1935 (which was broadened three times in the late-1930s) to assert its power over U.S. foreign policymaking.[127] In response, to circumvent Congress on a number of issues, FDR employed executive agreements—international commitments between himself and other heads of state. Such agreements are as binding as treaties and, through a series of federal court cases, they assumed the same constitutional status. Unlike treaties, however, executive agreements do not require ratification by the U.S. Senate. As such, executive agreements empower the president more broadly with respect to U.S. foreign policymaking, which was FDR's design. This presidential tool was one means by which FDR expanded the powers and size of the office of the presidency more than perhaps any other president in U.S. history.[128] As political scientist James Lindsay notes, "executive agreements became the method of choice for concluding international agreements after the end of World War II."[129] The Charter of the IMT was one such international agreement. Domestic politics, a critical component of prudentialism, thus helps explain the nature of this transitional justice option.

IV. Conclusion

As the foregoing indicates, the Allies instituted various transitional justice options alongside and in addition to the IMT. As well as cooperating with other states to support unilateral prosecution and lustration for particular Germans, the USG provided conditional amnesty to some and even employed others, including Nazis suspected of committing some of the most heinous crimes or otherwise facilitating Nazi aggression and ideology.

This case study, which also examines the reasons the USG supported the IMT after WWII, teaches several lessons about the etiology of the tribunal's establishment. For example, the IMT might not have been created without Stalin's early, constant, and forceful lobbying. The IMT experience reveals much about U.S. foreign policy on one of the first and most significant cases of transitional justice in history. Specifically, and of particular relevance to this book, it suggests that almost every major decision regarding the transitional justice methods for addressing the principal Nazi suspects (including which general options the USG supported and the forms those options took) was made from a combination of politics, pragmatics, and normative beliefs—in other words, prudentialism.

The decision to "do something" was motivated by all three factors. USG officials were conscious of the domestic ramifications of such a decision, as the American public demanded that Nazis be held accountable. Domestic political pressure thus helped drive U.S. decision-making to act. As a pragmatic concern, the USG held in custody many of the principal Nazis and thus faced pressing choices about how best to deal with them. Even simply keeping them imprisoned or letting them go would have been decisions to "do something"; the former would have constituted indefinite detention, in itself a violation of due process, and the latter would have represented implicit unconditional amnesty. Finally, many USG officials held strong normative beliefs. Apart from the necessity of addressing the large number of Nazi prisoners of war in U.S. custody, USG officials, such as FDR, Wallace, and certain congressional leaders, also felt it was their *duty* to do so. They were compelled by a belief, which many of their constituents shared, that individual Nazis should be held accountable for their heinous crimes. Moreover, these officials deemed it appropriate to execute at least some Nazis for their atrocities. (A difference among these USG officials is that those who shared Truman and Stimson's views believed such capital punishment should occur only after a legal conviction.)

The ultimate decision to prosecute many of the chief Nazis also was motivated by a combination of all three concerns. Several domestic political factors helped to build a consensus around prosecution. A lack of clear early direction from FDR enabled Stimson to assume leadership on this transitional justice issue and to amass support for his favored option: prosecution. FDR was persuaded by his misreading of American public outrage against the Morgenthau Plan to abandon his initial preference for summary execution in favor of prosecution—the option that Stalin, like Stimson, advocated. USG officials also were compelled by another concern rooted in American legal tradition. Jackson noted that the due process guarantees sacrosanct in the United States would be instrumental toward convincing Americans that prosecution was legitimate. The December 1944 Malmédy Massacre of American soldiers inspired USG officials to rally around the most developed proposal to date, the Bernays Plan for prosecution. Finally, FDR's April 1945 death enabled a former judge,

Truman, to assume the presidency and assert his preference for confronting senior Nazis in a courtroom.

USG officials also favored prosecution because of pragmatic concerns and normative beliefs. Practically, even if USG officials prosecuted some of the Nazis, the USG still could pursue other options as well, such as conditional amnesty and lustration, which it did. The USG also wanted to use the discovery features of a trial to collect evidence and establish a historical account of Nazi atrocities, in part to rebut any future criticisms of American involvement in or conduct during WWII. Many USG officials, such as Marshall, Cramer, and Frankfurther, were driven by strong normative convictions. This faction of the USG—led by Stimson and eventually championed by Truman—felt that it was more just to put Nazis on trial than to subject them to the other option that was being seriously considered: lethal force through extrajudicial execution.

Although at one point during his frustration with the Soviet contingent Jackson suggested that the Allies hold separate trials for prosecuting senior Nazis, the USG ultimately decided to cooperate with its allies on establishing and operating an international military tribunal. The USG's decision reflected both external diplomatic calculations and internal politics involving the precarious balance of power among the different branches of government. The Soviet Union lobbied strongly for a joint trial. Despite disagreements with the Soviets, which foreshadowed the ideological conflict of the approaching Cold War, the USG ultimately concurred. Failing to reach accord would have strained relations with this powerful ally. Furthermore, if the USG had pursued a unilateral or more narrowly multilateral trial, it would have violated its earlier commitment to hold a joint trial, and it might have been politically risky not to honor that public pledge. The USG also was disinclined to permit domestic trials in Germany itself, which were considered a failure after WWI. Moreover, pursuing an ICT enabled the U.S. president to establish and operate this transitional justice option through executive agreement, thus circumventing the U.S. Senate—with which FDR had disagreed so often on foreign policymaking. Finally, the USG's decision to support the creation of the ICT as a military instead of civilian court was driven by an additional political desire to facilitate compromises among the participating states.

Pragmatic factors also played a role in the USG's decision to prosecute suspected Nazi atrocity perpetrators through an ICT. Creating multiple tribunals, rather than concentrating and coordinating efforts among the Allies, would have strained each ally's resources on an already logistically difficult and draining enterprise. Furthermore, although the USG held in custody and thus could contribute the majority of defendants to what would become the IMT, only by joining forces could the USG have participated in the trial of other senior Nazis. The USG also believed that a unified effort was necessary to illustrate the conspiracy driving Nazi atrocities in the first place. Finally, because the IMT was established to address only a few of the most egregious perpetrators of Nazi atrocities, the

USG would not be precluded from addressing the majority of its Nazi prisoners through the other prosecutorial mechanisms (unilateral trials) and non-prosecutorial methods (lustration and conditional amnesty) described above.

The IMT origin narrative also reveals the explanatory limitations of certain factors. Most significant, it is apparent that normative beliefs alone did not drive the USG's transitional justice approach to Nazis. That FDR, who favored summary execution, differed so greatly in his initial preference from Truman indicates that USG officials held no consistent normative belief regarding post-WWII transitional justice, and that U.S. decision-makers had seriously considered non-legalistic options for even the principal Nazis. The large number of Nazis the USG not only did not prosecute but either addressed through lustration or conditional amnesty (sometimes even by employing them) demonstrates that the USG was not universally committed to a normative view of prosecuting suspected atrocity perpetrators.

The significance of the IMT is felt not just in its role as the first major ICT, but also that it greatly impacted parallel transitional justice considerations, the most important of which related to atrocities committed by Japanese during WWII. The next chapter discusses the establishment of the IMT's sister ICT, the IMTFE.

The United States Role in
Transitional Justice for Japan

I. Background

Shorthand references to transitional justice for Nazi Germany, as discussed in the previous chapter, are similarly misleading as those for Imperial Japan. What is popularly known as "Tokyo" is actually a series of trials that took place in Tokyo, Japan, and elsewhere in East Asia from 1945 to 1951.[1] Like with "Nuremberg," these proceedings can be divided into two sets. The first was the "trial and punishment of the major war criminals in the Far East" before the IMTFE in Tokyo between 1946 and 1948 (what is commonly referred to as the "Tokyo Tribunal").[2] The second set was the proceedings by ad hoc, unilateral Allied military commissions throughout the Far East between 1945 and 1951. And, as will be discussed, like the IMT and NMT in the case of Germany, the IMTFE and the Allied military commissions were two of only several transitional justice options the USG supported for addressing Japanese suspected of committing atrocities during WWII.

A. NEGOTIATIONS LEADING TO "TOKYO"

As with the IMT, the creation of the IMTFE was not preordained.[3] In fact, much like their decision-making regarding suspected Nazis, the Allies, including the USG, considered alternative transitional justice options for addressing Japanese atrocities at various points during WWII. Six major diplomatic steps ultimately led to the creation of the IMTFE.

1. Early American Responses to
Japanese Atrocities During WWII

Imperial Japan, which officially allied with both Nazi Germany and Fascist Italy under the Tripartite Pact of September 27, 1940,[4] invaded and occupied various parts of Asia and committed other acts of aggression against some Western powers in the first few years of WWII.[5] In response, FDR froze all of Japan's assets in the United States, terminated the U.S.-Japanese Treaty of Commerce and Navigation, placed an embargo on Japan's oil supply, and threatened to suspend diplomatic relations between the two states. Japan then launched a surprise attack on Pearl Harbor on December 7, 1941, damaging the U.S. Pacific Fleet, killing over 2400 Americans, and wounding 1100 more.[6] The United States (joined by the United Kingdom) declared war on Japan the following day. The United States, Japan, and their respective allies fought in the Pacific Theater (and in Europe) over the following four years.[7]

The Allies, including the United States, claimed that, in addition to illegally waging an aggressive war, Japan committed widespread atrocities (war crimes, crimes against humanity, and crimes against peace) during WWII, including against American prisoners of war (POWs) (for example, during the notorious 1942 Bataan Death March) but worst of all against Chinese and Korean combatants and civilians. The total number of victims of Japanese atrocities may never be known, but it is clear that the Japanese murdered, mutilated, tortured, beat, poisoned, starved, raped, enslaved (for both sexual and labor purposes), cannibalized, decapitated, burned alive, buried alive, froze, hanged by the tongue of, impaled the genitals of, pillaged from, and performed medical experiments on millions of men, women, and children.[8] The brutality of the Japanese was so severe that, for example, upon witnessing the infamous 1937 Rape of Nanking, even the Nazi chargé d'affaires stationed there remarked: "The Japanese Imperial Army is nothing but a beastly machine."[9] This Nazi and his colleagues eventually provided sanctuary to Chinese refugees and lodged complaints about Japan's behavior to more senior Nazi officials in Germany.[10]

As information about Japanese atrocities emerged during WWII, the USG gradually took public and private steps to deter these crimes and to hold their perpetrators accountable. FDR and his vice president, Henry Wallace, voiced the earliest significant public pronouncements to this effect. As discussed in the previous chapter, FDR delivered a speech on August 21, 1942, denouncing Japanese (and German) atrocities,[11] a point he later reiterated on March 24, 1944.[12] FDR also used the earlier speech to warn Japanese (and Germans) suspected of perpetrating atrocities that they would be prosecuted.[13] On a related point, in a December 28, 1942, speech, Wallace declared that the USG—without pursuing pointless, purely retributive punishment—would seek to prove the guilt of suspected Japanese leaders, holding them responsible for crimes they committed during WWII.[14]

Other states also joined the USG in publicly condemning and threatening Japanese suspected of committing atrocities. On December 1, 1943, the USG partnered with the governments of China and the United Kingdom to issue the Cairo Declaration (the outcome of a conference held in Cairo among the three states four days earlier). This meeting apparently generated the first Allied war crimes policy concerning Japan. The joint proclamation by these self-described "Three Great Allies" and "three great powers" declared their intention to "restrain and punish the aggression of Japan."[15] The Allies explicitly asserted that they would punish Japan by stripping it of the territory it had acquired since the beginning of not just WWII, but also WWI, with specific reference to Chinese and Korean lands. Although the declaration was not explicit on the topic of atrocities, it nevertheless did not preclude holding Japanese individuals accountable for them.[16]

During WWII, the USG also issued private threats and promises about its intention to punish Japanese leaders for offenses they committed during the war, especially against Americans. For example, a few days after the Japanese attack on Pearl Harbor, FDR asked the Japanese government to abide by the law of armed conflict and international agreements concerning POWs.[17] FDR's aforementioned August 21, 1942, statement emphasized that the USG was aware of the Axis powers' war crimes in both Europe and Asia, and pledged prosecution for them.[18] On April 12, 1943, Hull communicated a message to the Japanese government via Swiss emissaries that if American POWs were mistreated or illegally abused, then "the American government [would] visit upon the officers of the Japanese Government responsible for such uncivilized and inhumane acts the punishment they deserve."[19] Hull reiterated his position in late January 1944, issuing a simultaneous warning with the British government in which the two countries promised not to forget acts such as the recent Bataan Death March and vowed to mete out "just punishment."[20] Hull's messages were sufficiently vague as to imply virtually any transitional justice mechanism except inaction or amnesty. At one point during WWII, Hull communicated to his British and Soviet counterparts his preference for dealing with suspected atrocity perpetrators from Japan (and Germany and Italy): the Allies "would take [German Chancellor Adolf] Hitler and [Italian Prime Minister Benito] Mussolini and [Japanese Prime Minister Hideki] Tōjō and their arch accomplices and bring them before a drumhead court-martial. And at sunrise the following day there would occur an historic incident."[21] As discussed in the previous chapter, some USG officials (along with U.K. government officials) thus initially favored summary execution for leaders of the Axis powers, including the Japanese, suspected of committing atrocities during WWII.

In addition to these unilateral and multilateral efforts to denounce and deter Japanese atrocities, the USG also partnered with other states to investigate offenses. On May 10, 1944, the USG and some of its allies established the Special Far Eastern and Pacific Committee of the UN War Crimes Commission (UNWCC).[22] This committee—which was created largely because of lobbying by Herbert Pell, the U.S. representative on the UNWCC[23]—was a significant international entity that observed, reported on, and made recommendations about responding to Japanese atrocities. On August 28, 1945, the Committee issued its final report, finding that the Japanese had committed various atrocities in violation of existing international law (e.g., the 1907 Hague Conventions).[24] The report also recommended that senior Japanese political, military, and economic officials "should be surrendered to or apprehended by the United Nations for trial before an international military tribunal."[25] The report further suggested that other

> Japanese who have been responsible for, or have taken a consenting part in, the crimes or atrocities committed in, or against the nationals of, a United Nation should be apprehended and sent back to the countries in which abominable deeds were done or against whose nationals crimes and atrocities were perpetrated in order that they may be judged in the courts of those countries and punished.[26]

Moreover, the report stated that the Supreme Commander of the Allied Powers (SCAP) should appoint "one or more International Military Tribunals for the trial of the war criminals" and that the SCAP should assume responsibility for appointing its members and adopting its rules of procedure.[27] As occurred during the transitional justice process that birthed the IMT, the Allied Powers thus precluded a civilian prosecutorial option for the principal suspected atrocity perpetrators in the Far East. However, according to historian Donald Cameron Watt, compared to the London Agreement, which provided for the "Prosecution and Punishment of the Major War Criminals of the European Axis,"[28]

> The novelty [of the UNWCC report] . . . [was in] recognize[ing] the military supremacy of the United States in the Far East by laying the responsibility for setting up one or more international military tribunals to try the Japanese major war criminals squarely on the shoulders of the American Supreme Allied Commander in the Pacific and left it to him to select the members of the tribunals.[29]

2. July 1945: Potsdam Declaration

The Allies did not jointly formalize their general policy toward suspected Japanese atrocity perpetrators until WWII was ending. In the section of the Potsdam Declaration of July 26, 1945 (a proclamation signed in the German city of Potsdam by Truman, Churchill, and Chinese Generalissimo Chiang Kai-shek) that defined the terms of Japan's surrender and provided for the Allied occupation of Japan, the signatories declared:

> Following are our terms. We will not deviate from them. There are no alternatives. We shall brook no delay . . . . There must be eliminated for all time the authority and influence of those who have deceived and misled the people of Japan into embarking on world conquest, for we insist that a new order of peace[,] security[,] and justice will be impossible until irresponsible militarism is driven from the world . . . . We do not intend that the Japanese shall be enslaved as a race or destroyed as a nation, but stern

justice shall be meted out to all war criminals, including those who have visited cruelties upon our prisoners.[30]

With this declaration, the Allies publicly made clear that, without negotiation or hesitation, they would seek removal of suspected Japanese war criminals from public office and hold them accountable. The precise form the transitional justice mechanism would take remained undefined, but the Allies continued to rule out inaction and amnesty. John Dower, the Pulitzer Prize-winning historian of post-WWII Japan, contends that this decision was intentional: The Potsdam Declaration "was highly generalized, and necessarily so, for the victors were still deliberating about how to handle Japanese war crimes right up to the end of the war."[31] The Japanese did not immediately respond to this ultimatum.

3. August–September 1945: Critical Developments

August 1945 witnessed a momentous evolution in U.S.-Japanese relations and the development of a coherent transitional justice strategy for addressing Japanese suspected of committing atrocities. First, hostilities in the Pacific Theater climaxed that month with the U.S. atomic bombings of Hiroshima on August 6, 1945, and of Nagasaki three days later. Five days afterward, Japan accepted the unconditional surrender demanded in the Potsdam Declaration, thus ceding to the Allies three months after Germany did.[32]

Second, after surrendering and before the Allied occupation, the Japanese attempted to thwart Allied efforts to prove their atrocities. During August 1945, the Japanese government employed a massive campaign within the country and its occupied territories to doctor, damage, or destroy (mostly by burning) much of the incriminating evidence (records, witnesses, and corpses) of their atrocities.[33]

Third, on August 4, Truman appointed Douglas MacArthur (General of the U.S. Army since December 18, 1944) to be the SCAP. In that role, MacArthur oversaw the Allied occupation of Japan, which commenced on August 28, including the transitional justice system. MacArthur's broad authority essentially rendered him the dictator, or "American Caesar," of postwar Japan.[34] Truman eventually relieved MacArthur of his command as SCAP on April 11, 1951, because of insubordination.[35] However, by that time, the IMTFE had concluded, and so MacArthur was the only SCAP to possess and use all of the powers of appointment and judicial review enumerated in the IMTFE's Charter.[36] The Allies would occupy Japan until all parties signed a peace treaty in San Francisco on April 8, 1952.[37]

Fourth, Japanese political and military officials engaged in mass suicides during this eventful month. They presumably did so because they felt guilty for their collective crimes, they were ashamed of their defeat by the Allies, they wanted to demonstrate their loyalty to their conquered leaders, or they wanted to avoid being held accountable by the Allies. Other Japanese either faked or, in the case of Tōjō, failed in their attempts to commit suicide. In total, over 1000 Japanese committed suicide, usually using pistol, poison, or pointed blade.[38]

The following month also proved decisive for efforts to pursue transitional justice in Japan. On September 2, more than two weeks after unconditionally surrendering, Japan accepted all of the remaining Potsdam Declaration provisions at a ceremony aboard the USS *Missouri* in Tokyo Bay.[39] Four days later, the USG issued a "Statement of the Initial Surrender Policy for Japan," proclaiming:

> Persons charged by the [SCAP] or appropriate United Nations Agencies with being war criminals, including those charged with having visited cruelties upon United Nations prisoners or other nationals, shall be arrested, tried[,] and if convicted, punished. Those wanted by another of the United Nations for offenses against its nationals, shall, if not wanted for trial or as witnesses or otherwise by the [SCAP], be turned over to the custody of such other nation.[40]

This statement clarified that the USG and its allies had selected prosecution as the general transitional justice option and that MacArthur would exercise primary jurisdiction over all Japanese suspects. Like the Potsdam Declaration, this statement explicitly and exclusively mentioned citizens of the United States and its allies among the United Nations as alleged victims. Two days later, on September 8, MacArthur established his office in Tokyo.[41]

Later that month, on September 22, the U.S. Joint Chiefs of Staff, at the direction of Truman and with the approval of all governments occupying Japan, sent orders to MacArthur to create an international military tribunal for prosecuting alleged Japanese atrocities. The Joint Chiefs also instructed MacArthur to apprehend, investigate, prosecute, and—if convicted—punish Japanese suspects, who were to be divided into three classes. Class A war criminals were suspected of committing the most egregious offenses: planning, initiating, and waging aggressive war; Class B war criminals allegedly committed conventional war crimes; and Class C war criminals were suspected of committing crimes against humanity.[42]

4. October–December 1945:
Negotiating the Specific Features of Transitional Justice

Transitional justice policy continued to develop apace through the autumn of 1945. On October 25, the USG distributed to its allies its "Policy of the United States in Regard to the Apprehension and Punishment of War Criminals in the Far East." This proposal outlined the SCAP's many powers and indicated that allies would be significantly involved in transitional justice issues in Japan through advisory roles to the SCAP and as staff on an international military tribunal. American allies, including Australia, the United Kingdom, and the Soviet Union, accepted the proposal more or less as a fait accompli.[43]

As most initiatives concerning the occupation of Japan, including transitional justice issues, had been led to date by the USG, its allies began lobbying for a broader and more substantive decision-making authority. On October 30, a Far Eastern Advisory Commission (FEAC), comprising the USG and several of its allies in the war against Japan, met in Washington, DC. However, the Soviet government expressed concerns about the mere advisory nature of the commission and lobbied for a greater voice in decisions concerning the occupation of Japan.[44] While the USG worked with its allies to expand their occupational roles, the pursuit of transitional justice for alleged Japanese atrocity perpetrators endured. On November 30, Truman appointed Joseph Keenan to be the IMTFE's chief prosecutor, called Chief of Counsel.[45] Because of his distinguished military and legal service to the United States and his expertise in criminal law, Keenan was well-respected by senior USG officials, including Truman and MacArthur.[46]

Keenan arrived in Tokyo on December 6 with forty aides, and MacArthur established the IMTFE's International Prosecution Section (IPS) two days later.[47] As an American citizen was serving as the chief prosecutor, each of the other ten United Nations parties that had waged war with Japan[48]—and which were thus members of what would become the Far Eastern Commission (FEC)—had the power to appoint one of its citizens to serve as an Associate Counsel.[49] Still, more staff members were needed to undertake the great amount of investigative and prosecutorial work. In total, the IPS would be comprised of fifty attorneys, half of whom were American.[50]

5. December 1945: Moscow Agreement and American Reflections

The Moscow Agreement of December 27 signified a crucial development in Allied cooperation concerning the occupation of Japan and the more specific issue of transitional justice. Several highly relevant portions of the agreements were solidified during meetings held in Moscow from December 16 to 26. At these meetings, the Allies agreed to establish the FEC, headquartered in Washington, DC.[51] The FEC, which held its first meeting on February 26, 1946, replaced the FEAC and had more teeth.[52] Participating states endowed the FEC with the authority to review any directive or action the SCAP took within the FEC's jurisdiction, including the future IMTFE's operations.[53] The Allies also agreed at this conference to establish an Allied Council for Japan (ACJ), chaired by MacArthur as the SCAP, which would consult with and advise the SCAP on his overseeing the occupation of Japan.[54] The ACJ would be comprised of one representative each from China, the United States, and the Soviet Union, and one member jointly representing Australia, India, New Zealand, and the United Kingdom.[55]

The Moscow Agreement declared the SCAP to be "the sole executive authority for the Allied Powers in Japan"; instructed the FEC to "respect existing control machinery in Japan, including the chain of command from the [USG] to the [SCAP] and the [SCAP]'s command of occupation forces"; and agreed that the USG would prepare and transfer the FEC's directives to the SCAP and could, under certain circumstances, issue interim directives directly to the SCAP.[56] Consequently, the Moscow Agreement cemented the roles of MacArthur specifically and the USG generally in overseeing the Allied occupation of Japan and related transitional justice issues, including those concerning the IMTFE. In addition to the USG's already implicit oversight of the Japanese occupation, the United States, along with China, the Soviet Union, and, to a lesser extent, the United Kingdom, explicitly possessed a disproportionately greater voice in the FEC and the ACJ than the other represented states.[57]

The December 30 report of U.S. secretary of state James Byrnes regarding the conference and agreement in Moscow earlier that month provides crucial insight into why the USG favored the inclusion of certain states in an unequal decision-making structure for the occupation and transitional justice system in Japan. Byrnes described the USG position that all states that had fought Japan during WWII should participate in the post-conflict peacemaking, including the occupation.[58] At the same time, Byrnes conveyed the USG belief, reflected in the roster of permanent members of the recently established UNSC,[59] that "greater" powers, which shouldered a disproportionately heavy burden in defeating Japan, should play a greater role in postwar peacemaking.[60]

6. Early-1946: Establishment of the International Military Tribunal for the Far East

The IMTFE Charter, based in large part on the IMT Charter, was established by MacArthur's order on January 19, 1946.[61] USG officials, particularly Keenan, initially drafted the IMTFE Charter; the USG consulted its allies about the document only after MacArthur issued it.[62] The IMTFE's Rules of Procedure also were established on January 19 and were promulgated by the IMTFE on April 25.[63] According to Solis Horwitz, who served on the IMTFE's prosecution staff during the trial, the USG exclusively drafted the IMTFE Charter. It did so because Keenan, as the IMTFE's Chief of Counsel, was tasked with preparing the details of the IMTFE, and none of the associate prosecutors had arrived in Japan before the Charter was promulgated.[64] However, on April 26, the Charter was amended slightly to reflect the views of the Allied delegations.[65]

The Charter indicated that Tokyo would be the permanent seat of the tribunal. The proceedings were held in the auditorium of the old Japanese War Ministry in the Ichigaya neighborhood of Tokyo. This venue was symbolic: it had been the auditorium of the Imperial Army Officers School and then temporary headquarters of the Japanese military during WWII.[66]

On February 15, MacArthur appointed eleven judges to the IMTFE,[67] one nominated by each of the nine members of the Instrument of Surrender[68] plus one judge each from India and the Philippine Commonwealth.[69] MacArthur did not reject any of the judicial nominees.[70] These eleven judges thus represented the eleven-state membership of the FEC. The first American judge was John Higgins, Chief Justice of the Superior Court of Massachusetts.[71] He was compelled to return (or chose to, because, according to Dower, his qualifications had been criticized) to the United States in July 1946 and therefore resigned.[72] Major General Myron Cramer, former Judge Advocate General of the U.S. Army, replaced Higgins.[73] MacArthur also had the power to appoint the IMTFE's president, or chief judge, from among the judges at-large,[74] and he chose the Australian representative, Sir William Webb. Whenever Webb was absent—not an uncommon event—Cramer served as acting president.[75]

Four months after the IMTFE's IPS was established, three months after the IMTFE was created, and just before the IMTFE's proceedings started in April, an International Defense Panel was created.[76] Japanese citizens and, at the request of the Japanese government to the USG, Americans, too, served as defense counsel.[77]

Exercising its authority with respect to the Japanese occupation, the FEC issued a statement on April 3 concerning the "Apprehension, Trial[,] and Punishment of War Criminals in the Far East," which was communicated to MacArthur twenty days later.[78] This statement basically included all of the USG's original directives to MacArthur—apparently a mere rubber stamp of USG policy.

B. THE INTERNATIONAL MILITARY TRIBUNAL FOR THE FAR EAST'S TRIALS

On April 29, 1946, Keenan and the ten associate prosecutors issued a joint indictment on behalf of all eleven states that had been at war with Japan and thus comprised the FEC.[79] The indictment charged twenty-eight men[80] with three sets of crimes[81] (crimes against peace, war crimes, and crimes against humanity) comprising fifty-five counts.[82]

The IMTFE's trial structure and procedure borrowed directly from the IMT's.[83] Opening statements preceding the arraignment, including Keenan's introduction of the indictment, were delivered on May 3.[84] What Webb called "the trial of the century"[85]—so momentous in his view that he believed "[t]here has been no more important criminal trial in all history"[86]—had commenced and would not conclude until the IMTFE's judges rendered their verdicts two-and-a- half years later, between November 4 and November 12, 1948.[87] As a result, the IMTFE's proceedings started about a year and a half after the IMT's began and ended approximately two years after the IMT concluded;[88] the IMTFE earned the distinction at that time as "the longest continuous trial in history."[89] The trial also earned the distinction of "absorb[ing] one-quarter of the paper consumed by the Allied Occupation forces in Japan during the Trial."[90] The IMTFE eventually sentenced seven defendants to death by hanging,[91] sixteen to life imprisonment,[92] one to twenty years imprisonment,[93] and one to seven years imprisonment.[94]

None was acquitted.[95] Three individuals were not sentenced: two died during the trial,[96] and one had been judged unfit for trial.[97]

On November 24, 1948, MacArthur affirmed the convictions.[98] Some of the convicted Japanese immediately filed habeas petitions with the U.S. Supreme Court.[99] On December 6, exactly three years after Keenan arrived in Tokyo, the Supreme Court approved oral argument in the matter (thus staying the sentences).[100] Justice Jackson—having returned to the Supreme Court from his post as the IMT's chief U.S. prosecutor—filed a memorandum in that decision explaining his reluctant agreement, because of his involvement in negotiating the IMT Charter and then representing the United States at that trial, to cast the tie-breaking vote.[101] Oral arguments were then delivered on December 16 and 17, and the Court, without Jackson's participation, announced its per curiam decision three days later.[102] The Court denied the motions for jurisdictional reasons. Specifically, the IMTFE was an international military tribunal and thus not a U.S. court; rather, it had been established by a U.S. general (MacArthur) acting as the agent of the Allied Powers, including the USG.[103] The Court reasoned that these circumstances limited the Supreme Court's power to intervene: "[T]he courts of the United States have no power or authority to review, to affirm, set aside or annul the judgments and sentences imposed on these petitioners . . . ."[104] Three days later, the Japanese petitioners the IMTFE had sentenced to death were executed at their place of confinement: Sugamo Prison in the Ikebukuro district of Tokyo.[105]

II. Transitional Justice Options Seriously Considered and Actually Implemented for Alleged Japanese Atrocity Perpetrators

Like the IMT for Nazis, the IMTFE was one of only several transitional justice options seriously considered and actually implemented to address Japanese suspected of committing atrocities during WWII. This Part summarizes what transitional justice options the Allied Powers—in particular, the USG—considered and then implemented for these Japanese. Part II.A describes the impact the existing and ongoing IMT precedent made on deliberations concerning Japanese. Parts II.B and II.C discuss the transitional justice options seriously considered and actually implemented for the primary and lower-level Japanese war criminals, respectively. As discussed below, for each group of alleged atrocity perpetrators, the general options implemented were the same: prosecution, amnesty, and lustration.[106] Figure 5.1 shows the general transitional justice options the USG supported for addressing Japanese, whereas Figure 5.2 displays the specific prosecutorial transitional justice options the USG supported in this case.

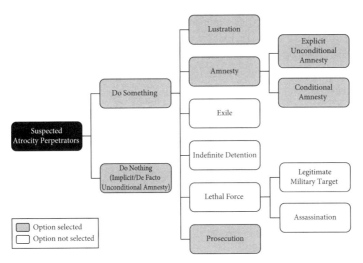

FIGURE 5.1 *U.S. Government Transitional Justice Options Tree for Suspected* Japanese *Atrocity Perpetrators—General.*

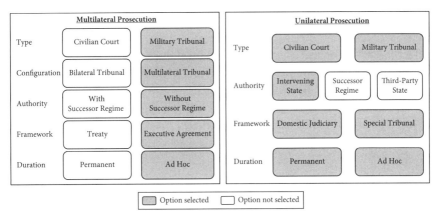

FIGURE 5.2 *U.S. Government Transitional Justice Options Table for Suspected* Japanese *Atrocity Perpetrators—Prosecution.*

A. THE PRECEDENT OF ADDRESSING NAZIS

Because negotiations leading to the IMT's establishment effectively doubled as negotiations for creating the IMTFE, options seriously considered for addressing principal Nazi suspects were also implicitly or explicitly considered for addressing the principal Japanese suspects. However, because the IMT set a precedent for prosecuting atrocity leaders through an ICT established by executive fiat, there is little indication that the use of lethal force through extrajudicial execution, prosecution in an ICT established via treaty, or unilateral or bilateral prosecution by individual Allied Powers were considered as seriously for the principal Japanese as they had been for the principal Nazis. As in the case of dealing with the principal Nazis, the Allied Powers never seriously considered unilateral prosecution for Class A Japanese war criminals by Japan or even a third-party state (e.g., a neutral country during WWII hostilities).

B. PRIMARY JAPANESE WAR CRIMINALS

Part I demonstrated that two transitional justice mechanisms USG officials seriously considered for addressing the principal suspected Japanese atrocity perpetrators—the designated Class A Japanese war criminals—were (1) prosecution in an ICT established through executive agreement and (2) lustration. The Allies implemented both of these mechanisms, along with a third: unconditional amnesty.

1. Prosecution

For the Class A war criminals the USG and its allies decided to hold accountable through prosecution, the forum was a newly established, ad hoc international military tribunal created outside the UN through an executive order by MacArthur acting as the SCAP.[107] This tribunal had limited subject-matter (crimes against peace, war crimes, and crimes against humanity), temporal (crimes committed since 1928, when Japanese assassinated Chang Tso-lin, a Chinese warlord), and personal (major war criminals in the Far East) jurisdiction. Unlike the immediate post–Cold War ad hoc tribunals would,[108] the IMT and the IMTFE did not feature any institutional overlap.

2. Unconditional Amnesty

Unlike the case of the principal suspected Nazi atrocity perpetrators, the USG seriously considered at least one other option for addressing some Class A Japanese war criminals and Hirohito: unconditional amnesty. While the Allies, including the USG, were trying thousands of Classes A, B, and C Japanese suspected of committing atrocities during WWII, the USG also provided amnesty to other Japanese who were suspected of similarly heinous crimes.[109]

The USG explicitly extended unconditional amnesty to Japanese Emperor Hirohito, who was never taken into Allied custody.[110] The U.S. Joint Chiefs of Staff specifically ordered MacArthur not to attempt to apprehend Hirohito as MacArthur sought to capture individuals who would eventually be tried before the IMTFE.[111] MacArthur thus declined to request or even support Hirohito's abdication.[112] As a result, on June 18, 1946, Keenan announced that Hirohito would not be charged, thus publicly and officially exonerating the emperor of responsibility for Japan's actions during WWII.[113]

A second grant of amnesty occurred after MacArthur selected twenty-eight individuals to indict before the IMTFE from all of the Class A war criminals he detained at Sugamo Prison.[114] The Allies, led by the USG, eventually released (by December 24, 1948) and never held accountable the more than fifty Class A war criminals remaining, many of whom eventually returned to Japanese politics.[115] Thus, for those Japanese Class A war criminals the USG arrested but then decided *not* to hold accountable through the IMTFE, the USG implicitly extended unconditional amnesty.

3. Lustration

The Allied Powers adopted a lustration policy, which MacArthur administered as the SCAP, purging the principal Japanese war criminals, at least temporarily, from public office. The Class A war criminals not prosecuted were not permitted to immediately serve again in government.[116] Some Japanese implicated in or convicted of atrocities, however, would later return to public life, even rising to prominent senior political roles. For example, Mamoru Shigemitsu, whom the IMTFE had convicted on six counts and sentenced to seven years imprisonment,[117] was appointed Japanese foreign minister in 1954.[118] In addition, Nobusuke Kishi, an unindicted Class A war criminal, became prime minister in 1957.[119] The USG later would collaborate with many of these convicted or suspected war criminals in efforts to combat communism.[120] That the USG "embraced many erstwhile war criminals in the common cause of anticommunism," Dower states, "gave a perverse binational coloration to this repudiation of the [IMTFE's] verdict."[121]

C. LOWER-LEVEL JAPANESE WAR CRIMINALS

The USG and some other Allies seriously considered and implemented at least five transitional justice options for addressing Japanese suspected of committing lesser atrocities: (1) prosecution in U.S. military tribunals, (2) appeal in a U.S. civilian court, (3) prosecution in military courts established by other states, (4) de facto conditional amnesty, and (5) lustration. Those Japanese whom the USG and its allies decided to hold accountable were prosecuted through unilateral, ad hoc Allied military tribunals (options 1 and 3). Some of those cases were (unsuccessfully) appealed to the USG's permanent domestic federal judiciary, including the U.S. Supreme Court (option 2). Many of these and other Japanese Classes B and C war criminals also were the targets of lustration (option 5). Others whom the USG did not hold accountable, including several thousand Japanese involved in medical experimentation, were effectively provided de facto conditional amnesty (option 4) because the USG presumably would have revoked immunity had they not cooperated.

1. Prosecution in U.S. Military Tribunals

Although the decision was made to prosecute only some of the Class A war criminals before an international military tribunal, the USG addressed suspects of Classes B and C through an alternative transitional justice option. On September

12, 1945, Truman ordered the U.S. Joint Chiefs of Staff to instruct MacArthur to try apprehended Japanese suspected of committing atrocities before unilateral ad hoc U.S. military tribunals.[122] This directive, aimed at "smaller fish" (Classes B and C), was thus separate from the one that established the IMTFE for the principal (Class A) alleged Japanese atrocity perpetrators.

From 1945, a year before the IMTFE began operations, to 1951, several years after the IMTFE had rendered its verdict, the USG held trials of Classes B and C Japanese before these ad hoc U.S. military tribunals in Japan and in other territories the Japanese formerly occupied, including China and the Philippines. Through these tribunals, the USG prosecuted 1409 Japanese, convicting 1229 of them; 163 received death sentences.[123] As such, the United States officially prosecuted more Japanese through bona fide trials than any other state.[124] Some argue that, because of their organizing authority (under MacArthur as the SCAP), these U.S. military tribunals were technically Allied tribunals.[125] According to Dower, unlike the IMTFE, "these local trials established no precedents, attracted no great attention, and left no lasting mark on popular memory outside Japan."[126] Some, however, stress these military tribunals' significance. As historian Philip Piccigallo observes:

> [F]or all its importance, the IMTFE constituted but a small part of a much larger process . . . [the Allied military trials] by far exceed[ed] in scope and ambition those of the IMTFE . . . . The Tokyo Tribunal, in short, was a constituent part of the entire Allied Eastern war crimes operation, albeit the most celebrated, longest, most discussed and, some felt, most important single component.[127]

2. Appeal in a U.S. Civilian Court

Some convictions before these ad hoc military tribunals achieved additional prominence when the affected defendants appealed to the U.S. Supreme Court. The most famous of these cases was the trial of Tomoyuki Yamashita, the Commanding General of the Fourteenth Army Group of the Imperial Japanese Army in the Philippine Islands from October 9, 1944, until September 3, 1945 (the date he surrendered to the U.S. Army). In his official capacity, Yamashita oversaw the commission of mass atrocities. He was subsequently categorized as a Class B war criminal for his alleged command responsibility during these offenses. He was then tried by an ad hoc U.S. military commission in Manila from October 8 to December 7, 1945, and sentenced to death by hanging. Yamashita appealed his conviction to the U.S. Supreme Court, which heard his argument on January 7 to 8, 1946. He claimed that the U.S. military commission that had tried, convicted, and sentenced him possessed neither the authority nor the jurisdiction to do so, and that he had been denied due process of law.[128] The Court rendered its judgment in the *Yamashita* case on February 4, 1946, upholding the jurisdiction of the U.S. military commission and therefore dismissing Yamashita's appeal.[129] He was subsequently executed on February 23, after MacArthur decided not to exercise his authority to intervene.[130] Because the *Yamashita* case was the first war crimes trial charging a military officer (who had not been accused of personally committing atrocities) with a failure to exercise control over persons under his command who allegedly had perpetrated the underlying offenses, it established the U.S. legal standard concerning "command responsibility."[131] For this reason—and also because it was a high-profile forerunner to the IMTFE—the *Yamashita* case is better known in some circles than the IMTFE itself.[132]

3. Prosecution in Military Courts Established by Other States

Six other Allied states—Australia, China, France, the Netherlands, the Philippines, and the United Kingdom—also held their own unilateral ad hoc military tribunals.[133] In total, between 1945 and 1951, 2200 ad hoc Allied military tribunals tried approximately 5700 Classes B and C war criminals, convicting 4400 of them.[134] Of the remaining suspects, 1018 were acquitted and 279 were either never tried or not sentenced.[135] Approximately 75 percent of all of these defendants were charged with offenses against POWs.[136] These trials were not wholly disconnected from the IMTFE; in fact, some of the records of the unilateral ad hoc military trials were used in the proceedings of the IMTFE.[137]

The unilateral proceedings conducted by the Soviet Union are particularly noteworthy given how many were mostly show trials. The Soviet Union conducted these trials summarily, after which the Soviet government probably executed as many as 3000 Japanese.[138] These trials were propaganda tools. As former U.S. Army attorney and legal academic Robert Barr Smith recounts:

> The Russian trials were mostly pulpits for propaganda attacks on the West. The "imperialist policy" of their erstwhile allies, said the Russians, had led them to abandon "the struggle against war criminals." The Russians never tired of harping on Western decisions not to try the "greedy capitalists," the *zaibatsu* of Japanese industry . . . . [The] Communist media let the world know that "Japan and its American allies" were plotting to use . . . hideous [biological] weapons against Russia . . . . The West had "unleashed the most inhuman carnage in history, warfare with the assistance of microbes, fleas, lice and spiders . . . ."[139]

Unilateral prosecution through ad hoc Allied military tribunals thus served not only to supplement the IMTFE's proceedings but also to foreshadow—and even, because of Soviet propaganda, to foment—the coming Cold War.

4. De Facto Conditional Amnesty

The USG offered immunity and other incentives—including money, food, and entertainment—to over 3600 Japanese government agents, physicians, and scientists involved in Japanese experiments performed during WWII on thousands of civilians and Allied soldiers. The Imperial Japanese Army's Unit 731, led by Lieutenant General Shiro Ishii, conducted the most notorious research in Manchuria. These experiments, sometimes referred to as the "Asian Auschwitz," included vivisections, dissections, weapons testing, starvation, dehydration, poisoning, extreme temperature and pressure testing, and deliberate infection with numerous deadly diseases (such as bubonic plague, cholera, anthrax, smallpox, gangrene, streptococcus bacteria, and syphilis). Had WWII continued, the Japanese planned to use biological weapons developed from these experiments to attack the U.S. military in the Pacific Theater and possibly even the West Coast of the United States itself. After being granted immunity, some Japanese participants in these experiments assumed prominent roles—including senior positions in the health ministry, academia, and the private sector—in postwar Japanese society, allegedly with the assistance or at least knowledge of the USG.[140]

Through its conscious decision not to hold these alleged atrocity perpetrators accountable, the USG provided amnesty to thousands of Japanese suspected of direct involvement in some of the most horrific crimes of WWII, including those who planned offenses against Americans. As discussed below, because the USG sought information in return for granting these Japanese immunity, such amnesty was implicitly conditional.

5. Lustration

Finally, through the Allied lustration policy, by mid-1948 more than 200,000 Japanese had been removed or barred, at least temporarily, from public office.[141]

III. The United States Role in "Tokyo"

The United States was the most critical actor in what became known as "Tokyo." The USG served as the foremost proponent and host of discussions leading to the creation of the IMTFE, including by successfully lobbying for the creation of the UNWCC's Special Far Eastern and Pacific Committee. The 1945 Moscow Agreement laid out the general role of the USG in postwar Japan's occupation, including its transitional justice process. This function included, inter alia, the USG's responsibilities with respect to the FEC. The USG was tasked with hosting the FEC's headquarters in Washington, DC, and, on behalf of the four signatories to the Moscow Agreement, presenting the Terms of Reference of the FEC to other specified governments and inviting them to participate.[142]

The USG was responsible for producing the initial draft of the IMTFE Charter and then for lobbying the other Allies to accept it with minimal changes.[143] As such, the USG effectively made all of the design decisions, modeled on the IMT, and then presented its plan to the other Allies as a fait accompli. Yves Beigbeder, who served as legal secretary to the IMT's French judge, thus calls the IMTFE

Charter "essentially an American project."[144] The USG also asserted its cultural dominance in the design of the IMTFE, by having English serve as the only official language other than Japanese, and in having so much of the tribunal's design and operation based on the American system of law and criminal justice (as represented in the IMT, as well).[145] The USG had such significant—even unilateral—authority over the transitional justice process for Japan largely because of the practical fact that it led the Japanese occupation, at least in the short-term. As Dower recounts of the September 1945 USG orders to MacArthur,

> The original directives, although known and approved by the other allied
> nations, represented unilateral action on the part of the United States. This
> method of operation was not limited to the question of war crimes. It was a
> temporary device for conducting a joint occupation under the command of
> a national of one of the allied nations until the joint machinery for carrying
> on such an occupation could be perfected.[146]

The USG dominated prosecution at the IMTFE. An American served as the sole chief prosecutor, and Americans comprised not only the plurality of nationalities represented on the IPS's Executive Committee, but also half of the IPS itself.[147] The USG provided the first legal staff to arrive in Tokyo, thus leading the early work of the IMTFE.[148] Furthermore, the USG supplied a significant share of eyewitnesses, experts, and senior political and military officials who testified at the IMTFE.[149]

The USG also contributed a great amount of assistance to the IMTFE defendants. Unlike at the IMT, the USG furnished Americans to serve as defense counsel alongside the Japanese at the IMTFE. Not only did the USG pay the salaries of all American defense counsel, but it also spent millions of U.S. dollars on the transportation and accommodation of *all* defense counsel in their overseas trips (to China, Germany, the United Kingdom, and the United States) to obtain evidence and locate witnesses.[150] As such, the USG involvement in the defense led the Dutch judge on the IMTFE, Bernard Röling, to conclude that "[t]he Americans ... dominated the defen[s]e ...."[151] Furthermore, the USG saved Tōjō's life after his failed suicide attempt.[152] As Arnold Brackman, a journalist who covered the IMTFE trials, reported on the incident: "The tough old warrior was rushed to a U.S. Army field hospital and given transfusions of American blood."[153]

In addition to dominating the prosecution and arguably also the defense, the USG eventually would lead the most important aspect of the bench. For reasons unknown (because they are not documented), the power of presiding over the drafting of the IMTFE's decision shifted from the Australian chief judge/president, Webb, to the American judge, Cramer, who chaired the seven-member Majority Drafting Committee.[154]

Perhaps the most obvious way that the USG dominated the establishment of the IMTFE was the fact that a senior American military officer served as the SCAP. As Piccigallo observes, the IMTFE "functioned throughout under the all-pervading shadow of SCAP."[155] The IMTFE provided enormous powers to MacArthur. He was responsible for appointing most of the senior officers of the tribunal: the judges,[156] including the president (chief judge) of the tribunal,[157] the General Secretary,[158] and the Chief of Counsel (chief prosecutor).[159] In addition to choosing, as noted, an American to serve as chief prosecutor, MacArthur also chose an American, Colonel Vern Walbridge, to serve as the General Secretary.[160] The USG (through MacArthur) also possessed the right to refuse all other staffing decisions, such as appointments for IPS associate prosecutors from the other member states of the FEC. In addition, MacArthur could exercise judicial review, so he literally held the power to make decisions over life and death.[161] In this sense, MacArthur therefore wielded a power similar to that in the United States of a governor or the president to grant clemency for a convict on death row. As yet another example of USG influence over the IMTFE, the chairman of the ACJ, which consulted with MacArthur during the sentencing review process, was William Sebald, the U.S. representative.[162] Moreover, it was the USG that made the decision to release the remaining Class A war criminals who were not indicted by the IMTFE.[163]

The USG therefore was the most crucial actor in the establishment of the IMTFE. As political scientist Howard Ball argues: "The United States was the prime mover in the creation and implementation of the [IMTFE]."[164] Dower concurs, arguing, "the American control of prosecution policy and strategy bordered on the absolute."[165] Some tribunal participants agree. As Röling observes, the IMTFE "was very much an American performance . . . ."[166] Even those who reviewed appeals from the IMTFE shared these sentiments. As U.S. Supreme Court Justice William Douglas observed, "the [IMTFE] is dominated by American influence . . . ."[167] The fact of U.S. supremacy was not lost on the other countries participating in establishing these trials. Anticipating criticisms of the USG's heavy influence, these other states also proactively sought to undermine this charge for fear of how the perception might affect the IMTFE's functioning and success. Referring to whatever courts (including the IMTFE) the SCAP created, the FEC urged that the "international character of the courts and of the authority by which they were appointed and under which they act should be properly recognized and emphasized, particularly in dealings with the Japanese people."[168]

Some analysts even suggest that the USG's dominance in the establishment of the IMTFE was so great that it defined the tribunal itself. First, some argue that the IMTFE was a misnomer. As Dower contends,

> The top-level war-crimes trials that accompanied the occupation, formally known as the International Military Tribunal for the Far East . . . were misleadingly named. An international panel of judges did preside and the president of the tribunal was Australian, but the Tokyo trial was a predominantly American show. Americans dominated the [IPS] that set the

agenda for the tribunal, and they brooked scant internal dissent from other national contingents.[169]

Others claim that the USG's dominance of the IMTFE exceeded that of the IMT. As commentator Wu Tianwei states: "Although the United States played a major role in both the Nuremberg and Tokyo trials, having had her legal views and opinions well pronounced, she virtually dominated the latter, in which her policy toward Japan took precedence."[170] The IMTFE appears to be one of—if not the— most unilateral, in terms of the establishment, design, staffing, and procedure of all ICTs ever created. Consequently, the United States would forever be linked with evaluations of the IMTFE. As IMTFE defense counsel Ben Blakeney, an American, argues, "it is to the United States that will inure, in great measure, the credit or discredit which history will attach to the proceedings of the [IMTFE]— and not history only, but contemporary opinion."[171]

Beyond the USG writ large, the role of individual USG officials in the establishment of the IMTFE cannot be overstated. As the IMT served as the model for the IMTFE, all of those who contributed to the establishment of the IMT thus implicitly contributed to the creation of the IMTFE. Those individuals include Bernays, Jackson, Stimson, Morgenthau, Jr., FDR, and Truman. In the case of the IMTFE, several other individuals made important contributions. Pell, as the U.S. representative on the UNWCC, prompted the coordinated international investigation of alleged Japanese atrocities by successfully lobbying for the establishment of the UNWCC's Special Far Eastern and Pacific Committee. Pell's leadership was so widely known that international efforts to investigate alleged Japanese atrocities were referred to by some American allies as "Pell's cause."[172] Keenan played an incalculably critical role in leading the IMTFE's investigation and prosecution, and in negotiating decisions on which Japanese to indict in the first place.[173] MacArthur's influence was felt through his various establishment, appointment, and review powers. Also, although Keenan led the Allied decision-making on which Japanese to indict, MacArthur (in consultation with Truman and other senior USG officials) made the decision against indicting Hirohito.[174] The individual justices of the U.S. Supreme Court played a critical role in deciding against reviewing the IMTFE's judgment. Finally, Truman decided to appoint MacArthur as the SCAP and issued numerous directives to him, thus overseeing the overall establishment and operation of the IMTFE.

Besides the United States, certain other states played important roles in the establishment of the IMTFE. According to Horwitz, the IMTFE indictment "was largely a British document," owing in large part to the fact that the U.K.'s associate prosecutor, Arthur Comyns-Carr, headed the subcommittee tasked with preparing the charging document.[175] The United Kingdom also exercised significant influence because Comyns-Carr chaired the chief prosecutor's Executive Committee, which oversaw the selection of IMTFE defendants.[176] In addition, Australia significantly impacted the proceedings, as MacArthur appointed its representative on the bench to be the IMTFE's president. Finally, as the IMTFE's Charter was almost wholly a copy of the IMT's Charter, those states involved in drafting the latter document—France, the Soviet Union, the United Kingdom, and the United States—implicitly contributed to drafting the former document.

IV. Explaining the United States Role in Transitional Justice for Japan

A. THE UNITED STATES GOVERNMENT'S MOTIVATIONS TO LEAD THE PRIMARY TRANSITIONAL JUSTICE INSTITUTION FOR JAPAN

First, why did the USG take such a leading role in the establishment of the IMTFE? The USG's involvement was, in many ways, even greater than its role in the creation of the IMT. This is somewhat unexpected, especially considering that the United States suffered more casualties in the European Theater[177] and that Americans were (and still are) more familiar with individual Nazi leaders and their crimes.[178]

There are three likely, perhaps mutually supportive, political reasons for the USG's motive to lead the transitional justice process for Japanese suspected of committing atrocities during WWII. First, the USG was undoubtedly highly sensitive to the fact that Americans suffered in some ways more at the hands of Japanese than Germans. In the European Theater, the United States incurred comparatively fewer deaths than its allies, whereas in the Pacific Theater, Americans bore as many or more deaths than many of their allies.[179] In particular, the United States had withstood Japan's surprise attack on Pearl Harbor. Japanese treatment of American POWs was arguably more brutal than the Axis powers' practices in Europe. While 4 percent of Allied POWs captured by Germans and Italians died while imprisoned, almost seven times as many Allied POWs (27 percent) detained by the Japanese died (mostly from murder, disease, starvation, or torture). Death rates among Americans imprisoned by the Japanese even exceeded the average among the Allies as a whole: of 21,580 American POWs held by the Japanese, 7107, or 32.9 percent, died.[180] Consequently, according to Dower: "Long after the war had ended, and notwithstanding the revelation of the enormity of Nazi atrocities, great numbers of Americans, British, and Australians continued to believe that the enemy in Asia had been even more heinous than the German one."[181] As a result of this perceived disparity, some believe that the IMTFE was "a vehicle for America's taking revenge" against the Japanese.[182] As Beigbeder observes, some experts believe that "MacArthur's real aim was to avenge the treacherous attack on Pearl Harbor, which had brought humiliation on the US nation and its military forces . . . ."[183]

The USG likely was motivated not only by retrospective but also prospective concerns. Thus, a second explanation is that the USG wished to assert its presence in Asia, where American and Soviet spheres of influence were less defined, in large part to stem the spread of communism from the Soviet Union. In fact, some commentators connect this very objective—intimidating the Soviet Union and demonstrating American military preeminence—to the USG's deployment of atomic bombs in Japan.[184] By leading the transitional justice institution for Japan, along with a greater role in the occupation, the United States could raise its stature and position in Asian—and global—affairs.

Third, racism probably also drove USG decision-making, at least subconsciously. Dower contends that because of its "reflective ethnocentrism," the USG "excluded Japan's Asian antagonists from any meaningful role in the occupation."[185] Not content to allow Asians (particularly Chinese)—who had suffered as much or more than Americans—to play a leading role in establishing and operating the IMTFE, the USG seized the initiative.

Beyond the likely reasons that motivated the USG to take such a leading role in the establishment of the IMTFE, there are some unlikely ones as well. International law scholar Antonio Cassese stated that some believe that the IMTFE was "a means of assuaging American national guilt over the use of atomic weapons in Japan."[186] I have found no evidence to suggest that USG officials held this motive or that many scholars believe this assertion.

B. OTHER STATES' MOTIVATIONS TO DEFER TO THE UNITED STATES IN LEADING THE PRIMARY TRANSITIONAL JUSTICE INSTITUTION FOR JAPAN

Just because the USG may have wanted to lead the transitional justice institution for Japan need not have meant that other states would follow suit. A second question, therefore, is why the USG's allies decided to defer to the USG taking such a prominent role in the establishment of the IMTFE. As Dower observes, "[a]lthough the countries Japan had invaded and occupied were all Asian, and although the number of Asians who had died as a consequence of its depredations was enormous, only three of the eleven judges were Asians .... The trial was fundamentally a white man's tribunal."[187] The United States' commanding role was especially unanticipated considering that some of the USG's allies suffered much more from Japanese activities than the United States. Most significantly, China was the greatest victim of Japanese atrocities, with approximately 6 million Chinese having been killed, in what is sometimes referred to as "the forgotten Holocaust."[188]

The authority to lead Japan's transitional justice process was not based, though, solely on victimhood. Instead, it was grounded at least as much in global power. The USG's allies were content to defer to it because the USG was both willing and able to oversee the post-conflict occupation and administration of

Japan, including the IMTFE. In contrast to the European Theater, in which the victorious powers each played a substantial role and each placed a significant military presence in postwar Germany, it was almost exclusively the United States that led the Allied defeat of Japan and that stationed a disproportionate amount of troops on Japanese territory. In some ways, precisely because the USG deferred to other states to shoulder the burden of fighting Japan earlier in WWII, those states' resources were then depleted and so they deferred to the USG to shoulder the burden of dealing with post-conflict Japan. The United States not only won the Pacific War but also established itself, with the atomic bombings of Nagasaki and Hiroshima and its subsequent occupation of and overwhelming military presence in Japan, as by far the strongest power in Asia, if not the world. Thus the USG's dominance in the IMTFE reflected the fact that the USG also dominated the occupation of Japan.[189] Specifically referring to the fact that the IMTFE's single chief prosecutor was American, whereas the IMT featured four chief prosecutors (one from each of the quadripartite Allied powers), Horwitz observes:

> While this plan was wholly consonant with the principles governing the occupation of Japan, it was an unusual departure from ordinary international practice. For the first time eleven nations had agreed in a matter other than actual military operations to subordinate their sovereignty and to permit a national of one of them to have final direction and control.[190]

American postwar hegemony, at least regionally, was therefore clear. As Watt argues: "That America should lead in matters concerned with war crimes trials was only one facet, albeit an important one, of that fact."[191] The United States even had enough resources to provide much of the funding for, and staff of, the IMTFE, which further compelled its allies to let the United States lead the IMTFE effort.[192] American prosecutors at the IMTFE made similar arguments at the time, pointing out the USG's "predominant contribution" to defeating Japan, and therefore claiming that "it was the universally admitted right and duty of the United States" to oversee Japanese war crimes trials.[193] The United States' WWII Asian allies, crippled by and suffering from the war, deferred to it on the occupation of, and transitional justice process for, Japan, mostly because there was nothing else they could do about the inertia built from, and the hierarchy derived by, the USG's leadership in winning the Pacific Theater.

C. THE APPOINTMENT OF A NON-AMERICAN AS PRESIDENT OF THE INTERNATIONAL MILITARY TRIBUNAL FOR THE FAR EAST

A particularly puzzling feature of the establishment of the IMTFE was the selection of its president. Why did MacArthur, who, according to the IMTFE Charter held the unilateral power to appoint whomever he wished, select a non-American (Webb) to serve as the head jurist and presiding officer of the tribunal? MacArthur's choice is especially unanticipated given the following circumstances: (1) MacArthur need not have consulted any other state in this appointment, (2) the tribunal's president held significant power because his vote could break any ties in the tribunal's decisions and judgments (including convictions and sentences),[194] and (3) the IMT already featured a non-American (U.K. Colonel Sir Geoffrey Lawrence) as its president.[195]

MacArthur initially did, in fact, plan to appoint the American judge as the IMTFE's president. However, that plan was foiled by Keenan's outrage at the selection of Higgins, whom Keenan did not consider prominent enough to assume his seat on the IMTFE's bench. Keenan had instead lobbied for the appointment of any of the following, in descending order of preference: Willis Smith, president of the American Bar Association; Roscoe Pound, dean of Harvard Law School; a federal appellate judge; or a military official holding a rank no less than major general.[196] In Keenan's view, the selection of a member of the Superior Court of Massachusetts was not on par with the prestige and position of the nominees from each of the other states represented on the IMTFE's bench, or the USG's own senior members of the IMT. Indeed, the chief prosecutor, Jackson, was a member of the U.S. Supreme Court, and one of the judges, Francis Biddle, was the U.S. attorney general.

By the time MacArthur was to appoint the IMTFE's president, the USG's allies had already expressed interest in playing a more direct and prominent role in post-conflict occupation and transitional justice issues in Japan; several of them had recently lobbied for a more directly and officially involved FEC to replace the FEAC. Precisely because MacArthur had already appointed an American to be the IMTFE's single chief prosecutor, the only senior role left to fill with a non-American was the tribunal's president. If MacArthur wanted to accommodate the USG's allies by broadening the decision-making authority of transitional justice for Japan and to dampen allegations and criticisms that the process was dominated by the USG, this was the prime opportunity.

MacArthur was familiar with Webb's work and views on Japanese atrocities. Webb had been involved in the Australian War Crimes Commission, through which, between 1943 and 1945, he produced three prominent reports on Japanese wartime atrocities.[197] Webb's home country of Australia had been a victim of Japanese atrocities, and it was a strong ally of and had a similar judicial system (at least more so than Asian states) to the United States. Perhaps most crucially, Webb was MacArthur's personal friend.[198] MacArthur was therefore sufficiently informed about Webb's background and views to be reasonably confident that Webb would preside similarly to any American jurist MacArthur would otherwise appoint. And, just in case, MacArthur appointed Cramer (Higgins's successor as the American representative on the IMTFE's bench) to be the tribunal's acting president whenever Webb was absent or otherwise unable or unwilling to carry out his duties.[199] Webb was therefore the ideal candidate to make the tribunal appear less dominated by the USG without really losing much, if any, USG influence or violating MacArthur's assumptions about how the bench would behave and rule.

D. AMERICAN PROVISION OF AMNESTY TO ALLEGED JAPANESE ATROCITY PERPETRATORS

Perhaps the most shocking aspect of the transitional justice process in Japan is that the USG provided amnesty to thousands of individuals suspected of committing atrocities, including offenses planned and perpetrated against Americans. In the case of Hirohito, this policy can be explained by three political factors. First, the occupying authorities (especially MacArthur) were, according to legal scholar Mark Osiel, "convinced that the Japanese public, although willing to blame the Emperor's underlings, would not tolerate the punishment and consequent dethronement of Hirohito himself."[200] Therefore, these USG officials imagined that indicting Hirohito would have provoked a violent insurgency in Japan, one that would have required vast resources to suppress. Second, other senior USG officials believed that Hirohito, as Japan's emperor, was the "best ally" of the Allies' occupation and would be essential to combating Soviet-led "communization of the entire world."[201] Third, some Allied leaders opposed Hirohito's indictment, fearful that his removal would trigger a contentious succession struggle among his relatives, which would further complicate postwar reconstruction and reconciliation efforts.[202]

Some scholars suggest that an additional reason the Allies did not indict Hirohito before the IMTFE was his "figurehead" status, which would have effectively precluded accountability for Japan's wartime atrocities.[203] On the contrary, many thought that Hirohito's indictment by the IMTFE would have been appropriate or even helpful. For example, in delivering their opinions, both Webb and Henri Bernard, the French representative on the IMTFE bench, suggested that the prosecution should have indicted Hirohito, and criticized the fact that he had been granted immunity.[204] Scholarly research supports their contention that Hirohito was directly involved in the Japanese commission of atrocities during WWII.[205]

As with Hirohito, the USG's provision of amnesty to more than four dozen Class A war criminals was driven by political considerations. The USG wished to facilitate Japan's re-entry into the international community, particularly as a partner in the USG's postwar efforts to prepare for rising tension with the Soviet Union.[206] As historian James Bowen argues,

> With the Cold War intensifying, the government of President Harry S. Truman felt that Japan needed to be moulded into an American ally and a bulwark against the spread of communism. Truman believed that these

aims would be difficult to achieve if the Japanese people were alienated by continuing prosecutions of their war criminals . . . . The decision to halt the prosecutions was entirely based on political expediency. It had nothing to do with issues of legality, morality, or humanity.[207]

Of these amnesties, Dower observes: "Ordinary people . . . could be excused for failing to comprehend exactly where justice left off and political whimsy began."[208]

The most unlikely group granted immunity may be the numerous Japanese involved in medical experimentation on humans. To be sure, providing de facto conditional amnesty to these suspected perpetrators was identical to the USG's treatment of certain Nazi scientists (including some suspected of conducting medical experiments on humans) as well as counterintelligence and anti-communist assets. However, three distinctions merit attention. First, among the Japanese human guinea pigs were American POWs,[209] whereas no similar allegation is made against Nazi scientists. Such offenses presumably would have bolstered the USG's resolve to hold Japanese scientists accountable. Not doing so directly violated USG pledges that were both unilateral (such as Hull's statement on April 12, 1943, and the USG's September 6, 1945, "Statement of the Initial Surrender Policy for Japan") and multilateral (such as the Potsdam Declaration of July 26, 1945) specifically warning that the Japanese would be severely punished if American POWs were mistreated. Second, the sheer number of Japanese involved in human experiments who were granted conditional amnesty was much greater than in the German case, where the number of Nazi scientists as a whole (including those suspected of conducting human experiments) offered immunity (over 1600) was a fraction of the amount of Japanese involved in just human experiments who were offered amnesty (over 3600). Finally, these Japanese were treated the opposite of how the USG handled certain other Nazis suspected of conducting medical experiments on humans. The USG convicted sixteen such Nazis in *United States v. Brandt* (also known as the "Doctors' Trial"), the first case before the NMT, sentencing six to death and the remaining ten to prison terms ranging from ten years to life.[210]

Recently declassified USG documents and testimony from Japanese involved in or knowledgeable about the human experiments reveal that the USG was interested in the potential utility of the work of Ishii and other Japanese, however unethical, to the U.S. military.[211] Senior USG officials felt that obtaining data from the experiments was more valuable than bringing those involved to justice, because the information could be used to advance the USG's own weapons development program. USG officials also were concerned about preventing other countries, particularly the Soviet Union, from obtaining the data. Unlike Josef Mengele and some of his Nazi cohorts who performed similar experiments on humans but who were, according to a former U.S./DoJ official and an investigative reporter, "too well known for their war crimes" to become collaborators with the United States,[212] the Japanese human experimenters were all relatively anonymous. As a result, the USG could pursue its strategy undetected, and USG policymakers could partner with implicated Japanese officials without much fear of a public relations backlash.[213]

The incipient Cold War—and the superpowers' attendant desire to secure competitive advantages and scientific advancements—thus chilled the USG's enthusiasm for investigating and prosecuting Japanese human experimenters. USG officials believed that their research would be useful in the arms race developing between the Soviet Union and the United States. Apparently untroubled by medical ethics—consistent with its own postwar human experiments in Guatemala[214]— the USG reasoned that it could keep its deal with involved Japanese secret. Even if it could not, the exchange would be worth the fallout. In other words, one can presume the USG genuinely believed it could benefit from the pain and death of Japanese victims of medical experiments, experiments that included Americans, and that the USG could maintain confidentiality over its profiting from the attendant misery and casualties. Regardless, one U.S. soldier who served in immediate postwar Japan argues that the U.S. deal with Japanese involved in wartime human medical experimentation was not only unethical but also unnecessary:

> No matter what the American authorities believed those research papers contained, the objectives cannot possibly justify their actions. The research was in any case crude, backward, and barbaric. Any nation that had a monopoly on nuclear power certainly did not need this kind of research information—nor did we need to embarrass ourselves in such a despicable manner.[215]

And embarrass the USG this deal did. As Beigbeder argues, "the later discovery that the USA had secretly bargained with and granted immunity to the leaders of Unit 731 could only be taken as an affront to any human rights concern, besides making the USA a belated accomplice to a particularly odious war crime and crime against humanity."[216]

V. Conclusion

The Allies, including the USG, implemented the same three general transitional justice options—prosecution, amnesty, and lustration—for both Nazis and Japanese in the immediate aftermath of WWII. Several lessons emerge from this case study about the etiology of the IMTFE—one of the first and most significant, yet least studied, occurrences of transitional justice in history. Specifically, this chapter reveals that almost every major decision regarding the transitional justice method for addressing the principal Japanese suspected of committing atrocities during WWII was made primarily from a combination of political and pragmatic factors—as prudentialism would suggest. USG officials' norma-tive beliefs feature, sometimes inconsistently, as influences in very few of these decisions—cutting against legalism. The recent establishment of the IMT and the unfolding Cold War were ever-present factors driving U.S. foreign policy on this issue.

The USG, as the lead occupier of postwar Japan, had no choice but to "do something." The USG's initial pragmatic concern was thus the same as with the Nazis: the USG held in custody many of the principal Japanese and had to determine what to do with them. As with the Nazis, even keeping the Japanese imprisoned or letting them go would have been decisions to "do something"; the former would have constituted indefinite detention, and the latter would have represented implicit unconditional amnesty. Some USG officials, such as Hull, initially preferred summary execution for Japanese suspects. However, these USG officials later changed their minds or were overruled, and this transitional justice option does not seem to have been a popular or serious USG consideration with respect to Japanese. The recent establishment of the IMT prompted the USG to act similarly for comparable atrocities elsewhere in the world. Had the USG not acted consistently in the case of Japanese atrocities, it likely would have been vociferously criticized for being regionalist and racist.

Also consistent with their treatment of the Nazis, USG officials were conscious of the domestic political ramifications of their decisions. The American public demanded that Japanese be held accountable, especially after the Japanese gov-ernment's devastating sneak-attack on Pearl Harbor. USG officials, concerned about the developing threat of communism, sought to bolster American pres-ence and influence in Asia—a battleground for the approaching ideological clash. Establishing and leading a high-profile transitional justice institution provided a clear opportunity toward that end.

The decision to prosecute many of the chief Japanese also was driven by a com-bination of political and pragmatic concerns. The IMT precedent again served as an important political factor. As with the decision to "do something," the prece-dent of prosecuting atrocity perpetrators from Germany significantly influenced the decision to extend that precedent—independent of nationality, ethnicity, or location—to the Japanese case. Pragmatically, even if the USG prosecuted some of the Japanese, the USG still would have been able to pursue other options as well, such as amnesty and lustration, which were indeed instituted.

The USG's decision to support an *international* military tribunal stemmed from a combination of politics, pragmatics, and normative beliefs. Again, the IMT and the Cold War featured prominently. Pragmatically, the USG already had the IMT as a working model for a transitional justice system, which facili-tated a quick application to Japan with minimal structural changes, under the assumption that all those who supported the IMT design for Germany would probably do so for Japan. Path dependency thus underlays this transitional jus-tice decision.

At the same time, it is clear what pragmatic factor did *not* persuade the USG to support an international transitional justice option: burden-sharing. Given that the USG provided most of the staff and financial support for the IMTFE, involving other states in the process probably had little to do with the extent of the USG's resource contributions. Instead, the USG supported an international tribunal because it wished to maintain positive political relations with wartime allies, especially in light of its increasingly troubled affairs with the Soviet Union. Prosecution through a broadly multilateral institution also promoted the legitimacy of the transitional justice process, especially at a time when other states criticized the USG for its dominant occupation of Japan. USG officials held a normative belief that states involved militarily with Japan should also be involved in peace efforts, including transitional justice, further driving the USG to favor a multilateral transitional justice option.

Just as with the U.S. role in transitional justice for Germany, the U.S. role in transitional justice for Japan reveals the limitations of certain explanatory factors. Most significant, it is apparent that normative beliefs played only a partial and inconsistent role. Although many USG officials felt obliged to hold Japanese accountable for their heinous crimes, they chose not to when they believed certain Japanese—including Hirohito, more than fifty Class A war criminals, and over 3600 officials, scientists, and physicians involved in human experiments—were potentially useful. The large number of Japanese the USG helped escape justice or addressed through lustration demonstrates that the USG was not committed to a principled conception of justice through legal prosecution, even for those suspected of direct involvement in planning and perpetrating offenses against Americans. Notwithstanding the lofty rhetoric the USG employed in establishing the IMTFE, the emerging Cold War, which had served as one of the principal factors driving the USG to establish the IMTFE, simultaneously chilled the USG's enthusiasm for investigating and prosecuting some Japanese. USG officials envisioned greater benefit from an alliance with postwar Japan against the looming communist threat and to prevent the Soviet Union from obtaining advantages in weapons technology. Not until the Cold War thawed half a century later would the next ICT—the ICTY—be established.

The United States Role in Transitional Justice for Libya, Iraq, and the Former Yugoslavia

I. Background

During the Cold War, the international community and individual states took steps to formalize the process for holding alleged atrocity perpetrators accountable, yet ultimately failed to do so. Atrocities in the FRY peaked just as the Cold War ended, providing the means, motivation, and opportunity to establish the ICTY.

Other atrocities were also perpetrated around this time. On December 21, 1988, Pan Am flight 103 exploded over Lockerbie, Scotland. Two Libyans (also known as the "Lockerbie 2" or "pair") subsequently were accused of bombing the plane, the passengers of which were mostly American and British nationals.[1] Less than two years later, during its August 1990 invasion of Kuwait and subsequent occupation of the country through 1991, Iraq allegedly perpetrated atrocities against Kuwaitis. A U.S. Army report concluded that these atrocities were "widespread and systematic."[2] At approximately the same time, the Saddam administration perpetrated atrocities against Kurds in its own country. As this chapter discusses, the USG approach to addressing the 1988 bombing of Pan Am flight 103 and the 1990–1991 Iraqi offenses against Kuwaitis is intricately intertwined with USG policy on transitional justice for the FRY.

A. INTERNATIONAL IMPUNITY FOR ATROCITIES DURING THE COLD WAR

Immediately after the IMT delivered its judgment in 1946, the campaign to establish a permanent ICT (what would become the ICC) gained traction, albeit in fits and starts. In late-1946, an international congress, comprising the quadripartite Allied powers from WWII and eighteen other states, called for the establishment of a permanent ICT. The next year, the French judge from the IMT suggested that, in addition to creating a permanent ICT, the ICJ should feature a dedicated criminal chamber.[3] Following this proposal, in a resolution adopted on December 9, 1948 (approximately one month after the IMTFE delivered its judgment), the UNGA requested the recently established International Law Commission (ILC) to consider the possibility of establishing a permanent ICT, including through this very option of creating a specific criminal chamber of the ICJ.[4]

These and other calls for the establishment of a permanent ICT were stalled by the complications that the Cold War introduced. This period was characterized by a lack of international cooperation because of a diplomatic and military stalemate between the two antagonistic superpowers, the United States and the Soviet Union.[5] Their political impasse obstructed the UNSC's attempt to establish mechanisms, including ICTs, for addressing atrocities in states such as Cambodia, Haiti, and Chile.[6] These chilly relations were, according to Benjamin Ferencz, a former prosecutor at the NMT, "an excuse to put international criminal court proposals on ice."[7] When the Soviet Union collapsed in 1991, so too did this deadlock.

The creation of ICTs (permanent or otherwise) was inhibited by this American-Soviet tension as well as the nature of Cold War conflicts. One commentator surmised in 1991 that the USG had not conducted war crimes trials since the end of WWII "not for lack of war criminals, but because the unsuccessful conclusion of the Korean and Vietnam wars did not permit the U.S. to bring the offenders to trial."[8] Others also have suggested that China would have used its veto in the UNSC during the Cold War to block any progress on international efforts to investigate and prosecute atrocities.[9] In the absence of a permanent, global ICT, if the world wanted to establish a multilateral criminal tribunal to address atrocities after the end of the Cold War, only ad hoc solutions were possible.[10]

B. CODIFYING GENOCIDE

Although progress on creating post-IMT/IMTFE ICTs was frozen during—and in large part because of—the Cold War, advancements on relevant fronts still occurred. On the same day as and coupled with its request to the ILC to consider the possibility of establishing a permanent ICT, the UNGA passed resolution 260(III), which approved and proposed for signature and ratification or accession the Convention on the Prevention and Punishment of the Crime of Genocide (also known as the Genocide Convention).[11] Even though the Genocide Convention received sufficient state support to enter into force on January 12, 1951, it did so without the approval of the USG. Because of concerns over sovereignty constraints, the USG did not ratify the treaty until November 25, 1988, and, even then, limited its obligations through official reservations.[12]

The Genocide Convention embodies multiple objectives, one of which is to define the crime of genocide in international law.[13] The treaty enumerates the responsibility of signatories when genocide is afoot: that "they undertake to prevent and to punish" the crime.[14] Moreover, the Convention describes the two forums in which individuals charged with genocide or other enumerated crimes shall be tried: either "a competent tribunal of the State in the territory of which the act was committed" or "by such international penal tribunal as may have jurisdiction with respect to those Contracting Parties which shall have accepted its jurisdiction."[15]

The USG ratified the Genocide Convention in 1988, before atrocities were committed in the FRY. Thus, if these offenses rose to the level of genocide, then the USG was obligated not only to respond proactively but also to do so through supporting a prosecutorial mechanism. Yugoslavia, for its part, became a party to the Genocide Convention in 1948; USG officials highlighted this point when justifying international intervention as the Balkan atrocities unfolded and when seeking to bring perpetrators to justice.[16] By emphasizing the Convention, the USG implicitly called attention not only to the nature of the crimes enumerated in the treaty but also to the possible form the corresponding transitional justice solution could take, including an ICT.

C. DOMESTIC ACCOUNTABILITY FOR ATROCITIES DURING THE COLD WAR

Some states demonstrated an interest during the Cold War—sometimes insincerely or because of political calculations—in bringing to justice individuals they considered atrocity perpetrators, either unilaterally or through narrow multilateralism. Perhaps the most prominent example of USG efforts in this respect was the trial of Lieutenant William Calley in 1970–1971. Calley was accused and convicted by a U.S. military court of ordering numerous civilian murders in what became known as the 1968 "My Lai Massacre" during the Vietnam War. Despite being sentenced to life imprisonment, Calley ultimately served only three-and-a-half years under house arrest because many viewed him as a mere scapegoat for the massacre.[17]

Other countries besides the United States also attempted to bring alleged atrocity perpetrators to justice during or at the end of the Cold War. For example, the USG believes that Iraq sought in 1990 to establish a multilateral court in Algeria to prosecute Bush, Sr. for allegedly committing atrocities.[18]

D. THE BALKAN ATROCITIES

Atrocities that occurred in the Balkans during the early-1990s leading directly to the formation of the ICTY were only the latest in a string of regional horrors.[19] For many years, Josip Tito had managed to stave off the deep-seeded ethnic tensions within and among Yugoslavia's six republics (Bosnia and Herzegovina, Croatia, Macedonia, Montenegro, Serbia, and Slovenia) and two autonomous provinces (Kosovo and Vojvodina). When he died in 1980, the relative peace and order in the region disintegrated. Spewing Serb ethnonationalism, Slobodan Milošević became the Serbian Communist Party Chief in 1986. Milošević sought to unify Yugoslavia under Serbian rule, an effort resisted and resented by Milan Kučan and Franjo Tudjman, the presidents of Slovenia and Croatia, respectively. Both countries declared independence in 1991. Recalling the genocidal campaign Croatia's Ustashi, a fascist group, waged against Serbs (among others) in WWII, Milošević expressed concern for the approximately half a million Serbs residing in these newly independent states. His rhetoric turned into action when he began sending the Serb-dominated Yugoslav National Army (Jugoslavenska narodna armija, or JNA) into Slovenia and then Croatia.

The people of Bosnia and Herzegovina witnessed what was occurring else-where within Yugoslavia, and many desired to secede as well. Despite a boycott by Bosnian Serbs, on February 29 and March 1, 1992, the Muslims and Croats of Bosnia and Herzegovina voted for independence. As before, Serbs responded rhetorically and violently. After establishing an independent "Serbian Republic of Bosnia and Herzegovina" in April 1992, under the leadership of Radovan Karadžić and with the assistance of the JNA, Bosnian Serbs started attacking Croats and Muslims throughout Bosnia and Herzegovina.

Serbs pursued a widespread, organized campaign of murder, rape, torture, internment, deportation, and destruction and confiscation of property against Croats, Bosniaks, and Albanians, effectively an "ethnic cleansing."[20] Serb-run concentration camps resembled similar efforts by the Nazis to collect and ware-house their victims in life-threatening conditions. However, Serbs were by no means the only party that allegedly committed atrocities.[21]

E. THE INTERNATIONAL TRANSITIONAL JUSTICE RESPONSE TO THE BALKAN ATROCITIES

The international community's, including the USG's, transitional justice response to atrocities committed in the FRY fit within a larger effort to address conflict in the Balkans. A key feature of this response was the USG's initiatives, initially resisted by other UNSC members, to pursue a multilateral transitional justice solution.

1. General Chronology

In early- to mid-1992, the UN began its most meaningful efforts to address FRY turmoil, including through the use of force. On April 7, 1992, the UNSC author-ized the deployment of the UN Protection Force (UNPROFOR) in Bosnia and Herzegovina.[22] In addition, on July 13, 1992, the UNSC threatened suspected atrocity perpetrators with individual responsibility for violations of international humanitarian law.[23]

The Bush, Sr. administration prompted some of the international commu-nity's first attempts to address atrocities in the FRY. In August 1992, the USG called for the first emergency meeting of the UN Human Rights Commission, to discuss unconfirmed reports of death camps in the FRY.[24] At approximately the same time, the USG began drafting a UNSC resolution, eventually adopted on August 13, 1992,[25] requesting states and organizations to collect information about violations of humanitarian law within the FRY and to submit that information to the UNSC.[26] Later that month, as part of the West's more general threat to prosecute Serbs for war crimes trials in addition to other sanctions if the conflict did not end, Acting U.S. Secretary of State Lawrence Eagleburger warned that unless Serb leaders stopped the "ethnic cleansing" campaign, their people would face "a spectacularly bleak future."[27]

The international community, too, became increasingly involved with the situation in the FRY. In late-August 1992, the United Kingdom hosted an international conference on the FRY, at which participants approved a "Statement of Principles." This document compelled all persons to comply with international humanitarian law, noted personal responsibility for violations, included a pledge "to carry forward a study of the creation of an international criminal court," and announced that governments and international organizations should "take all possible legal action to bring to account those responsible for committing or ordering grave breaches of the Geneva Conventions."[28] Moreover, conference participants decided to merge the UN's and Europe's mediation efforts under the cochairmanship of former U.S. secretary of state Cyrus Vance, who was serving as UNSG Boutros Boutros-Ghali's special envoy to the FRY, and British Lord David Owen.[29] On August 28, 1992, the UN Commission on Human Rights's Special Rapporteur on the FRY issued a report recommending the establishment of a commission to evaluate and investigate particular violations of international humanitarian law in the FRY that might warrant prosecution.[30]

The following month, the international community expanded its attempt to address the situation in the FRY through force. On September 14, 1992, the UNSC enlarged UNPROFOR's "mandate and strength."[31] That same month, the USG continued its multilateral initiatives to collect data on and otherwise prepare to deal with the situation. On September 15, 1992, Bush, Sr. announced that the USG was collaborating with other states to create a UN Commission of Experts (CoE) that would prepare for the possible prosecution of alleged atrocity perpetrators from the FRY,[32] and submitted a resolution to the UNSC for that purpose.[33] The USG announced the next week that it had submitted to the UNSC its initial report concerning violations of international law in the FRY.[34] At the same time, the USG declared that it was collaborating with other states on a UN resolution to establish a commission of experts on the FRY.[35]

As the USG submitted these public announcements, some senior USG officials sought to raise awareness among their colleagues in the government about, and to prompt more meaningful action regarding the situation in, the FRY. On September 25, 1992, U.S. ambassador to the UN in Geneva Morris Abram testified about war crimes in the FRY on behalf of the U.S./DoS before the Commission on Security and Cooperation in Europe (CSCE).[36] The following month, Warren Zimmerman, the U.S. Ambassador to Yugoslavia from 1989 to 1992, testified before the same commission about the USG's efforts to address the situation in the FRY, stating: "Governments have a responsibility to ensure that each person's guilt is established in accordance with basic notions of decency and due process. This respect for law must be a central part of America's message to the world, as new democracies emerge around the globe."[37]

By the fall of 1992, the UNSC's commitment to document atrocities in the FRY became more concrete, starting with the creation of the first international institution dedicated to investigating such offenses. On October 6, 1992, the UNSC voted unanimously to request that the UNSG establish a CoE to provide the UNSG with conclusive information on international humanitarian law violations in the FRY, and also requested the UNSG to report to the UNSC on the CoE's conclusions when making any recommendations for next steps.[38] Edward Perkins, U.S. delegate to the UN, said the resolution "sen[t] a clear message that those responsible for the atrocities and gross violations, including violations involved in the process of 'ethnic cleansing' and other war crimes in former Yugoslavia, must be brought to justice."[39] The USG also stated that the CoE was "a first necessary step before moving ahead with prosecution, perhaps before an international tribunal."[40] The USG additionally warned against "show trials of absent defendants when the purpose of a trial is to reiterate the importance of respect for law."[41] The CoE was first proposed by the Bush, Sr. administration and modeled on the Allied War Crimes Commission, established in 1943 and responsible for collecting evidence used at the IMT and other Allied tribunals after WWII.[42] In late-October 1992, the UN War Crimes Commission, the formal name for the CoE, held its organizational meeting in New York.[43]

While the international community focused on atrocities committed in the FRY, more general efforts arose to address atrocities worldwide. On October 28, 1992, the UNGA's Sixth Committee (Legal) considered the ILC's report recommending the establishment of an international criminal court.[44] As discussed below, efforts in the early-1990s to establish what would become the ICC were stillborn, in part because of USG opposition.

The following month, UN bodies increased their focus on personal culpability for atrocities committed in the FRY. On November 16, 1992, the UNSC condemned "ethnic cleansing" in Bosnia and Herzegovina and warned "that those that commit or order the commission of such acts will be held individually responsible . . . ."[45] By the end of November, while the CoE considered exhuming a possible mass grave, one CoE member, legal scholar M. Cherif Bassiouni, indicated that the CoE eventually would recommend to the UNSC the possible creation of an ad hoc or permanent ICT with jurisdiction over atrocities in the FRY.[46] Bassiouni also stated that, because of the nature of the atrocities, their suspected perpetrators could be tried in virtually any country, under a claim of universal jurisdiction.[47]

The USG's public, unilateral efforts to seek individualized justice for atrocities in the FRY peaked in mid-December 1992. On December 16, 1992, Eagleburger, in what became known as the "naming names speech,"[48] announced at a meeting in Geneva a list of ten Serbs and Croats the USG believed should be prosecuted before an ICT.[49] His announcement, the first time the USG had publicly condemned specific FRY officials, included individuals such as Milošević, Karadžić, Ratko Mladić, and Zeljko Razjatovic (more popularly known as Arkan), and organizations such as Arkan's Tigers.[50] This list perfectly mirrored one that Eagleburger's subordinates within the U.S./DoS had provided him in a confidential memorandum two days earlier.[51]

In what had become a virtuous cycle of USG and UN action, on December 18, 1992, the UNSC demanded the immediate closure of all detention camps in Bosnia and Herzegovina. The same day, the UNGA adopted two measures to protect and promote human rights more generally: the Declaration on the Protection of All Persons from Enforced Disappearance[52] and the Declaration on the Rights of Persons Belonging to National or Ethnic, Religious and Linguistic Minorities.[53]

Bush, Sr. lost his re-election campaign to Clinton in November 1992, but the USG's efforts regarding transitional justice in the FRY continued unabated. The newly installed Clinton administration's first major action toward establishing an ICT for the FRY occurred on January 27, 1993, when U.S. Secretary of State Warren Christopher asked his senior advisers to prepare a report on the best method of trying suspected atrocity perpetrators in the FRY.[54] That same day, the USG sent the UN its fifth report documenting atrocities in the Balkans.[55] On February 9, 1993, U.S. ambassador to the UN Human Rights Commission Richard Schifter stated that "the horrors of Bosnia are surely among the greatest tragedies to befall humankind in the second half of the 20th Century."[56]

In February 1993, agencies that the UN created specifically to address the Balkans crisis submitted key reports that focused the international community's attention on the precise forms the transitional justice institution for the FRY could take. On February 9, 1993, CSCE rapporteurs issued a report that proposed the creation of an ICT for the FRY.[57] The same day, the UNSG sent a letter to the UNSC president,[58] which included the CoE's interim report (dated January 26, 1993) as well as the UNSG's review of the report and his own proposals. Finding that violations of international humanitarian law had been committed in the FRY, the report concluded with the following:

> 72. Jurisdiction for war crimes is governed by the universality principles and, hence, is vested in all States, where parties to the conflict or not.

Although the Genocide Convention emphasizes territorial jurisdiction, it also establishes the jurisdictional basis for an international tribunal. It is well recognized that the principle of universality can also apply to genocide as well as to other crimes against humanity.

73. States may choose to combine their jurisdiction under the universality principle and vest this combined jurisdiction in an international tribunal. The [IMT] may be said to have derived its jurisdiction from such a combination of national jurisdictions of the States parties to the London Agreement setting up that Tribunal.

74. The [CoE] was led to discuss the idea of the establishment of an ad hoc international tribunal. In its opinion, it would be for the [UNSC] or another competent organ of the United Nations to establish such a tribunal in relation to events in the territory of the former Yugoslavia. The [CoE] observes that such a decision would be consistent with the direction of its work.[59]

Through these statement, the CoE seemingly proposed at least five transitional justice options for handling atrocities in the FRY: (1) unilateral state prosecution through a claim of universal jurisdiction; (2) an ICT established through a treaty, perhaps outside the UN system; (3) an ICT established through executive agreement (such as the IMT or, though it was not explicitly mentioned, the IMTFE); (4) an ad hoc ICT established by the UNSC; and (5) an ad hoc ICT created by "another competent organ of the United Nations" (such as the UNGA, though it was not explicitly mentioned).

By mid-February 1993, the UNSC narrowed the spectrum of transitional justice institutions it would consider to address the Balkans crisis. On February 18, the UNSC unanimously approved a draft resolution calling for the UNSG to propose an ICT for the FRY with jurisdiction dating from June 25, 1991, when the FRY began disintegrating.[60] Four days later, the UNSC announced "that an international tribunal shall be established for the prosecution of persons responsible for serious violations of international humanitarian law committed in the territory of the former Yugoslavia since 1991," and requested the UNSG to submit a report, including proposals and options, to the UNSC on the matter, "taking into account suggestions put forward in this regard by Member States . . . ."[61] In an accompanying speech, Madeleine Albright, then the U.S. ambassador to the UN, declared:

There is an echo in this chamber today. The Nuremberg principles have been reaffirmed. We have preserved the long-neglected compact made by the community of civilized nations 48 years ago in San Francisco: to create the [UN] and enforce the Nuremberg principles. The lesson that we are all accountable to international law may have finally taken hold in our collective memory. This will be no victors' tribunal. The only victor that will prevail in this endeavor is the truth.[62]

In a letter dated April 5, 1993, the USG expressed its views and proposals to the UNSG regarding the establishment of an ICT for the FRY. In two annexes to the letter, the USG articulated general principles it held with respect to the creation of an ICT for the FRY[63] and proposed a draft charter for such a tribunal.[64] The USG explicitly described its reasoning for its preferred ICT structure under the draft charter. In particular, the letter explained why the USG believed that a tribunal for the FRY should be international. The USG argued that "the Tribunal should be established by the international community to enforce international standards," which included "substantive and procedural law that is internationally accepted."[65] These laws and principles included fairness; the perception of fairness; basic due process, such as independent and impartial trial and appellate courts and prosecutorial authority; and the observance of fundamental rights of defendants, such as the rights to counsel, cross-examination, and appeal.[66] The letter also described the USG's belief that a tribunal for the FRY should be established by the UNSC. The UNSC, the USG argued, had the authority under Chapter VII of the UN Charter and was the appropriate body to create such a tribunal, as "[t]he process should not be limited to a single regional group."[67]

The letter also explained why the USG favored the speediest creation of a tribunal for the FRY as possible. This premium on rapid action justified ICT creation through the UNSC instead of through a treaty, as the latter tends to follow a more lumbering process. Furthermore, establishing the tribunal through the UNSC had the added potential benefit of greater inclusivity. "[T]he process for establishing the Tribunal," the USG argued,

> should be designed to bring it into existence at an early date. The [UNSC] is in a position to do so in accordance with the procedure set forth in Resolution 808 (1993). The alternative of establishing a tribunal by treaty would, in our view, be much less effective and take much more time. This alternative would require a lengthy process of negotiation, conclusion and ratification; and it might lead to the absence of important States at the time the tribunal begins its work.[68]

The second annex, the draft charter, was a detailed proposal for the structure and operation of an ICT for the FRY.[69] The USG deliberately designed the charter to reflect four particular points: "the Tribunal should be international (e.g., not regional); it should be fair and be seen as fair; it should be established by the [UNSC]; and it should be available as a model if additional [ICTs] are established."[70] Importantly, the USG viewed the ICT for the FRY as a model for future ICTs, which the ICTY would indeed become just a year later in response to the Rwandan genocide.[71]

While the UN and the USG pushed ahead with their efforts to pursue transitional justice for the Balkans crisis, other actors were only plodding along. By April 23, 1993, the CoE had analyzed data provided by governments and NGOs but was only just beginning its own investigation.[72]

In May 1993, the UNSC finalized details on the ICTY and formally created the tribunal. On May 3, the UNSG sent its report, which contained a draft statute for the ICTY, to the UNSC.[73] USG officials were concerned about some of the draft statute's elements, such as the definition and scope of certain legal concepts (e.g., crimes against humanity, command responsibility, defense of superior orders), but ultimately decided not to object, given the USG's priority of establishing the ICTY as soon as possible to address the intensifying conflict in the FRY.[74] Instead, the USG announced an interpretative statement on the statute and persuaded other UNSC members to follow suit.[75]

Toward the end of the month, negotiations over a transitional justice institution for the FRY finally came to fruition. On May 22, the foreign ministers of France, Russia, Spain (then a rotating member of the UNSC), the United Kingdom, and the United States issued a statement declaring that they "support[ed] the rapid establishment of the War Crimes Tribunal, so that those guilty of atrocities may be brought to justice."[76] Three days later, the UNSC invoked the UN Charter's Chapter VII to officially establish an ad hoc ICT

> for the sole purpose of prosecuting persons responsible for serious violations of international humanitarian law committed in the territory of the former Yugoslavia between 1 January 1991 and a date to be determined by the Security Council upon the restoration of peace and to this end to adopt the Statute of the International Tribunal annexed to

the UNSG's May 5, 1993, reports, which this resolution explicitly approved.[77]

2. The Commission of Experts and the Tribunal

Internal USG documents reveal much about the USG's timing and rationale for supporting the creation of the CoE. On August 31, 1992, U.S./DoS officials sent two virtually identical confidential memorandums to Eagleburger recommending that he authorize the Department to support UNSC efforts to establish a war crimes commission on the FRY with a limited mandate.[78] The authors of these memoranda stated that "[a]ctive U.S. participation in this process" is important and "can bring the initiative into line with longstanding US positions."[79]

Specifically, these memos' authors argued that an ICT should not be established prematurely and that, once initiated, the tribunal should have limited temporal, subject-matter, and geographic jurisdictions. Regarding the timing of the creation of the ICT, the authors of both memos suggested that "appropriate defendants should be in custody before any such tribunal is created."[80] Regarding the form of the ICT, the authors proposed that "if an international court is established, it should be an *ad hoc* tribunal with jurisdiction limited to appropriate war crimes in the former Yugoslavia rather than a standing international criminal court."[81]

In addition, the authors indicated that early USG support for a war crimes commission could help avert undesirable outcomes proposed by other states and even other parts of the USG. The authors of one of the memos stated:

> Supporting a war crimes commission should also be helpful in Congress and in responding to a proposal that Germany and Denmark have told us they intend to make in the [UNGA] on the creation of an international tribunal to deal with the former Yugoslavia. As you know from the [August 1992] London [International] Conference [on the FRY], German Foreign Minister [Klaus] Kinkel is personally committed to the proposal to create an international criminal court and it is possible that the proposal will garner widespread support in the UNGA. The Senate voted recently to support the creation of an international tribunal, and we have been invited to testify at Congressional hearings on this issue later this month. Supporting a war crimes commission that could investigate war crimes and make recommendations to the [UNSC] should assist us in preventing the premature or unwarranted establishment of international tribunals.[82]

3. The U.S. Government's Multilateral Intentions and Frustrations

During his congressional confirmation hearing on January 13, 1993, to become the 63rd U.S. secretary of state, Christopher discussed atrocities in the FRY and Iraq, and whether and how to hold their perpetrators accountable. In particular, Christopher stated that the Clinton administration supported war crimes trials for both Iraqis suspected of committing atrocities in Kurdistan and alleged perpetrators of atrocities in the FRY.[83] Christopher suggested two venues for such trials: (1) before the ICJ, and (2) before a tribunal created in the United States.[84] Whichever method the USG pursued, Christopher pledged the USG's intentions to participate in a multilateral transitional justice process.[85]

However, the USG's early efforts did not garner much support among its allies, some of which resisted imposing stronger measures in the Balkans, even through a multilateral UN initiative. In an episode reminiscent of the etiology of the IMT, according to one observer, "[t]he British, in particular, have expressed reservations to the United States about the purpose and feasibility of moving toward war-crimes trials."[86] Instead of advocating for summary executions in this case (as the United Kingdom had done for Nazis), however, the British resisted prosecutions in the Balkans out of concern that such proceedings would endanger UN peacekeepers and the overall humanitarian effort.[87] Other members of the UNSC also opposed the initial USG lobbying to establish an ICT for the FRY. France, like the United Kingdom, believed a peace settlement merited a higher priority than prosecutions. China worried that creating an ICT for the FRY might establish a precedent that could backfire on them for their own alleged atrocities. The Russians, who shared similar concerns as China, resisted prosecuting their historic allies and Slavic brethren, the Serbs.[88]

The USG was particularly disappointed in the lack of support its efforts received from the CoE. Many commentators criticized the structure of the CoE as well as the performance and attitude of some of its members; the commission suffered from leadership problems and disruptive transitions early in its operation. The CoE Chairman, retired legal scholar Frits Kalshoven, "resigned midstream" to be replaced by Bassiouni, another CoE member.[89] Kalshoven certainly did not expect to assume the chairmanship, in part because he was unsure about whether he even supported trials for atrocity perpetrators in the FRY.[90] Moreover, he was not necessarily supportive of the ICTY or optimistic about its success, even after the UNSC provisionally approved its creation. He reportedly stated:

> There is no way a tribunal could work in the present atmosphere of anti-Serb propaganda, which is rampant all over the world . . . . It will never be possible to have an objective procedure . . . . And by the way, a tribunal can take place only at the end of the conflict,

which Kalshoven then predicted might not occur for more than a decade.[91]

Five months after its establishment, journalist and author Roy Gutman described the CoE as "bogged down in confusion" and having "achieved next to nothing."[92] Gutman reported that USG officials were "livid" that the CoE had accomplished so little since its establishment: "It hasn't held a hearing or sent a mission into Bosnia, or even requested the news media to provide copies of their stories and videotapes."[93] In particular, Gutman referenced Abram's assertions that the CoE had been delinquent in its duties:

> They meet once in a while . . . . They don't have a staff to amount to anything. They don't have resources, people right now interviewing witnesses, who can tell you about who the camp guards were . . . . If this is serious you've got to have a large number of people involved. And moreover, you've got to start dealing with the problem before the trail gets cold.[94]

Gutman suggested that descriptions of atrocities in the CoE's interim report were lacking, because the body "did not say where they had occurred or where the principal responsibility might lie."[95]

4. A Permanent or Ad Hoc International Criminal Tribunal

The CoE's potential impact on the creation of a permanent ICT in the early 1990s rankled the USG and some of its allies. As Melinda Kimble, Deputy U.S. Assistant Secretary of State for International Organization Affairs, and U.S./DoS Legal Adviser Edwin Williamson discussed in a confidential memorandum dated September 25, 1992: "Belgium expressed concern that the proposed resolution [establishing the CoE] would conflict with the work of the UN Sixth

Committee on the creation of an international criminal court ...."[96] Several states, including from the European Community, advocated in mid-September 1992 for a permanent ICT that would have jurisdiction over atrocities allegedly committed in the FRY.[97]

In the same confidential U.S./DoS memorandum, Kimble and Williamson stated three reasons they believed "the question of bringing Yugoslavia war criminals to justice and the Sixth Committee efforts to create a broader, more permanent, international criminal court should be kept on two different tracks."[98] First, Kimble and Williamson argued that a non-international judicial process would be more appropriate: "we do not believe that Yugoslavia war criminals should necessarily be prosecuted in an international tribunal, rather than a domestic or regional tribunal."[99] Second, Kimble and Williamson were concerned about the implications an ICT for the FRY might have for the transitional justice forum used to address those suspected of bombing Pan Am flight 103: "we want to avoid the suggestion that the Libyans responsible for the bombing of Pan Am 103 could be tried in an international court rather than returned to the U.S. or U.K. for trial pursuant to [UNSC] Resolution 748."[100] Third, Kimble and Williamson did not want to hasten the process of creating a permanent ICT, especially as the USG believed a permanent ICT might pose greater threats to USG interests than an ad hoc one.[101] In fact, Kimble and Williamson were so concerned about the form and function of a permanent ICT that they contended: "the current [UNGA] resolution should contain no language endorsing the creation of an international criminal court."[102] Further, the U.S./DoS sought "to persuade other countries to adopt our position ...."[103]

An internal U.S./DoS memorandum indicates that, as of January 12, 1993, U.S./DoS officials retained concerns about a permanent ICT, but that they did not oppose its creation in principle at a later date.[104] By the time this memorandum was circulated, the USG essentially considered the emergence of a permanent ICT with jurisdiction over atrocities committed in the FRY to be a moot issue. The memo argued: "The UN is not expected to be in a position to establish such a [permanent ICT] based on the ILC's work any time soon. Thus, it would not be of use with regard to suspected Yugoslav or Iraqi war criminals or the two Libyans indicted for the bombing of Pan Am 103."[105]

II. Transitional Justice Options Seriously Considered and Actually Implemented for Alleged Balkan Atrocity Perpetrators

As with the IMT and the IMTFE after WWII, the ICTY was one of only several transitional justice options seriously considered and actually implemented for addressing individuals suspected of committing atrocities in the Balkans. As discussed in this Part, the USG also may have offered conditional amnesty to—and certainly did, at least temporarily, implicitly extend unconditional amnesty to—individuals not only suspected but also indicted by the ICTY for perpetrating some of the worst atrocities in the Balkans. As a result, the USG violated political and legal obligations it voluntarily assumed less than a decade earlier under the Genocide Convention to punish genocide perpetrators, and specifically to do so through a prosecutorial mechanism. Figure 6.1 shows the general transitional justice options the USG supported for addressing alleged Balkan atrocity perpetrators, whereas Figure 6.2 displays the specific prosecutorial transitional justice options the USG supported in this case.

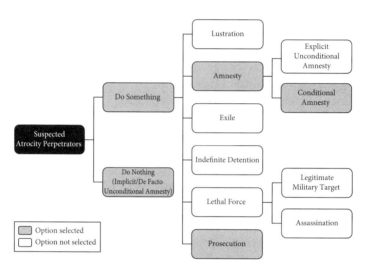

FIGURE 6.1 *U.S. Government Transitional Justice Options Tree for Suspected* Balkan *Atrocity Perpetrators—General.*

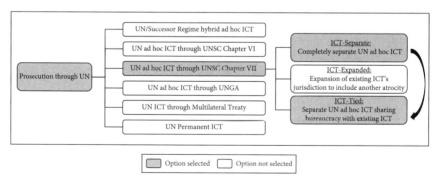

FIGURE 6.2 *U.S. Government Transitional Justice Options Tree for Suspected* Balkan *Atrocity Perpetrators—Prosecution.*

A. TRANSITIONAL JUSTICE OPTIONS SERIOUSLY CONSIDERED

1. Transitional Justice Options the UN Seriously Considered

By signing the Genocide Convention, members of the international community—including the United States—committed themselves not only to addressing suspected genocide perpetrators punitively, but also to adopting one of two prosecutorial mechanisms. Specifically, trials had to occur either domestically (in the state where atrocities were perpetrated) or internationally (through an ICT). Hence, signatory states were unsurprisingly predisposed to these particular transitional justice options, at least for instances of genocide, by the time the Balkan atrocities were perpetrated. These states were obligated by treaty not to implement other transitional justice options—such as inaction, amnesty, exile, lustration, indefinite detention, or lethal force—for suspected genocide perpetrators from the FRY.

Almost immediately after atrocities in the FRY came to light, the international community, operating through the UN, declared that it would seek to prosecute the culprits. Echoing the Genocide Convention's provisions, this rhetoric apparently ruled out inaction and other non-prosecutorial mechanisms as serious options. The only remaining question concerned the type of prosecution to implement.

In addition to the two basic options the Genocide Convention required, the international community also considered whether an ICT, if chosen, would be ad hoc or permanent; under the auspices of or outside the UN; and, if under the UN aegis, via the UNSC or another UN organ, such as the UNGA.

2. Transitional Justice Options the U.S. Government Seriously Considered

Like other members of the international community, the USG almost immediately sought to prosecute individuals suspected of perpetrating atrocities in the Balkans. However, unlike other states, such as Belgium and Germany, the USG was less flexible regarding the ultimate form that prosecution could take. The USG appears only to have seriously considered prosecutions through an ICT, and preferred that the ICT be ad hoc and established through the UNSC.

Also, as discussed in the next section, in opposition to the preferences of other members of the international community, the USG seriously considered a particular non-prosecutorial transitional justice option for addressing some Balkan atrocity perpetrators: amnesty. Specifically, compelling evidence suggests that the USG offered Karadžić conditional amnesty, and did offer Karadžić, Milošević, Mladić, and other suspected (and even indicted) atrocity perpetrators at least temporary unconditional amnesty. Unlike its treatment of suspected atrocity perpetrators during WWII, the USG apparently did not seriously consider either lethal force or lustration as a means of addressing Balkan atrocity perpetrators.

1. Conditional Amnesty

On July 25, 1995, the ICTY indicted Karadžić, charging him with atrocities committed at Srebrenica and in other parts of the Balkans. After successfully evading capture for many years, he was finally arrested on July 21, 2008, and transferred to the ICTY nine days later.[106]

Karadžić, often referred to as the "Butcher of Bosnia,"[107] claims that, in July 1996 (between his indictment and arrest), USG officials, particularly former U.S. ambassador Richard Holbrooke, promised him that the ICTY would drop its case if he left politics. Karadžić's claim is supported by, among others, three senior U.S./DoS officials, two of whom agree that "Holbrooke did the right thing and got the job done." As a result of Holbrooke's alleged promise, Karadžić asserted (because he voluntarily resigned from office and withdrew from public life) that he is entitled to immunity before the ICTY. The ICTY ruled this assertion to be inaccurate even if Holbrooke had made the deal because Karadžić's alleged offenses were so egregious that he could not be immunized. Holbrooke denied ever having offered Karadžić this deal.[108] Scheffer supports Holbrooke's account of the matter.[109]

2. Implicit Unconditional Amnesty

The USG resisted sending troops into the Balkans to arrest suspected atrocity perpetrators, even after many of those suspects were indicted by the ICTY. In a policy described by Carl Bildt, the former prime minister of Sweden who served as the civilian representative under the Dayton peace accords on Bosnia, as "benign neglect,"[110] the USG refused to command its forces to apprehend these individuals, despite having as many as 60,000 of its own and NATO troops already deployed in the Balkans.[111] During this time, Karadžić, Milošević, Mladić, and other suspected atrocity perpetrators remained in office or in hiding.[112]

USG officials insisted that prevailing orders required that if any of their troops "encounter people who they know to be indicted war criminals they are to detain them for transfer to civilian authority so they may be arrested and then turned over to The Hague for prosecution."[113] Some observers argued that this particular mandate prevented the USG and its allies from more aggressively pursuing indicted war criminals.[114] Others note that the passive arrest policy was rooted in fear of provoking violence among the local population, especially toward American and other NATO peacekeepers themselves.[115] Consequently, when NATO (including U.S. troops) did not confront an indicted war criminal, which was most of the time, those individuals remained free. Similarly, NATO left other indicted war criminals, such as Milošević, who held high office, to carry out their business.

III. Explaining the United States Role in Transitional Justice for the Former Yugoslavia

This Part first considers USG decision-making at each of the most critical decision points leading to the establishment of the ICTY and then identifies and resolves certain puzzles in that decision-making process.

A. DECISION POINTS

In the course of endorsing what would become the ICTY, the USG backed general and specific transitional justice options. This section discusses the USG's rationale for each of those decisions, namely (1) to support action, (2) to support punitive action, (3) to support prosecution, (4) to support multilateral prosecution, and (5) to support multilateral prosecution organized by the UNSC.

1. U.S. Government Support for Action

The USG claimed its motivation to "do something" in response to the deteriorating situation in the FRY was because of U.S. officials' outrage over the violence. For example, as part of its announcement supporting the establishment of a war crimes commission through the UN, the USG stated: "We are appalled by the crimes alleged in [the FRY]."[116] As Michael Matheson, then the Principal Deputy Legal Advisor at the U.S./DoS, also argues: "One motivation for wanting to do something about the Balkan atrocities was of course the general moral revulsion against these crimes, which I think was the main factor for everyone I dealt with."[117] John Shattuck, then the Assistant Secretary of State for Democracy, Human Rights, and Labor, concurs, stating that USG officials were "appalled" at atrocities in the FRY.[118]

But there were other, possibly more important factors that drove USG involvement. Specifically, the international community, including the USG, identified a political opportunity. The outrage the USG expressed had not been sufficient to prompt an earlier, more robust American intervention in the FRY. Consequently, some scholars theorize that the effort by the USG and others to support some transitional justice mechanism for the FRY served to compensate for the muddied and highly criticized approach adopted during the crisis. As Bass argues, "the establishment of the [ICTY] was an act of tokenism by the world community, which was largely unwilling to intervene in [the FRY] but did not mind creating an institution that would give the *appearance* of moral concern. The world would prosecute the crimes that it would not prevent."[119] Stephen Walker, the U.S./DoS's Croatia Desk Officer in 1993, agrees, arguing:

> Public/media pressure created the need to appear to do something, but policy makers wanted to avoid committing US troops or political capital. ICTY

was the ideal substitute for real action . . . . The Clinton Administration was desperate to create a Potemkin Village policy—look like they were doing something without actually doing anything to stop the genocide.[120]

Walker resigned from the USG on August 24, 1993, stating that he did so in protest over the Clinton administration's policy toward the FRY. Walker viewed that policy as a weak response to the atrocities, one that legitimized aggression and genocide.[121]

For certain USG officials, this political opportunity may have been particularly salient. Bush, Sr. may have viewed greater involvement in transitional justice issues in the FRY as a strong response to opponent Clinton's criticism during the 1992 presidential campaign. During that election season, Clinton repeatedly called for a more effective and aggressive USG response, including military intervention if necessary, to the Balkan atrocities.[122] Bush, Sr.'s decision to support the creation of an ICT for the FRY thus may have partially been an attempt to head off criticism of his foreign policy decision-making while seeking re-election, especially after his historically high public approval rating plummeted when he reneged on his 1988 presidential campaign pledge of "no new taxes." Likewise, after entering office himself, Clinton pursued an active Balkans policy reportedly because he felt obligated to carry out his campaign "promise to address human rights issues" in the FRY.[123]

Some individuals who served in the USG at the time, however, reject the explanation that the USG supported the creation of an ICT for the FRY to substitute for military intervention. Scheffer, for example, who then served as Senior Adviser and Counsel to Albright, responds directly to Bass's assertion of tokenism by arguing:

> discussions and decisions regarding military and other enforcement options . . . were not propelled by the excuse that establishment of the criminal tribunal covered our backside. The failure to act militarily resulted from policies and circumstances that coexisted with the [ICTY] but were not driven by its presence in The Hague.[124]

Regardless of the political opportunity, the USG certainly believed that involvement in the FRY represented a pragmatic one. The USG consciously sought to seize the occasion of the Balkans crisis to combat the creation of transitional justice mechanisms the USG considered problematic. Foremost in the minds of USG officials was a potentially flawed transitional justice institution stemming from the 1990–1991 Persian Gulf War. To counteract this development, establishing a transitional justice institution for the FRY that would be unbiased and followed the rule of law was a high priority. According to U.S./DoS talking points,

> Saddam Hussein attempted to convene a multilateral forum in Algeria in December 1990, to try President Bush for war crimes, inter alia. Such

perversions of the concept reiterate the importance of establishing a responsible procedure [for the FRY] in which allegations will be investigated impartially and, if a tribunal is established, due process is observed.[125]

2. U.S. Government Support for Punitive Action

As with the decision to "do something," the USG's choice to punish the suspected perpetrators of the Balkan atrocities resulted from an understanding of its legal obligations, reinforced by a combination of political and pragmatic factors. First, the USG believed—or at least claimed to believe—that it had a duty to punish violators of international law. As part of the USG's announcement that it would support the establishment of a war crimes commission through the UN, the USG stated: "Those who violate the Nuremberg principles, which are reflected in international humanitarian law, must be punished."[126]

The USG vociferously opposed various alternative methods for addressing suspected perpetrators of the Balkan atrocities. When confronted with the prospect of defending its support for prosecution over amnesty, for example, the U.S./DoS prepared talking points that emphasized normative beliefs and pragmatic reasons for opposing the latter transitional justice option. The U.S./DoS argued that amnesty was foreclosed out of an obligation to punish violators of international law, especially for the case of the FRY:

> We believe that persons responsible for serious human rights abuses should be punished. This is particularly true of those people whom states have positive international legal obligations to prosecute or extradite, including those who are responsible for: grave braches of the Geneva Conventions; acts of genocide; violations of the Torture Convention; crimes against internationally protected persons; and crimes against citizens of other states.[127]

The U.S./DoS also argued that the ongoing peace process would not necessitate amnesty, and that prosecution was indeed a distinct enterprise:

> Even if the parties to the conflict agreed to an amnesty among themselves, this would not bind other states. We believe that the peace talks are not actively considering the possibility of an amnesty. In fact, the leaders of the talks have asked that the [ICTY] proceed on a track separate from the peace talks.[128]

Finally, the USG, through prepared talking points, doubted the effectiveness of amnesty in this case. The script expressed "skepticism about an amnesty's contribution to peace in that region" and stated that "[o]ur best chance to break the cycle of vengeance is to make the people responsible for crimes individually accountable before a court that scrupulously observes due process."[129]

A little less than a year after the ICTY's establishment, Albright offered a further reason to preclude amnesty: to combat apathy over enforcing international law. In a speech on April 12, 1994, at the U.S. Holocaust Memorial Museum, Albright declared: "We all have a stake in the success of this Tribunal .... We oppose amnesty for the architects of ethnic cleansing .... And there is no more appropriate place than here to sound a clarion call against the indifference and towards the harder choice of dedication to the rule of law."[130]

3. U.S. Government Support for Prosecution

Of the punitive options available, the USG supported prosecution, again for a combination of reasons. For one, the USG's repetitive invocation of "Nuremberg" suggests that the USG believed that prosecution was the most appropriate way of addressing alleged perpetrators of Balkan atrocities. Moreover, the USG, as a signatory to the Genocide Convention, was legally obligated to prosecute at least those individuals suspected of perpetrating genocide.

Second, the USG sought to deter regional atrocities. In response to a possible question about whether investigating and prosecuting war crimes was essential to deterring violence elsewhere in the Balkans, the USG's talking point stated belief "that the principle of deterrence is very important. It should be brought into operation in this tragic situation."[131] The USG reiterated this argument in other documents concerning an ICT for the FRY,[132] and Walker recalls this rationale in retrospect.[133] So, too, does Scheffer.[134]

The USG also sought to delegitimize suspects through their indictment for atrocities. The USG argued that merely issuing warrants for particular suspects could dramatically undermine their authority, regardless of whether they were ever apprehended. As the USG stated, "the international community will not accept as legitimate leaders of the [FRY] any persons sought by the [ICTY]."[135] Shattuck agrees, recalling that he and his colleagues favored prosecution in order to turn "indicted war criminals into international pariahs."[136]

4. U.S. Government Support for Multilateral Prosecution

The USG favored multilateral prosecutions for reasons that turned on politics, pragmatics, and normative beliefs. First, the USG argued that prosecution through an ICT would be diplomatically beneficial, by promoting a durable end to conflict. In response to a possible question about whether investigating and prosecuting war crimes would help the opposing sides establish long-term harmony, the U.S./DoS's talking point was that "[a] multilateral approach to war crimes will help set the foundations for a last[ing] peace. It will show that justice, and not violent retribution, is an available response."[137] As part of that lasting peace, the USG stressed that an ICT could facilitate reconciliation among the warring factions: "The [ICTY] can also promote reconciliation in the [FRY], by holding individuals—rather than ethnic groups—responsible for atrocities. Retribution through due process of law can, we hope, break the cycle of vengeance many have noted in the [FRY]."[138]

Path dependence was a prominent pragmatic factor in determining the USG's preferred ICT form for the FRY. The USG noted that the UNSC already was addressing the situation and so should continue doing so. In response to a possible question about why the USG did not prosecute alleged atrocity perpetrators from the FRY in the USG's own courts, the U.S./DoS explained that "[t]he [UNSC] has taken the initiative in addressing war crimes in [the FRY]. It should decide whether persons accused of war crimes are to be prosecuted and, together with the nations in which war crimes have occurred, in what tribunals."[139] Path dependence also factored into the USG's preference for a multilateral transitional justice option because multilateral efforts had successfully uncovered evidence of war crimes. The U.S./DoS therefore reasoned that "[i]nformation concerning war crimes will be gathered and developed by the [UNSC], through the [CoE] we advocate. Unilateral action on the basis of internationally-held information may prove difficult and would not send an appropriate signal."[140]

The USG cited its own possible lack of jurisdiction as an additional pragmatic factor favoring a multilateral approach to prosecution, despite Bassiouni's and the CoE's claims about invoking universal jurisdiction for these offenses. In explaining why the United States likely could not prosecute alleged atrocity perpetrators from the FRY in its own courts, the USG claimed that

> It is clear that we have jurisdiction to prosecute enemy prisoners of war (EPWs) under the Uniform Code of Military Justice [(UCMJ)], which would provide the basis for conducting prosecutions of persons accused of war crimes. Persons accused of war crimes but who are not EPWs—that is, who are not captured by our military in hostilities or, after being captured by others in combat, are transferred to our government in accordance with the Geneva Convention—might not fall within the UCMJ.[141]

The USG reiterated this point a few months later when it stated in a classified memorandum that "[i]t is unlikely that U.S. courts would have jurisdiction under current domestic law to try persons who committed war crimes in . . . the [FRY]."[142] More important, even if the USG *had* jurisdiction, it would not necessarily have sought to exercise that power. Walker recalls that the USG favored an ICT because "the US did not want to take responsibility." [143]

Indeed, USG officials did not believe that the FRY itself should or even could exercise jurisdiction over alleged atrocity perpetrators. Walker asserted that "[t]here were no local courts that were viable in the region . . . ."[144] Shattuck agrees, recalling: "Because national institutions of justice in the [FRY] were increasingly affected by the war, the only possible instrument of justice that might be used to prosecute war criminals had to be international."[145]

Yet another pragmatic factor the USG cited in supporting multilateral prosecution was the effect this broad-based effort would have on both specific and general deterrence of potential atrocity perpetrators. In response to a question about whether "the effort and expense are worth" an ICT for the FRY, the U.S./DoS's prepared response was: "The international tribunal will deter violations . . . . Deterrence can only grow as the prospect of prosecution grows more realistic, as it will over the coming months."[146] Pointing to the CoE's deterrent effect just a few months after it was established bolstered the U.S./DoS's faith in the deterrent effect of an ICT for the FRY. As the U.S./DoS's talking points observed: "after the [UNSC] established a [CoE] to investigate violations of international humanitarian law in the [FRY][,] some detention facilities were made accessible to relief workers and some combatants expressed concern over their exposure to prosecution."[147] The USG also touted the ability of an ICT for the FRY to promote general deterrence: "we must not forget that this Tribunal may send a message to other regions where ethnic fighting has begun. We should make it clear that the international community will insist upon respect for international humanitarian law."[148]

5. U.S. Government Support for Multilateral Prosecution Organized by the UN Security Council

Explaining the exact forum in which the USG would support multilateral prosecutions of suspected Balkan atrocity perpetrators is a function of the USG's pragmatism about the UNSC's unique role and influence in international relations and international law. The UNSC was a natural venue for administering transitional justice for the FRY, in part because of the path dependence arising from the fact that it was already addressing atrocities in the region, but also because of its Chapter VII powers, which dictate that UN members "shall join in affording mutual assistance in carrying out the measures decided upon by the [UNSC]."[149] An internal U.S./DoS memorandum from January 12, 1993, indicates that the U.S./DoS preferred that, if an ICT were created, that "it be established by the [UNSC]" as the UNSC was "already seized of this matter and . . . has the authority to compel Member States to cooperate in prosecutions before such a tribunal."[150] The USG also publicly acknowledged the UNSC's ability to require states to comply with the UNSC's orders. The USG championed the UNSC on this dimension by stressing difficulties in voluntary, unilateral apprehension of suspects.[151] Scheffer adds that haste in addressing the ongoing atrocities in the FRY also factored into this decision: "time was not on the side of a multiyear endeavor to create a war crimes tribunal for the Balkans along the conventional path [of a treaty.]"[152]

Independent experts recognized that, as a pragmatic matter, the UNSC possessed the proper authority to create and staff an ICT. Jerome Shestack, chairman of the International League for Human Rights, noted: "The [UNSC] has the power under the U.N. Charter to establish a tribunal, appoint the judges[,] and designate the procedures for indictment and trial."[153] Combined with the relative speed with which the UNSC could create an ICT, especially compared to more lumbering processes (e.g., negotiating and ratifying a treaty), using the UNSC as the authorizing body was almost universally acknowledged and desired. As Ferencz observes: "Almost all States recognized that creation of the [ICTY] by [UNSC] resolution pursuant to Chapter VII of the Charter had distinct advantages: it was expeditious, it could be effective immediately, and it was legally binding on all States."[154]

No doubt the USG also had a particular political interest in favoring the establishment of the ICTY through the UNSC. The USG holds a privileged permanent seat on the UNSC and corresponding veto over resolutions with which it disagrees. Some USG officials from the time recall that the USG was conscious not only of limiting the scope of the ICTY but also of the precedent it was setting in the creation of ICTs. These officials believed that if the UNSC served as the ICT's locus, the USG could assert control over the tribunal. Walker, for example, argues that the USG favored the UNSC forum "to have the US veto available to limit the mandate of the tribunal and any future courts."[155] Shattuck agrees, recalling that "[t]he U.S. regarded the [UNSC] as the only effective governing body of the U.N., which would also preserve U.S. sovereign prerogatives through the veto process."[156]

B. PUZZLES

1. Defendants in Custody

In the course of negotiations leading to the establishment of the ICTY, some USG officials contended that it would be premature to create an ICT for the FRY before apprehending suspects. For example, the USG invoked the Nuremberg precedent as a rationale for establishing the CoE, which enabled war crimes investigators first to collect evidence, followed by "a tribunal [that] was convened *only after* defendants could be brought into custody . . . ."[157] Senior USG officials also argued internally that an ICT for the FRY should not be established unless and until "appropriate defendants" were in custody.[158]

Nevertheless, the ICTY's formation predated the capture of some relevant suspects, including many of the allegedly most egregious offenders. The ICTY indicted both Karadžić and Mladić in 1995, but Karadžić was not caught until 2008, and Mladić was not arrested until 2011. The ICTY indicted Milošević in 1999 but he was not apprehended until 2001.[159] Indeed, only relatively "small fish" were in custody early on, and even by 1996—three years *after* the ICTY was established—fifty-six of the more serious indictees were still fugitives.[160] Why, then, did the USG continue supporting the establishment of the ICTY in 1993 despite the fact that some USG officials implied that they would not?

One explanation for this seeming inconsistency is that USG officials working toward the establishment of the ICTY did not universally hold the view that the tribunal should not be created until potential defendants were caught. Matheson, for example, denies recalling this view, and emphasizes that he did not share the sentiment in any event.[161]

Another, stronger explanation is that, in the face of difficulty apprehending "big fish," the USG's priorities for the ICTY fluctuated over time. According to Michael Scharf, legal scholar and former U.S./DoS Attorney-Adviser for UN Affairs, USG officials "never really thought they'd get Milošević, Karadžić, or Mladić . . . ."[162] Instead, some USG officials settled for the more general significance of creating the ICTY. As Shattuck argued: "Justice doesn't have to ultimately mean putting people behind bars . . . . I would not measure [the] [ICTY] in terms of how many people go to jail, or top-level people, because the number is going to be very low. Success is a commitment to establish principles of accountability, getting out the truth."[163] From the standpoint of 1993, that only some suspects would likely be tried was therefore not necessarily a reason to oppose the creation of an ICT for the FRY. And the fact that many of the "big fish" were eventually apprehended and prosecuted by the ICTY rewarded ICTY advocates' early optimism in the tribunal's ultimate reach.

2. Near-Contemporaneous Potential Transitional Justice Demands

While atrocities in the Balkans raged and the USG considered how to respond, crises erupted elsewhere in the world that presented the USG with other compelling transitional justice problems. In particular, the U.S./DoS remained conscious of how supporting a war crimes commission for the FRY would implicate situations concerning Libya and Iraq. Ultimately, though, the USG compartmentalized the conflicts and prioritized the FRY; the U.S./DoS argued in a confidential memorandum: "We believe the situations [concerning Libya and Iraq] can be distinguished [from the FRY] and the political imperative with regard to the situation in Yugoslavia outweighs these concerns."[164] This section considers why the USG did not lobby for addressing Libyan and Iraqi cases in an international forum (i.e., an ICT) under the same standards from which the USG advocated for the FRY.

A. LIBYA

Why did the USG rule out the use of an ICT to address the bombing of Pan Am flight 103, yet seek to prosecute alleged atrocity perpetrators from the FRY through that option at approximately the same time?

The U.S./DoS believed that supporting a war crimes commission on the FRY would elicit pressure from Libya and its sympathizers to do so for the Pan Am tragedy. As a confidential U.S./DoS memorandum on August 31, 1992, argued:

> [f]ollowing the efforts by the United States to obtain passage of [UNSC] Resolution 748 [(invoking the UN Charter's Chapter VII authority to compel Libya to cooperate with the investigation of the alleged terrorist attack and to impose sanctions on Libya until it complied[165])], we have been

fending off repeated proposals by Libya and its [Non-Aligned Movement] supporters to resolve the Pan Am 103 problem by referring the matter to an international tribunal.[166]

The same memorandum stressed the origin of the lobbying and its potential outcome: "There may be pressures from Arab countries to find an international forum for the Lockerbie pair; this could be an undesirable diversion from our preferred course of action."[167] That preferred course of action, according to a different confidential U.S./DoS memorandum, was to have the Lockerbie pair "extradited to the United States or United Kingdom as required by [UNSC] Resolution 748."[168] It was this plan, already established with the imprimatur of the UNSC, which ultimately led the U.S./DoS to conclude that the USG could persuasively make the case that the FRY and Libya could be treated distinctly. In making this argument, USG officials stressed differences between Libya and Iraq. According to a confidential U.S./DoS memorandum, "the Libyan case is more distinguishable [from the Iraqi one] since the [UNSC] has already laid out a clear course of action to be followed."[169]

A set of U.S./DoS talking points addressed the potential question of why the USG did not favor the creation of an ICT to prosecute the suspected terrorist attackers of Pan Am flight 103. The talking points first stressed that "[o]ur position consistently is that defendants should be tried before appropriate tribunals, with due process, whether those tribunals are national or international."[170] The talking points then went on to state that "[UNSC] Resolution [731[171]] called upon Libya to surrender the suspects. This reflects a decision by the international community that national tribunals are appropriate for those defendants."[172] Matheson agrees, recalling: "There was no need for an international tribunal in the PA 103 case—U.S. and British courts had jurisdiction, had issued indictments, and were perfectly proper and normal places for prosecution."[173] The phrasing of the talking points as well as Matheson's statement leave open the possibility that ICTs could be appropriate for other suspects, such as in the case of the FRY. As a result, the phraseology suggests that USG officials did not possess a normative belief favoring international over domestic tribunals, but that political and pragmatic issues dictated the USG's preference in this particular context.

Scharf argues even further that normative beliefs (in, for example, the rule of law) had little to do with the USG's policy on this matter. Claiming that the USG used the bombing of Pan Am flight 103 as an opportunity to impose economic sanctions on Libya through the UNSC in order to "isolate Libya and strangle it economically," Scharf contends that "[t]here really wasn't much interest in a justice mechanism" within the USG.[174]

Scharf offers an additional reason the USG supported the creation of an ICT to address the FRY but not the bombing of Pan Am flight 103. He points out that, during the late-1980s and early-1990s, the USG considered a terrorist plane attack distinct from atrocities allegedly committed in the FRY, thereby requiring an alternative response. He explains:

> in Bosnia you had basically international crimes. You had grave breaches of the Geneva Conventions, crimes against humanity, genocide. What is the bombing of Pan Am flight 103? At the time, it was just a regular domestic criminal matter. Yes, over 300 people died, but it wasn't seen as invoking international law.[175]

Shattuck agrees, arguing that, as compared to the bombing of Pan Am flight 103, the "scale of atrocities [were] much larger in [the] Balkans," thus necessitating a different approach.[176] From the perspective of the USG at the time, then, the nature and number of casualties in the Pan Am flight 103 and FRY contexts merited different categorizations and, thus, responses. Now, however, especially since the attacks on September 11, 2001, the USG as well as many other members of the international community increasingly consider terrorism to qualify as an international crime even if the number of victims involved is far less than in a situation like the FRY.[177]

B. IRAQ

In October 1990, as the Gulf War unfolded, Bush, Sr. and others in his administration openly discussed the idea of trying Iraqi leaders in a war crimes tribunal and publicly threatened Saddam in particular with prosecution in such a forum.[178] Not only would a trial hold Iraqi leaders accountable for alleged atrocities, but Bush, Sr. also may have issued the prosecution warning for purely political and pragmatic reasons. First, some commentators have suggested that the USG may have pursued prosecution as a preemptive self-defense against Iraqi efforts to embarrass the Bush, Sr. administration. Because the administration knew of "plans announced by the Iraqi regime to conduct a show trial of Mr. Bush for his campaign against Iraq," expediency dictated that "the president may have wanted to raise the threat of war-crimes trials to counter" those plans.[179] Second, the Bush, Sr. administration may have thought that a war crimes tribunal would deter Iraqis from using POWs as human shields.[180] Along with the Bush, Sr. White House, the UNSC effectively threatened to prosecute Iraqis who violated international humanitarian law.[181]

The following year, however, Bush, Sr. explicitly offered Saddam amnesty in exile, which the Iraqi leader rejected.[182] The Clinton administration that soon followed returned, at least rhetorically, to the Bush, Sr. administration's earlier prosecutorial approach. As previously mentioned, in the course of his 1993 confirmation hearing to become secretary of state, Christopher echoed Bush, Sr.'s initial statement proposing that Iraqis be tried for war crimes.[183]

But Iraqis were not tried. Saddam thus remained in power until April 9, 2003 (when he was deposed by the USG-led coalition invasion and occupation of Iraq) and was subsequently executed on December 30, 2006 (after a domestic war crimes tribunal, the IST, handed down a conviction and death sentence).[184]

Why did the United States support the establishment of an ICT for the FRY after not supporting one for Iraq at approximately the same time (during or after the first Gulf War)? After all, some of the atrocities committed in the FRY and Iraq were of a similar nature and scope (as compared to the bombing of Pan Am flight 103). Moreover, in neither case was the leader allegedly overseeing the atrocities—Milošević and Saddam—in USG custody, let alone deposed, while a tribunal was under consideration. Furthermore, Iraq's invasion of Kuwait in 1990 was the first clear act of aggression by a state actor after the Cold War ended. International cooperation already had been achieved through the UNSC to oust Iraq, which was plundering Kuwait and violating the rights of civilians and POWs, including Americans.[185] In addition, at least some of the UNSC resolutions concerning Balkan atrocities were modeled on those previously passed regarding Iraq.[186] Finally, in mid-1992, the U.S./DoS Office of the Legal Adviser (U.S./DoS/L) actively considered a proposal to establish an international commission to investigate atrocities allegedly committed by Iraqis during the Gulf War.[187]

Beyond these facial similarities and connections between the situations in the FRY and Iraq, the U.S./DoS was conscious of legislative branch criticism over inaction regarding atrocities allegedly committed by Iraqis generally and by Saddam and other Ba'ath Party members specifically.[188] As with the response to the bombing of Pan Am flight 103, the U.S./DoS believed that supporting a war crimes commission on the FRY also would elicit congressional pressure to do so for Saddam and his co-conspirators, albeit perhaps from domestic rather than international sources.[189] A separate confidential U.S./DoS memorandum observed that this comparison was perhaps inevitable and thus demanded attention.[190]

Perhaps the most obvious reason the USG decided not to prosecute Saddam and his co-conspirators in the early 1990s was because it *could not*. The United States had not defeated and occupied Iraq, nor had it deposed and captured Saddam or members of his regime. Other political and pragmatic factors were also at play. Some media sources reported that the USG did not want trials to interfere with a possible coup from within, whereas others claimed the USG backed away due to logistical concerns over the location of an ICT for Iraq and potential backlash from Arab states.[191] Indeed, some commentators cited the latter concern to argue against the idea of trying Saddam, whether or not he was apprehended. A former U.S. ambassador cautioned against "the danger of making a martyr of Saddam, of giving him a platform to call for 'jihad' and of inflaming further passions against the U.S. and the coalition in the Islamic world."[192]

Although international law had developed significantly in the preceding decades, some suspect that it had not yet progressed enough to provide appropriate tools for addressing particular mass crimes committed by the Saddam

regime. Matheson argues that, by the time an ICT for Iraq would have been created, there was not yet consensus, domestically or internationally, on the wisdom
of such a transitional justice institution: "the idea of international prosecution
had not yet taken hold, either in the US or internationally."[193] Even if true, the
notion of a multilateral prosecutorial transitional justice institution certainly
had high-profile precedents in the forms of the IMT and the IMTFE, and would
soon take hold in the cases of the FRY and Rwanda.

Citing a different concern about international approaches to transitional justice, Theodor Meron, a legal scholar and judge (including former chief judge) of
the ICTY, suggests that atrocities committed in Iraq against Kurds did not occur
within the context of an international war, and thus counseled against prosecution. "Internal strife and civil wars," Meron observed, "are still largely outside
the parameters of war crimes and the grave breaches provisions of the Geneva
conventions."[194] Not until the establishment of the ICTR would an ICT be created
to address a purely domestic atrocity.[195] In any case, though, Meron's argument
does not explain why prosecution was not pursued for Iraq's atrocities against
Kuwaitis, which did occur in the context of an international war.

The classic, supposed tension between peace and justice is another cited reason Saddam and his cohorts were not prosecuted after the 1990–1991 Gulf War.
As Meron observes, "the U.N. coalition's war objectives were limited, and there
was an obvious tension between negotiating a ceasefire with Saddam Hussein
and demanding his arrest and trial as a war criminal."[196] Meron recalls, in referring to UNSCR 687 of April 3, 1991,[197] "the ceasefire resolution did not contain a
single word regarding criminal responsibility. Instead, the U.N. resolution promulgated a system of war reparations and established numerous obligations for
Iraq in areas ranging from disarmament to boundary demarcation."[198] Matheson
points to two different ways the USG abandoned prosecutions to prioritize peace
over justice: "In part, there was reluctance in some quarters to conduct trials
of senior Iraqi leaders who might have initiated a coup against Saddam or succeeded him in a more favorably-inclined Iraqi government. In part, there was a
desire to end the conflict, exchange prisoners, and move on."[199]

Anticipating congressional criticism over USG treatment of alleged Iraqi
atrocities, the U.S./DoS prepared talking points on the USG's ongoing approach
to the atrocities and how that situation differed from the one in the FRY. This distinction, the USG claimed, justified greater resolve for prosecuting Balkan atrocities. Regarding Iraqi atrocities, the U.S./DoS prepared three separate talking
points. The first concerned the USG's collection of data on alleged Iraqi atrocities:

> The US had an aggressive policy on Iraqi war crimes. It began collecting
> information on war crimes in early August 1990 and activated two U.S.
> Army Judge Advocate Reserve units to collect war crimes information in
> a systematic manner so that evidence would be preserved regardless as to
> what kind of trials would take place.[200]

Second, the USG stated its preference for particular transitional justice options under certain circumstances:

> The US policy was that those guilty of war crimes could be charged in domestic courts of the country concerned (e.g., Kuwait, Saudi Arabia, or US court-martials of enemy soldiers). The US also indicated that international tribunals could be established if appropriate, such as an Arab tribunal, but only favored the creation of such a court if defendants actually came into custody.[201]

Third, the USG proactively sought to address alleged Iraqi atrocities through the UN, but that effort was limited by political considerations. Specifically, when collaborating in an international forum, prioritization becomes necessary: "The US supported language on war crimes in UN resolutions, but the perception at the time was that countries would be reluctant to go much further on war crimes, and the US did not want to expend precious capital in the UNSC on this matter."[202] In short, the USG argued that, although it supported transitional justice for addressing alleged Iraqi atrocities, and even had initiated that process by collecting evidence and endorsing relevant UN resolutions, establishing an ICT was unlikely unless suspects could be apprehended and more states supported the initiative.

As with the case of the bombing of Pan Am flight 103, the U.S./DoS concluded that the USG could persuasively argue that the FRY and Iraq should be treated differently. The reason was due, in part, to the fact that other states involved in the respective conflicts held opposing views on whether to pursue transitional justice. According to a confidential U.S./DoS memorandum, USG officials "believe[d] that the Iraqi situation can be distinguished [from the FRY]. None of the Arab states most affected have shown the slightest interest in further pursuing the issue of war crimes. By contrast, states neighboring Yugoslavia have been active in their support for additional action."[203]

A separate, confidential U.S./DoS memorandum makes an even more detailed case for why "Yugoslavia is different [than Iraq],"[204] listing five reasons the two situations are dissimilar and should be treated as such. First, the nature of the investigations was different:

> Unlike Iraq, there as [sic] been no active, professional investigation of war crimes (such as that conducted by the US Army). In Yugoslavia, we will only have reports by individual states to the UN of so-called substantiated information. This information (and similar information provided to the UN in connection with Iraq) is not the kind of detailed evidence needed for trials.[205]

Second, the consequences of the USG's passive stance toward the atrocities were different: "Unlike Iraq, a failure to act (such as by creating a commission) [for the FRY] will mean that those who are suspected of war crimes will probably escape trials because no one systematically investigated and preserved evidence."[206] Third, the USG's confidence in the domestic courts of the two countries differed: "Unlike Iraq, it is not clear that appropriate domestic courts [in the FRY] will be available to try war criminals. In particular, the courts and prosecutors of states of the [FRY] do not appear to be appropriate at this time."[207] Fourth, the amount of pressure from the international community for the UN to address alleged atrocities varied: "Unlike Iraq, there is in fact substantial international pressure for UN action on war crimes [in the FRY], in particular the creation of a war crimes commission."[208] Finally, the perceived relationship between justice and peace was different in the two contexts: "Unlike Iraq, it is possible that trial of war criminals [from the FRY] can be integral to obtaining and maintaining a peace settlement. Some experts suggest that a failure to try war criminals [from the FRY] will lead to private vendettas, which could disrupt a settlement."[209]

A separate set of U.S./DoS talking points illuminates why evidence collection for Iraq and the FRY differed, which was related to whether the USG participated in the conflict. According to those talking points, "When US forces are involved in hostilities, the Department of Defense investigates allegations of war crimes. Obviously, there has been no basis for such investigations in [the FRY]. Consequently, unlike Iraq, there has been no expert investigation of allegations of war crimes."[210] In contrast to Iraq, where U.S. troops had been involved in the 1990–1991 Gulf War, no U.S. troops entered the FRY until after the UNSC established the ICTY in 1993.[211]

This same set of U.S./DoS talking points addressed the potential question of why the USG did not press for an ICT to confront alleged Iraqi atrocity perpetrators, including Saddam. The official viewpoints first stressed agreement that "Iraqi war criminals should be prosecuted, as was called for in [UNSC] Resolution 674."[212] However, the talking points went on to state that an international forum was not the default solution: "National tribunals are the common first resort for the prosecution of war criminals."[213] As evidence of this claim, the USG cited WWII: "After WWII, most defendants were prosecuted in national tribunals. For example, only 22 persons were tried before the [IMT], for crimes that had 'no particular geographical location.'"[214] In the case of Iraq, the USG cited a domestic jurisdiction that was willing and able to prosecute: "Kuwait, as the state in which Iraqi war crimes were primarily committed, expressed its intention to conduct war crimes prosecutions of Iraqis in its custody . . . . We urged other concerned nations to take similar steps."[215] The USG sought to distinguish Iraq and the FRY on this point, the availability of an appropriate domestic forum, arguing that "[u]nlike Iraq, there does not appear to be a suitable national tribunal [in the FRY]. The war crimes have occurred in the territory of [the FRY], but tribunals in [the FRY] itself do not appear to be appropriate venues for trials of war criminals."[216] Why the USG considered the proper analogy for a domestic court in the FRY to be a domestic court in Kuwait rather than in Iraq itself is unclear, especially as Saddam and his cohorts remained in power in Iraq. Finally, the USG talking points cited pragmatic concerns and normative beliefs in response to its decision not to initiate proceedings against some of the chief alleged atrocity perpetrators from Iraq: "We have not taken action with regard to Saddam Hussein or other senior Iraqi officials we can't lay our hands on. A prerequisite to a fair tribunal is that the defendant be present and able to assist in the preparation of his defense."[217] Of course, that position contradicted the approach later taken for the FRY, where, as previously discussed, the ICTY indicted Karadžić, Mladić, and Milošević all before they had been apprehended.

Perhaps the most charitable explanation for the different responses to the FRY and Iraq is that USG officials actually intended to prosecute the Iraqi regime but then changed course based on their experience with the FRY. As Shattuck observes, "there was strong sentiment among [USG] human rights officials that an ad hoc Iraqi tribunal should be established once the ICTY was seen as a success. Start-up difficulties with ICTY shelved the Iraqi tribunal effort."[218]

Not only did efforts to address suspected atrocities in the FRY bear on those in the Iraqi and Libyan cases, but the Middle East situations also impacted each other. The U.S./DoS perceived that Libyan and Iraqi issues were interrelated, as any action regarding one could (through path dependence) elicit or even require similar action for the other. A confidential U.S./DoS memorandum argued: "Despite Congressional pressures, we have refrained from proposing establishment of such a War Crimes Commission in connection to Iraq for fear of immediate demands for the creation of an international tribunal for the Lockerbie 2."[219] As a separate confidential U.S./DoS memorandum noted: "The Department did not [propose the establishment of a war crimes commission on Iraq] . . . because of concern over Libya and did not want the internal domestic issue of war crimes action to endanger the extraditions sought in that situation."[220]

3. The Present "Nuremberg" Precedent and Absent "Tokyo" Precedent

The USG and other international actors cited various aspects of "Nuremberg" as precedents during the process of establishing the ICTY. The USG invoked the 1943 Allied War Crimes Commission that preceded the IMT as a basis for creating the CoE that preceded the ICTY. The USG also pointed to the IMT as a precedent for establishing—and model for designing—the ICTY. Finally, the USG referenced the principles the IMT established as principles guiding the creation and operation of the ICTY.

The process of establishing the IMT appeared critical to the process of establishing a transitional justice institution for the FRY. U.S./DoS talking points reflected a belief that the sequence of events leading to the IMT, in which an investigatory commission was first established, offered "the best means to justice" in the FRY.[221]

The USG consciously modeled the CoE largely on the 1943 commission. Two internal U.S./DoS memoranda each twice refer to "the 1943 War Crimes

Commission" as a model on which a war crimes commission for the FRY could be based.[222] Another U.S./DoS memorandum notes that the creation of a UN War Crimes Commission on Yugoslavia "would follow the Nuremberg precedent," where a war crimes commission in 1943 was created "to receive and collate information pertaining to war crimes allegations" and led to the 1945 decision to establish the IMT and other tribunals.[223] U.S./DoS talking points from September 15, 1992, echo this sentiment.[224]

Yet another U.S./DoS memorandum, which first provides background information on the 1943 commission, declares that "[s]everal aspects of the Commission's work are most relevant to the commission [for the FRY] now proposed."[225] The memorandum proceeds by listing four such considerations. The first concerns the scope of each commission:

> although the 1943 Commission focused on gathering information, it also made recommendations on policy questions. For example, it recommended that "crimes against humanity" (i.e., acts that arguably did not violate the laws of war as understood at that time) be described as a separate war crime; for the proposed Commission, a possible comparable question is whether "ethnic cleansing" is an independent war crime. The Commission now proposed should have comparable breadth.[226]

The second matter related to limits on that authority: "the participating governments retained decisionmaking authority on all policy questions, including individual prosecutions, nature of tribunals, and definitions of war crimes. For the [CoE] now proposed, the [UNSC] might be appointed to play this role. In any event, the [CoE] itself should not have decisionmaking authority."[227] On this point and to delineate further the CoE's powers, the memorandum added: "The [CoE] should not serve as a prosecutor. Decisions about whom to prosecute, and in what forum, should be made by the [UNSC]."[228] The third issue concerned the CoE's ability to determine the jurisdictional scope of a potential follow-up tribunal over certain defendants:

> like the 1943 Commission, the proposed Commission should have the latitude to recommend whether an international tribunal is appropriate for every defendant. In keeping with previous declarations by the [UN], only twenty-two defendants—those whose war crimes had no "particular geographic location"—were tried before the [IMT], twenty-five before the [IMTFE]. The remainder were tried under the auspices of the states concerned (i.e., those with custody of the defendant or in whose territory the alleged war crime occurred).[229]

The fourth matter related to the investigatory scope of the CoE:

> the 1943 Commission was primarily a clearinghouse for information provided by the governments concerned. The proposed Commission,

conversely, should have authority to conduct independent investigations and resources adequate to that task. Allegations received by the 1943 Commission had often been investigated and evaluated by experts in the participating governments before the Commission received them. No comparable process has occurred with regard to war crimes violations in the [FRY].[230]

The IMT itself then served as a critical precedent to the ICTY. The USG prepared talking points to answer affirmatively the question of whether the Nuremberg trials were a "useful precedent" to a transitional justice institution for the FRY.[231] The USG even referred to what would become the ICTY as a "second Nuremberg."[232]

The USG publicly reinforced the importance of the IMT precedent in two senses. The IMT episode provided a rationale for pursuing transitional justice for the FRY in the first place. The precedent also shaped the USG's rationale for the type of transitional justice it pursued for the FRY. The USG cited the general principles embodied in the IMT as a helpful model for the transitional justice institution for the FRY. According to U.S./DoS talking points, "the basic lessons of Nuremberg—deterrence and individual responsibility—should guide us today."[233] The USG also cited "the Nuremberg principles" for requiring atrocity perpetrators in the FRY to be punished.[234] In a separate set of talking points, the USG noted the IMT's categories of crimes when describing the subject-matter jurisdiction an ICT for the FRY could claim.[235]

The strong reference in these USG talking points to the "Nuremberg" precedent is somewhat puzzling, given that precedent's problematic history. For example, even though the 1943 Commission was widely regarded as a "failure,"[236] USG officials still embraced it as the model—in structure, function, and name—for the CoE established in 1992.

Finally, even though the USG cited the "Nuremberg" precedent in its arguments *to* create the ICTY, the USG also cited the "Nuremberg" precedent in its arguments *not to* create other ICTs. For example, as discussed above, the USG referenced the IMT's prosecution of "only" twenty-two defendants as a reason that domestic prosecution should be the default transitional justice option for handling alleged Iraqi atrocity perpetrators.[237]

Although the USG cited multiple institutional and procedural elements of "Nuremberg" to justify certain decisions regarding the FRY, "Tokyo" is conspicuously absent from its analogical reasoning with respect to the FRY.[238] Various explanations might resolve this oversight paradox. First, "Nuremberg" is often used as shorthand to refer to the negotiations leading to, the operation of, the results from, and other developments surrounding *both* the IMT and the IMTFE.[239]

Second, USG officials intentionally may have neglected to mention the IMTFE because they felt that the IMT was a more successful institution. If so, pragmatism would suggest coupling the transitional justice institution for the FRY with a more positive historical example than one that provoked mixed feelings. Scharf recalls this sentiment as the reason "Tokyo" was not invoked in the course of creating the ICTY. Recalling that the UNGA adopted the Nuremberg principles in 1946,[240] that the IMT's verdict achieved greater consensus than that of the IMTFE, and that the creation of the IMT was a collaborative effort (compared to the IMTFE, which was created by MacArthur's "executive fiat"), Scharf maintains that "history was never all that excited about the Tokyo experience. So, it was Nuremberg we looked to and not Tokyo. We had read up on Tokyo and used it as an example of what *not* to do."[241] Scharf's perspective contradicts the previous explanation of using "Nuremberg" to refer to both the IMT and the IMTFE, as those who shared Scharf's view did, in fact, deliberately attempt to differentiate the two tribunals.

Third, the IMT, like the ICTY, was a truly pathbreaking institution, on which the sister tribunal created shortly thereafter (in the case of the IMT, the IMTFE, and in the case of the ICTY, the ICTR) was modeled. Consequently, the IMT experience could properly be thought of as the fundamental guide on which the ICTY could be based, just as the IMTFE was. To that end, the IMT was the more famous, novel institution,[242] and citing to it was done for that reason (without necessarily any criticism of the IMTFE).

Finally, USG officials may have deliberately focused on the IMT rather than the IMTFE for geographic reasons: the IMT operated and responded to atrocities perpetrated in Europe, just as the ICTY would. The USG might have thought that mentioning the IMTFE was irrelevant or at least peripheral.

4. Change in Presidential Administrations

The series of events leading to the establishment of the ICTY commenced during the Bush, Sr. administration, when the USG began compiling detailed reports on atrocities in the Balkans, sent them to the UN, and began working (publicly and privately) on the creation of an ICT for the FRY. The Clinton administration continued USG support for the establishment of what would become the ICTY. Thus, the change in presidential administrations had no significant impact on this tribunal's genesis, in contrast to the effect the transition from FDR to Truman had on the transitional justice response to Nazi atrocities.[243] This fact is especially noteworthy given that continuity was maintained for the FRY when successive presidents were members of different parties whereas policy goals changed for Nazi Germany when successive presidents shared partisan affiliation.

One explanation offered for why the Bush, Sr.-Clinton transitional justice policy remained consistent was because of overlapping staff representation in both administrations; therefore, these staff members' preferred policies remained the same.[244] Moreover, the staffers who crafted the USG's transitional justice policies for the FRY were largely career civil servants rather than senior political appointees. As these low- to mid-level bureaucrats were primarily responsible for drafting policy toward the ICTY, one might infer that the USG considered the matter less a priority than their predecessors in the 1940s. In comparison, the decision over addressing Nazis was debated at the highest levels of the USG. The scope of atrocities and the presence or absence of U.S. troops distinguish the two cases and help explain the different levels of attention and controversy their transitional justice responses received.

IV. Conclusion

The creation of the ICTY held great significance, and continues to, for the more general pursuit of transitional justice. The tribunal truly represents an institutional evolution, if not revolution, in transitional justice. According to Ferencz, the ICTY "constitutes an improvement over Nuremberg in that it is an independent body created by the world community; it also has improved procedural rules and impartial judges."[245] Moreover, the ICTY represents a political progression in transitional justice. The ICTY's creation demonstrates just how much U.S.-Russian relations had improved in the immediate aftermath of the Cold War, and not merely because the two powers cooperated through the UNSC to establish the ICTY. As atrocities in the FRY came to light, the United States asked Russia to pressure the Serbs—with whom the Soviet Union had developed a strong relationship through the Warsaw Pact—to permit international inspectors into detention camps.[246] While some suspected atrocity perpetrators were running for office, the United States and Russia sought to influence democratic elections in Serbia through a joint statement.[247] Beyond the thawing of U.S.-Russia relations, the ICTY represents a further political development. As the UNSC's first subsidiary judicial body, the ICTY exemplifies the potential for achieving consensus in the post–Cold War world among the UNSC's five permanent members.

The establishment of the ICTY also illustrates again how the USG's transitional justice decision-making has been determined by a combination of politics, pragmatics, and normative beliefs. First, the USG was motivated (or at least claimed to be motivated) by certain normative beliefs. USG officials stated outrage at atrocities allegedly being committed in the FRY. They argued that implementing a high, internationally recognized standard of due process was the only appropriate method of responding to suspected perpetrators, and that the USG had an obligation to punish them for violating international law. As demonstrated by, for example, Zimmerman's October 1992 testimony before the CSCE, the USG claimed to support the creation of what would become the ICTY out of a commitment to and desire to promote the rule of law in the post–Cold War's "New World Order."

Other normative beliefs played a role in the Libya and Iraq cases. USG officials felt that, because the bombing of Pan Am flight 103 was not on par with the nature or scale of other atrocities that should prompt an international forum (specifically, in the FRY), an ICT was unnecessary and undesirable. At that time, then, USG officials apparently held the normative belief that terrorism should be addressed exclusively in domestic contexts. In the case of Iraq, USG officials also apparently held the normative belief that perceived tensions between peace and justice should be resolved in favor of the former.

But normative beliefs were not the only factor at work. If that were the case, the perpetrators of other atrocities that occurred at approximately the same time, such as the bombing of Pan Am flight 103 and Iraq's crimes during the 1990–1991 Gulf War, would more likely have been handled through a similar transitional justice option of prosecution through an ICT or, at least in the case of Iraq, not through amnesty. Instead, the U.S./DoS sought to distinguish those cases along pragmatic and political dimensions to justify their disparate treatment. In response to the bombing of Pan Am flight 103, the USG favored domestic trials in the United States or the United Kingdom for the two Libyan suspects. USG officials believed that competent courts were already available and appropriate in the United States and the United Kingdom, civilian nationals of which represented the overwhelming majority of the bombing's victims. In the case of Iraq, various political and pragmatic concerns—including the ongoing status of the Saddam regime, hope for domestic regime change, opposition from key regional powers, the context in which crimes were perpetrated, and prioritization of peace over justice—stifled USG support for prosecution, whether domestically or through an ICT.

Furthermore, if the USG had been committed to a legalistic transitional justice method, the USG would not have permitted implicit unconditional amnesty (and possibly also conditional amnesty) for some perpetrators of atrocities in the FRY itself. Pragmatic concerns over the safety of their own and other NATO troops dampened the USG's support for apprehending suspected atrocity perpetrators.

Moreover, a normative belief in upholding legal obligations does not explain the form that prosecution took. Some of the USG's beliefs—liberal or otherwise—shifted over time or were inconsistently held. For example, from the perspective of the USG according to its late-September 1992 confidential U.S./DoS memorandum, there is nothing necessarily superior about using an ICT rather than a regional or domestic war crimes tribunal. That position rests in tension with the USG's perspective, voiced elsewhere during the road to establishing the ICTY, that certain crimes so shock the conscience of mankind that they should be addressed collectively by the international community (perhaps through an ICT, whether ad hoc or permanent). As another example, though the USG nodded to the UNSC's efforts to address Balkan atrocities as a reason to create a transitional justice institution for the FRY through the UNSC, the USG did not favor this approach when handling either the Libya or Iraqi case, despite the fact that both situations were already being dealt with through the UNSC.

The ultimate USG decision to favor an ad hoc UNSC-sponsored ICT for the FRY was therefore motivated, at least in part, by political concerns. The USG, in particular because Bush, Sr. was seeking re-election, viewed the choice of transitional justice solution for the FRY as a way to combat criticism over its, and in particular his, foreign policy failures in the region and elsewhere. The USG's role in and design of the ICTY was partly politically self-interested, as the USG (unlike some of its allies, such as Belgium and Germany) opposed the establishment at that time of a permanent ICT with greater jurisdiction. Instead, the USG wanted the ICT for the FRY to be a model for future ICTs while serving to preempt—and prevent—in 1993 the establishment of a permanent, global ICT or other transitional justice institutions the USG deemed potentially problematic. And the USG considered the exact form the ICTY was to take—an institution created by the UNSC—to be politically desirable, as the UNSC could obligate all states to honor its mandates, which would be critical to the tribunal's success.

Issue linkage is a further political factor that drove USG decision-making in the Balkans case. The strategy pursued to create the CoE and then the ICTY itself reflects a great amount of issue linkage, at least from the USG's perspective, regarding disparate transitional justice issues. The USG had concerns about issue linkages among institutions: that the creation of the CoE and/or ICTY could prompt the establishment of a permanent, global ICT. The USG also had concerns about issue linkages across regions: that the establishment of a transitional justice institution to address atrocities allegedly committed in one region (e.g., the FRY, the Middle East) or by citizens of a particular state (e.g., Libya) might negatively impact calls for addressing atrocities allegedly committed in other regions or by other states' nationals.

Pragmatic considerations, alone or in combination with politics, also drove the USG's eventual policy. The USG used this opportunity to combat apathy toward atrocities; to promote regional, global, specific, and general deterrence of atrocities; and to isolate and stigmatize their suspected perpetrators. USG officials further argued that their favored transitional justice solution of an ICT was the best method of promoting a lasting peace in the region, in part because the USG itself might not have jurisdiction. Relative to other options, such as a treaty, and relative to almost any other potentially sponsoring body, the USG argued that the UNSC provided the quickest, most authoritative, and most politically forceful mechanism for establishing what would become the ICTY.

Path dependence was another noteworthy pragmatic factor that influenced the form and shape of the transitional justice option for the FRY that the USG would support. The USG cited path dependence as a compelling reason to support the creation of a transitional justice institution through the UNSC, both because the UNSC already was addressing the matter of Balkan atrocities and because the UNSC was being used as a coordinating body to collect relevant evidence.

Finally, the "Nuremberg" precedent should not be overlooked, although it is arguably less significant than path dependence as a salient pragmatic factor. It is not clear whether this precedent exerted independent force on the nature and shape of what transitional justice option the USG would support for responding to the Balkan atrocities, or whether it merely reflected or strengthened what the USG would have supported even without it.

The study of the origins of the ICTY provides crucial insight into the USG position on the creation of a permanent, global ICT, what would eventually become the ICC. As discussed in this chapter, the USG opposed the creation of a permanent international criminal court, at least in response to atrocities perpetrated in the FRY. Near-contemporaneous atrocities, particularly stemming from Libya and Iraq, convinced the USG to prevent those crimes from falling under the jurisdiction of whatever ICT was going to be established at that time for the FRY. Where Americans had been killed, as in the case of the bombing of Pan Am flight 103, the USG wanted to exert greater control over the judicial process than an ICT would afford. The USG thus deliberately took a leading role in the design of the ICT for the FRY in part to prevent it from becoming a permanent ICT with global reach. The USG strongly favored transitional justice options, including ICTs, which it was confident would not threaten its interest in preserving maximum flexibility to oversee crimes involving Americans. Given that the Rome Statute establishing the ICC was not adopted until 1998 and did not enter into force until 2001, the USG achieved its dual goals in 1993 of establishing an ad hoc ICT with jurisdiction limited to the FRY and inhibiting the creation of a global, permanent ICT at that time.

Some political factors that played a role in earlier USG policy on transitional justice issues were not significant in the creation of the ICTY. For example, the change in presidential administrations, including the switch from one governing political party to another, did not affect the path toward the ICTY. Unlike the shift from FDR to Truman, the Clinton administration continued the Bush, Sr. administration's support for its preferred transitional justice option for the FRY.

The USG's previously classified documents, discussed in this chapter, acknowledged that the process of establishing the ICTY was a mix of politics, pragmatics, and normative beliefs. As one internal memorandum observed in April 1993: "Depending on prevailing circumstances and the attitudes of members of the [UNSC] on various aspects of [adopting a statute for and establishing and organizing an ICT for the FRY] . . ., this task may be difficult and require close coordination among the Perm[anent] Five [members of the UNSC] and other States."[248] Also, as one observer of the ICTY creation process noted at the time, "setting up a tribunal for war crimes . . . depends as much on favorable political winds as on legal precepts."[249] Rather than a normative belief reflecting legalism, this chapter has yet again demonstrated that political and pragmatic considerations so central to prudentialism factored significantly (and probably more so) into the USG's calculus on transitional justice issues, in this case arising from atrocities concerning Libya, Iraq, and the FRY. As discussed in the final case study of this book, the Rwanda experience further bolsters that conclusion.

The United States Role in
Transitional Justice for Rwanda

I. Background

The case of the Rwandan genocide is particularly significant for analyzing transitional justice responses to atrocities because of the egregious nature and specific characteristics of the mass killing and its consequences.[1] First, an extraordinarily high number and percentage of Rwandans participated in committing the genocide.[2] Second, despite evidence of mass atrocities and the likelihood that even minimal efforts would have mitigated the scope of the genocide,[3] neither the UN nor the world's sole superpower, the United States, intervened.[4] After the genocide, however, the UN, acting through the UNSC—where the USG took a proactive role and on which the GoR coincidentally held a nonpermanent seat during 1994—actively engaged in the post-conflict transitional justice process in Rwanda.

The USG's decision to support the creation of the ICTR met with no serious internal opposition. Then-U.S. National Security Advisor Anthony Lake recalls: "We thought it was a good idea. There were no high level arguments or concerns—simply approval and 'let's get it done in the [UNSC].'"[5] Some USG officials involved in the debate remember that the only counterarguments to the ICTR, which were minimal, concerned whether creating the tribunal might incite more violence—the opposite of the intended effect. As Shattuck recalls: "The other side of the debate was that it would be a potentially incendiary device at a time when there had been plenty of bloodshed already, and that it would not prove to be the instrument of peace that we thought it would be."[6] However, these concerns were minor, and were certainly not held among senior officials. In the end, according to Scheffer, "[t]here was no faction under the executive or legislative branches standing in the way of creating the ICTR."[7] This near-unanimous approval within the USG to support the establishment of the ICTR is puzzling

given the USG's inaction during the genocide; the number, merits, and precedence of alternative transitional justice options; the GoR's ultimate opposition to
this proposal; and the fact that the USG did not initially favor this option.

A. APRIL–JULY 1994: DURING THE GENOCIDE

USG support for the ICTR's creation began both publicly and privately well
before the genocide had concluded. Immediately after the killing started on
April 6, 1994, the USG began publicly issuing general statements denouncing the
atrocities and declaring a need for accountability for the genocide.[8] Indeed, the
day after the genocide began, Clinton declared that he was "shocked and deeply
saddened . . . [and] horrified that elements of the Rwandan security forces have
sought out and murdered Rwandan officials . . . ."[9] He "condemn[ed] these actions
and . . . call[ed] on all parties to cease any such actions immediately . . . ."[10] That
same day, the UNSC President (UNSC/P) for April 1994, Colin Keating, who
was the UN Permanent Representative (UN/PR) from New Zealand, issued a
statement supported by the USG (as UNSC/P statements are unanimous), similarly condemning "these horrific attacks and their perpetrators, who must be
held responsible."[11] A week and a half later, Lake called on "the leadership of the
Rwandan armed forces, including Army Commander-in-Chief Col. Augustin
Bizimungu, Col. [Léonard] Nkundiye, Capt. Pascal Simbikangwa[,] and Col.
[Théoneste] Bagasora . . . to do everything in their power to end the violence
immediately."[12] According to historian and Human Rights Watch senior adviser
Dr. Alison Des Forges, that statement "was the first by a major international actor
to publicly assign responsibility for the ongoing killing to specific individuals,
but it stopped short of calling the slaughter genocide."[13] Perhaps the most forceful early public statement by the USG concerning accountability for the genocide
came on April 28. That day, U.S./DoS spokesperson Christine Shelly read a prepared statement that the USG "strongly condemns the massacres"; she mentioned
that the USG was communicating with all parties to the conflict and would be
"working very strongly through the United Nations."[14] During that press briefing, Shelly also indicated four general transitional justice options: domestic prosecutions within Rwanda, use of an ICT, referral to the UN, and use of the ICJ.[15]

Private USG efforts to condemn and seek accountability for the genocide
started at approximately the same time. On April 26, the U.S./DoS decided that
Prudence Bushnell, Principal Deputy Assistant Secretary of State for African
Affairs, would call GoR officials leading the genocide as well as rebel leaders.
Bushnell spoke to Bagasora on April 28, Bizimungu and Rwandan Patriotic
Front (RPF) Major General Paul Kagame on April 30, and again to Kagame on
May 1. She tried unsuccessfully to call Bagasora again that week but spoke to
Bizimungu several more times in early May.[16] Bushnell told Bizimungu: "I am
calling to tell you President Clinton is going to hold you accountable for the kill-
ings."[17] In her conversation with Bagasora on April 28, Bushnell urged him to "end

the killings," emphasizing that "in the eyes of the world, the Rwanda military engaged in criminal acts" and stressing that "it would behoove the GOR military to show some responsible leadership and a willingness to compromise ... we were looking to him personally to do the right thing."[18] U.S. Assistant Secretary of State for African Affairs George Moose also repeatedly spoke by telephone to representatives of the GoR and the RPF.[19] The discussions clearly signaled that the USG was watching the genocide and taking note of its perpetrators, with the intention of eventually holding them individually accountable for their crimes. Further reflecting that view, on April 29, at a meeting of the U.S. National Security Council (U.S./NSC) Deputies Committee, Scheffer proposed a UN-led investigation of the crime of genocide in Rwanda.[20]

The USG and the UNSC/P were not alone in calling for perpetrators to be brought to justice. Some Rwandans did, too, though they were much more specific (and, as it would turn out, prescient) about the precise form the accountability mechanism should take. Although not in power, Rwandans opposed to the genocidal Hutu regime almost immediately began demanding that the UN catch and try *génocidaires*. One week after the genocide began, Claude Dusaidi, the RPF representative to the UN, wrote to the UNSC/P that a "crime of genocide" had been committed in Rwanda and requested that the UNSC immediately establish an ICT and apprehend those responsible for the killings.[21] After the genocide, the five reasons cited by the RPF-led GoR for its ICT request were:

(1) "to involve the international community, which was also harmed by the genocide and by the grave and massive violations of international humanitarian law" and "to enhance the exemplary nature of a justice that would be seen to be completely neutral and fair";

(2) "to avoid any suspicion of its [the GoR's] wanting to organize speedy, vengeful justice";

(3) "to make it easier to get at those criminals who have found refuge in foreign countries";

(4) to emphasize that "the genocide committed in Rwanda is a crime against humankind and should be suppressed by the international community as a whole"; and

(5) "above all ... to teach the Rwandese people a lesson, to fight against the impunity to which it had become accustomed since 1959 and to promote national reconciliation."[22]

Two weeks later, on April 30, the UNSC suggested that prosecutions be used to determine responsibility for atrocities in Rwanda, but did not endorse a specific forum. The UNSC/P's statement called "on the leadership of both parties ... to commit themselves to ensuring that persons who instigate or participate in such attacks are prosecuted and punished."[23] The statement further recalled that "persons who instigate or participate in such acts are individually responsible. In this context, the [UNSC] recall[ed] that the killing of members of an ethnic group with the intention of destroying such a group in whole or in part constitutes a crime punishable under international law."[24] The statement then requested the UNSG "to make proposals for investigation of the reports of serious violations of international humanitarian law during the conflict."[25] Without employing the word "genocide," this statement alluded to its definition under international law.

RPF officials were not satisfied, however, with the UN's slow progress, and therefore lobbied publicly for an ICT by alleging racism and regionalism. In May, RPF Prime Minister-designate Faustin Twagiramungu posed a rhetorical question at a press conference: "Is what is happening different from what happened in Nazi Germany? Was a war crimes court not set up in Germany? Is it because we're Africans that a court has not been set up?"[26]

The same month, the USG began preparing daily intergovernmental agency briefings on Rwanda.[27] Many of these discussions occurred in the U.S. Interagency War Crimes Working Group (U.S./IWCWG), which emerged in response to the Balkans crisis. A classified internal discussion paper of May 1 outlined goals, tactics, and options for the daily intra-USG briefings on Rwanda. On the topic of "Genocide Investigation: Language that calls for an international investigation of human rights abuses and possible violations of the genocide convention," the paper cautioned: "Be careful. [The Office of the] Legal [Adviser] at [U.S./DoS] was worried about this yesterday—Genocide finding could commit USG to actually 'do something.'" On the topic of "Pressure to Punish Organizers of Killings" the paper also cautioned: "NO. Hold till Ceasefire has been established—don't want to scare off the participants."[28] At this point, political considerations about automatic USG involvement and disruption of peace negotiations prevented the USG from calling for an investigation into and punishment for the massacres.

Two weeks later, on May 16, Joan Donoghue, U.S./DoS Assistant Legal Adviser for African Affairs, prepared a legal analysis for Christopher, finding that "[t]here can be little question that the specific listed acts [of genocide] have taken place in Rwanda."[29] Shortly thereafter, Toby Gati, U.S. Assistant Secretary of State for Intelligence and Research, sent a memorandum to Moose and U.S./DoS Legal Adviser Conrad Harper concluding that "[t]here is substantial circumstantial evidence implicating senior Rwandan government and military officials in the widespread, systematic killing of ethnic Tutsis, and to a lesser extent, ethnic Hutus who supported power-sharing between the two groups."[30] On May 21, several U.S./DoS officials, including Moose, Shattuck, Assistant Secretary of State for International Organization Affairs Douglas Bennet, and Harper sent a memorandum titled "Has Genocide Occurred in Rwanda?" to Christopher recommending that he authorize U.S./DoS officials to use the formulation "acts of genocide have occurred" in Rwanda, noting that "[t]his is the same formulation that we use with respect to Bosnia."[31] The memorandum, featuring the file name of "nonamerwandakilllgs"[32] (which appears to be a shortened version of "no name Rwanda killings"), also noted that such a statement

> would not have any particular legal consequences. Under the [Genocide] Convention, the prosecution of persons charged with genocide is the responsibility of the competent courts in the state where the acts took place or an [ICT] (none has yet been established); the U.S. has no criminal jurisdiction over acts of genocide occurring within Rwanda unless they are committed by U.S. citizens or they fall under another criminal provision of U.S. law (such as those relating to acts of terrorism for which there is a basis for U.S. jurisdiction).[33]

Similarly, in response to a May 27 note from U.S./NSC Senior Director for African Affairs Donald Steinberg to Lake indicating that no additional legal obligations would follow from Clinton's use of the term "genocide" in referring to the situation in Rwanda, Lake stated: "No. Raises stakes even further beyond possible remedies."[34] Publicly and internally, the USG was thus careful not to describe the conflict as "genocide," in part for fear of that term's legal, political, and perhaps moral implications. Namely, its use could trigger the USG's obligation to apprehend and prosecute perpetrators.[35] While Hutu *interahamwe* (paramilitary mobile killing squads) slaughtered Tutsi men, women, and children by the hundreds of thousands, the U.S./DoS continued wrestling with the precise language for the killings.[36]

During this same month (May 1994), the USG began urging the UN to take a more proactive role in responding to the genocide.[37] Human rights advocate Holly Burkhalter implies that Shattuck's pressure on UN officials resulted in the appointment of a special rapporteur on Rwanda.[38] The UN responded to such external pressure in other ways, such as by sending UN High Commissioner for Human Rights (UN/HCHR) José Ayala Lasso to Rwanda on May 11–12 to investigate allegations of serious violations of international humanitarian law and to publish a report on his findings. Thus, even before the genocide had concluded, various agents and agencies of the UN—such as the UN/HCHR, the UN Commission on Human Rights (UN/CHR), and the UNSC (including the USG)—had launched an investigation and made known that criminal perpetrators would be held individually responsible. Importantly, these UN agencies' efforts received the RPF's imprimatur.[39]

Also in May, the USG held bilateral meetings with relevant non-state actors to explore issues concerning pursuing transitional justice for Rwanda. Among other efforts, U.S. Ambassador to Belgium Alan Blinken met with ICJ Judge Raymond Ranjeva to explore "the notion of an international inquiry into gross violations of human rights in Rwanda."[40] USG officials also consulted NGOs, such as the International Committee of the Red Cross, on the possibility of creating an ICT for Rwanda and recruiting witnesses to testify.[41] Shortly thereafter, the USG also consulted and lobbied UN officials, including Lasso, to create an ICT for Rwanda. Specifically, the USG advocated expanding the jurisdiction of the ICTY to encompass atrocities in Rwanda (what I refer to as the "ICTY-Expanded" option).[42]

According to Scheffer, it was not until the middle of the following month that serious planning for establishing an ICT for Rwanda commenced.[43] During June, momentum developed within the UN to establish a "commission of experts to gather evidence related to breaches of the genocide convention and other violations of international humanitarian law in Rwanda." This commission would eventually become the UN Independent Commission of Experts on Rwanda (UN/ICER). On June 10, Spain circulated a draft resolution calling for the establishment of such a commission.[44] Spain's initiative prompted further internal USG discussion about whether and how to support the commission, and whether to propose or at least support a transitional justice option. At the time, the USG was considering at least three options: ICTY-Expanded, the creation of an entirely separate ICT for Rwanda (what I refer to as the "ICT-Separate" option), and the establishment of a permanent international criminal court.[45] Later that month, the USG decided to co-sponsor a UNSC resolution establishing a commission of experts for Rwanda.[46]

From June 9 to 20, the UN conducted another investigation of atrocities in Rwanda. René Degni-Ségui, who had recently been appointed UN/CHR Special Rapporteur on the situation of human rights in Rwanda, visited Rwanda and its neighboring countries, Burundi, Zaire (now the DRC), and Kenya. Bacre Waly Ndiaye, UN/CHR Special Rapporteur on extrajudicial, summary, or arbitrary executions, and Nigel Rodley, UN/CHR Special Rapporteur on torture, accompanied Degni-Ségui. Their mission was to investigate allegations of human rights violations, particularly crimes against humanity and genocide.[47] On June 28, after their return, Degni-Ségui issued a report that "recommend[ed] ... the establishment of an ad hoc international criminal tribunal or, alternatively, the extension of the jurisdiction of the [ICTY]."[48] This report marked the first public proposal supporting specific transitional justice options for Rwanda. Degni-Ségui mentioned ICTY-Expanded or a new ICT, which implicitly included ICT-Separate and an ICT for Rwanda that shared some bureaucracy with the ICTY (what I refer to as the "ICT-Tied" option). During this same period, the USG continued to publicly characterize the atrocities in Rwanda as "acts of genocide" (rather than unqualified "genocide"), to deny that it had any legal obligation to act, and to stress that it was supporting an active UN role to help stop the massacres.[49] Amid this June investigation, the USG had still not determined whether it would support an ICT for Rwanda.[50] On July 1, the UNSC took a further step toward pursuing transitional justice for Rwanda through voting for UNSCR 935, which declared that atrocity perpetrators would be held individually accountable and requested the UNSG to establish the UN/ICER to collect evidence of those crimes.[51]

The USG supported or supplemented these UN efforts, including the UN/ICER. Responding both to pressure and overwhelming evidence, and as opposed to characterizing the offenses through the less definitive construct of "acts of genocide," Christopher for the first time publicly called the slaughter in Rwanda "genocide" on June 10.[52] Several weeks later, on June 30, Christopher testified before the U.S. Senate Committee on Foreign Relations (U.S./SCFR), observing, "it's clear that there is genocide, acts of genocide in Rwanda, and they ought to be pursued" and also stating that, even though the USG had no unilateral responsibility, the international community had a collective obligation under the Genocide Convention to punish acts of genocide. Christopher also made an unsolicited comparison to Bosnia: "I have no hesitation in saying that there was genocide in Rwanda and had been genocide, is genocide, in Bosnia as well." He publicly stated for the first time during this testimony that the USG supported "the creation of an international war crimes tribunal" for Rwanda, and that he had recently met with the ICTY's deputy prosecutor to discuss the matter.[53] At this point, the USG envisaged the ICT taking one of two forms: an ICT specifically for Rwanda (although Christopher did not mention its relationship to the UN) or a permanent international criminal court.[54]

Shortly after the vote to establish the UN/ICER, the U.S. representative on the UNSC, Edward Gnehm, Jr., stated:

> Our goal must be individual accountability and responsibility for grave violations of international humanitarian law in Rwanda. We must fix responsibility on those who have directed these acts of violence. In so doing, we can transform revenge into justice, affirm the rule of law and, hopefully, bring this horrible cycle of violence to a merciful close.[55]

Also around that time, as Scheffer notes, the U.S./IWCWG began collecting its own evidence of the genocide, in part to assist the UN/ICER.[56] On July 15, the White House joined U.S./DoS in publicly supporting the establishment of an ICT for Rwanda, expressing hope "that the United Nations would act swiftly . . . to create a War Crimes Tribunal."[57] Four days later, Albright called for "quick action" within the UNSC to establish an ICT for Rwanda.[58] The USG was simultaneously pressuring individual states, such as Tanzania and France, to detain certain suspected *génocidaires*,[59] and the USG also began curtailing diplomatic relations with the GoR, including a refusal to recognize the current government, closing the GoR's embassy in Washington, DC, and freezing the GoR's assets in the United States.[60]

The selection of the ICTY chief prosecutor, who ultimately would also become the ICTR chief prosecutor, occurred parallel to these developments, although this broadened mandate was not decided at the time. During a July 6 meeting in Moscow, Shattuck and Russian deputy foreign minister Sergey Lavrov agreed to appoint Richard Goldstone, a prominent South African jurist, as the ICTY chief prosecutor.[61] Two days later, UNSC Resolution 936 formalized that decision,[62] and Goldstone began serving as ICTY chief prosecutor on August 15.[63]

B. JULY–SEPTEMBER 1994: AFTER THE GENOCIDE

The RPF defeated the remaining GoR troops in mid-July 1994, halting the genocide. The RPF then gave Dégni-Ségui a list of fifty-five people it considered to be the core group of *génocidaires*.[64] Meanwhile, Rwanda's new government was sworn in on July 19, after which it lobbied for the establishment of an ICT for Rwanda. France began withdrawing its forces (deployed under *Opération Turquoise*) later that month.[65] Also around this time, the Tanzanian government declared its willingness to cooperate "fully" with the international community in bringing *génocidaires* to justice,[66] a pledge that later would prove important both to apprehending suspected *génocidaires* and to establishing the ICTR within its borders.

Notwithstanding the White House's public and rhetorically unconditional endorsement of an ICT for Rwanda, the U.S./DoS in actuality remained only conditionally supportive. Senior U.S. Representative Tony Hall sent a letter on July 1 to Christopher advocating the immediate establishment of an ICT for Rwanda.[67] In response, one of Christopher's deputies, Wendy Sherman, stated that "[w]e will support the creation of an international tribunal if the [UN/ICER] confirms that violations of international humanitarian law have occurred."[68]

In the immediate aftermath of the genocide, the U.S./IWCWG actively considered two of the options outlined in Degni-Ségui's June 28 report to prosecute genocide leaders: ICT-Tied and ICTY-Expanded. At this point, the USG favored the latter option, which Matheson recommended, in part to facilitate the expansion of the ICTY into a permanent international criminal court.[69] The USG proposed that any ICT for Rwanda would not only share "common resources and registry staff" with the ICTY, but would also share with the ICTY a common statute, trial and appellate chambers[,] and chief prosecutor."[70] The USG also decided to declare its preference and commitment for domestic criminal justice efforts to prosecute other *génocidaires*.[71] As it could not assume that the ICTY and the ICTR would share a chief prosecutor, the USG also actively researched and considered candidates for the position of ICTR chief prosecutor.[72]

The USG undertook six main efforts to gather international support behind the establishment of an ICT for Rwanda, especially under the rubric of ICTY-Expanded. First, on July 26, the USG instructed its embassies around the world "to advise their host governments of the U.S. support of an international tribunal to prosecute violations of . . . international humanitarian law in Rwanda and to seek their support as well," and to declare that the USG's "present thinking" favored ICTY-Expanded or ICT-Tied; that the USG requested these governments to detain suspected *génocidaires*; and that ICTY chief prosecutor Goldstone "seems ready to supervise both the Yugoslav and Rwanda prosecutions" and had South African President "[Nelson] Mandela's personal endorsement for this position." The cable also requested its embassies to begin identifying African prosecutors and judges who could serve on an ICT for Rwanda.[73] Scheffer characterizes this cable as "the first clear summary of what I and others spent July intensively hammering out as the U.S. initiative . . . ."[74]

Second, from mid-July to November 8 (the date the ICTR was established), USG officials conducted frequent bilateral meetings with various governments to lobby for a Rwanda ICT, specifically according to the ICTY-Expanded proposal.[75] The USG's bilateral communication at this time with the Russian, French, South African, and Chinese governments is particularly noteworthy.

The USG focused its attention on the Russian and French governments because, as UNSC permanent members, their support was critical to establishing an ICT for Rwanda through that forum. Moreover, and to varying degrees, both of these states opposed the USG's preference for ICTY-Expanded, instead desiring the ICTR to constitute a legally separate ICT. Reaching agreement with France particularly concerned the USG because of the French government's history and association with Rwanda, a relationship the USG viewed as logistically critical to establishing a successful transitional justice mechanism. As one internal U.S./DoS document states:

> France is a key player on this issue, not only because of its current involvement in Rwanda, but because it may have the most complete information of any western government on war crimes in Rwanda and access to witnesses, evidence[,] and even perpetrators. France's support for the work of the [UN/ICER] may be critical to the success of its efforts, and France's views on next steps will be critically important in the [UNSC].[76]

By mid-September, while Russia and France continued to oppose ICTY-Expanded, the USG began employing tactics other than simply advocating the merits of the USG's preferred option. For example, the USG offered to support a Russian candidate for one of the new judgeships on an ICT in the form of ICTY-Expanded after having privately referred to the Kremlin as having "stubbornly defended" its opposition to this transitional justice option.[77] ICTY-Expanded would have jurisdiction over cases arising from both the Rwandan genocide and the conflict in the FRY, the latter of which was of historic and emotional concern to Russians due to Slavic ties with the Serb population.[78] The USG simultaneously appealed to the French government in a similar fashion: "the USG would welcome the appointment of a Deputy Prosecutor and staff prosecutors from other French-speaking countries to handle the Rwandan cases, as well as the election of an additional French-speaking judge to deal with both Rwandan and Yugoslav cases."[79]

The USG believed that garnering robust South African support behind an ICT for Rwanda (in particular from President Mandela and Foreign Minister Alfred Nzo) would "lend great credibility and momentum for this important effort."[80] In bilateral discussions with the South African government, including directly with Mandela (in which the USG addressed him as "Africa's most respected leader"), the USG further pressed the connection between Rwanda's and South Africa's national interests: "South Africa could and should play a prominent role in this effort, thereby promoting human rights and furthering its moral leadership in the international community. This will be particularly true if, as we hope, Justice Goldstone will oversee both Yugoslav and Rwanda war crimes."[81] Indeed, several African states, including South Africa, eventually agreed to provide support for an ICT for Rwanda, specifically the ICTY-Expanded option. The USG suspected that staffing selection, rather than the proposal's merits, played a decisive role in providing motivation. As an internal U.S./DoS document mused:

> we have received favorable preliminary reactions from key African governments for expanding the [ICTY] to include Rwanda. This is probably due, at least in part, to the fact that the current head of one of the two trial chambers [of the ICTY] (Judge Karibi-Whyte) is from Nigeria, and the current chief prosecutor [of the ICTY] (Judge Goldstone) is from South Africa and has the personal support of President Mandela.[82]

The USG also pressed China to support the establishment of an ICT for Rwanda, because, by mid-August, China was the only UNSC permanent member resisting the idea. China explained its hesitancy in terms of the international community potentially violating the GoR's sovereignty. In order to lobby China, the USG made direct bilateral appeals and also enlisted the support of various African states.[83]

The USG's third lobbying effort occurred in early August, when USG officials secured support from Goldstone for the ICTY-Expanded option.[84] Fourth, the USG convened meetings (on August 4 and 9) of the UNSC permanent members' legal advisers to discuss establishing an ICT for Rwanda and specifically to lobby for ICTY-Expanded. On August 4, Russia "strongly supported" and France "generally supported" the USG proposal, whereas China and the United Kingdom remained noncommittal.[85] By August 9, only China's position continued to be uncertain.[86] Another meeting of these legal advisers convened on August 18 at the behest of UN Legal Counsel Hans Correll. During that meeting, the USG reiterated its preference for ICTY-Expanded while Correll noted various transitional justice options for Rwanda, including the USG proposal (ICTY-Expanded), ICT-Separate (through either Chapter VI or Chapter VII of the UN Charter), or augmenting the GoR's national courts with foreign judges.[87] At this meeting, France (seconded by the United Kingdom) restated its preference for legally separate ICTs for Rwanda and for the FRY, but was "not, however, adamantly opposed to [the] US approach."[88] A few days later, UN Deputy Legal Adviser Ralph Zacklin told USG officials that he personally preferred two legally separate ICTs for Rwanda and for the FRY. Zacklin also said that, although he believed they could share an appeals chamber, he preferred separate trial chambers and chief prosecutors, as well as suggested that whatever part of an ICT for Rwanda were located in Africa should be in Nairobi or, as a second choice, in

Addis Ababa.[89] On August 30, the Chinese government informed the USG that it would support the USG's proposal for ICTY-Expanded.[90]

The fifth USG lobbying campaign unfolded from August 4 to 10, when four USG officials traveled to Uganda, Rwanda, Burundi, Zaire, and France for bilateral discussions about various USG objectives relating to post-genocide Rwanda.[91] In Rwanda, the delegation sought to convey the USG's strong support for an ICT for Rwanda—without specifying whether it be ICTY-Expanded or ICT-Tied—and also to persuade the GoR to support such a tribunal, in part by requesting that the UNSC establish it.[92] In Rwanda, the delegation met with Kagame (who had become vice president and minister of defense), Rwandan Minister of Justice Alphonse-Marie Nkubito, Twagiramungu, and Rwandan Minister of Rehabilitation and Social Integration Jacques Bihozagara.[93] The delegation arrived in Kigali on August 5, where they were joined by U.S. Ambassador to Rwanda David Rawson and Chairman of the Joint Chiefs of Staff General John Shalikashvili.[94] The stated purposes of the trip were to "seek Kagame's support for a [UNSC] resolution to establish an [ICT] for Rwanda to investigate the genocide and bring its leaders to justice . . . [and to] urge Kagame to work with the United States to rebuild the country's shattered justice system . . . ." Shattuck also delivered a USG-drafted letter to Kagame and Nkubito endorsing the establishment of an ICT for Rwanda, which he asked the GoR to send to the UNSC.[95] On behalf of the GoR, Nkubito submitted the letter to the UNSG on August 8,[96] and the UNSC issued a presidential statement on August 10 embracing its contents.[97]

The USG's sixth main maneuver toward an ICT for Rwanda (specifically as ICTY-Expanded) occurred on September 1, when the USG began circulating a draft resolution and annex including a statute to create an ICT for Rwanda through ICTY-Expanded.[98] The USG followed up by circulating another draft document to UNSC members on September 20 arguing that prosecution of the Rwandan cases "can be most effectively done by adding this responsibility to the mandate of the [ICTY]."[99]

After the USG delegation returned from its multistate trip, the U.S./DoS increased its focus on Rwandan criminal justice issues. On August 12, the U.S./DoS established a separate U.S./IWCWG on Rwanda and indicated that it would press for a speedy completion of the UN/ICER's work.[100] Almost two weeks later, Shattuck published an opinion piece in the *Washington Post*, stating "it is vital that the international community rapidly create a war crimes tribunal for Rwanda that will hold the perpetrators of genocide and other atrocities accountable to their victims and to the international community."[101] Also in mid-August, the USG began pressuring the UN/ICER and the UN/HCHR to support the establishment of an ICT for Rwanda, including a request that the UN/ICER issue an interim report with a recommendation to that effect.[102] The idea of the UN/ICER issuing an interim report apparently arose from this USG pressure, after an August 18 meeting between Matheson and three members of the

UN/ICER, including its chairman, Atsu-Koffi Amega.[103] The USG made several offers of assistance to the UN/ICER at this point, including legal staff, and urged the UN to provide adequate office equipment.[104]

Soon thereafter, Clinton sent a high-level delegation to Rwanda to investigate post-genocide issues in the region. Upon their return, delegation members briefed the White House, the U.S./NSC, and the U.S./DoS; appeared on various televised news programs; and were quoted in the media. Their conclusions and recommendations "track[ed] closely with U.S.G. policy," including the quick establishment of an ICT for Rwanda.[105] One mission member, Aspen Institute president S. Frederick Starr, published an opinion piece in the *Washington Post* on September 6 recommending the establishment of such an ICT.[106]

That same month, the USG sent another team to Rwanda—an interagency evidence-gathering team to assist the efforts of the UN/ICER, which had completed its preliminary work in Rwanda on September 5.[107] This team traveled to Rwanda to assess the political and security climate, to collect evidence, and to interview witnesses, all data and findings of which they provided to the UN/ICER.[108] The UN/ICER acknowledged these contributions in its October 1 interim report, stating that U.S./DoS "forwarded to the [UN/ICER] documents ... that prove the existence of a plan for genocide against Tutsis and the murder of moderate Hutus."[109] The USG sent yet a third mission to Rwanda later that month. In mid-September, Undersecretary of State for Global Affairs Timothy Wirth visited Rwanda for four days to investigate developments on the ground and to further lobby for the establishment of an ICT for Rwanda.[110]

The UN/ICER's interim report made recommendations on the prosecutions' format. The report suggested an international, rather than a "municipal," tribunal and, like Degni-Ségui's June 28 report, discussed only two options for dealing with suspected *génocidaires*: ICTY-Expanded and a new ICT, either ICT-Tied or ICT-Separate.[111] The UN/ICER stated its preference for ICTY-Expanded, arguing that

> [t]he alternative of creating an ad hoc tribunal alongside the already existing [ICTY] would not only be less efficient from an administrative point of view of staffing and use of physical resources, but would be more likely to lead to less consistency in the legal interpretation and application of international criminal law.[112]

The GoR remained dissatisfied with the international community's progress toward bringing *génocidaires* to justice. On September 28, the Rwandan UN/PR sent a letter to the UNSC/P noting "evident reluctance by the international community to set up an international tribunal."[113] On October 4, the GoR publicly declared its preferences, namely that proceedings occur in Rwanda and that convicted *génocidaires* receive the death penalty.[114] Two days later, Rwandan President Pasteur Bizimungu stated to the UNGA,

> it is absolutely urgent that this international tribunal be established. It will enable us to prosecute in a completely open setting those responsible for the genocide. Since most of the criminals have found refuge in various corners of the world, what we seek is a tool of justice that knows no borders. Moreover, the very nature of the events—considered to be crimes against humanity—warrants the international community's joining forces to prevent their reoccurrence.

Bizimungu also stated the GoR's preference for an ICT created by UNSC Chapter VII, so that the ICT could compel state compliance.[115] However, none of these GoR statements indicated its preference among the ICTY-Expanded, ICT-Tied, or ICT-Separate options.

C. SEPTEMBER–NOVEMBER 1994: THE NARROWING OPTION: ICT-TIED

Between the July 26 cable (indicating USG preference for ICTY-Expanded) and September 28, USG preferences shifted to ICT-Tied, a compromise solution New Zealand advocated on September 26.[116] Although the UN/ICER endorsed ICTY-Expanded in its interim report, several UNSC member states, most notably Russia and France, preferred ICT-Tied.[117] Russia and France favored ICT-Tied in part to avoid creating the institutional framework for a permanent international criminal court, which ICTY-Expanded would do more so.[118]

Because the USG harbored only a weak preference for ICTY-Expanded over ICT-Tied, and given the value of French and Russian support, the USG revised its own position to reflect the shifting preferences among these other UNSC permanent members.[119] The USG characterized its new position in favor of ICT-Tied as "the latest USG proposal for the [Rwanda] war crimes tribunal, based on the New Zealand approach."[120] That announcement occurred on September 28, with the caveat that "the appeals judges and prosecutor for the [ICTY] would serve also as the appeals judges and prosecutor for Rwanda," and reflected the USG's desire to "compromise in the interest of quick [UNSC] action on Rwanda prosecutions, which is essential in light of the situation . . . ."[121] The GoR advised the USG that it agreed with the "New Zealand approach" and wanted trials to be held in Kigali.[122] The French, British, and Belgian governments also advised the USG that they, too, supported the ICT-Tied option.[123] On September 28–29, the U.S. and New Zealand governments circulated among UNSC members and Zacklin a draft UNSC resolution for the establishment of the ICTR.[124] The U.S., New Zealand, and U.K. governments then introduced a revised text two weeks later.[125] The USG also decided to establish a ministerial-level operational support group, "The Friends of Rwanda," to coordinate further efforts to assist post-genocide Rwanda.[126]

Even after support for the ICT-Tied option emerged among the UNSC perma-
nent members and some other critical states—such as New Zealand, Uganda, and
Tanzania (the last of which, in October, offered Arusha as a venue for any ICT for
Rwanda[127])—other parties raised concerns. For example, Boutros-Ghali objected
to Goldstone as chief prosecutor, preferring instead a Francophone African.[128]
Furthermore, in mid-October, Japan's government expressed concern that the
UNSC apparently was engaged in the proliferation of ad hoc ICTs, a practice to
which it objected.[129]

In addition, the GoR remained an active lobbyist for a Rwanda ICT without
stating a preference for a particular ICT type (e.g., ICT-Tied, ICTY-Expanded).
Furthermore, GoR representatives voiced objections to Matheson and other USG
officials regarding the draft ICTR statute, including the temporal jurisdiction, the
number of judges, the seat of the tribunal, and the text of Articles 3 (on crimes against
humanity), 4 (on war crimes), 26 (on sentencing), and 27 (on pardon or commutation of sentences). The GoR also pressed for a voice in the selection of tribunal staff,
a veto over all releases and pardons, and a guarantee that all convicted *génocidaires*
be incarcerated in Rwanda.[130] The GoR demanded more control over a process perceived as crucial to its post-conflict reconstruction. The GoR moreover insisted that
atrocities committed before 1994 be included in the ICT's jurisdiction, because, the
GoR argued, these offenses should also be punished and were inextricably linked to
the genocide in 1994. Twagiramungu again publicly demanded the establishment
of an ICT for Rwanda around this time.[131] USG officials continued meeting with
their GoR counterparts from mid-October through early-November[132] but did not
discover "until the last day or so prior to the vote in the [UNSC] that the Rwandan
government would not budge on their objections to the ICTR statute."[133] Part of the
problem may have been communication difficulties the GoR delegation at the UN
claimed to have with their home government in Kigali, which prevented the GoR
delegation from receiving timely and thorough guidance.[134]

On November 3, the USG convened a meeting of the co-sponsors of a resolution to establish an ICT for Rwanda: France, New Zealand, Russia, Spain, the
United States, and the United Kingdom.[135] The group decided at that meeting
(1) to confer with GoR officials the following day to try to persuade them "to vote
in favor or not participate" in the resolution, (2) to bring the resolution to a vote on
November 7 "irrespective of Rwandan position," and (3) "that no changes would
be made in [the] text of resolution or statute unless Rwanda indicated one or
another minor cosmetic change would enable them to vote yes on the resolution."
Members of the group varied in terms of their strict adherence to these positions.
French and Russian representatives urged no further amendments to the resolution and insisted on a November 7 vote. U.S. and Spanish officials supported the
French/Russian position. However, the government of New Zealand was willing
both to negotiate further with the GoR and to delay any vote on the resolution.[136]

As planned, on November 4 the co-sponsors of the resolution met with GoR
officials, including Rwandan UN/PR Manzi Bakuramutsa. The group conveyed to

the Rwandan delegates its decisions from the previous day, including the planned November 7 vote on the proposed resolution, and expressed hope that the GoR either would vote affirmatively or abstain. GoR officials demurred, stating that they had not yet received instructions from more senior officials in Kigali. The delay partially arose because, according to a U.S./DoS cable, "time was differently perceived in Rwanda . . . it simply took weeks for them fully to grasp" the proposal. Bakuramutsa also reiterated some of the GoR's objections to the draft resolution. The co-sponsors responded that they were amenable to increasing the number of judges but not to increasing the GoR's involvement in their selection because the ICT "could not be seen as in any way prone to bias." The meeting concluded with an agreement to reconvene as soon as the GoR delegates received their instructions. Members of the co-sponsoring group continued to vary in terms of their resolve, with the French and Russians insistent on a November 7 vote over the extant version of the resolution, and New Zealand being most willing to compromise with the GoR and delay the vote. USG officials present at the meeting added that, although no agreement with the GoR had been reached, the meeting had been productive in conveying the "message to Rwandans that time had come to make their decision and slight firming up of New Zealand and UK resolve to act on Monday[, November 7]."[137]

Further meetings among GoR, USG, and UN officials on this topic did occur from November 5 to 7, but in Kigali rather than at UN headquarters in New York City. During this time, GoR officials in Kigali sent instructions to their representatives at the UN to vote against the proposed tribunal statute. Scheffer opines that the delay from November 7 to the next day did not significantly affect the ultimate vote on the UNSC resolution containing the tribunal statute. Instead, he suggests that such delays are common and, in this case, probably reflected the lag between last-minute meetings occurring in Kigali and the time it took to relay messages from there to New York City.[138]

D. NOVEMBER 8, 1994: THE DECISION TO CREATE THE ICTR

On November 8, the UNSC adopted Resolution 955, establishing the ICTR through the UN Charter's Chapter VII authority.[139] The vote was thirteen in favor, one abstention (China), and one against (Rwanda). Along with the United States, those voting in favor of the resolution were: Argentina, Brazil, Czech Republic, Djibouti, France, New Zealand, Nigeria, Oman, Pakistan, Russia, Spain, and the United Kingdom.[140]

China abstained from the vote, as explained by its UN/PR, both because it opposed in principle overreaching the UNSC's authority by invoking Chapter VII to establish an ICT via UNSC resolution, and also because China believed that the UNSC should have consulted further with the GoR.[141] It is unclear to what extent China's objection was based, as it claimed, on a principled opposition to this use of Chapter VII and deference to the GoR's concerns. Alternatively, these reasons could have masked China's unwillingness to cooperate with the ICTR, or China's desire to avoid a precedent that could later hold it responsible for its own alleged atrocities. (The GoR's negative vote is discussed later in this chapter.[142])

The subject-matter jurisdiction of the ICTR was limited to genocide, crimes against humanity, and violations of Article 3 common to the Geneva Conventions of August 12, 1949, for the Protection of War Victims, and of Additional Protocol II thereto of June 8, 1977. The temporal jurisdiction was restricted to crimes committed between January 1 and December 31, 1994. Finally, the personal and territorial jurisdictions were confined to crimes committed by Rwandans in the territory of Rwanda or of neighboring states, as well as by non-Rwandan citizens for crimes committed in Rwanda. UNSCR 977, adopted on February 22, 1995, designated Arusha, Tanzania, as the ICTR's seat.[143]

When established, the ICTR shared an appeals chamber and chief prosecutor with the ICTY and was endowed with UNSC Chapter VII powers to compel state compliance with arresting and extraditing suspected *génocidaires*. The ICTR marks a watershed in the development of international law and transitional justice because, in contrast to the ICTY, which treated the Balkans crisis as an ongoing *international* armed conflict, and the IMT and the IMTFE, which addressed the European and Pacific theaters of a *world* war, the ICTR is "the first international court having competence to prosecute and punish individuals for egregious crimes committed during an *internal* conflict."[144]

In the case of Rwanda, after issuing broad public statements condemning and calling for accountability of *génocidaires* and privately and directly threatening the genocide's leaders, the USG decided to act only after the genocide. Specifically, the USG decided to support prosecutions through ICT-Tied after abandoning its initial position of favoring ICTY-Expanded. The USG therefore chose to support a judicial process that would deal with only a few dozen *génocidaires*, would be relatively expensive compared to other transitional justice options, would be located outside the victimized country, would create the precedent of founding an ICT for a purely civil conflict, would share some resources and bureaucracy with an existing transitional justice institution (the ICTY), and would affirm the precedent (established by the ICTY) of the UNSC's use of its Chapter VII powers to investigate selectively and to prosecute alleged atrocity perpetrators.

E. ADDITIONAL TRANSITIONAL JUSTICE INSTITUTIONS

To supplement the ICTR, both the GoR and the international community later instituted various transitional justice institutions, primarily prosecutorial in nature. In total, there have been four main transitional justice mechanisms for Rwanda: two inside Rwanda—prosecutions by ordinary domestic courts and *gacaca* (also known as "*gacaca* courts" or "*gacaca* jurisdictions")—and two outside Rwanda—prosecutions through the ICTR and in foreign countries. As this Part has already discussed the ICTR, the three other mechanisms are summarized below.[145]

1. Rwandan Transitional Justice Institutions

After the genocide, the GoR imprisoned approximately 120,000 individuals suspected of perpetrating atrocities.[146] With the assistance of the UN, foreign governments, and NGOs, the GoR rebuilt its infrastructure. In the process, the GoR instituted two primary mechanisms for addressing *génocidaires* not prosecuted by the ICTR: domestic national prosecutions and *gacaca* (a revived and revised version of Rwanda's traditional conflict resolution system).

Rwanda's national court system began trying the most egregious genocide suspects not pursued by the ICTR, but often only after the suspects had sat in pretrial detention for several years. By 2000, more than 2500 people had been tried, 370 of whom had received the death penalty, 800 of whom had received life imprisonment, 500 of whom had been acquitted, and the remainder of whom had received prison sentences of various durations.[147]

In 2001, local Rwandan communities elected over 250,000 of their neighbors to serve as judges in 11,000 *gacaca* jurisdictions.[148] Over its decade of operation, *gacaca* addressed the overwhelming majority of suspected *génocidaires*.[149] One expert on *gacaca*, political scientist Phil Clark, describes the process as follows:

> Derived from the Kinyarwanda word meaning "the lawn" or "the grass"—in reference to the conducting of hearings in open spaces in full view of the community—gacaca is a traditional Rwandan method of conflict resolution that has been controversially revived and transformed to meet the perceived needs of the post-genocide environment. Gacaca gives respected individuals elected by the local population the duty of prosecuting cases and excludes professional judges and lawyers from participating in any official capacity.[150]

2. Foreign Transitional Justice Institutions

In addition to Rwanda's domestic prosecutions, other states have prosecuted suspected *génocidaires* on their territory, through a claim of universal jurisdiction and sometimes referred by the ICTR.[151] As an alternative to prosecutions for alleged conduct during the genocide, some countries in which suspected *génocidaires* sought refuge have tried those individuals for lying on their immigration applications about their whereabouts and activities during the genocide. For example, in 2013, a U.S. federal court convicted Beatrice Munyenyezi of making false statements in her asylum application and stripped her of American citizenship. The United States may eventually deport Munyenyezi to Rwanda to face trial for suspected crimes during the genocide.[152]

II. Transitional Justice Options Seriously Considered
and Actually Implemented for Alleged Rwandan *Génocidaires*

Unlike with the WWII and Balkan atrocities discussed in the previous three
chapters, neither the USG nor other members of the international community
implemented any significant transitional justice options aside from prosecution
in the immediate aftermath of the genocide. Based on the history detailed in
Part I above, this Part discusses what transitional justice options the UN and the
USG seriously considered and actually implemented for addressing the principal
individuals suspected of perpetrating atrocities in Rwanda.

A. TRANSITIONAL JUSTICE OPTIONS
THE UN SERIOUSLY CONSIDERED AND ACTUALLY IMPLEMENTED

Just as with the atrocities in the FRY, the Rwandan genocide occurred after most
members of the international community signed the Genocide Convention.
Consequently, states involved with Rwandan transitional justice were predisposed to two particular options: prosecution domestically in the state where
atrocities were perpetrated (here, Rwanda) or internationally through an ICT.

And just as with the atrocities in the FRY, almost immediately after atrocities
in Rwanda came to light, the international community (operating through the
UN) declared that it would seek to prosecute the perpetrators. This rhetoric again
generally ruled out inaction and other non-prosecutorial mechanisms as serious
options. The question that the international community thus confronted once
more was what type of prosecution to implement.

Unlike the case of the FRY, by the time of the Rwandan genocide, an ICT
(the ICTY) existed. The international community thus seriously considered three
main options: ICTY-Expanded, ICT-Tied, and ICT-Separate. These options represented a narrower array of choices than the international community seriously
considered in the case of the FRY. As discussed above, the UNSC ultimately
implemented ICT-Tied.

B. TRANSITIONAL JUSTICE OPTIONS THE U.S. GOVERNMENT
SERIOUSLY CONSIDERED AND ACTUALLY IMPLEMENTED

Just as with the FRY, the USG (like other members of the international community) almost immediately sought to arrange prosecution of Rwandan *génocidaires*.
Unlike with the FRY, however, the USG appeared more flexible regarding the ultimate form that prosecution could take. At various points, the USG apparently seriously considered supporting prosecution through ICTY-Expanded, ICT-Separate,
ICT-Tied, a permanent international criminal court, or the ICJ. Moreover, unlike

with either the Nazis or Japanese from WWII or the Balkan atrocity perpetrators, the USG seemingly did not seriously consider supporting any non-prosecutorial transitional justice options for Rwanda.

The USG ultimately supported the implementation of ICT-Tied through the UNSC. Figure 7.1 shows the general transitional justice option the USG supported for addressing alleged Rwandan *génocidaires*, whereas Figure 7.2 displays the specific prosecutorial transitional justice option the USG supported in this case.

In addition, the USG later instituted programs to support the GoR's confrontation of *génocidaires* through: (1) a U.S. Resident Legal Advisor to Rwanda to advise and materially assist the GoR in its national prosecutions,[153] and (2) financial, technical, and material assistance to *gacaca*.[154]

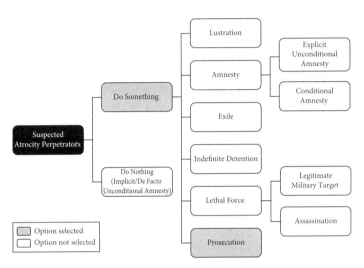

FIGURE 7.1 *U.S. Government Transitional Justice Options Tree for Suspected* Rwandan *Genocide Perpetrators—General.*

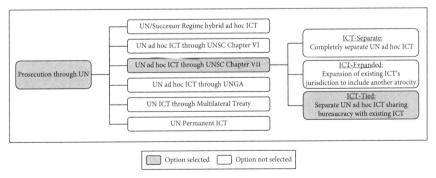

FIGURE 7.2 *U.S. Government Transitional Justice Options Tree for Suspected* Rwandan *Genocide Perpetrators—Prosecution.*

III. Explaining the United States Role in Transitional Justice for Rwanda

This Part considers, first, USG decision-making at each of the most critical decision points leading to the establishment of the ICTR. This Part then identifies and resolves certain puzzles in that decision-making process.

A. DECISION POINTS

In the course of endorsing what would become the ICTR, the USG backed general and specific transitional justice options. This Part discusses the USG's rationale for each of those decisions, namely (1) to support action, (2) to support prosecution, (3) to support prosecution through the UN, (4) to support prosecution through the UNSC's Chapter VII powers, and (5) to support prosecution through the ICT-Tied option.

1. U.S. Government Support for Action

It is not obvious that the USG would have decided to do something about Rwandan *génocidaires*. The USG had been proactive in the aftermath of some atrocities, such as by taking the initiatives regarding suspected German, Japanese, and Balkan perpetrators discussed in the preceding three chapters. However, the USG also was inactive in the immediate aftermath of other atrocities, such as the 1915 Armenian genocide that killed approximately 1 million people, and the mid-1970s Khmer Rouge genocide of Cambodians that claimed approximately 1.7 million lives.[155]

Furthermore, the USG not only decided to remain on the sidelines during the Rwandan genocide, but also proactively sought to block or minimize UN efforts.[156] Declassified USG documents reveal that:

> Contrary to later public statements, the US lobbied the UN for a total withdrawal of UN forces in Rwanda; Secretary of State Warren Christopher did not authorize officials to use the term "genocide" until May 21[, 1994], and even then, US officials waited another three weeks before using the term in public; [b]ureaucratic infighting slowed the US response to the genocide; [t]he US refused to "jam" extremist radio broadcasts inciting the killing because of costs and concern with international law; and US officials knew exactly who was leading the genocide, and actually spoke with those leaders to urge an end to the violence.[157]

The initial question then is why, given USG inaction and obstructionism during the genocide, the USG took an active role post-genocide.

One possible explanation lies in guilt. The USG decision to "do something" post-genocide may have been driven by personal responsibility felt by Clinton and other USG officials stemming from their recognition that even limited intervention by the USG could have significantly mitigated the genocide. Referring to the USG as a whole, a U.S. congressperson charged when advocating for the immediate establishment of an ICT for Rwanda in July 1994: "Any further delay clearly increases the burden of guilt on our account."[158] Indeed, some GoR officials have accused the USG in similar fashion.[159]

Some experts on the genocide outside the USG agree with this explanation. Des Forges believed that "the USG decided to support the ICTR because they felt so damn guilty," thinking "it was a 'least-we-can-do' kind of idea . . . they wanted to have some form of justice just because they needed to settle their own consciences . . . ."[160] Journalist Elizabeth Neuffer agreed: "How to assuage the West's guilt? The answer was the same as for the [FRY]: create a war crimes tribunal."[161]

Some USG officials who worked on the issue concur with these experts. Gregory Stanton, former Political Officer in the U.S./DoS Office for UN Political Affairs, former president of the International Association of Genocide Scholars, and current president of Genocide Watch, believes that USG officials were motivated by subconscious feelings of "guilt . . . . We were involved in the decision to throw out UNAMIR troops from Rwanda. The result of that decision was that hundreds of thousands of people were slaughtered. I think a lot of people in the USG realized that was a huge mistake."[162] Stanton specifically points to Clinton and other senior USG officials as being motivated by feelings of culpability to "do something" post-genocide.[163] Congressperson Maxine Waters, who accompanied Clinton to his March 25, 1998, speech at the Kigali International Airport, publicly stated her belief that Clinton felt remorse over the USG not intervening in the genocide.[164]

Shattuck acknowledges that he and others sensed a connection between USG inaction during the genocide and the desire to do something after the fact. As Shattuck explains, doing nothing was

> unthinkable, in my view, from the standpoint of having had the international community withdraw the UN forces that might well have been able to at least slow the genocide. Nothing was done to stop the genocide and it was unthinkable not to address the genocide after it occurred . . . [there were] certainly feelings of obligation and perhaps some guilt.[165]

Some senior USG officials discuss their feelings in terms of a missed opportunity to offer assistance without explicitly drawing connections to USG post-genocide policies. Albright reflected on the genocide by noting: "My deepest regret from my years in public service is the failure of the United States and the international community to act sooner to halt those crimes."[166]

However, other USG officials working on the issue emphatically deny that guilt was a motivating factor. As Scheffer declares, "it is a popular, erroneous presumption, and everyone likes to use it, that the ICTR was America's sop to what occurred in Rwanda or that it was somehow our contrition for letting the genocide occur."[167] (Even then, though, Scheffer has referred multiple times to the establishment of the ICTR as part of his then-USG colleagues and his own personal effort to seek "redemption"[168] after "the United States had abandoned Rwandan Tutsi to their fate in the genocide."[169]) Matheson is also skeptical of the remorse explanation, though he is less vehement in his denial, stating, "in terms of saying that the government feels guilt, well, the government is not a person, so it is hard to attribute that kind of motive to it."[170] While acknowledging, like Albright, that not intervening in Rwanda is his greatest regret,[171] Clinton, too, has explicitly denied feeling guilty about the genocide.[172]

It is unclear from the interviews I conducted, excerpted above, whether a major factor in the USG decision to "do something" was that USG decision-makers felt guilty (about not intervening, and obstructing other assistance during the genocide) and so wanted to "do something" in the aftermath to make amends. The USG, including the Clinton administration, declined to intervene in previous and subsequent atrocities (e.g., Sudan, the DRC), and has provided only minimal support to many transitional justice systems in their immediate aftermath, further raising questions about whether and, if so, to what extent feelings of guilt over humanitarian crises have driven foreign policy decision-making on transitional justice.

Another explanation for the USG's decision to "do something" post-genocide is that, with the progressive realization of the particularly egregious nature and scope of the atrocities, the USG felt that it should become involved as a logical, appropriate, and necessary response. Lake, Matheson, and Stanton all subscribe to that view.[173] This perspective denies that the UN, including the USG, knew the full extent of the genocide soon after it erupted—a view not without its skeptics and essentially debunked now. Indeed, declassified USG documents from the time and subsequent reports indicate that the USG was aware of the magnitude of the atrocities as they unfolded.[174]

Instead, USG officials such as Stanton and Scheffer believe that their colleagues pursued a transitional justice option for Rwanda to achieve a foreign policy success as compensation for recent USG failures in the region—during the Rwandan genocide itself as well as the disastrous October 1993 intervention in Somalia[175]—even without feelings of guilt about those failures.[176] Those involved may have viewed a genocide response that did not risk American lives and resources but rather supported the establishment of a post-conflict transitional justice solution as the less costly alternative, both politically and pragmatically (e.g., financially), although these two options need not have been mutually exclusive.

On the other hand, some USG officials involved do not believe that achieving a foreign policy success after Somalia and Rwanda factored into the calculus. Shattuck argues: "The impact of Somalia on U.S.-Rwanda policy was more a factor in having the U.S. decide not to support the continuation of the peacekeeping operation in Rwanda."[177] Others, such as Matheson, concur, arguing that even if the USG had attained foreign policy successes in Rwanda and Somalia, the USG still would have supported the establishment of the ICTR.[178]

A fourth possible explanation is that the USG wanted to become involved in the transitional justice solution for Rwanda for strategic reasons: (1) the solution's potential value as a precedent for handling future atrocities, (2) the overlap between the solution and the USG's interests, (3) a sense that USG involvement would ensure the solution's best possible outcome, and, finally, (4) the inevitably of some sort of transitional justice for Rwanda. Stanton, Matheson, and Scheffer hold this view, with Scheffer arguing that the USG decided

> to take the lead before another delegation seized the lead and the credit for it. A major reason for US leadership was the reality that it would allow us to control the drafting and ultimate structure of the [ICTR]. Ninety percent of the struggle is being the initial drafter, creating the draft that other delegations have to work from. We needed to be in the front door first with that draft resolution ... part of the game is for other delegations to recognize the US early as the country to look to for that initial draft.[179]

This concern also appears explicitly in internal USG documents. In response to the Spanish government's June 10 proposal for what would become the UN/ICER, a U.S./DoS cable stated that

> USUN anticipates that other countries will launch this human rights initiative as theirs .... [U.S./DoS] should undertake the necessary assessment and provide appropriate guidance so that we not be foreclosed out of the option of the U.S. taking the initiative on the issue by another delegation doing so first.[180]

The USG's posturing and desire to claim credit are also apparent at other steps in the process of seeking transitional justice for Rwanda.[181]

Furthermore, the USG did not view a transitional justice system for Rwanda as a threat to its pragmatic objectives. The temporary and limited ICTR would help achieve the USG's goals of promoting justice and atrocity deterrence. Crucially, the ICTR establishment would not create a permanent or broad institution that would affect American citizens and government activities or risk harm to U.S. interests from the possibilities of other state actors not complying.

USG officials believed that their involvement in the ICTR would ensure the best possible outcome. As Stanton argues:

> There were some people in the Clinton Administration and there are some people still in the U.S. government and I think in general who think of the U.S. as having a particularly good model to make justice on and so we have a duty to work in these settings to uphold due process and the rights of the defendant to make sure these things work well.[182]

Shattuck concurs: "There was the thought among us that if the ICTR was sponsored by the U.S., it stood a better chance of being adopted than if it was sponsored by some other government."[183] The USG believed that only the United States had the necessary will, resources, and mature judicial traditions to guide the successful development of Rwandan transitional justice. Moreover, USG officials believed that a transitional justice system would be established in any case for post-genocide Rwanda so, according to Stanton, "it was clearly a private part of the decision to support the establishment of the ICTR" to mold what it viewed as an inevitable outcome.[184]

Finally, some USG officials contend that USG action in post-genocide Rwandan was motivated partially by recent USG involvement in the immediate aftermath of the FRY conflict. The ICTY precedent provided a model and impetus for USG action in post-genocide Rwanda. According to Matheson, he and some other U.S./DoS officials "persuaded the [U.S./DoS] that we had to treat Rwanda the same way as Yugoslavia."[185] Scheffer agrees, stating that, in post-genocide Rwanda, "there had to be a judicial response at least as credible as that which the Balkans atrocities had inspired with the [ICTY]."[186]

Furthermore, the ICTY precedent caused USG officials to consider carefully the consistency with which they applied transitional justice solutions in different regions; they wanted the international community to view them as treating Africans similarly to Europeans. According to these officials, the USG would have found it politically difficult to justify inaction in post-genocide Rwanda, especially after the USG's precedent of proactive involvement in the arguably less egregious Balkans crisis. Had the USG not acted, it likely would have faced criticism as being racist and regionalist,[187] as Twagiramungu had suggested. As discussed in Chapter V, the USG faced similar pressures with respect to Japanese atrocity perpetrators after the USG had participated in establishing the IMT for Nazis.

2. U.S. Government Support for Prosecution

Some USG officials claim Washington preferred prosecution as a means of realizing the precise transitional justice goals USG officials sought. Among those goals, deterrence against future violence, both in the short-term and long-term and both locally and throughout the region, was prioritized highly.[188]

The USG clearly also sought to punish the *génocidaires*. Clinton declared in a 1998 speech in Rwanda: "We must punish the [genocide] leaders, and then we can have justice for everyone else."[189] Most USG officials, including Scheffer, Stanton, Matheson, and Lake, viewed prosecution as a likely mechanism for meting out optimal punishment.[190] Besides its retributive nature, punishment (e.g, through imprisonment) featured the added benefit of incapacitating *géno-cidaires* in the region, which was a third transitional justice goal of the USG.[191] USG officials involved in the decision also sought as a fourth transitional justice goal to establish the historical record, which was considered crucial to determining what occurred during the genocide and to delegitimize the regime that had been in power at that time.[192] Prosecution had yet another benefit in that it could accomplish most of the transitional justice goals that alternatives would have yielded. For example, prosecution, like amnesty, can establish the truth and provide accountability.[193]

Besides fulfilling certain transitional justice goals, a second main reason explaining the road to prosecution was that it was the only legal option available.[194] Christopher's June 30, 1994, testimony to the U.S./SCFR had stated that the international community, including the USG, had an obligation under the 1948 Genocide Convention to punish acts of genocide. That treaty also requires all signatories, including the United States, to prosecute genocide perpetrators.[195]

Some USG officials, such as Matheson, claim that a third reason underlying the USG's preference for prosecution was the lack of urgency to make any deal or to be lenient with *génocidaires* as part of a power transfer as they were no longer in power. This situation, Matheson stated, rendered amnesty, exile, and lustration unnecessary.[196]

Fourth, USG officials such as Bushnell, Stanton, and Bennet, claim that support for prosecutions followed from the U.S. tradition to investigate and prosecute after a crime.[197] As a fifth argument, USG officials contend that the logistical challenges of dealing with a large number of *génocidaires* generated a belief that some alternatives to prosecution were impractical, even impossible. Regarding exile, Shattuck argues, "[g]iven the enormous number of people involved in the genocide, there was just no practical way to imagine exile."[198] Similarly, regarding the use of lethal force, Matheson states, "it is not as though we could have sent in individual assassins. The *génocidaires* were too numerous and they had to be dealt with in other ways."[199]

A sixth rationale concerns the USG's foreign policy toolbox. War crimes prosecutions clearly have been an effective arrow in that quiver; thus, the USG was equipped and institutionally prepared to support prosecutions for Rwanda. Indeed, no other option was as prominent in the toolbox. For example, Bushnell claims that the USG did not support one of the alternatives to prosecution—lethal force—specifically because it was not part of the USG foreign policy repertoire.[200]

Shattuck and Scheffer argue that the ongoing precedent of prosecuting suspected perpetrators of the FRY atrocities served as a final reason USG officials sought to prosecute *génocidaires*, especially as the Rwandan genocide was considered even more horrendous than the Balkans crisis.[201]

Even though some governments, such as in Tanzania,[202] floated the idea of amnesty, and some individuals, such as the GoR's own Minister for Rehabilitation and Social Integration, suggested it as a mechanism for "passive participants in the violence,"[203] the international community (including the USG) did not widely or seriously consider amnesty as an alternative to prosecution in post-genocide Rwanda. Given that supporting amnesty featured in USG decision-making as recently as three years earlier (when the USG contributed 40 percent of the budget for El Salvador's 1991 Commission on the Truth[204]), it is important to understand why the USG never seriously considered the same policy for Rwanda. In addition, the USG apparently did not consider any of the other proactive but non-prosecutorial transitional justice options: exile, lustration, indefinite detention, and lethal force.

Some alternatives to prosecution, such as amnesty, were not considered because USG officials saw them as incapable of providing optimal transitional justice and possibly capable of fomenting additional conflict and impunity. Shattuck argues that, if *génocidaires* were granted amnesty, their victims would have sought revenge, leading to further violence.[205] Similarly, Stanton argues that, if *génocidaires* were allowed to flee into exile, more violence would have occurred, as *génocidaires* would have continued killing.[206] Some USG officials, such as Shattuck, also regarded the use of lethal force as lacking deterring force against further conflict or, even worse, perhaps facilitating it.[207] The USG also did not consider alternatives such as exile, amnesty, and lustration because, according to Lake, Matheson, Shattuck, and Stanton, the USG viewed these options as inappropriate and incapable of providing sufficient punishment for the egregiousness of the genocide.[208]

3. U.S. Government Support for Prosecution through the UN

The USG's support for UN-led prosecutions finds purchase in the political and pragmatic benefits the United States would accrue by cooperating on a broadly multilateral transitional justice solution rather than pursuing a unilateral, bilateral, or narrowly multilateral option. The ICTR ensured burden-sharing by distributing the costs and responsibilities of trying *génocidaires* through collective participation in the UN system.[209] Moreover, the ICTR created issue linkages between the investigation and prosecution of *génocidaires* and stability and post-conflict reconstruction and reconciliation in Rwanda and the Great Lakes region of East Africa. For example, the USG believed that the creation of an ICT for Rwanda would facilitate the repatriation of refugees.[210] As a result, some USG officials (including Bennet) involved in the decision to establish the ICTR perceived its creation as a mutually beneficial endeavor among the USG and other UN member states.[211]

Lake, Matheson, and Stanton claim that the USG's decision to support prosecution through the UN furthered the political objective of bolstering the legitimacy of prosecutions in Africa and elsewhere with greater force than a narrower coalition or single state could produce.[212] International—and, particularly, UN-led—prosecutions would obviate a sense that the Rwanda trials were merely political instruments. As Stanton recalls, unilateral GoR prosecutions "would be seen as victor's justice . . . ."[213] For this reason, some states, such as Tanzania, which were critical to the process of bringing *génocidaires* to justice, were hesitant to cooperate with a transitional justice option pursued outside the UN.[214]

As a third reason, Matheson argues that the USG preferred international prosecutions to promote Rwanda's national stability and reconciliation by ensuring that the transitional justice would not lie in the hands of "any one ethnic group," referring to Tutsi.[215] USG officials feared that any perceived bias in the transitional justice process might provoke further hostilities, such as vigilante justice.[216] Prosecuting through the near-universal international body of the UN would supposedly allay this concern.

Fourth, USG officials pointed to Rwanda's lack of viability as a functioning state to prosecute unilaterally or even in a multilateral partnership as a reason to support international prosecution. Matheson and Scheffer, for example, believed that the Rwandan judiciary did not have the capacity for such trials, at least not immediately post-genocide.[217] Beyond the inability of the GoR to prosecute, USG officials such as Matheson cite the undesirability of its doing so. USG officials claim that they had little familiarity and experience with the post-genocide GoR government and thus could not predict its actions.[218] Other USG officials argued that, beyond a lack of information, a lack of trust between the USG and the new GoR permeated their relations. Among other things, the USG was particularly concerned about the GoR's knowledge of, or even participation in, supporting the RPF's alleged post-genocide reprisal mass killings of Hutu.[219] Other observers arrived at the same conclusion: the GoR could not and should not manage the trials. Bass states: "The [ICTR] was established partly because of dissatisfaction with the quality of justice likely to be dispensed by the overburdened, penniless, and understandably vengeful Rwandan regime."[220]

Stanton cites a fifth reason for the USG's international prosecution preference: that the entire world, not just Rwanda, shouldered the responsibility to respond to the genocide.[221] Prosecuting through the near-universal international body of the UN, instead of through a unilateral or more narrowly multilateral option, would ensure that most of the world, which had failed to intervene, would at least assume responsibility for assisting Rwanda post-genocide. The political and pragmatic benefits of broad multilateralism, then, could not be understated.

USG officials such as Scheffer cite, as a sixth reason, the GoR's own preference for a UN-led ICT to explain why the USG supported prosecutions through the UN.[222] A seventh explanation offered for USG support for UN-led prosecution is that the UN already was dealing with the genocide. The UN therefore was considered the natural, path-dependent forum for seamless decision-making immediately after the genocide, including regarding any transitional justice institution.

An eighth explanation for USG support for UN-led prosecution was that, in the absence of triumphant occupying forces, the UN was the default, indeed the only appropriate forum. USG officials such as Bushnell, Matheson, Shattuck, and Stanton referred to the Allies' victory in WWII and their decision to establish the IMT as distinguishable from Rwanda, where no members of the international community intervened.[223]

Bennet offers a ninth reason for USG support for UN-led prosecutions: at that time, USG-UN relations were positive enough that USG officials opted as a first resort to work through the UN on international issues.[224] Not only had the USG

supported the UNSC's 1993 establishment of the ICTY, but the USG also had col-
laborated recently through the UN in the 1991 Gulf War.

USG officials also claim, as a tenth reason, that they supported UN-led prosecutions because this option allowed them to pursue other prosecutorial mechanisms for some *génocidaires* outside the UN. According to USG officials such as
Albright, Scheffer, and Stanton, during the mid-1994 negotiations to establish
the ICTR, the USG also offered the GoR support in dealing with *génocidaires*
through its domestic judicial process.[225] Indeed, as early as August 1994, USG
officials began conducting bilateral talks with the GoR about how the former
could help "reconstitute the Rwandan justice system . . . ."[226]

Finally, USG officials involved in the decision argue that the recent and existing precedent of prosecuting suspects in the FRY through the UN triggered USG
support for a plan to prosecute *génocidaires* through the same forum.[227]

4. U.S. Government Support for Prosecution through the UNSC's Chapter VII Powers

As noted above, the USG eventually decided to prosecute *génocidaires* through
the UNSC's Chapter VII powers. Matheson recalled that the USG supported the
creation of an ICT for Rwanda via Chapter VII because that provision obligates
potentially uncooperative governments to extradite suspects residing in their
countries and to comply with the ICTR in other ways, which was crucial given
the number of *génocidaires* who sought refuge abroad.[228]

Some USG officials, such as Lake, stated that the USG also supported UNSC
prosecutions to maximize the USG's control over the process through its veto-
wielding, permanent seat on the UNSC.[229] A third explanation lies in the fact that
not just the UN in general but the UNSC specifically already was dealing with the
genocide. The UNSC had sent UNAMIR troops to Rwanda and was debating further action during the genocide. Bushnell recalls that, as a result, the USG viewed
the UNSC as the expected and path-dependent forum for continued discussions
post-genocide over whether and how to prosecute *génocidaires*.[230]

A further reason some USG officials offer for their choice to support UNSC-
led prosecutions related to the end of the Cold War, which created a permissive atmosphere for the Great Powers to reach agreement on transitional justice
issues.[231] A fifth explanation contends that the USG believed a UNSC-led prosecution was especially superior to at least one of the alternatives at this decision
point: a hybrid UN/Rwanda ICT. The USG perceived the GoR to be an unwilling and undesirable partner for the international community on a hybrid court
because, as Shattuck explains, the GoR "was both skeptical and weak."[232]

A sixth impetus for supporting UNSC-led prosecutions was that the establishment of a post-ICTY, UNSC-led ICT would reinforce or even increase the
legitimacy of the ICTY and of the UNSC's Chapter VII powers to establish
ICTs.[233] Finally and relatedly, the ongoing ICTY precedent again provided a focal
point for decision-making, in this case a UNSC-led prosecution. USG officials

argue that the political climate favored replicating or expanding the ICTY over alternatives for four reasons. First, a UNSC-created ICT for the FRY predisposed the UNSC (including the USG) to support the same option for Rwanda to ensure equal treatment of the two atrocities.[234] Second, the ICTY precedent established the acceptability and legitimacy of that option.[235] Third, the perceived need to make a decision quickly to promote the USG's transitional justice goals (e.g., deterrence, punishment) constrained innovation, perhaps by creating a hybrid UN/GoR tribunal or a permanent international criminal court.[236] Finally, the ICTY precedent laid the political groundwork for this option. The UNSC could easily replicate in the ICTR the theoretical, legal, procedural, and structural design of the ICTY.[237]

5. U.S. Government Support for Prosecution through the ICT-Tied Option

Through the UNSC, the USG could have supported ICT-Separate, ICTY-Expanded, or ICT-Tied. The USG did not seriously consider ICT-Separate and initially favored ICTY-Expanded for four reasons. First, USG officials antici-pated that ICT-Tied or ICTY-Expanded would facilitate greater burden-sharing and cost efficiency than ICT-Separate. An ICT for Rwanda that bureaucrati-cally overlapped with the ICTY presumably would reduce financial and trans-actional costs. USG officials argue, for example, that a single chief prosecutor would limit cost (e.g., time, money) in recruiting senior staff for trying offend-ers of both atrocities. Bushnell and Stanton contend that the exhaustive—and exhausting—negotiations over ICTY chief prosecutor candidates discouraged states from repeating the process for the ICTR.[238] The USG thus initially favored ICTY-Expanded to maximize institutional overlap, especially considering the difficulties the ICTY had faced.[239] The USG additionally was concerned that any delays in appending Rwanda to the ICTY would lead to further conflict in Rwanda through vigilante justice.[240]

Second, USG officials viewed both ICTY-Expanded and ICT-Tied as advan-tageous relative to ICT-Separate because they could maintain the consistent development of international law and prosecutorial process. Prosecuting per-petrators of the Balkan and Rwandan atrocities through at least a common appeals chamber would facilitate the harmony of international jurisprudence. If the prosecution of *génocidaires* occurred in an ICT unassociated with the ICTY, multiple and potentially conflicting bodies of international criminal law could develop.[241]

The USG initially favored ICTY-Expanded to create an institution whose jurisdiction could be broadened to include atrocities beyond the Balkans and Rwanda.[242] In particular, some USG officials envisioned and supported the estab-lishment of a permanent international criminal court.[243] Incidentally, the USG supported an expandable institution in 1994 because it would be subject to USG veto in the UNSC, but the USG would not support the ICC four years later in part because it was created through a non-UN multilateral treaty and therefore would not be subject to USG veto in the UNSC.[244]

Finally, the ICTY precedent created momentum for ICTY-Expanded or ICT-Tied over ICT-Separate. USG officials recalled the difficulty in creating the ICTY and desired not to reinvent the wheel through a completely separate ICT for Rwanda.[245] Riding the momentum of the existing ICTY meant that the international community already had a chief prosecutor in Goldstone who was willing and, many thought, able to take on oversight of the Rwanda cases. Furthermore, Goldstone was a former prominent official from a powerful African state—South Africa, a country simultaneously employing a transitional justice process to handle past atrocities—which presumably would ensure his acceptance throughout Africa and make his work within the continent run smoothly.[246]

Ultimately, the USG voted for the option that the ICTR embodies: ICT-Tied. There are four main reasons the USG eventually favored this option, especially over ICTY-Expanded. First, although other UNSC permanent member states, especially France[247] and Russia, opposed ICTY-Expanded because it might evolve into a permanent international criminal court, the USG was able to forge a compromise with the dissenters by sharing some bureaucratic infrastructure between the ICTY and an ICT for Rwanda (represented by ICT-Tied).[248]

Second, some USG officials suggest that the United States chose ICT-Tied as a compromise solution because other states felt ICTY-Expanded was insufficient to deal with the enormity and importance of the Rwandan genocide.[249] Scheffer specifically cites the GoR's preference for ICT-Tied over ICTY-Expanded as a reason the USG ultimately favored ICT-Tied, not only because the GoR represented the victims of the genocide but also because, at that time, it sat on the UNSC and opposed having the Rwandan genocide merely tacked on to the ICTY.[250]

Third, USG officials also suggest that workload and other capacity factors compelled the USG's ultimate preference for ICT-Tied over ICTY-Expanded. Some felt it was pragmatically too difficult to have the ICTY prosecute *génocidaires* in addition to its own caseload.[251] Furthermore, the USG also was concerned about the capacity of the ICTY to retain custody over suspected *génocidaires* in The Hague.[252]

A final reason that USG officials ultimately preferred ICT-Tied to ICTY-Expanded was that the former could be located in Africa, near Rwanda. As a result, ICT-Tied, which could be centralized in Africa, would ease management of the investigations and prosecutions compared to ICTY-Expanded, which would have been based in the ICTY's existing offices in The Hague.[253] ICT-Tied also better ensured credibility and enabled Rwandans more easily to observe or follow the trials, which may have been as much a symbolic motive as it was pragmatic.[254]

This final decision point—the USG's determination to support prosecution through ICT-Tied—presents the following puzzles.

At the final decision point, the USG did not achieve its initial goal of establishing an ICT for Rwanda through ICTY-Expanded, raising questions about why the superpower compromised.

Two political factors, both mentioned above, caused the USG to shift its support to ICT-Tied. One was that some UNSC permanent members, notably France and Russia, opposed an institution that might lead to the creation of a permanent international criminal court. Another was that some states, including Rwanda, favored ICT-Tied over ICTY-Expanded as being more appropriate for dealing with the genocide. However, these states' influence on the USG's overall policy should not be overstated given that the USG held only a weak initial preference for ICTY-Expanded over ICT-Tied. The USG's primary political and pragmatic objective was ensuring that other powerful states would vote and provide financial and administrative resources for the establishment of a relatively low-cost (in terms of diplomacy and finances) ICT through the UNSC that the USG could influence. If the USG had pursued its initial preference for ICTY-Expanded, other UNSC permanent members might have voted against it, blocking its creation. In that case, multiple states may have pursued isolated prosecution of *génocidaires* under competing assertions of "universal jurisdiction," thus fomenting discord over jurisdictional claims to suspects, witnesses, and evidence, further delaying and driving up the cost of a post-genocide transitional justice solution. The effect of this chaotic scheme would have been reduced efficiency, legitimacy, and impact of whichever transitional justice solution, if any, had been established. Furthermore, the USG might also have risked the political capital it needed from the other UNSC permanent members to address broader matters of international peace and security, such as its desire to restore Jean-Bertrand Aristide to power in Haiti in 1994.[255] Therefore, between the two options (ICTY-Expanded and ICT-Tied), neither of which conflicted with the USG's interests, the USG ultimately favored the one that most of the other UNSC permanent members preferred. To be clear, the implication is not that other states compelled the world's sole superpower to act against its preferences. The USG's eventual decision to back an option with strong support from others in the international community, without expending crucial American political capital, ensured that the ICTR would be established through the UNSC's Chapter VII powers and would receive support from and the cooperation of other powerful states and Rwanda.

B. UN/ICER'S OPPOSITION

A second puzzle considers why the USG ultimately supported ICT-Tied when the UN/ICER's interim report recommended against this option, and instead advocated for ICTY-Expanded. There are two possible political explanations. Some USG officials suggest that the UN/ICER's recommendations had little impact on the USG's ultimate decision because that UN body, like other ad hoc UN commissions, exerts little influence on USG decisions generally. As Scheffer recalls: "The fact that a Commission of Experts recommends something is very interesting, but it has absolutely no—it has very little determinative effect on how governments decide to make sovereign decisions."[256] Matheson and Bushnell agree.[257] An anonymous former USG official similarly argues that independent commissions such as the UN/ICER "don't necessarily or typically have any direct impact on U.S. policy." This may have been particularly true for the UN/ICER because, given its limited mandate and short time frame, it was apparently a fact-finding commission that held little weight. Rather, it may have been merely a cosmetic aspect of a standard operating procedure established during the creation of the ICTY. As Bassiouni argues:

> The [UNSC] may establish a Commission because it sees the need, at that time, for that issue to go through a particular process. The [UN/ICER] was one such case .... Its function was essentially window dressing. At the time, the [UNSC] wanted to follow its precedent of the Yugoslavia Commission that preceded the [ICTY] and that called for its establishment as stated in Resolution 808.[258]

Another explanation, offered by Scheffer, is that the UN/ICER's recommendation to support ICTY-Expanded was nothing more than a reflection of the USG's own initial position. By the time it published its preliminary report, the UN/ICER simply had not amended its recommendations to match the USG's revised position in favor of ICT-Tied.[259] This theory rests on the lag time between the date, if ever, that the UN/ICER received the U.S./DoS/US-UN's guidance indicating the USG's revised position in favor of ICT-Tied, and the publication of the UN body's preliminary report. Bassiouni supports Scheffer's theory: "More frequently than not, the reports produced [by UN independent commissions] are designed to please ... certain governments, particularly the three Western permanent members [of the UNSC] and a number of Western European countries that champion human rights."[260]

Given its limited mandate, especially compared to the UN Independent Commission of Experts on the former Yugoslavia (UN/ICEfY), and the fact that USG officials seem not to hold these bodies in high esteem, it should not be surprising that the UN/ICER lacked influence over USG decision-making regarding the precise form of the Rwanda ICT. It appears that the UN/ICER was created mostly to mirror the process of establishing the ICTY. As a result, USG officials had no qualms about rejecting the UN/ICER's recommendations, especially as those recommendations may have been nothing more than a reflection of the USG's own initial preferences. Competing interests—such as addressing Russian and French concerns, locating the ICT near Rwanda, and creating a separate ICT that could handle the Rwandan caseload—trumped what little influence the UN/ICER may have exerted.

C. GOVERNMENT OF RWANDA'S OPPOSITION

A third puzzle is why the USG decided to support ICT-Tied even though the GoR opposed it. As described above, commentators consider the GoR's preferences to have been influential in most decision points (except the final one), mostly out of deference to its people's suffering, especially when the international community (including the USG) had done little to help them during the genocide. As Bushnell explains,

> you have an international community that did nothing to stop the geno-
> cide. And you have the victims who end up being the next government . . . .
> [T]he victims/victors had their own sense of what needed to be done and
> they felt very, very strongly . . . . [T]he international community, if not in
> agreement with them, was certainly not in any position to say no.[261]

But the international community did say no. Despite the GoR's vote against UNSCR 955, the USG (and all other UNSC member states except China) voted for it.

Before examining the reasons the USG opposed the GoR, it is important to understand the GoR's vote. The GoR publicly offered seven objections or concerns: (1) the temporal jurisdiction of calendar year 1994 was inadequate to encompass previous planning and practice massacres; (2) the ICTR did not include enough trial chamber judges, and inappropriately shared an appeals chamber and chief prosecutor with the ICTY; (3) the subject-matter jurisdiction was overly broad and did not prioritize any of the crimes, including genocide, as the most important; (4) UNSC member states that participated in the Rwandan civil war (which the GoR stated "need not be named" but likely referred to France[262]) would inappropriately be able to propose and vote on judicial candidates; (5) suspects and convicts would inappropriately be held in states outside of Rwanda and those states would make decisions regarding these detainees; (6) the ICTR should include the death penalty as a potential sentence; and (7) the ICTR should be located in Rwanda.[263] Of the reasons offered, some believe that the lack of capital punishment was the GoR's main objection,[264] even though the country's Justice Minister, Nkubito, personally opposed its use.[265]

Yet some experts believe that there may have been other reasons for the GoR's negative vote. One theory, proposed by Shattuck, is that the GoR did not trust the UN to prosecute *génocidaires*, as the UN had proven unreliable and inept during the genocide.[266] A second theory, offered by Des Forges, is that the GoR feared that the ICTR could backfire on it by prosecuting RPF officials for their retaliations against Hutu during and immediately after the genocide.[267]

One explanation for why the USG voted for UNSCR 955, despite the GoR's opposition, is that the USG viewed some of the GoR's objections as impractical or insufficient to compel USG opposition to the resolution. As Scheffer argues: "We believed at that stage we had done all we could with the Rwandans, who after all would not in the end dictate the UNSC process or decision-making."[268] For

one, the GoR wanted the ICTR to include the death penalty as a possible punishment notwithstanding the fact that many members of the UNSC were and are
in principle opposed to capital punishment. The GoR felt that execution was an
appropriate punishment, and believed it would be inconsistent if the ICTR did
not make this sentence available because judges overseeing less serious offenses
tried in the domestic Rwandan judiciary could and did impose the death penalty.[269] As Scheffer recalls:

> The European states of the [UNSC] will never, ever support the creation of a
> court with the death penalty—it's off the table, it's not negotiable, it will not
> happen . . . . We were not going to fall over our sword defending Rwanda's
> desire to have the death penalty. It was simply an unrealistic proposal. It's
> like saying Rwanda desires the resurrection of Alexander the Great to pre-
> side over the Rwanda tribunal—it's not going to happen.[270]

Instead, the USG prioritized the creation of an ICT through the UNSC's Chapter
VII powers over including capital punishment among the possible penalties for
génocidaires. Although the USG considered capital punishment to be legitimate
in its own criminal justice system, it recognized that other states crucial to supporting the ICT vehemently opposed the penalty.

Another GoR objection the USG did not find compelling concerned the ICTR's
proposed location. The GoR wanted the ICTR to be in Kigali, Rwanda's capital.
However, because the USG viewed post-genocide Rwanda as unstable and inhos-
pitable to hosting the ICTR, the USG did not agree.[271] In sum, Scheffer recalls:

> at the end of the day, we were going to stand with the vast majority of the
> [UNSC] as to how the ICTR was going to be structured as opposed to take
> an extreme minority and, frankly, surreal, unrealistic position, which is, in
> the end, what the Rwandan government was arguing.[272]

Matheson concurs.[273]

A third explanation for the USG vote, according to Shattuck, is that the USG
suspected GoR officials or their associates of committing some of the crimes,
specifically in the Kibeho massacre, that would come under the jurisdiction of
the ICTR. Consequently, the USG did not want to bend to GoR demands about
reconfiguring the ICTR's temporal jurisdiction or prioritizing the tribunal's
subject-matter jurisdiction that would bar those crimes and individuals from the
tribunal's ambit.[274]

A fourth reason for the USG's vote, according to Scheffer, Stanton, and
Shattuck, was that the GoR was so late in voicing its objections to UNSCR 955
that the USG found it difficult to resist the momentum that had been building
to pass it.[275] Scheffer claims it was not until the day before the vote that the USG
learned that the GoR would cast a negative vote.[276] In other words, the international community's investment of diplomatic and political capital up to that

point had created path dependency and policy inertia in favor of establishing the ICTR over any remaining GoR concerns.

A fifth explanation is that the GoR reflected, or did not oppose, the USG's position on earlier decision points. Yet when the GoR resisted the USG's preference for ICT-Tied, the USG decided to go forward with its intentions. As Scheffer observes, "we were constantly seeking for [the GoR] to adjust their position so that they could support the consensus or the near-consensus position."[277] When convenient, the USG supported GoR preferences; when inconvenient, the USG ignored them.

A final explanation for the USG decision to support the establishment of the ICTR over the GoR's objections is that the USG received assurance that the GoR would cooperate with the ICTR regardless of the latter's negative vote. As scholar Virginia Morris and Scharf argue: "Kagame indicated that Rwanda would cooperate fully with the tribunal if it were set up over Rwanda's objections. This assurance of cooperation by Rwanda cleared the way for the [UNSC's] decision to establish [the ICTR]."[278] Scheffer agrees, stating: "I knew from my consultations that Rwandan officials intended to support the tribunal following the vote."[279] Not only did the GoR signal these intentions, but the fact that the ICTR had been created through Chapter VII also compelled the GoR to cooperate regardless. As Albright, then the UNSC/P, declared after the vote to establish the ICTR, "we urge the [GoR] to honor its obligation to cooperate fully with the [ICTR] and the investigation it must undertake in order to prosecute those guilty of the unspeakable acts of genocide and other atrocities."[280]

Given that GoR preferences were cited at all decision points except the last one (regarding the type of ICT the UNSC would establish), one of two rationales might explain the ultimate divergence of views between Rwanda and the United States. Either the USG followed the GoR's preferences up to a limit beyond which it would be impractical, illegitimate, unacceptable, or unnecessary to do so, or the GoR's preferences reflected the USG's own except at the final decision point. Considering that each of the first four decision points was overdetermined, independent of GoR preferences, the latter explanation is likely correct.

D. NARROW FOCUS

A fourth puzzle questions why, given the large number of *génocidaires*, the USG decided to support an option—ICT-Tied—that would focus on only a small fraction of alleged perpetrators, even if they were the suspected leaders of the genocide. One explanation, offered by Lake, is that the ICTR could only handle a narrow focus.[281] Scheffer concurs, citing experience:

> we were at least practical enough in 1994 to understand that going beyond the leadership is nuts, you can't do it, there are no resources for it .... That is one of the clear lessons of the 1990s with respect to international criminal

justice: that personal jurisdiction cannot be practically undertaken unless it is limited.[282]

Stanton agrees:

It was recognized right from the start that the UN court wouldn't have the capacity to handle the huge numbers of people that had been involved in the Rwandan genocide, that most of the prosecutions would have to be handled by the Rwandan national courts. So the idea was to go after the planners and the leaders and the conspirators, like Nuremberg . . . and then let other prosecutions go forward in Rwandan courts.[283]

In this respect, the USG's approach to the ICTR mirrored its approach to the IMT, the IMTFE, and the ICTY, which also tried only a small fraction of the larger group of suspected atrocity perpetrators.

A second explanation for the ICTR's limited scope, offered by Lake and Scheffer, is that the GoR wished to prosecute the majority of *génocidaires* and preferred that the ICTR prosecute only a small number of them.[284] This request was underscored by the list identifying only fifty-five suspected *génocidaires* that the RPF provided to Dégni-Ségui immediately post-genocide, which suggested that the GoR wanted the international community to focus only on this finite group.

A third explanation for the ICTR's restricted scope would suggest that the USG never intended for UNSC-led prosecutions to be the USG's only method of dealing with *génocidaires*. Moreover, on this account, the USG always planned to support addressing a much greater number of *génocidaires* through additional transitional justice solutions, which it has done.

Because the ICTR was constrained by capacity, and because the USG already planned to support other transitional justice options for dealing with *génocidaires*, the ICTR was designed to focus narrowly on a few dozen of the most egregious *génocidaires*. As discussed above, the GoR's preferences may have affected or merely reflected the USG's position. Given that this decision point was not as determined as others, it is possible that the GoR's preferences were more influential on this issue.

F. ICTY PROGRESS

Finally, why did the USG support ICT-Tied despite having reason to be concerned about the ICTY precedent and operations? The USG was discouraged by the ICTY's progress at the same time it was considering an ICT for Rwanda that would share at least some bureaucracy with the ICTY. Between May 25, 1993, when the ICTY was established, and November 8, 1994, when the ICTR was created, the ICTY suffered significant delays and setbacks. Among the more critical problems, the first ICTY chief prosecutor, Ramón Escovar-Salom, resigned almost immediately after his appointment on October 21, 1993,[285] and the UN/

ICEfY was terminated on April 30, 1994, "prematurely," according to Bassiouni, its chairman.[286] The ICTY did, however, achieve some progress between May 25, 1993, and November 8, 1994, including the election of judges,[287] the meeting of the first plenary session, the ICTY president's affirming of state obligations to cooperate with the ICTY,[288] the entering into force of the tribunal's Rules of Procedure and Evidence,[289] and Goldstone's appointment as the second chief prosecutor.[290] The ICTY then took more steps forward, especially in the cases against Duško Tadić and Dragan Nikolić.[291]

Despite these signs of improvement, the ICTY's overall lack of progress raised serious doubts among USG officials about its prospect for lasting success. As Albright recalls: "There seemed a real possibility that the [ICTY] would flop and that, once again, the world community would be accused of promising much while delivering little."[292] Shattuck recollects discussions over whether the ICTY was even a worthwhile model for Rwandan transitional justice.[293] Scheffer remembers condemnations hurled at the ICTY, especially after Escovar-Salom's resignation,[294] and Matheson recalls many early challenges.[295] Stanton recollects that

> [ICTY officials] had, up to that point, failed to get their hands on the top perpetrators of the crimes in the [FRY] and there hadn't been any trials yet. So they were looking very impotent at this point .... Up to the date we established the ICTR, the results from the ICTY were disappointing.[296]

Some outside observers also have noted the poor progress the ICTY made during its first eighteen months. As political scientist Howard Ball observes: "Although there was a formal opening ceremony in the Hague in November 1993, the ICTY immediately adjourned, for there were no judges, no chief prosecutor, and no prosecutorial staff."[297]

At least two theories might explain the USG decision to support the ICTY model for Rwanda despite the ICTY's minimal progress and the real possibility of its failure. One, offered by Scheffer and Stanton, is that the USG recognized that the period between May 25, 1993, and November 8, 1994, was not sufficient to determine the likelihood of the ICTY's ultimate success.[298] An ICTY official from that time agrees, arguing: "Anybody who claimed that they based the decision to establish the ICTR on the success—or lack thereof—of the ICTY is kidding themselves. It was much too soon to make any reasonable assessment of the ICTY's work."[299]

Another explanation is that the USG had no reason to believe that alternative options would be any less problematic, or that investment to date in the ICTY, even though the tribunal had difficulties, would be more than merely a sunk cost. Furthermore, the problems the ICTY had faced related to implementation and not to institutional design; organizational execution theoretically could be rectified over time for both the ICTY itself and an ICT for Rwanda. As Matheson recalls:

> The problem was not the concept but the practicalities of getting people appointed and resources provided and so on. Those problems would have been equally if not more serious in any other potential option. At least we had begun to address them in the Yugoslav context. And so we had some reason to believe we could do the same for Rwanda. But if we had started completely differently, there would have been no [UNSC] support for it legally, and there would have been no UN funding. No other option gave any greater hope, and in most ways a lot less hope, in providing a quick, efficient startup.[300]

Consequently, the USG supported ICT-Tied despite having reason to be concerned about the ICTY precedent because the ICTY had not yet had enough time to work out its early missteps, and because there was no obviously better alternative to the ICTY model.

IV. Conclusion

The ICTR's establishment, in which the USG played a leading role, was a momentous advancement in international law and politics. Along with the ICTY, founded just the previous year, the creation of the ICTR marked a significant development in international cooperation, especially among Great Powers. The ICTR's birth (and that of the ICTY), particularly the bilateral cooperation between the United States and Russia on Goldstone's appointment as the ICTY and then the ICTY/ICTR chief prosecutor, illustrates significant progress in international cooperation during the immediate post–Cold War period. Shortly beforehand, the bilateral superpower rivalry paralyzed the UNSC and otherwise prevented effective collaboration on international issues, including transitional justice.

The ICTR's creation also represents a significant development in transitional justice. The ICTR established a precedent for the international community's response to crimes limited to an internal conflict. It also affirmed the power and legitimacy of the UNSC, initially demonstrated during the ICTY episode, to use its Chapter VII powers to create ad hoc ICTs for prosecuting suspected atrocity perpetrators.

As with the previous case studies—on the U.S. role in transitional justice for Nazi Germany, Imperial Japan, Libya, Iraq, and the FRY—a combination of politics, pragmatics, and normative beliefs drove the USG's decision-making regarding transitional justice for Rwanda. Some of the USG's individual motivations related to more than one of these factors.

That the USG did not intervene in the Rwandan genocide affected both political and pragmatic calculations over its subsequent transitional justice decision-making. The USG's political and legal resistance to intervention affected the timing and nature of its denouncements of the genocide. That the USG did not send troops or other assistance to Rwanda perversely may have increased the likelihood of involvement in the immediate aftermath. A desire to compensate for its foreign policy failures in Rwanda, if not also feelings of guilt over not intervening, apparently motivated at least some USG officials to support a transitional justice institution for Rwanda. The USG's stated pragmatic desire to avoid disrupting potential peace negotiations further affected the timing and nature of its rhetoric.

The extent of the USG's role in the transitional justice process for Rwanda was determined further by another political goal, namely a desire to claim credit for Rwanda's transitional justice solution before any other state could seize the initiative. Driven by that competitiveness, USG officials took the lead on designing and lobbying for the creation of an institution they felt was inevitable. Their goal of ensuring the most favorable design of that institution relative to U.S. interests further motivated the USG to become involved in a leadership capacity.

Certain political and pragmatic objectives influenced the USG's choice over the general transitional justice option. USG officials believed that prosecution, particularly through a respected international forum such as the UN, would bolster the legitimacy of war crimes trials, prevent further conflict and impunity, and promote local stability and reconciliation by removing the transitional justice process from the GoR's exclusive control.

The USG's preexisting treaty agreements also affected its transitional justice decision-making politically. USG officials stated that they were partly motivated to support prosecution over alternative transitional justice options because of the USG's obligations under the Genocide Convention to try suspected genocide offenders before competent tribunals.

Particular features of the Rwandan genocide exerted pragmatic influence on the USG's role in transitional justice for Rwanda. Given that *génocidaires* were no longer in power, prosecution was seen as a suitable option, whereas responses such as amnesty and exile and extreme solutions such as lethal force were seen as unnecessary. Furthermore, the sheer number of *génocidaires* rendered exile and lethal force impractical, if not impossible.

The USG was motivated to support prosecutions in the case of Rwanda because of particular political and pragmatic objectives USG officials held. These officials sought to bolster the legitimacy of war crimes trials, facilitate the repatriation of refugees, deter additional atrocities, remove the most egregious perpetrators from the region, and establish a historical record of the genocide.

The natures of the successor regime and its relationship with the USG were yet further political engines driving the transitional justice process. From the USG's perspective, the RPF-led GoR was unfamiliar, unpredictable, and untrusted. As a result, the USG did not want to leave the transitional justice process, even if it were prosecutorial, solely in the GoR's hands. For similar reasons, the USG did not want to partner with the GoR on a transitional justice institution through the UN, such as a GoR-UN hybrid tribunal.

How the conflict ended was a crucial pragmatic factor driving the transitional justice process. The absence of victorious occupying forces led the USG to support a transitional justice option through the UN as a default forum. And the USG's relationship with the UN at that particular point in history helped determine politically whether that default forum would be embraced. As the USG had positive relations with the UN at the time, USG officials viewed the UN as an attractive option.

The USG's ability to reach agreement with former adversaries and current allies on key matters significantly affected the post-genocide transitional justice process politically. The USG viewed the support of Russia and South Africa as critical to the selection of the ICTR's chief prosecutor. Moreover, the USG knew that it was necessary to obtain agreement from Russia, China, France, and the United Kingdom because of their equal veto power over the creation of any ICT through the UNSC. Fortunately for the USG, the end of the Cold War provided the political opportunity to reach consensus with Russia on transitional justice in Rwanda (as similarly occurred with transitional justice for the FRY). The USG was also concerned about France because of its historical ties to and ongoing involvement in Rwanda. Indeed, France likely had the best access of any country (other than Rwanda itself) to witnesses, evidence, and even suspected *génocidaires*. The USG knew that the UNSC's permanent members, including the USG itself, could compel the cooperation of states that were important to transitional justice in Rwanda and still retain veto power over that process. Reaching that consensus was so important to the USG that it abandoned the transitional justice option it initially preferred in favor of one other permanent UNSC members also supported.

The USG's power to overrule those states with which it ultimately disagreed, namely Rwanda itself, also helped shape transitional justice for Rwanda politically. The USG cited the GoR's preference for the international community to create an ICT through the UNSC as part of the reason the USG supported that option. Moreover, USG officials noted their desire to placate the GoR and defer to it to prosecute the overwhelming majority of *génocidaires* as a reason that the USG supported a transitional justice option that would address only a small fraction of the suspected genocide perpetrators. However, the USG did not honor the GoR's wishes about the precise design and function of the ICT for Rwanda. Unlike with the permanent members, the GoR did not wield a veto on the UNSC, and so the USG could choose which of the GoR's preferences it would support—and which it would not.

The perceived need to move quickly on a transitional justice response to the ferocious pace of the genocide served as a key pragmatic motivation leading to the eventual form that response would take. The USG thus decided to withdraw its initial, weak preference for ICTY-Expanded because negotiations with other critical states to generate more support would have required additional time. For the same reason, the USG decided to adopt or otherwise apply the existing ICTY model instead of pursuing innovative options, such as a hybrid GoR-UN ICT, which would have taken extra time to design. The USG decided it could not entertain additional GoR requests for modifications to the design of the ICT-Tied option, in part because such amendments would further delay the process.

A pragmatic desire to limit the cost of the chosen prosecutorial transitional justice option convinced the USG to support prosecution not only through the UN, which would enable the USG to share burdens with other members of the international community, but also through an option that shared at least some bureaucracy with the existing ICTY infrastructure. Pragmatic budgetary concerns also prompted USG officials to support a transitional justice option that could address only a few dozen *génocidaires*. Additionally, connecting the ICT for Rwanda to that of the ICTY was attractive to the USG for two more pragmatic reasons: (1) it satisfied USG preferences to promote the consistent development of international law and prosecutorial process; and (2) the ICTY already had a respected chief prosecutor—and one from sub-Saharan Africa to boot—who could be commissioned, as well, by the ICTR.

Enacting a transitional justice option for Rwanda through the UNSC presented a further pragmatic advantage: the UNSC could compel states to comply with critical requests for cooperation. Certain additional pragmatic factors further influenced the ultimate transitional justice option the USG supported. The USG's objectives to avoid adding to the ICTY's already significant caseload and limited detention capacity, and the USG's goal to locate the ICT for Rwanda in Africa, both played a role in the USG's decision to support ICT-Tied over ICTY-Expanded.

Overall, the single most important pragmatic determinant of the USG's support for the creation of the ICTR, at least for the first four decision points, was the path dependency created by the ICTY. This precedent—and the analogical reasoning following from it, despite known problems and setbacks—implicitly applied pressure on the USG to formulate a consistent policy on suspected atrocity perpetrators, regardless of their nationality, ethnicity, or location. In other words, just as the IMT precedent had done in the case of post-WWII Japan, the ICTY precedent served as a model compelling both the impetus for, and the shape of, USG action in post-genocide Rwanda.

All USG officials involved in the decision emphasize the pragmatic and political significance of the ICTY precedent to the creation of the ICTR. As Scheffer argues:

> If there had not been an ICTY, I think the presumption of considering an ICTR may not have occurred in 1994. In other words, the ICTY paved the

way for the issue to arise very quickly within the councils of the UN and in Washington. The ICTY had an enormous influence on creating the context within which an ICTR could be contemplated.[301]

In fact, many USG officials, such as Bushnell, Shattuck, and Stanton, believe that the ICTY was the "single most important factor" molding the form of the USG's decision to "do something" in post-genocide Rwanda.[302] Scholars also have noted the pragmatic importance of the ICTY precedent to the ICTR and other tribunals. Legal academic Peter Burns opines that the ICTY "is clearly a prototype for other such tribunals and it carries with it the moral and political force of the world community."[303] Not only were the pragmatic reasons and normative beliefs driving the USG's support for the establishment of the ICTR based in many ways on the ICTY (e.g., support for prosecution as a more appropriate solution than amnesty, exile, lustration, or lethal force; pursuing an option through rather than outside the UN), but much of the process leading to the eventual creation of the ICTR borrowed from the Balkans case as well. For example, the decision to establish the UN/ICER that preceded UNSCR 955 mirrored the UNSC's decision to ask the UNSG to establish the UN/ICEfY that conducted an investigation in the Balkans and issued recommendations that led to the creation of the ICTY.[304]

USG officials differ on the necessity of the ICTY precedent to the establishment of the ICTR. Some USG officials believe that the ICTR would have materialized even without the ICTY precedent. As Matheson theorizes: "If there had been no ICTY . . . I guess there still would have been an ICTR. All the same elements were there. I don't see why a different solution would have emerged."[305] Other USG officials, such as Shattuck, believe that had the ICTY not existed, the ICTR would not have either, in part because the USG would have felt less political pressure to "do something" in post-genocide Rwanda and to do so through an ICT.[306] Some UN officials involved in the decision favor this latter view, though perhaps not as strongly. As UN Legal Officer Daphna Shraga and Zacklin argue, "it is questionable whether the [ICTR] would have been established without the Yugoslav precedent . . . ."[307] Some scholars concur, assuming that the transitional justice response for Rwanda, if any, would have been much less significant without the ICTY precedent. Therefore, the ICTR was not established to reflect the supposedly benevolent motives of the international community when it established the ICTY. "In view of this hard reality," legal scholar Payam Akhavan argues on account of disparate treatment for black Africans and white Europeans in response to other atrocities, "there is little room for celebration, and even less for triumphalism."[308]

As the ICTY served as such an important precedent for the ICTR, it follows that the USG decision to establish the ICTR derives much of its origin from its earlier decision to support the ICTY's creation. Perhaps counterintuitively, then, many of the political factors, pragmatic features, and normative beliefs about establishing a UN ad hoc ICT for Rwanda through the UNSC's Chapter VII powers are represented in the debate to establish the ICTY, and occur during the Balkans crisis (when the decision to create the ICTY was made), *not* during and immediately after the Rwandan genocide. Again, the creation of the ICTY thus helps to explain both the USG's decision to support the establishment of the ICTR and the form the resulting ICT took. As discussed in Chapter V, the USG embraced similar path dependency in adopting the IMT framework as a working model for what would become the IMTFE.

Path dependency also served as both a pragmatic and political factor driving the USG's decision-making on transitional justice for Rwanda in another way. As the forum in which the international community was addressing the Rwandan genocide, the UN's (particularly the UNSC's) extant role compelled the USG to think of the UNSC as the most appropriate forum for dealing with the genocide's aftermath, including the transitional justice institution. The existing model of the ICTY and the existing UN and UNSC discussions about the Rwandan genocide stifled creative thinking about alternative transitional justice solutions. The ongoing precedent and negotiations also suggested that emulating the ICTY model and working through these forums was bureaucratically and politically easier and more desirable than pursuing an alternative option, which would raise difficult and sensitive questions about why the Rwandan genocide was being treated differently than the Balkans crisis. The existing ICTY machinery provided a blueprint of a UNSC-led ICT that could quickly and easily be adapted for the Rwandan genocide. The ICTY's statute, rules of procedure and evidence, chief prosecutor, appeals chamber, and supervisory authority (the UNSC) all were readily available to use for the Rwandan transitional justice institution.

Besides political and pragmatic factors, normative beliefs contributed to the USG's decision to support the creation of the ICTR. The USG's growing awareness over time about the nature and scope of the atrocities compelled officials to become involved out of a normative belief that such atrocities should be addressed through transitional justice. Some USG officials strongly favored on principle a particular means for confronting some genocide perpetrators. These USG officials believed that the most egregious *génocidaires* must be prosecuted and punished for their heinous acts. A further normative belief relates to U.S. domestic traditions. Some USG officials stated that the U.S. practice of prosecution in dealing with criminal offenders necessitated a legal process for addressing suspected Rwandan genocide perpetrators.

Nevertheless, there are limits to the persuasiveness of USG officials' explanations of the normative beliefs driving the U.S. role in transitional justice for Rwanda. Although some officials argued that prosecution was the only legal, mainstream, and appropriate option for dealing with *génocidaires,* and that the USG tradition of domestic prosecutions influenced its decision to favor this option for Rwanda, these explanations are dubious. As discussed in Chapters II, IV, V, and VI, the USG had and has since supported alternative transitional justice options for responding to atrocities. The argument that the USG does not use lethal force on suspected atrocity perpetrators is, as also discussed in Chapter II, inaccurate and therefore not a compelling explanation for the decision to prosecute in this case.

Now that these six cases—Germany and Japan in the immediate aftermath of WWII as well as Libya, Iraq, the FRY, and Rwanda in the immediate aftermath of the Cold War—have been examined, I proceed in the following, final chapter to consider them as a whole. That chapter will evaluate these cases' similarities and differences as well as assess whether legalism or prudentialism better accounts for the U.S. role in the cases' transitional justice.

Conclusion

I. Introduction

In this final chapter, I summarize the key findings from this book. In addition, I assess which of the two explanatory theories articulated in Chapter III—legalism or prudentialism—better accounts for U.S. policy on transitional justice in the six cases discussed in Chapters IV through VII: Germany and Japan in the immediate aftermath of WWII as well as Libya, Iraq, the FRY, and Rwanda in the immediate aftermath of the Cold War.

II. Summary of Findings

Chapter II demonstrated the wide array of transitional justice options—including inaction, amnesty, lustration, exile, lethal force, prosecution, indefinite detention, and each of their various permutations—and how the USG has employed many of them in the past. Especially recently (since September 11, 2001), however, the USG has most often supported only four of these options to address suspected atrocity perpetrators: inaction, indefinite detention, lethal force, and prosecution.

Chapter III explored the particular problems and challenges transitional justice represents for international relations, focusing on security and cooperation. After reviewing two prominent traditional international relations theories—realism and liberalism—and concluding that they do not specifically relate to transitional justice issues, I illustrated how variants of those theories—my prudentialism and Bass's legalism—are useful frameworks to explain state behavior regarding transitional justice. Legalism analyzes liberal states' transitional justice behavior by explaining their commitment to a normative belief, based on the rule of law, that it is both correct and necessary to prosecute war criminals. Conversely, prudentialism asserts that states, regardless of their liberal posture, formulate policies on transitional justice not out of a principled commitment to the rule of law, but rather as a result of a case-specific balancing of politics, pragmatics, and normative beliefs. The chapter also compared hypotheses that each framework would proffer, some of which conflict while others do not. The four most significant dueling hypotheses are: (1) legalism contends that states will consistently pursue transitional justice and will do so in the form of trials, whereas prudentialism postulates that states will not necessarily formulate consistent policies on whether or how to pursue transitional justice; (2) legalism contends that only liberal states support bona fide war crimes tribunals whereas prudentialism postulates that any state—liberal or illiberal—may support such tribunals; (3) legalism contends that liberal states would not support non-legalistic transitional justice options, whereas prudentialism postulates that any state—liberal or illiberal—may support such options; and (4) legalism offers no contention on the type of legalistic transitional justice options states would support, whereas prudentialism postulates that any state—liberal or illiberal— may support variation among forms of such options.

Chapters IV through VII then focused on the role that a particular liberal state, the United States, played in transitional justice for Germany and Japan in the immediate aftermath of WWII as well as for Libya, Iraq, the FRY, and Rwanda in the immediate aftermath of the Cold War. As indicated at the end of Chapter III, puzzling aspects of U.S. policy on transitional justice required explanation. What accounts for the USG's preference for certain transitional justice options over others in particular cases? Why would the USG support non-legalistic transitional justice options over or alongside legalistic transitional justice options for responding to the same atrocity? Why and how did the particular transitional justice options the USG supported vary among the six cases?

Each of the six case studies revealed that a combination of politics, pragmatics, and normative beliefs drove U.S. decision-making on transitional justice. For example, in all four primary cases (Germany, Japan, the FRY, and Rwanda), USG officials believed that cooperating through a multilateral initiative (specifically, in the case of the Germany and Japan, using WWII alliances, and, in the case of the FRY and Rwanda, using the UNSC) would generate certain political and pragmatic benefits: resources; credibility and legitimacy; access to suspects, witnesses, and evidence; and the approval and participation of former adversaries, current allies, and other crucial international actors. At the same time, both secondary cases (Libya and Iraq) highlight circumstances in which USG officials viewed certain political and pragmatic aspects of multilateral initiatives as hindering, rather than helping, transitional justice processes. Where the primary targets of the atrocity included nationals of their own country, as in the bombing of Pan Am flight 103, USG officials preferred a unilateral, domestic response. And where key international actors were unsupportive of a multilateral initiative, as in Iraq, the USG disfavored such a configuration.

Path dependency stands out as a significant pragmatic and political factor, both among and between the pairs of ICTs (the IMT/the IMTFE and the ICTY/the ICTR). This pattern of path dependency compelled decision-makers to embrace existing, available models for enacting transitional justice. For each pair of ICTs, the latter's existence and form were due in large part to the strong influence of its predecessor's creation and design. In addition, path dependency arising from the IMT (and possibly also the IMTFE) narrowed the transitional justice option and design that the ICTY (and thus also the ICTR) would embody. Path dependency also propelled decision-makers to work within the forum already involved in the corresponding atrocities to pursue transitional justice. In the case of Germany and Japan, those fora were international alliances from WWII, and the UNSC played the same role in the case of the FRY and Rwanda.

Whether the USG already held suspected atrocity perpetrators in custody served as a further pragmatic factor driving its transitional justice decision-making. The political dynamics of the Cold War's beginning and ending (particularly the relationship between the United States and the Soviet Union and then Russia) also feature prominently in transitional justice for Germany/Japan and the FRY/Rwanda, respectively.

In all four primary cases, a normative belief that at least some suspected atrocity perpetrators should be punished for their offenses shaped USG officials' preferences. In the cases of Nazi and Japanese suspects from WWII, USG officials were also driven by the normative belief that convicted perpetrators should suffer capital punishment. When it came to Iraq and Rwanda, however, it appears that a normative belief in resolving the perceived tension between peace and justice in favor of the former temporarily dampened USG officials' efforts to pursue punishment.

In three of the four primary case studies (Germany, Japan, and the FRY), the USG not only supported the creation of an ICT, but also simultaneously or sequentially supported non-legalistic transitional justice options for addressing suspected perpetrators of the same atrocities. For Nazis and Japanese, besides prosecutorial transitional justice options (the multilateral tribunals and unilateral trials), the USG supported amnesty and lustration. For individuals suspected of committing atrocities in the FRY, aside from the prosecutorial option of the ICTY, the USG temporarily supported amnesty. In each instance, the USG employed amnesty as a means of addressing known atrocity perpetrators the USG considered useful. In addition, the USG sought to prosecute alleged atrocity perpetrators from the FRY and Rwanda through an ICT after not doing so for near-contemporaneous atrocities concerning Libya and Iraq.

The remainder of this concluding chapter considers whether legalism or prudentialism provides a more compelling explanation for why and how the USG pursued transitional justice in this book's six case studies.

III. Legalism Versus Prudentialism

A core aim of this book has been to determine which theoretical approach—legalism or prudentialism—better accounts for U.S. policy on transitional justice. As discussed above, the primary factors that influenced USG decision-making on particular transitional justice options were politics, pragmatics, and normative beliefs. This finding suggests that prudentialism, rather than legalism, is a superior explanatory framework. More generally, legalism is susceptible to some of the same flaws noted by those who question Democratic Peace Theory[1] (another prominent liberal paradigm, which Bass uses to introduce legalism by claiming his "argument is related to the democratic peace school."[2]). In particular, there are problems with legalism's empirical claims and causal logic.

A. EMPIRICAL CLAIMS

This book's findings challenge Bass's legalism by interrogating his theory's empirical claims about liberal and illiberal states and the homogeneity he imposes on war crimes tribunals themselves.[3]

1. Liberal States

This book reveals several crucial examples in which liberal states *did not* seek to investigate, apprehend, prosecute, and, when convicted, punish suspected atrocity perpetrators. Those examples undermine Bass's legalist claims that—in reference to, among other situations, the IMT, the IMTFE, the ICTY, and the ICTR—rather than "merely to purge[,] ... [v]ictorious liberals saw their foes as war criminals deserving of just punishment."[4]

As discussed in four of this book's six cases (Germany, Japan, Iraq, and the FRY), the USG (and, to varying extents, other liberal states) sought non-prosecutorial transitional justice options for many—including some of the worst—suspected atrocity perpetrators. Bass asserts that "at the end of America's most brutal war ever, the Germans would be accorded the benefit of legal procedure as it had evolved in America . . . ."[5] Overall, Bass claims, "*legalism* meant that, at the end of the greatest conflagration in human history, the victors extended the *protection of due process* to their defeated enemies in Nuremberg and Tokyo."[6] Although it is true that the victorious Allied powers extended the protection of due process to a few dozen of their defeated Axis enemies via the IMT and the IMTFE as well as to others through related unilateral war crimes trials, most of the Allies' other Axis enemies were not treated similarly. As discussed in Chapters IV and V, the USG not only deliberately granted amnesty to, and even employed, thousands of Axis scientists and officials, but also broadly instituted lustration throughout postwar Germany and Japan.

Bass makes a similar claim with respect to atrocities committed in the 1990s. He asserts that "[w]hen war and massacre tore apart Yugoslavia and Rwanda, the reaction of the great liberal powers was *legalist*."[7] It is true that the United States and several other liberal-state members of the UNSC reacted to those atrocities— in part—by establishing the ICTY and the ICTR. This book substantiates Bass's claim about Rwanda, since the USG did not support non-legalistic transitional justice options in that case. However, this book repudiates Bass's claim about the FRY, where, as with during the immediate post-WWII era, the response of intervening states included non-legalistic options. As discussed in Chapter VI, the USG may have granted conditional amnesty and did implicitly grant uncon- ditional amnesty to alleged and indicted atrocity perpetrators in the FRY. And around the same time (as also discussed in Chapter VI), the USG explicitly offered Saddam Hussein, who directed atrocities against Kurds and Kuwaitis, amnesty in exile.

Bass partly acknowledges the limits of his theory. "Even the British govern- ment," he states, "soured on trials by Leipzig, would only hear of executing fifty to one hundred top Axis leaders at the end of World War II."[8] Recalling Churchill's and other senior British officials' initial demands for the extrajudicial execution of major Nazi officials, Bass observes that "British officials . . . were sharply skeptical about legalism for the top German leaders."[9] He thus appends the following caveat to his theory of legalism: "This book does not argue that liberal states will always be legalist, but that they will overwhelmingly *tend* to be legalist."[10] Bass thus por- trays Churchill's strongly held initial preference for a lethal, non-legalistic means of addressing suspected atrocity perpetrators as "an uncomfortable exception" to his overall theory, rather than a case that undermines it.[11] However, British war crimes policy in 1944–1945 *does* undermine the explanatory power of legalism. First, this episode actually presents not one but two "exceptions" to Bass's theory. Indeed, as discussed in Chapter IV, some USG officials (e.g., FDR, Morgenthau) initially supported Churchill's preference for extrajudicial execution. Certain lead- ers of *both* the United States and the United Kingdom thus preferred a lethal, non- legalistic transitional justice option. Second, in articulating his theory, Bass does not make the case that it is consistent with legalism for a liberal state—let alone two—to consider extrajudicially executing "only" up to 100 of an atrocity's most egregious suspected perpetrators. To the contrary, that impulse is consistent with prudentialism, particularly as one of the reasons the British held the position was to avoid mistakes made at Leipzig, where only a few suspected atrocity perpetra- tors were held accountable. This impulse was motivated not by a principled com- mitment to the rule of law but by a political and pragmatic desire to prevent errors that occurred during the course of such past efforts.

I argue instead that prudentialism better explains American and British war crimes policy in 1944–1945 and other examples drawn from U.S. policy on tran- sitional justice (the focus of this book). In fact, as discussed in Chapter II, the

United States, as just one liberal state, has pursued all general transitional justice options, including those that are non-legalistic in nature: inaction, amnesty, lustration, lethal force, exile, and indefinite detention. As a result, it appears inaccurate to claim, as Bass does, that liberal states "will overwhelmingly *tend* to be legalist."[12] Indeed, as this book has demonstrated, a prominent liberal state (the United States) apparently tends *not* to be legalist in addressing suspected atrocity perpetrators much of the time. As this book has also shown, contrary to other scholarship on this subject,[13] the USG has often pursued transitional justice options that are not retributive.

This book's findings suggest that future research should examine U.S. transitional justice policy in cases beyond the six studied here to determine how the USG confronted suspected atrocity perpetrators in those other instances. This book's findings also suggest that future research should examine the transitional justice policy of liberal states aside from the United States to understand how politics, pragmatism, and normative beliefs might have influenced their handling of suspected atrocity perpetrators.[14] If these inquiries reveal other instances in which liberal states (including the United States) supported non-legalistic transitional justice options, then prudentialism's explanatory power would be further bolstered at the expense of legalism's.

2. Illiberal States

Although this book focuses on liberal states—and one, the United States, in particular—some observations still can be made about illiberal states. Bass argues that "illiberal [states] *never* have" pursued war crimes tribunals.[15] Elsewhere he states that "it is *only* liberal states, with legalist beliefs, that support bona fide war crimes tribunals."[16] Bass also refers to legalism as an "odd trait of . . . liberal countries"[17] and claims that "liberal states . . . treat[] their humbled foes in a way *utterly divorced* from the methods practiced by illiberal states."[18] This book challenges Bass's empirical claims about illiberal states,[19] stressing not only that illiberal states sometimes have, in fact, pursued bona fide war crimes trials, but also that they have been at least as crucial to the establishment of some ICTs as have liberal states.

As discussed in Chapter IV, the illiberal Soviet Union initially was more supportive of establishing the IMT—which Bass describes as "legalism's greatest moment of glory"[20]—than were the liberal American and British polities. After all, the USG initially supported Churchill's proposal to execute or exile Nazi leaders without trial—the epitome of non-legalistic transitional justice. Moreover, as Chapter IV illustrated, it was the illiberal Soviet Union that helped persuade the liberal Anglo-American allies to pursue trials rather than summary executions. As Gaddis reminds us, "the Nuremberg trials were conducted jointly with the Soviet Union, whose own crimes were certainly comparable to those of the Nazis and, in terms of the number of victims, even worse."[21] Likewise, the Soviet

Union supported and staffed the IMTFE (discussed in Chapter V); it was joined by, among others, China (also an illiberal state).[22]

Similarly, China and other illiberal states were crucial to the UNSC's establishment of the ICTY and the ICTR. As discussed in Chapter VI, the UNSC resolution establishing the ICTY was adopted unanimously in 1993, which meant that permanent member China and nonpermanent member Djibouti,[23] both of which were illiberal at the time, each voted in favor. As discussed in Chapter VII, three nonpermanent members—Djibouti, Nigeria, and Oman— all of which were illiberal at the time, voted for the UNSC resolution establishing the ICTR. Then-illiberal permanent member China[24] chose to abstain rather than vote against the resolution, meaning that its ability to wield a veto did not block the ICTR's creation. Thus, although Bass is correct that "great liberal powers" supported these two tribunals, illiberal powers—great and small—also supported their creation by voting for them or at least not preventing their emergence.

In addition, illiberal states have supported bona fide war crimes tribunals not considered in this book's case studies. For example, some of the most illiberal states in the world have ratified or acceded to the Rome Statute, the treaty establishing the ICC, and did so as illiberal states.[25]

As with liberal states, this book's findings suggest that future research should examine the transitional justice policies of illiberal states to determine how they have confronted suspected atrocity perpetrators. If these inquiries reveal that illiberal states have supported legalistic transitional justice options in other cases, then legalism's empirical basis again would be called into question and prudentialism's further strengthened.

3. War Crimes Tribunals

Legalism thus fails to account for the fact that liberal states often have pursued transitional justice options other than war crimes tribunals, and that illiberal states have indeed supported bona fide war crimes tribunals. Legalism is also unable to explain why, as this book has shown, states—liberal and illiberal—have pursued a variety of forms of war crimes tribunals.

B. CAUSAL LOGIC

The weaknesses in legalism's empirical claims in turn call into question the causal logic underpinning the theory.[26] As this book has shown, legalism fails to account both for why at least one liberal state, the United States, supports war crimes tribunals over or alongside other transitional justice options, and for why the same liberal state supports some types of war crimes tribunals over or alongside others in particular contexts. In addition, legalism's concession about the concern liberal states have for their own soldiers and citizens further undermines legalism's overall contention. And that concession relates to one of the biggest distinctions between legalism and prudentialism: whether the theory accounts for a country's security interests in formulating policy on transitional justice.

1. War Crimes Tribunals Versus Other Transitional Justice Options

Although liberal states may have provided the overwhelming support to establish war crimes tribunals, they have not necessarily done so *because* they are liberal. As discussed in Chapter III, legalism argues that liberal ideals—such as a belief in the rule of law under which it is correct and necessary to bring alleged atrocity perpetrators to justice—drive liberal states to put those individuals on trial. Specifically referring to the post-WWII prosecution of Nazis through the IMT, legalism asserts that the USG was motivated to support this transitional justice option "because of an American belief in the rightness of its own domestic legalism."[27] Prudentialism, by contrast, suggests that liberal states may not be motivated by this normative belief at all, or perhaps only partially. Even then, prudentialism contends, normative commitments remain less significant factors than politics or pragmatics.

This book directly challenges legalism's assertion that a sense of outrage and responsibility necessarily drives liberal states to investigate, prosecute, and, when convicted, punish suspected atrocity perpetrators through war crimes tribunals. As this book has shown, liberal states, including the United States, often have pursued *non*-prosecutorial transitional justice options instead of or in addition to prosecutorial ones for the same atrocity. The same outrage and responsibility that would have compelled these states to support the creation of a war crimes tribunal (as Bass might argue) presumably also would have motivated these states to pursue more consistent prosecution of suspected atrocity perpetrators. Rather, as discussed in Chapter II, the USG supported each of the other general transitional justice options—inaction, amnesty, lustration, lethal force, exile, and indefinite detention—in cases besides the six investigated in this book. Moreover, as discussed in Chapters IV, V, and VI, the USG supported non-prosecutorial transitional justice options for at least some—and, in the case of WWII, the overwhelming majority—of the suspected atrocity perpetrators in four of the six cases analyzed (Germany, Japan, Iraq, and the FRY).

This phenomenon confirms that factors other than a principled commitment to the rule of law actually motivated USG officials to support the establishment and operation of the IMT, the IMTFE, the ICTY, the ICTR, and perhaps other war crimes tribunals as well. Additional factors beyond normative beliefs clearly are included in liberal states' calculus when they are confronted with suspected atrocity perpetrators.

As discussed in Chapter II, the war crimes tribunal is but one of many transitional justice options. Like the other possibilities, the war crimes tribunal may be a legal tool, but the decision to implement it in the first place is, as Beigbeder notes, a "political process."[28] As Justice Jackson remarked in discussing the fate of Nazis after WWII:

> It's a political decision as to whether you should execute these people without trial, release them without trial, or try them and decide at the end of the trial what to do. That decision was made by the President, and I was asked to run the legal end of the prosecution.[29]

Like Beigbeder and Justice Jackson, Bass concedes that it is a political judgment to use legalistic options to address suspected atrocity perpetrators; he writes: "*Once a president or prime minister has turned the judgment of defeated enemies over to the judges, the outcome is in the hands of laws that developed from domestic traditions.*"[30] As discussed above, Bass further concedes that political authorities only "sometimes" opt to do so.[31] Prudentialism contends that, quite separate from or at least in addition to normative beliefs, there are political and pragmatic reasons *any* state—liberal or illiberal—will become involved in the establishment of a war crimes tribunal (or, for that matter, any transitional justice response to an atrocity). Prudentialism, unlike legalism, thus accounts for the political decisions and processes Beigbeder, Justice Jackson, and even Bass acknowledge are at play in U.S. policymaking on transitional justice. Further, prudentialism does so without reference to the frequency of any particular outcome.

2. Types of Prosecution

One of legalism's "basic questions" is: "What makes governments support international war crimes tribunals?"[32] But that question neglects the multitude of tribunal designs, as discussed in Chapter II and as illustrated in Chapters IV, V, VI, and VII. This book has sought to determine not only what made a particular government—the USG—support ICTs *in general*, but also why the USG supported *specific types* of ICTs over time. This additional question is one of the most important ways in which prudentialism differs from legalism.

As a theory, legalism offers only general propositions; it does not offer an explanation for the more particular policy choices liberal states make in the realm of transitional justice. Bass's work refers very generally to "war crimes tribunals," but does not seek to specify the particular forms they can take. As discussed in Chapter II (and illustrated in Figure 2.2), there are several different types of prosecution, including a variety of war crimes tribunals (e.g., through versus outside the UN, military versus civilian courts, unilateral versus multilateral scope, with or without the successor regime, domestic versus international versus hybrid construct). A liberal state could pursue—and many liberal states, including the United States, have pursued—any one of these types of tribunals. The type of prosecution dictates which authorities are involved and what procedures and penalties they employ. These features, in turn, determine whether the different forms of prosecution are—and are perceived to be—legal and just in addition to the consequences of using them. For example, as discussed in Chapters IV and V, alongside the IMT and the IMTFE, respectively, the USG and the other quad-ripartite Allies imposed unilateral prosecution on their defeated Axis enemies.

Prudentialism contends that liberal states, if they choose to prosecute sus-pected atrocity perpetrators at all, do so not out of a principled commitment to the rule of law, as legalism argues. Rather, prudentialism asserts that when seek-ing to try alleged atrocity perpetrators, states impose a case-specific balancing of three factors—politics, pragmatics, and normative beliefs—to decide among the various types of war crimes tribunals and other prosecutorial transitional justice options. As this book uncovered, the USG was motivated by a combination of these three factors in deciding (1) *whether* to support a war crimes tribunal, and (2) if so, *which type* of war crimes tribunal.

3. Concern for Own Soldiers and Citizens

Bass states that there are at least two factors that limit whether and when liberal states will support the prosecution of alleged atrocity perpetrators. "First," he claims, "even liberal states almost never put their own soldiers at risk in order to bring war criminals to book."[33] Chapter VI of this book bolsters this contention, as the USG avoided arresting indicted Balkan war criminals for fear of reprisals against its troops. "Second," Bass acknowledges, "even liberal states are more likely to seek justice for war crimes committed against their own citizens, not against innocent foreigners."[34] This book presents evidence suggesting, as Bass theorizes, that at least one liberal state, the United States, appears more likely to pursue justice for atrocities committed against its own citizens. However, Chapter V presents a glaring excep-tion to this general rule by documenting that the USG granted amnesty to: (1) the Imperial Japanese emperor, Hirohito, despite his likely involvement in the Japanese commission of atrocities during WWII, (2) more than fifty other Japanese suspected of perpetrating some of the most egregious offenses during the war, and (3) several thousand additional Japanese who may have experimented on American POWs. Bass's acknowledged limitations of legalism, which this book reinforces, suggest that there are factors other than a principled commitment to the rule of law driving the transitional justice decision-making of at least one liberal polity, the United States.

4. Security Interests

As one of those additional factors driving transitional justice decision-making, prudentialism, rather than legalism, correctly accounts for U.S. security interests in formulating the country's policies. As this book has shown, preventing further conflict, protecting American soldiers, and bolstering U.S. scientific and coun-terintelligence capabilities have all factored into U.S. policymaking in this issue area. That the USG faced no security interests in the case of Rwanda[35] accounts for why legalism and prudentialism do not differ in predicting a legalistic response to the genocide. At the same time, as discussed above, legalism is silent on the type of legalistic response the USG supported in this case, whereas prudentialism, as the theory does in all of the cases studied in this book, explains the USG's specific response as a balancing of politics, pragmatics, and normative beliefs.

IV. Conclusion

Recent efforts to bring to justice suspected perpetrators of atrocities in various countries (e.g., Burma, Burundi, Cambodia, the CAR, Chad, Chile, the DRC, East Timor, the FRY, Iraq, Kenya, Liberia, Libya, Mexico, Nigeria, Rwanda, Sierra Leone, South Sudan, Sudan, Syria, Uganda, the United States[36]) and by certain transnational groups (e.g., al-Qaeda, Daesh/ISIS/ISIL, Lord's Resistance Army) demonstrate how relevant and crucial issues of transitional justice are today, and, unfortunately, will remain for the foreseeable future. As a result, it is all the more important to determine which theories best explain transitional justice decision-making.

Legalism, Bass contends, is a compelling theory for explaining transitional justice decision-making. He concludes in his book:

> The actions of liberal states . . . cannot be explained convincingly with-out an account of their principled ideas. Liberal states have taken a legal-istic approach to the punishment of war criminals, even when so doing has greatly complicated international diplomacy. If the historical episodes in this book are typical, then legalism seems to arise exclusively in liberal states, ones where civil rights are respected at home.[37]

On the contrary, as this book has shown, the actions of a prominent liberal state, the United States, cannot be explained convincingly without taking into account political and pragmatic factors, as separate from normative beliefs. At least this single liberal state has taken a prudentialist approach to the punishment of war criminals. Even if the historical episodes in Bass's book—and particularly if the historical episodes in this book—are typical, then prudentialism seems to arise at least in the United States, regardless of the extent to which the USG respects civil rights at home.

Despite the power of legalism in explaining transitional justice policy in some cases, there are a number of factors for which Bass's theory cannot account. First, legalism does not account for why some liberal states (e.g., the United States) often seriously consider and even pursue *non-legalistic* transitional justice options instead of or in addition to legalistic transitional justice options.

Second, legalism does not account for the fact that, even in instances where liberal states have instituted war crimes trials, those trials have not applied to all suspected atrocity perpetrators from the same conflict. In other words, legalism does not account for what transitional justice options liberal states seriously con-sidered or, more importantly, actually implemented to address suspected atrocity perpetrators beyond the few prosecuted by war crimes tribunals.

Third, with its general suggestion that liberal states support bona fide war crimes trials, legalism fails to explain which of the many types of war crimes trials or tribunals a liberal state would support in a given context. There are myriad legalistic transitional justice options, and legalism does not theorize why liberal states sometimes prefer one to another.

Finally, legalism does not acknowledge that illiberal states such as the Soviet Union (one of the most illiberal in history) have, in fact, supported what even Bass considers to be bona fide war crimes trials.

In contrast to legalism's hedged claim—that liberal states "tend to be legalist"—given how seldom war crimes trials or tribunals have been established and used, it appears that at least one liberal state, the United States, tends *not* to be legalist. And when the USG occasionally *does* institute legalistic transitional justice options, it does not necessarily do so out of any principled commitment to the rule of law. Instead, drawing from this book's six case studies, prudentialism offers a more robust and accurate explanation for the USG's transitional justice policies.

Although Bass makes at least three concessions about his theory of legalism, these admissions are so central and critical that they in fact severely undermine his theory. These concessions indicate that even those who subscribe to legalism acknowledge strategic factors in liberal states' decision-making with respect to supporting the establishment of war crimes tribunals. First, Bass recognizes the political nature of transitional justice decisions, implicitly conceding that a principled commitment to the rule of law is not the only—or perhaps even primary—rationale behind liberal authorities confronting suspected atrocity perpetrators. Second, Bass grants that endangerment of their own soldiers dampens, whereas victimization of their own citizens spurs, liberal states' desires to prosecute suspected atrocity perpetrators. Third, Bass confesses the limits of legalism in explaining British policy regarding transitional justice of Nazis after WWII despite unpersuasively dismissing this occurrence as "an uncomfortable exception."

To paraphrase a critique of Democratic Peace Theory,[38] Bass's admission that "the selfishness of states, even of liberal ones,"[39] and other non-legalistic factors matter to states' transitional justice policies is a concession from legalism's architect that not only gives the game away to but ends the game decisively in favor of prudentialism.

Given that prudentialism is the more explanatorily powerful theory about the cases of U.S. policy on transitional justice investigated in this book, what implications can be drawn for the future? The USG is unlikely to take a principled or consistent approach to transitional justice. Rather, the USG will prioritize political and pragmatic factors, particularly concerning security. The USG will thus continue to vary its support across and within the panoply of legalistic and non-legalistic transitional justice options.

{ NOTES }

Chapter 1

1. ROBERT JACKSON, THE CASE AGAINST THE NAZI WAR CRIMINALS 4 (1946). At the time, Jackson was on leave from his permanent position as an Associate Justice of the U.S. Supreme Court.

2. BENJAMIN VALENTINO, FINAL SOLUTIONS 1 (2004).

3. *Id.* For related sources, see "Multiple Atrocities" in the Bibliography.

4. The International Alliance to End Genocide, Genocide Watch, http://www.genocidewatch.org/alliancetoendgenocide/about.html (last visited July 26, 2015).

5. SAMANTHA POWER, "A PROBLEM FROM HELL": AMERICA AND THE AGE OF GENOCIDE 306 (2002) (quoting U.S. Secretary of State Warren Christopher).

6. DAVID SCHEFFER, ALL THE MISSING SOULS: A PERSONAL HISTORY OF THE WAR CRIMES TRIBUNALS 429–30 (2012) [hereinafter SCHEFFER, ALL THE MISSING SOULS]. For more legalistic and detailed criteria and discussion, see *id.* at 421–40.

7. Sarah Sewall, Under Sec'y of State for Civilian Sec., Democracy, & Human Rights, Charting the U.S. Atrocities Prevention Board's Progress, Address at the Council on Foreign Relations (Mar. 30, 2015), *available at* http://www.cfr.org/human-rights/charting-us-atrocities-prevention-boards-progress/p36332. Sewall has also defined "mass atrocities" as "the widespread and systematic use of violence by state or non-state armed groups against non-combatants." SARAH SEWALL ET AL., MASS ATROCITY RESPONSE OPERATIONS: A MILITARY PLANNING HANDBOOK 17 (2010).

8. *See, e.g.*, ENCYCLOPEDIA OF GENOCIDE AND CRIMES AGAINST HUMANITY (Dinah Shelton ed., 2005); WILLIAM SCHABAS, GENOCIDE IN INTERNATIONAL LAW (2d ed. 2009); WILLIAM SCHABAS, WAR CRIMES AND HUMAN RIGHTS (2008); Elena Baylis, *Parallel Courts in Post-Conflict Kosovo*, 32 YALE J. INT'L L. 1, 3 (2007); Adrienne Bernhard, *Response: Sara L. Seck, Home State Responsibility and Local Communities*, 11 YALE H.R. & DEV. L.J. 207, 212 (2008).

9. In 1998, at a conference in Rome, Italy, diplomats included the crime of aggression in the subject-matter jurisdiction of the ICC's underlying treaty (named after the city in which the treaty was adopted). *See* Rome Statute of the International Criminal Court art. 5(1), July 17, 1998, 2187 U.N.T.S. 90 [hereinafter Rome Statute]. However, the crime itself was left undefined. Twelve years later, at a conference in Kampala, Uganda, to review the Rome Statute, the ICC's Assembly of States Parties (ASP) adopted an amendment concerning the crime of aggression. *See* ICC, Assembly of States Parties, Review Conference, 13th plen. mtg., U.N. Doc. Resolution RC/Res.6 (June 11, 2010), *available at* http://www.icc-cpi.int/iccdocs/asp_docs/Resolutions/RC-Res.6-ENG.pdf. Specifically, the ASP defined "crime of aggression" to mean:

> the planning, preparation, initiation or execution, by a person in a position effectively to exercise control over or to direct the political or military action of a State,

of an act of aggression which, by its character, gravity and scale, constitutes a manifest violation of the Charter of the United Nations.

Id. at Annex I, para. 2. The ASP went on to define "act of aggression." *Id.* In addition, the ASP described conditions for the exercise of jurisdiction over the crime of aggression. *Id.* at Annex I, paras. 3, 4. These provisions were incorporated into the Rome Statute as articles 8 *bis*, 15 *bis*, and 15 *ter*, and other portions of the Rome Statute were adjusted accordingly.

10. Rome Statute, *supra* note 9, art. 5; *see also* Zachary D. Kaufman, *The United States, Syria, and the International Criminal Court: Implications of the Rome Statute's Aggression Amendment*, 55 HARV. INT'L L.J. ONLINE 35 (2013).

11. *See, e.g.*, U.S. DEP'T OF STATE, FACT SHEET: AL QAEDA AND TALIBAN ATROCITIES (2001), *available at* http://wfile.ait.org.tw/wf-archive/2001/011123/epf503.htm.

12. *See, e.g.*, 2005 World Summit Outcome, G.A. Res. 60/1, ¶ 138–39, U.N. Doc. A/RES/60/1 (Oct. 24, 2005) (declaring that states have the responsibility to protect their populations from ethnic cleansing in addition to genocide, war crimes, and crimes against humanity).

13. SCHEFFER, ALL THE MISSING SOULS, *supra* note 6, at 424–28.

14. The International Center on Transitional Justice (ICTJ), a prominent NGO in the field, defines the term "transitional justice" as "the set of judicial and non-judicial measures that have been implemented by different countries in order to redress the legacies of massive human rights abuses." ICTJ, What Is Transitional Justice, http://ictj. org/about/transitional-justice (last visited July 26, 2015) [hereinafter ICTJ Definition]. *But see* Phil Clark, Zachary D. Kaufman & Kalypso Nicolaïdis, *Tensions in Transitional Justice, in* AFTER GENOCIDE: TRANSITIONAL JUSTICE, POST-CONFLICT RECONSTRUCTION, AND RECONCILIATION IN RWANDA AND BEYOND 381–82, 390–91 (Phil Clark & Zachary D. Kaufman eds., 2009) (arguing that "transitional justice" may be a misnomer because the context may not result in any sort of "transition" and because "justice" does not necessarily encompass other objectives pursued in the aftermath of a conflict, such as reconciliation, peace, healing, forgiveness, and truth).

15. One definition of "international criminal justice"—offered by legal scholar and former ICTY Senior Legal Officer Gideon Boas, who describes it as "broadly accepted"—is: "the response of the international community—and other communities—to mass atrocity." Gideon Boas, *What Is International Criminal Justice?, in* INTERNATIONAL CRIMINAL JUSTICE: LEGITIMACY AND COHERENCE 1, 1 (Gideon Boas et al. eds., 2012).

16. *Id.*

17. *See, e.g.*, Symposium, *The Role of International Criminal Justice in Transitional Justice,* 7 INT'L J. TRANSITIONAL JUST. 383 (2013); Naomi Roht-Arriaza, Editorial Note, *in id.* at 383, 383 (referring to "the key, and often fraught, relationship between transitional justice (TJ) and [international criminal justice]") [hereinafter Roht-Arriaza, Editorial Note].

18. *See infra* Chapter II of this book.

19. RUTI G. TEITEL, GLOBALIZING TRANSITIONAL JUSTICE xii, 3 (2014).

20. *See, generally id.*; RUTI G. TEITEL, TRANSITIONAL JUSTICE (2000).

21. *See, e.g.*, KATHRYN SIKKINK, THE JUSTICE CASCADE: HOW HUMAN RIGHTS PROSECUTIONS ARE CHANGING WORLD POLITICS (2011); Naomi Roht-Arriaza, *The New Landscape of Transitional Justice, in* TRANSITIONAL JUSTICE IN THE TWENTY-FIRST CENTURY 1 (Naomi Roth-Arriaza & Javier Mariezcurrena eds., 2006).

22. Encyclopedia of Transitional Justice (Nadya Nedelsky & Lavinia Stan eds., 2012).

23. Zachary D. Kaufman, *International Criminal Tribunal for Rwanda, in id.* at 233.

24. *See, e.g.*, Roman David, *International Criminal Tribunals and the Perception of Justice: The Effect of the ICTY in Croatia*, 8 Int'l J. Transitional Just. 476 (2014); Patrick Vinck & Phuong N. Pham, *Outreach Evaluation: The International Criminal Court in the Central African Republic*, 4 Int'l J. Transitional Just. 421 (2010); James Gondi, *War Crimes Tribunals, Mass Atrocities and the Role of Humanity's Law in Transitional Justice*, 8 Int'l J. Transitional Just. 162 (2014) (reviewing William Schabas, Unimaginable Atrocities (2012); Charles Anthony Smith, The Rise and Fall of War Crimes Trials (2012); Ruti Teitel, Humanity's Law (2011)); Rachel Kerr, Book Review, 5 Int'l J. Transitional Just. 319 (2011) (reviewing Kamari Maxine Clarke, Fictions of Justice: The International Criminal Court and the Challenge of Legal Pluralism in Sub-Saharan Africa (2009); Tim Kelsall, Culture Under Cross-Examination: International Justice and the Special Court for Sierra Leone (2009)).

25. *See, e.g.*, Michèle Laborde-Barbanègre et al., *Case Against Thomas Lubanga*, May 1, 2014, https://www.ictj.org/sites/default/files/ICTJ-Briefing-DRC-Lubanga-2014.pdf; Michèle Laborde-Barbanègre & Roxane Cassehgari, *Reflections on ICC Jurisprudence Regarding the Democratic Republic of the Congo*, Sept. 2014, https://www.ictj.org/sites/default/files/ICTJ-Briefing-DRC-ICCReflections-2014.pdf; *Prosecuting International and Other Serious Crimes in Kenya*, Apr. 30, 2013, https://www.ictj.org/publication/prosecuting-international-and-other-serious-crimes-kenya.

26. *See, e.g.*, Roht-Arriaza, Editorial Note, *supra* note 17, at 385 (noting that the ICC encourages "domestic legal systems to incorporate international crimes domestically and to try most crimes at home" and includes "victim access, participation and reparations").

27. The norm supporting the idea that sovereignty is a responsibility, not a privilege, has come to be known as "The Responsibility to Protect." *See* Int'l Comm'n on Intervention and State Responsibility, The Responsibility to Protect (2001), *available at* http://responsibilitytoprotect.org/ICISS%20Report.pdf; The Responsibility to Protect: Overcoming the Challenges of Atrocity Prevention (Serena Sharma & Jennifer Welsh eds., 2015); Jennifer Welsh, *The Rwanda Effect: Development and Endorsement of the "Responsibility to Protect," in* After Genocide, *supra* note 14, at 333.

28. For related sources, see "Pol Pot / Khmer Rouge / ECCC" in the Bibliography.

29. *See, e.g.*, Paul Collier & Anke Hoeffler, *Greed and Grievance in Civil War*, 56 Oxford Econ. Papers 563 (2004); James Fearon & David Laitin, *Ethnicity, Insurgency, and Civil War*, 97 Am. Pol. Sci. Rev. 75 (2003).

30. The genocide against the Tutsi will be discussed further in Chapter VII of this book.

31. Philip Gourevitch, We Wish to Inform You That Tomorrow We Will Be Killed with Our Families 3 (1998) ("nearly three times"); Gérard Prunier, The Rwanda Crisis 261 (1995) ("at least five times").

32. The atrocities committed in the FRY will be discussed further in Chapter VI of this book.

33. *See generally* David Rohde, Endgame: The Betrayal and Fall of Srebrenica, Europe's Worst Massacre Since World War II (2012).

34. A growing literature exists concerning whether the USG should support particular ICTs or ICTs generally. Especially recently, this literature has focused on the ICC. *Compare* The American NGO Coalition for the International Criminal Court, http://www.amicc.org/ (last visited July 26, 2015) (advocating USG support for the ICC), *with* BRETT SCHAEFER & STEVEN GROVES, THE U.S. SHOULD NOT JOIN THE INTERNATIONAL CRIMINAL COURT (2009), *available at* http://www.heritage.org/research/reports/2009/08/the-us-should-not-join-the-international-criminal-court (advocating USG opposition to the ICC).

35. The term "prudentialism" has been used in other, sometimes related contexts, particularly by international relations scholar Andrew Hurrell. *See, e.g.*, Andrew Hurrell, *Order and Justice in International Relations: What Is at Stake?, in* ORDER AND JUSTICE IN INTERNATIONAL RELATIONS 24, 29 (Rosemary Foot et al. eds., 2003) (arguing that historian John Gaddis provides examples in U.S. foreign policy of a "prudentialist" approach to order and justice); Andrew Hurrell, *Vattel: Pluralism and Its Limits, in* CLASSICAL THEORIES OF INTERNATIONAL RELATIONS 233, 243 (Ian Clark & Iver Neumann eds., 1996) (arguing that philosopher Emerich de Vattel employs "prudentialism" in his approach to the balance of power); Scott Idelman, *A Prudential Theory of Judicial Candor*, 73 TEX. L. REV. 1307, 1310 (1995) (defining "prudentialism" as "the view that judicial decisionmaking may properly rest on political and institutional considerations"); Vincent Samar, *Justifying the Use of International Human Rights Principles in American Constitutional Law*, 37 COLUM. HUM. RTS L. REV. 1, 25 (2005) (defining "prudential argument" in U.S. constitutional law as assessing "various possible decision-results utilizing a cost/benefit analysis").

36. GARY BASS, STAY THE HAND OF VENGEANCE: THE POLITICS OF WAR CRIMES TRIBUNALS 7 (2000); *see also* Gary J. Bass, *Atrocity & Legalism*, DAEDALUS 73 (2003); Gary Jonathan Bass, *War Crimes and the Limits of Legalism*, 97 MICH. L. REV. 2103 (1999) (reviewing MARTHA MINOW, BETWEEN VENGEANCE AND FORGIVENESS: FACING HISTORY AFTER GENOCIDE AND MASS VIOLENCE (1998); MARK OSIEL, MASS ATROCITY, COLLECTIVE MEMORY, AND THE LAW (1997)). Like "prudentialism," the term "legalism" has been used in other, sometimes related contexts, which Bass acknowledges. *See* BASS, *supra*, at 314 n.12 (citing JUDITH SHKLAR, LEGALISM (1986)); *see also* ROBERT KAGAN, ADVERSARIAL LEGALISM (2001).

37. When *Stay the Hand of Vengeance* was first published, in 2000, Bass was Assistant Professor of Politics and International Affairs at Princeton University. The book received prestigious recognition and glowing reviews in both popular and scholarly periodicals. The Association of American Publishers bestowed upon the work honorable mention for its 2000 award for Best Professional/Scholarly Book in Government and Political Science. Book reviews called *Stay the Hand of Vengeance* "[o]ne of the most valuable books to appear about doing justice" (Aryeh Neier, *The Quest for Justice*, N.Y. REV. BOOKS, Mar. 8, 2001, at 31); "[t]he best work yet on the politics of justice after war" (G. John Ikenberry, *Political and Legal*, FOREIGN AFF., Nov.–Dec. 2000, at 173, 173); "impressive," "a gem," and "probably the most masterful exposition yet produced about historical attempts at international criminal justice" (David J. Scheffer, *The Tool Box, Past and Present, of Justice and Reconciliation for Atrocities*, 95 AM. J. INT'L L. 970, 970-71 (2001)); "a solid, lively, and readable contribution to the politics of international criminal justice" (Antonio Cassese, *Gary Jonathan Bass's Stay the Hand of Vengeance*, 24 INT'L HIST. REV. 238, 240 (2002)); "provid[ing] excellent scholarly analysis" and "a first rate scholarly volume" (Stephan Landsman, *Those Who Remember the Past May Not Be Condemned to Repeat It*, 100 MICH.

L. Rev. 1564, 1565, 1581 (2002)); "excellent . . . a worthwhile acquisition for anyone and any library, but it is an essential one for those concerned with international law, international organization, and war crimes" (Arthur W. Blaser, *Gary Jonathan Bass's Stay the Hand of Vengeance*, 96 Am. Pol. Sci. Rev. 255, 255 (2002)); "timely and exhaustive" with an argument presented "compellingly" and "convincingly" (Chuck Sudetic, *Justice Is Better than Revenge*, N.Y. Times Book Rev., Oct. 29, 2000, at 29); "compelling" (*Gary Jonathan Bass's Stay the Hand of Vengeance*, New Yorker, Nov. 6, 2000, at 99); "compelling" and that Bass "argues convincingly" about his legalism theory (David Manasian, *Gary Jonathan Bass's Stay the Hand of Vengeance*, Economist, Sept. 9, 2000, at 106); "exhaustive and magisterial" (Jesse Berrett, *Evil on Trial*, Salon.com, Oct. 11, 2000, http://www.salon.com/2000/10/11/warcrimes/); and "impressive scholarly work" (*Gary Jonathan Bass's Stay the Hand of Vengeance*, Publishers Wkly., July 3, 2000, http://www.publishersweekly.com/978-0-691-04922-9). In one of the blurbs on the back cover of the book itself, political scientist Stanley Hoffmann called the work "brilliant" and "the best book on the subject" of the politics of war crimes tribunals.

A minority of responses has been more neutral or balanced but still notes the book's precedent-setting contributions. Former ICTR legal adviser Kingsley Moghalu refers to Bass's conception of legalism as the "conventional wisdom" on "the phenomenon of war crimes trials and tribunals in international law and politics." Kingsley Chiedu Moghalu, Global Justice: The Politics of War Crimes Trials 171 (2008). Moghalu offers the "international society" approach of the "English School" of international relations, exemplified by the work of Hedley Bull (particularly his seminal book, *The Anarchical Society: A Study of Order in World Politics*), as an alternative to legalism. *Id.* at 8–10. International law scholar Frédéric Mégret described Bass's monograph as "the first book-length attempt . . . to try to fit into contemporary international relations theory a phenomenon that otherwise remains curiously unaccounted for," namely states' creation of ICTs. Frédéric Mégret, *The Politics of International Criminal Justice*, 13 Eur. J. Int'l L. 1261, 1267 (2002). Moghalu and Mégret also raised counterarguments to Bass's theory and claims, as did a senior U.S. soldier and attorney in her book review. *See* Susan K. Arnold, *Stay the Hand of Vengeance: The Politics of War Crimes Tribunals*, 172 Mil. L. Rev. 195, 195 (2002).

Regardless, *Stay the Hand of Vengeance* continues to be highly influential in international relations, international law, transitional justice, history, anthropology, and related fields. For instance, in the *Oxford Handbook of Genocide Studies*, Bass is listed as the first of six examples of "political scientists who study justice mechanisms." Scott Straus, *Political Science and Genocide*, *in* The Oxford Handbook of Genocide Studies 163, 165 n.3 (Donald Bloxham & A. Dirk Moses eds., 2010). *Stay the Hand of Vengeance* has been required reading in recent academic courses, including at Georgetown University, Harvard University, the Massachusetts Institute of Technology, New York University, and the University of Michigan. The book has also been cited in over 400 law review articles (as of a July 26, 2015, search of WestlawNext's "Law Reviews & Journals" directory).

38. The Oxford Handbook of International Relations 69 (Christian Reus-Smit & Duncan Snidal eds., 2008) [hereinafter Oxford IR Handbook].

39. *See id.* at 583, 585.

40. Bass, *supra* note 36, at 7.

41. *See* Oxford IR Handbook, *supra* note 38, at 585–87 (observing some of the many factors influencing individual decision-makers).

42. That said, some scholars have begun to address the connections (through rights and duties) between intervention and post-conflict involvement. *See, e.g.*, MARTHA FINNEMORE, THE PURPOSE OF INTERVENTION (2003); HUMANITARIAN INTERVENTION AND INTERNATIONAL RELATIONS (Jennifer Welsh ed., 2004); INTERNATIONAL INTERVENTION IN THE POST-COLD WAR WORLD (Michael Davis et al. eds., 2004); MICHAEL WALZER, JUST AND UNJUST WARS (4th ed. 2006); NICHOLAS WHEELER, SAVING STRANGERS (2000).

43. Throughout this book, I use "unilateral" to mean "performed or undertaken by one party," and "multilateral" to denote "performed or undertaken by more than one party." For a discussion of these terms and their specific application to U.S. foreign policy, see UNILATERALISM AND U.S. FOREIGN POLICY: INTERNATIONAL PERSPECTIVES (Yuen Foong Khong & David Malone eds., 2003).

44. For example, a search on July 26, 2015, of WestlawNext's "Law Reviews & Journals" directory of the phrase "transitional justice" returned 1930 hits. In 2007, Oxford University Press began publishing what many experts consider to be the leading periodical dedicated to the field: *The International Journal of Transitional Justice*.

45. *See, e.g.*, ROBERT KEOHANE, AFTER HEGEMONY (1984).

46. Statute of the International Court of Justice art. 34(1), June 26, 1945, 59 Stat. 1055, 1060.

47. *See, e.g.*, Rome Statute, *supra* note 9, at art. 25(1).

48. Other studies include: HOWARD BALL, PROSECUTING WAR CRIMES AND GENOCIDE (1999); BASS, *supra* note 36.

49. *See, e.g.*, COUNCIL ON FOREIGN RELATIONS, TOWARD AN INTERNATIONAL CRIMINAL COURT? (1999); LEE FEINSTEIN & TOD LINDBERG, MEANS TO AN END: U.S. INTEREST IN THE INTERNATIONAL CRIMINAL COURT (2009); BRADLEY SMITH, THE AMERICAN ROAD TO NUREMBERG (1982); JAMES F. WILLIS, PROLOGUE TO NUREMBERG: THE POLITICS AND DIPLOMACY OF PUNISHING WAR CRIMINALS OF THE FIRST WORLD WAR (1982).

50. *See, e.g.*, MOGHALU, *supra* note 37; SIKKINK, *supra* note 21; CHARLES ANTHONY SMITH, THE RISE AND FALL OF WAR CRIMES TRIALS: FROM CHARLES I TO BUSH II (2012); THE SWORD AND THE SCALES: THE UNITED STATES AND INTERNATIONAL COURTS AND TRIBUNALS (Cesare P.R. ed., 2009).

51. ANNIE R. BIRD, US FOREIGN POLICY ON TRANSITIONAL JUSTICE (2015) (focusing on Cambodia, Liberia/Sierra Leone, and Colombia and arguing that U.S. officials' approach to transitional justice is retributive based on greater familiarity with this form of justice as well as pride in and a desire to export the U.S. justice system).

52. Solis Horwitz, *The Tokyo Trial*, 28 INT'L CONCILIATION 473, 475 (1950).

53. *See* NEIL BOISTER & ROBERT CRYER, THE TOKYO INTERNATIONAL MILITARY TRIBUNAL: A REAPPRAISAL 1 (2008) (noting that the IMTFE is "relatively unstudied"); Zachary D. Kaufman, *The Nuremberg Tribunal v. The Tokyo Tribunal: Designs, Staffs, and Operations* 43 J. MARSHALL L. REV. 753, 753–54 (2010) [hereinafter Kaufman, *IMT v. IMTFE*] (observing that some scholars and practitioners completely overlook the IMTFE's existence, incorrectly referring to the ICTY as the first ICT since the IMT); Zachary D. Kaufman, *Transitional Justice for Tōjō's Japan: The United States Role in the Establishment of the International Military Tribunal for the Far East and other Transitional Justice Mechanisms for Japan After World War II*, 27 EMORY INT'L L. REV. 755, 755 (2013) (establishing that, although significant scholarly attention has focused on the creation of the first ICT, the IMT, much less has addressed the establishment of the second such body, the IMTFE). Interest in the IMTFE is increasing elsewhere,

however. On September 2, 2013, the Shanghai Jiao Tong University ("SJTU") Press released an eighty-volume, nearly 50,000-page set of books about the IMTFE that was co-compiled by the National Library of China and the SJTU. *80-Volume Tokyo Trials Account Debuts in Beijing*, CHINA DAILY, Sept. 2, 2013, http://usa.chinadaily.com.cn/china/2013-09/02/content_16937887.htm.

54. Statute of the International Tribunal for Rwanda art. 8(1), Nov. 8, 1994, 33 I.L.M. 1602.

55. *See* Warren Hoge, *U.S. Lobbies U.N. on Darfur and International Court*, N.Y. TIMES, Jan. 29, 2005, at A8; Nicholas Kristof, Op-Ed., *Why Should We Shield the Killers?*, N.Y. TIMES, Feb. 2, 2005, at A21.

56. 1 & 2 ESSAYS ON THE ROME STATUTE OF THE INTERNATIONAL CRIMINAL COURT (Flavia Lattanzi & William A. Schabas eds., 1999); WILLIAM SCHABAS, AN INTRODUCTION TO THE INTERNATIONAL CRIMINAL COURT (4th ed. 2011); WILLIAM SCHABAS, THE INTERNATIONAL CRIMINAL COURT: A COMMENTARY ON THE ROME STATUTE (2010).

57. Int'l Criminal Court, Situations and Cases, http://www.icc-cpi.int/en_menus/icc/situations%20and%20cases/Pages/situations%20and%20cases.aspx (last visited July 26, 2015); William Schabas, *First Prosecutions at the International Criminal Court*, 25 HUM. RTS. L.J. 25 (2006).

58. Int'l Criminal Court, Preliminary Examinations, http://www.icc-cpi.int/en_menus/icc/structure%20of%20the%20court/office%20of%20the%20prosecutor/comm%20and%20ref/Pages/communications%20and%20referrals.aspx (last visited July 26, 2015).

59. DAVID SCHEFFER, U.S. INST. OF PEACE, SPECIAL REPORT 78: OPTIONS FOR PROSECUTING INTERNATIONAL TERRORISTS (2001), *available at* http://www.usip.org/publications/options-prosecuting-international-terrorists.

60. Thom Shanker & David Johnston, *U.S. Lists Iraqis to Punish, or to Work With*, N.Y. TIMES, Feb. 26, 2003, at A1.

61. *See, e.g.*, SENATE SELECT COMM. ON INTELLIGENCE, COMMITTEE STUDY OF THE CENTRAL INTELLIGENCE AGENCY'S DETENTION AND INTERROGATION PROGRAM (2014), *available at* http://www.intelligence.senate.gov/study2014.html; ADVOCATES FOR U.S. TORTURE PROSECUTIONS, SHADOW REPORT TO THE UNITED NATIONS COMMITTEE AGAINST TORTURE ON THE REVIEW OF THE PERIODIC REPORT OF THE UNITED STATES OF AMERICA (2014), *available at* http://hrp.law.harvard.edu/wp-content/uploads/2014/10/CAT-Shadow-Report-Advocates-for-US-Torture-Prosecutions.pdf.

62. For further discussion of military tribunals/commissions, see Chapter II of this book.

63. For explanation of the U.S. vote against the Rome Statute from the senior American diplomat involved in the treaty's negotiations, see SCHEFFER, ALL THE MISSING SOULS, *supra* note 6, at 163–247; David Scheffer, *Staying the Course with the International Criminal Court*, 35 CORNELL INT'L L.J. 47 (2001–2002); David J. Scheffer, *The United States and the International Criminal Court*, 92 AM. J. INT'L L. 12, 17–22 (1999); *see also* William Schabas, *United States Hostility to the International Criminal Court: It's All About the Security Council*, 15 EUR. J. INT'L L. 701 (2004).

64. William Glaberson & Eric Lichtblau, *Guantanamo Detainee's Trial Opens, Ending a Seven-Year Legal Tangle*, N.Y. TIMES, July 22, 2008, at A12.

65. *Yemen Frees Bin Laden Driver After Jail Term Ends*, REUTERS, Jan. 11, 2009.

66. *Ex Parte* Quirin, 317 U.S. 1 (1942).

67. Hirota v. MacArthur, 338 U.S. 197, 201–04 (1948) (Douglas, J., concurring).

68. *Id.* at 204.

69. Martha Minow & Robert Post, Op-Ed., *Trust in the Legal System Must Be Regained*, Bos. Globe, Dec. 9, 2014, at A13.

70. These "tribunals" include the ad hoc 1967 Russell Tribunal, the Permanent Peoples' Tribunal established in 1979, the ad hoc 1991–1992 International War Crimes Tribunal, the ad hoc 1999–2000 International Tribunal on U.S./NATO War Crimes Against Yugoslavia, the ad hoc 2000 Women's International War Crimes Tribunal, the ad hoc 2003–2005 World Tribunal on Iraq, and the ad hoc 2009–2013 Russell Tribunal on Palestine. *See, e.g.*, Zachary D. Kaufman, *Transitional Justice Delayed Is Not Transitional Justice Denied: Contemporary Confrontation of Japanese Human Experimentation During World War II Through a People's Tribunal*, 26 Yale L. & Pol'y Rev. 645, 649–55 (2008). For related sources, see "International Citizens' War Crimes Tribunals" in the Bibliography.

71. *See, e.g.*, Scheffer, All the Missing Souls, *supra* note 6.

72. For relevant sources, see "ICC" and "Foreign Policy Analysis/U.S. Foreign Policy" in the Bibliography.

73. *See, e.g.*, Michael Hogan, The Marshall Plan (1987).

74. *See, e.g.*, Larry Minear & Philippe Guillot, Soldiers to the Rescue 111–28 (1996); Scheffer, All the Missing Souls, *supra* note 6, at 67; *see also* Document 57.

75. *See, e.g.*, ICTJ Definition, *supra* note 14; *see also* Martha Minow, Between Vengeance and Forgiveness: Facing History after Genocide and Mass Violence 23 (1998); William Schabas, *Compensation and Reparations*, *in* Reining in Impunity for International Crimes and Serious Violations of Fundamental Human Rights 445 (Christopher Joyner ed., 1998). For a consideration of such initiatives led by civil society, see Social Entrepreneurship in the Age of Atrocities: Changing Our World (Zachary D. Kaufman ed., 2012).

76. For additional discussion of transitional justice research methodology, see Zachary D. Kaufman, *Steven D. Roper & Lilian A. Barria's Designing Criminal Tribunals: Sovereignty and International Concerns in the Protection of Human Rights*, 10 Yale Hum. Rts. & Dev. L.J. 209, 210–13 (2007) (book review).

77. For an overview of case study research, see, e.g., Alexander George & Andrew Bennett, Case Studies and Theory Development in the Social Sciences (2005); Gary King et al., Designing Social Inquiry (1994); Martyn Hammersley & Roger Gomm, *Introduction* to Case Study Method 1 (Roger Gomm et al. eds., 2000).

78. George & Bennett, *supra* note 77, at 5. Other political scientists have noted that there are various definitions of case study research, which give rise to misunderstandings and disagreements. *See, e.g.*, John Gerring, *What Is a Case Study and What Is It Good for?*, 98 Am. Pol. Sci. Rev. 341 (2004).

79. Alexander L. George & Timothy J. McKeown, *Case Studies and Theories of Organizational Decision Making*, *in* Advances in Information Processing in Organizations 21, 35 (Robert F. Coulam & Richard A. Smith eds., 1985); *see also* King et al., *supra* note 77, at 226–28; Andrew Bennett & Alexander L. George, *Case Studies and Process Tracing in History and Political Science: Similar Strokes for Different Foci*, *in* Bridges and Boundaries: Historians, Political Scientists, and the Study of International Relations 137 (Colin Elman & Miriam F. Elman eds., 2001); Jeffrey T. Checkel, *Process Tracing*, *in* Qualitative Methods in International Relations: A Pluralist Guide 114 (Audie Klotz & Deepa Prakash eds., 2008).

80. For a debate about whether case study research can have general relevance, see CASE STUDY METHOD, *supra* note 77, at 19–115.

81. GEORGE & BENNETT, *supra* note 77, at 7.

82. David Collier & James Mahoney, *Insights and Pitfalls: Selection Bias in Qualitative Research*, 49 WORLD POL. 56, 71 (1996).

83. For more information on the pitfalls of single-case research designs, see, e.g., GEORGE & BENNETT, *supra* note 77, at 32–33; KING ET AL., *supra* note 77, at 208–11.

84. Of course, not all scholars agree that the post–Cold War era was ever one of unipolarity, or that, even if it was, that it is now or will endure. *See, e.g.*, Samuel Huntington, *The Lonely Superpower*, FOREIGN AFF., Mar.–Apr. 1999, at 35; Charles Krauthammer, *The Unipolar Moment*, FOREIGN AFF., Winter 1990–1991, at 23; Christopher Layne, *The Unipolar Illusion: Why New Great Powers Will Arise*, 17 INT'L SECURITY 5 (1993); Christopher Layne, *From Preponderance to Offshore Balancing: America's Future Grand Strategy*, 22 INT'L SECURITY 86 (1997); Michael Mastanduno, *Preserving the Unipolar Moment: Realist Theories and U.S. Grand Strategy after the Cold War*, 21 INT'L SECURITY 44 (1997); William Wohlforth, *The Stability of a Unipolar World*, 24 INT'L SECURITY 5 (1999).

85. For additional discussion of similarities and differences between the IMT and the IMTFE, see Kaufman, *IMT v. IMTFE, supra* note 53.

86. For more on selection bias, see, e.g., CHRISTOPHER ACHEN, THE STATISTICAL ANALYSIS OF QUASI-EXPERIMENTS (1986); Christopher Achen & Duncan Snidal, *Rational Deterrence Theory and Comparative Case Studies*, 41 WORLD POL. 143 (1989); Collier & Mahoney, *supra* note 82; Barbara Geddes, *How the Cases You Choose Affect the Answers You Get: Selection Bias in Comparative Politics, in* 2 POLITICAL ANALYSIS 131 (James Stimson ed., 1990); KING ET AL., *supra* note 77, at 128–39.

87. David Collier and Ronald Rogowski have defended this approach. *See* David Collier, *Translating Quantitative Methods for Qualitative Researchers: The Case of Selection Bias*, 89 AM. POL. SCI. REV. 461 (1995); Ronald Rogowski, *The Role of Theory and Anomaly in Social-Scientific Inference*, 89 AM. POL. SCI. REV 467 (1995); *see also* Collier & Mahoney, *supra* note 82, at 72–75.

88. *See, e.g.*, Joanna Walters, *American Families of Lockerbie Victims Still Convinced Libya Behind Attack on Flight*, TELEGRAPH (London), Mar. 11, 2014, http://www.telegraph.co.uk/news/uknews/terrorism-in-the-uk/10689479/American-families-of-Lockerbie-victims-still-convinced-Libya-behind-attack-on-flight.html.

89. All interviews are listed in the Bibliography, along with a shorthand I employ for referring to them throughout this book. I conducted a total of twenty-eight interviews with a total of twenty people.

90. All declassified documents are listed in the Bibliography, along with a shorthand I employ for referring to them throughout this book. These documents include 194 declassified and released to me, in whole or in part, from the U.S./DoS.

91. As indicated in the Bibliography, the U.S./DoS withheld in whole forty documents and in part thirty-one documents that it found to be responsive to my FOIA requests. The U.S./DoJ and the U.S./DoD claimed that they had no documents responsive to my requests.

92. For a discussion of elite interviewing, see, e.g., H. W. PERRY, JR., DECIDING TO DECIDE 8 (1991).

93. For example, Henry King, who served as a U.S. prosecutor of Nazis after WWII, was unwell while I was researching this book, and died in 2009. *See* Dennis Hevesi, *Henry*

T. King Jr., Prosecutor at Nuremberg, Dies at 89, N.Y. TIMES, May 12, 2009, at A25 (noting that almost all of "about 200 American prosecutors who helped bring dozens of Nazi leaders to trial from 1945 to 1949" were dead).

94. *See* DEBORAH LARSON, ORIGINS OF CONTAINMENT 17 (1989).

95. *Id.*

96. *See, e.g.,* Paulette Rothbauer, *Triangulation, in* 2 THE SAGE ENCYCLOPEDIA OF QUALITATIVE RESEARCH METHODS 892, 892–94 (Lisa Given ed., 2008).

97. YUEN FOONG KHONG, ANALOGIES AT WAR 63 (1992).

Chapter 2

1. For an analysis of case studies (e.g., lustration in Iraq, exile in Nigeria) outside this book's scope that reflect the breadth of problems and controversies involved in choosing among various transitional justice options, see Zachary D. Kaufman, *The Future of Transitional Justice,* 1 ST. ANTONY'S INT'L REV. 58 (2005) [hereinafter Kaufman, *The Future of Transitional Justice*].

2. GARY BASS, STAY THE HAND OF VENGEANCE: THE POLITICS OF WAR CRIMES TRIBUNALS 7 (2000).

3. There has been at least one instance of a public trial of a deceased individual. In January 897, in what became known as the "Cadaver Synod," Pope Stephen VI presided over the trial of Pope Formosus, whom Stephen accused of crimes against the Roman Catholic Church, and then had exhumed, robed in papal vestments, and seated on a throne to be prosecuted and then desecrated nine months after his death. 5 NEW CATHOLIC ENCYCLOPEDIA 1024 (1967).

4. *See, e.g.,* William Schabas, *Conjoined Twins of Transitional Justice? The Sierra Leone Truth and Reconciliation Commission and the Special Court,* 2 J. INT'L CRIM. JUST. 1082 (2004); William Schabas, *The Relationship Between Truth Commissions and International Courts: The Case of Sierra Leone,* 25 HUM. RTS. Q. 1035 (2003). As one example of a single alleged atrocity perpetrator facing sequential transitional justice options, former Liberian president Charles Taylor voluntarily went into exile in Nigeria in 2003 before being arrested in 2006 to face prosecution by the SCSL. *See* Zachary D. Kaufman, Op-Ed., *Liberia: Charles Taylor's Exile, Disappearance, Arrest, and Transfer,* LIBER. TIMES, May 20, 2006 [hereinafter Kaufman, *Charles Taylor*].

5. DAVID SCHEFFER, U.S. INST. OF PEACE, SPECIAL REPORT 78: OPTIONS FOR PROSECUTING INTERNATIONAL TERRORISTS (2001), *available at* http://www.usip.org/publications/options-prosecuting-international-terrorists.

6. For more information on action versus inaction in addressing suspected atrocity perpetrators, see, e.g., Kaufman, *The Future of Transitional Justice, supra* note 1, at 61–62.

7. Convention on the Prevention and Punishment of the Crime of Genocide art. 1, Dec. 9, 1948, 102 Stat. 3045, 78 U.N.T.S. 277, 280.

8. For a summary of and response to arguments against humanitarian intervention, see Jennifer Welsh, *Taking Consequences Seriously, in* HUMANITARIAN INTERVENTION AND INTERNATIONAL RELATIONS 52 (2004).

9. *See also* Phil Clark, Zachary D. Kaufman & Kalypso Nicolaïdis, *Tensions in Transitional Justice, in* AFTER GENOCIDE: TRANSITIONAL JUSTICE, POST-CONFLICT RECONSTRUCTION, AND RECONCILIATION IN RWANDA AND BEYOND 381 (Phil Clark & Zachary D. Kaufman eds., 2009).

10. Louis Henkin et al., International Law xxxiv (1987); R.J. Vincent, Nonintervention and International Order 13–16 (1974).

11. Vincent, *supra* note 10, at 379; Welsh, *supra* note 8, at 60–62.

12. Welsh, *supra* note 8, at 60.

13. *See, e.g.*, Jack Snyder & Leslie Vinjamuri, *Trials and Errors*, 28 Int'l Security 5, 33–36 (2003–2004).

14. David Scheffer, *The Future of Atrocity Law*, 25 Suffolk Transnat'l L. Rev. 389, 391 (2002).

15. *See, e.g.*, Human Rights Watch, *War in Iraq: Not a Humanitarian Intervention*, Jan. 26, 2004, http://www.hrw.org/news/2004/01/25/war-iraq-not-humanitarian-intervention; Edward Wong, *Hussein Charged with Genocide in 50,000 Deaths*, N.Y. Times, Apr. 5, 2006, at A1.

16. *See, e.g.*, Gary Bass, *At Saddam's Trial, the Law Is Just Part of the Picture*, Wash. Post, Jan. 18, 2004, at B3.

17. For related sources, see "Truth Commissions" and "Amnesty" in the Bibliography.

18. Truth Commissions and Courts: The Tension Between Criminal Justice and the Search for Truth (Shane Darcy & William Schabas eds., 2004).

19. *See generally* Zachary D. Kaufman & Pierre-Richard St. Hilaire, *The Rwandan Experience, in* Rwanda and South Africa in Dialogue: Addressing the Legacies of Genocide and a Crime Against Humanity 41, 41–45 (Charles Villa-Vicencio & Tyrone Savage eds., 2001). For related sources, see also "Truth Commissions" in the Bibliography.

20. Snyder & Vinjamuri, *supra* note 13, at 18.

21. For related sources, see "Armenian Genocide" in the Bibliography.

22. Virginia Morris & Michael Scharf, 1 The International Criminal Tribunal for Rwanda 691 (1998).

23. Michael Slackman, *Algerian Voters Said to Approve President's Postwar Plan*, N.Y. Times, Oct. 1, 2005, at A3.

24. For related sources, see "Truth Commissions" in the Bibliography.

25. Philip Rucker, *Leahy Proposes Panel to Investigate Bush Era; U.S. Attorney Firings Among Issues*, Wash. Post, Feb. 10, 2009, at A4.

26. Martha Minow & Robert Post, Op-Ed., *Trust in the Legal System Must Be Regained*, Bos. Globe, Dec. 9, 2014, at A13.

27. Charles Blow, Op-Ed., *A Kaffeeklatsch on Race*, N.Y. Times, Feb. 16, 2015, at A17.

28. Michael Scharf, *The Case for a Permanent International Truth Commission*, 7 Duke J. Comp. & Int'l L. 375 (1997).

29. Neil Kritz, *The Dilemmas of Transitional Justice, in* 1 Transitional Justice xix, xxiv (1995).

30. *See, e.g.*, Amy Waldman, *In Search of Baath Loyalists, U.S. Finds Itself in Gray Area*, N.Y. Times, July 22, 2003, at A1.

31. For related sources, see "Lustration" in the Bibliography.

32. For related sources, see "Exile" in the Bibliography.

33. Randal C. Archibold, *Jean-Claude Duvalier, 63, 2nd-Generation Dictator of Haiti*, N.Y. Times, Oct. 5, 2014, at A1; Marlise Simons, *Haiti Says It Will Seek Extradition of Duvalier*, N.Y. Times, Feb. 28, 1986, at A3.

34. Randal C. Archibold, *Just Days Before Election, Aristide Returns to Cheers and Uncertainty in Haiti*, N.Y. Times, Mar. 19, 2011, at A4; Tim Weiner & Lydia Polgreen, *Under Pressure, Aristide Leaves Haiti*, N.Y. Times, Feb. 29, 2004, at A1.

35. Michael Kaufman, *Idi Amin, Murderous and Erratic Ruler of Uganda in the 70's, Dies in Exile*, N.Y. TIMES, Aug. 17, 2003, at A32.

36. *Ex-Ethiopia Chief Reaches Zimbabwe*, N.Y. TIMES, May 23, 1991, at A9.

37. Kaufman, *Charles Taylor, supra* note 4; Somini Sengupta, *Sierra Leone War Crimes Trial Opens Without Chief Suspect*, N.Y. TIMES, June 4, 2004, at A4.

38. Lydia Polgreen & Marc Lacey, *Nigeria Will End Asylum for Warlord*, N.Y. TIMES, Mar. 26, 2006, at A11.

39. Lydia Polgreen, *Status of Liberia's Indicted Ex-President Is Unclear*, N.Y. TIMES, Mar. 28, 2006, at A9.

40. Lydia Polgreen, *Liberian Seized to Stand Trial on War Crimes*, N.Y. TIMES, Mar. 30, 2006, at A1. While Taylor was prosecuted under the aegis of the SCSL, his trial was physically held at the ICC in The Hague. *See* EVALUATING TRANSITIONAL JUSTICE: ACCOUNTABILITY AND PEACEBUILDING IN POST-CONFLICT SIERRA LEONE vii (Kirsten Ainley et al. eds., 2015).

41. Marlise Simons & Alan Cowell, *50-Year Sentence Upheld for Ex-President of Liberia*, N.Y. TIMES, Sept. 27, 2013, at A3.

42. Edward Mansfield & Jack Snyder, *Democratization and the Danger of War*, 20 INT'L SECURITY 5, 36 (1995).

43. Associated Press, *President Signs Legislation Ending Nazi Benefit Checks*, N.Y. TIMES, Dec. 18, 2014, http://www.nytimes.com/aponline/2014/12/18/us/politics/ap-us-nazi-social-security.html; David Rising et al., *Expelled Nazis Paid Millions in Social Security*, ASSOCIATED PRESS, Oct. 19, 2014, http://bigstory.ap.org/article/6ae3352f4d474b028c-84be0c627e7780/expelled-nazis-paid-millions-social-security.

44. For related sources, see "Lethal Force" in the Bibliography.

45. One example may be Russia's 2005 assassination of Aslan Maskhadov, who had been elected president of Chechnya in 1997. *See* Editorial, *The Wrong Chechen*, N.Y. TIMES, Mar. 16, 2005, at A22.

46. Benjamin Runkle, *The Age of the Manhunt*, FOREIGN POL'Y, May 9, 2011, http://www.foreignpolicy.com/articles/2011/05/09/the_age_of_the_manhunt; *see also* BENJAMIN RUNKLE, WANTED DEAD OR ALIVE: MANHUNTS FROM GERONIMO TO BIN LADEN (2011).

47. COLIN POWELL, MY AMERICAN JOURNEY 428 (1995).

48. *See, e.g.*, Karen DeYoung & Joby Warrick, *Under Obama, More Targeted Killings than Captures in Counterterrorism Efforts*, WASH. POST, Feb. 14, 2010, at A1.

49. Protocol Additional to the Geneva Conventions of 12 August 1949, and relating to the Protection of Victims of International Armed Conflicts art. 52, para. 2, *opened for signature* Dec. 12, 1977, 1125 U.N.T.S. 3, 27.

50. Harold Koh, Legal Adviser, U.S. Dep't of State, Speech at the Annual Meeting of the American Society of International Law (Mar. 25, 2010), http://www.state.gov/s/l/releases/remarks/139119.htm.

51. John Burns, *After Long Hunt, U.S. Bombs Kill Al Qaeda Leader in Iraq*, N.Y. TIMES, June 9, 2006, at A1.

52. Christine Hauser, *Bush Cautiously Notes Chance to "Turn the Tide,"* N.Y. TIMES, June 8, 2006, http://www.nytimes.com/2006/06/08/world/middleeast/07cnd-reaction.html.

53. *See, e.g.*, Editorial, *Defending Drones: The Laws of War and the Right to Self-Defense*, WASH. POST, Apr. 13, 2010, at A16; DeYoung & Warrick, *supra* note 48.

54. *Bush Gives CIA License to Kill Terrorist Leaders*, CHICAGO TRIB., Dec. 15, 2002, at 19.

55. Yochi Dreazen et al., *The Goal Was Never to Capture bin Laden*, ATLANTIC, May 4, 2011, http://www.theatlantic.com/politics/archive/2011/05/goal-was-never-to-capture-bin-laden/238330/; Mark Hosenball & Matt Spetalnick, *U.S. Team's Mission was to Kill bin Laden, not Capture*, REUTERS, May 2, 2011, http://www.reuters.com/article/2011/05/02/us-binladen-kill-idUSTRE7413H220110502.

56. Peter Baker et al., *Bin Laden Is Dead, Obama Says*, N.Y. TIMES, May 2, 2011, at A1.

57. Mark Mazzetti et al., *C.I.A. Strike Kills U.S.-Born Militant in a Car in Yemen*, N.Y. TIMES, Oct. 1, 2011, at A1.

58. Peter Finn, *In Secret Memo, Justice Department Sanctioned Strike*, WASH. POST, Sept. 30, 2011, at A9.

59. Scott Shane, *Targeted Killing Comes to Define War on Terror*, N.Y. TIMES, Apr. 8, 2013, at A1; *see also* Peter Bergen, Dir., Nat'l Sec. Studies Program, New Am. Found., Drone Wars: The Constitutional and Counterterrorism Implications of Targeted Killing, Testimony to the U.S. Senate Committee on the Judiciary (Apr. 23, 2013), *available at* http://newamerica.net/sites/newamerica.net/files/articles/TESTIMONY_BERGEN_DRONES.pdf.

60. The Bureau of Investigative Journalism maintains updated statistics by country, including Afghanistan, Pakistan, Somalia, and Yemen. *See* The Bureau of Investigative Journalism, http://www.thebureauinvestigates.com/category/projects/drones/drones-graphs/ (last visited July 26, 2015).

61. Charlie Savage, *Obama Team Split on Tactics Against Terror*, N.Y. TIMES, Mar. 29, 2010, at A1.

62. Jeffrey Toobin, *Killing Osama: Was It Legal?*, NEW YORKER, May 2, 2011, http://www.newyorker.com/online/blogs/newsdesk/2011/05/killing-osama-was-it-legal.html.

63. Yasir Qadhi, Op-Ed., *An Illegal and Counterproductive Assassination*, N.Y. TIMES, Oct. 2, 2011, at A25.

64. Micah Zenko, *An Inconvenient Truth*, FOREIGN POL'Y, Apr. 10, 2013, http://www.foreignpolicy.com/articles/2013/04/10/an_inconvenient_truth_drones.

65. *See, e.g.*, Richard Oppel, Jr., *Military Admits a Role in Killing*, N.Y. TIMES, Apr. 5, 2010, at A4.

66. *See, e.g.*, Jeffrey Gettleman, *The Hunted Become the Hunters as Uganda Enlists Former Rebels to End a War*, N.Y. TIMES, Apr. 11, 2010, at A10.

67. U.S. SENATE SELECT COMM. ON INTELLIGENCE, ALLEGED ASSASSINATION PLOTS INVOLVING FOREIGN LEADERS (1975); U.S. SENATE SELECT COMM. ON INTELLIGENCE, RESULTS OF THE 1973 CHURCH COMMITTEE HEARINGS, ON CIA MISDEEDS, AND THE 1984 IRAN/CONTRA HEARINGS (1984).

68. Letter from Jonathan Fanton and Kenneth Roth, Hum. Rts. Watch, to President George W. Bush, U.S. Policy on Assassinations (Sept. 20, 2001), *available at* http://www.hrw.org/press/2001/09/bushlet0920.htm.

69. Exec. Order No. 11,905, 41 Fed. Reg. 7703 (1976).

70. Exec. Order No. 12,036, 43 Fed. Reg. 3674 (1978).

71. U.S. SENATE INTELLIGENCE COMM. ON INTELLIGENCE (1984), *supra* note 67.

72. Exec. Order No. 12,333, 3 C.F.R. 200 (1982).

73. *See, e.g.*, Bob Woodward, *President Broadens Anti-Hussein Order; CIA Gets More Tools to Oust Iraqi Leader*, WASH. POST, June 16, 2002, at A1; Josh Rogin, *Top U.S. Admiral Admits We Are Trying to Kill Qaddafi*, FOREIGN POL'Y, June 24, 2011, http://thecable.

foreignpolicy.com/posts/2011/06/24/exclusive_top_us_admiral_admits_we_are_trying_
to_kill_qaddafi.

74. Qadhi, *supra* note 63.

75. *See, e.g.*, KATHRYN SIKKINK, THE JUSTICE CASCADE (2011); Diane Orentlicher,
Settling Accounts, 100 YALE L.J. 2537, 2542–44 (1991). For a skeptical consideration of how
prosecution, at least through ICTs, promotes stability, the rule of law, democracy, and
deterrence, see Snyder & Vinjamuri, *supra* note 13, at 20–25. On the unlikelihood of ICTs
to deter, see also Bernard Röling, *Introduction* to THE TOKYO WAR CRIMES TRIAL 15, 26
(C. Hoyosa et al. eds., 1986); John Yoo, *Prosecuting the Peace*, WALL ST. J., Jan. 6, 2012,
http://www.wsj.com/articles/SB10001424052970204720204577128610335846568 (reviewing DAVID SCHEFFER, ALL THE MISSING SOULS (2012); WILLIAM SHAWCROSS, JUSTICE
AND THE ENEMY (2011)).

76. For related sources, see "Transitional Justice," "Multiple War Crimes Tribunals,"
and "Multiple Hybrid Tribunals" in the Bibliography.

77. HANNAH ARENDT, EICHMANN IN JERUSALEM 253 (rev. ed. 1964).

78. *See generally* Zachary D. Kaufman, *Naomi Roht-Arriaza's The Pinochet Effect:
Transnational Justice in the Age of Human Rights*, 32 YALE J. INT'L L. 297 (2006) (book
review). For related sources, see also "Universal Jurisdiction" in the Bibliography.

79. *See, e.g.*, KINGLSEY CHIEDU MOGHALU, GLOBAL JUSTICE 82–83 (2008).

80. For related sources, see "Military Commissions/Tribunals" in the Bibliography.

81. *See, e.g.*, William Schabas, *National Courts Finally Begin to Prosecute Genocide, the
"Crime of Crimes,"* 1 J. INT'L CRIM. JUST. 39 (2003).

82. *See, e.g.*, JAMES Willis, PROLOGUE TO NUREMBERG (1982); BASS, *supra* note 2,
at 58–105.

83. *See, e.g.*, MICHAEL BELKNAP, THE VIETNAM WAR ON TRIAL (2002).

84. Neil Lewis, *First War-Crimes Case Opens at Guantánamo Base*, N.Y. TIMES, Aug. 25,
2004, at A14.

85. Saddam Hussein Trial, Library of Congress, http://www.loc.gov/law/help/hussein/
tribunal.php (last visited July 26, 2015).

86. Statute of the Iraqi Special Tribunal arts. 10–14, Dec. 10, 2003, *available at* http://
www.iraqcoalition.org/regulations/20031210_CPAORD_48_IST_and_Appendix_A.pdf.

87. *Id.*, art. 1, para. a.

88. 28 U.S.C. § 1350 (2012).

89. Torture Victim Protection Act of 1991, Pub. L. No. 102-256, 106 Stat. 73 (1992).

90. *See* Kadic v. Karadzic, 70 F.3d 232 (2d Cir. 1995); Doe v. Karadzic, 866 F. Supp. 734
(S.D.N.Y. 1994).

91. WHITNEY HARRIS, TYRANNY ON TRIAL 571 (rev. ed., 1999); Gregory S. Gordon,
*The Trial of Peter von Hagenbach: Reconciling History, Historiography and International
Criminal Law*, *in* THE HIDDEN HISTORIES OF WAR CRIMES TRIALS 13 (Kevin Jon Heller &
Gerry Simpson eds., 2013).

92. HOWARD BALL, PROSECUTING WAR CRIMES AND GENOCIDE 17–25 (1999).

93. As of July 26, 2015, 139 states had signed the Rome Statute and 123 countries had
ratified the treaty. *See* Rome Statute of the International Criminal Court, United Nations
Treaty Collection, https://treaties.un.org/Pages/ViewDetails.aspx?src=TREATY&mtdsg_
no=XVIII-10&chapter=18&lang=en (last visited July 26, 2015).

94. HARRIS, *supra* note 91, at 571.

95. In 1948, as part of the adoption of the Genocide Convention, the UNGA called upon the ILC to study "the question of an international criminal jurisdiction" by paying "attention to the possibility of establishing a Criminal Chamber of the International Court of Justice." G.A. Res. 260(III)(B) (Dec. 9, 1948). Because the ICJ is the UN's permanent, "principal judicial organ," creating a dedicated criminal chamber within it would be one method of establishing a permanent international criminal court through the UN. However, the jurisdiction of the ICJ is only over states and even then only consensually. Statute of the International Court of Justice, arts. 1, 34, 36, June 26, 1945, 49 Stat. 1055, 1060. Consequently, a permanent international criminal court subunit of the ICJ presumably would be subject to significant constraints on its jurisdiction; it would likely lack authority to try individuals at all or hear cases against states when their officials reject jurisdictional claims.

96. *See* WILLIAM SCHABAS, THE UN INTERNATIONAL CRIMINAL TRIBUNALS: THE FORMER YUGOSLAVIA, RWANDA, AND SIERRA LEONE (2006).

97. *See, e.g.*, INTERNATIONALIZED CRIMINAL COURTS (Cesare Romano et al. eds., 2004); William Schabas, *The Special Tribunal for Lebanon: Is a "Tribunal of an International Character" Equivalent to an "International Criminal Court"?*, 21 LEIDEN J. INT'L L. 513 (2008).

98. In 1994, when the ICTR was established, the ICTY, which then shared both an appeals chamber and chief prosecutor with the ICTR, evolved from representing option one to embodying option three. *See* Zachary D. Kaufman, *International Criminal Tribunal for Rwanda*, *in* 3 ENCYCLOPEDIA OF TRANSITIONAL JUSTICE 233, 235 (Nadya Nedelsy & Lavinia Stan eds., 2012); Zachary D. Kaufman, *The United States Role in the Establishment of the United Nations International Criminal Tribunal for Rwanda*, *in* AFTER GENOCIDE, *supra* note 9, at 229, 231, 233, 243, 248, 258.

99. Later, on August 28, 2003, the UNSC unanimously voted to divide the ICTY/ICTR chief prosecutor into two separate positions. *Prosecutor Loses Rwandan Role*, BBC NEWS, Aug. 29, 2003, http://news.bbc.co.uk/1/hi/world/africa/3189045.stm. However, because the tribunals continue to share an appeals chamber, they still represent instances of this third option, ICT-Tied.

100. *See, e.g.*, Benjamin Wittes & Jack Goldsmith, *The Best Trial Option for KSM: Nothing*, WASH. POST, Mar. 19, 2010, at A23.

101. Reuters, *Factbox: Has Obama Delivered on His 2008 Campaign Promises?*, MSNBC, Oct. 28, 2011, http://www.msnbc.msn.com/id/45076690/ns/politics/t/factbox-has-obama-delivered-his-campaign-promises (noting that, in August 2007, Obama stated: "As president, I will close Guantanamo, reject the Military Commissions Act, and adhere to the Geneva Conventions. Our Constitution and our Uniform Code of Military Justice provide a framework for dealing with the terrorists."); Mark Landler, *President Approves Defense Bill, Modified*, N.Y. TIMES, Jan. 1, 2012, at A22 (noting that Obama "said that he would never authorize the indefinite military detention of American citizens, because 'doing so would break with our most important traditions and values as a nation.'").

102. Human Rights Watch, Facts and Figures: Military Commissions v. Federal Courts, http://www.hrw.org/features/guantanamo-facts-figures (last visited July 26, 2015).

103. Authorization for Use of Military Force, S.J. Res. 23, 107th Cong. (2001).

104. National Defense Authorization Act for Fiscal Year 2012, H.R. 1540, 112th Cong. §§ 1021–1022 (2011).

105. For related sources, see "Indefinite Detention" in the Bibliography.

Chapter 3

1. For discussion of the traditional definition of security, see BARRY BUZAN ET AL., SECURITY: A NEW FRAMEWORK FOR ANALYSIS (1998); MARY KALDOR, NEW AND OLD WARS (2006); MICHAEL WILLIAMS, CULTURE AND SECURITY (2007); Mohammed Ayoob, *The Security Problematic of the Third World*, 43 WORLD POL. 257, 261–65 (1991); Mats Berdal, *How "New" Are "New Wars"? Global Economic Change and the Study of Civil War*, 9 GLOBAL GOVERNANCE 477 (2003); Emma Rothschild, *What Is Security?*, DAEDALUS, Summer 1995, at 53.

2. S. NEIL MACFARLANE & YUEN FOONG KHONG, HUMAN SECURITY AND THE UN: A CRITICAL HISTORY 14 (2006).

3. *Id.* at 2.

4. For a discussion of nonmilitary threats to security, see Richard Ullman, *Redefining Security*, 8 INT'L SECURITY 129 (1983).

5. For a discussion of environmental threats to security, see Jessica Mathews, *Redefining Security*, FOREIGN AFF., Spring 1989, at 162–77.

6. INT'L COMM'N ON INTERVENTION & STATE SOVEREIGNTY, THE RESPONSIBILITY TO PROTECT (2001), *available at* http://www.iciss.ca/pdf/Commission-Report.pdf; SECRETARY-GENERAL'S HIGH LEVEL PANEL ON THREATS, CHALLENGES & CHANGE, A MORE SECURE WORLD (2004), *available at* http://www.un.org/secureworld/; *see also* THE RESPONSIBILITY TO PROTECT: OVERCOMING THE CHALLENGES OF ATROCITY PREVENTION (Serena Sharma & Jennifer Welsh eds., 2015); Jennifer M. Welsh, *The Rwanda Effect: The Development and Endorsement of the "Responsibility to Protect," in* AFTER GENOCIDE: TRANSITIONAL JUSTICE, POST-CONFLICT RECONSTRUCTION, AND RECONCILIATION IN RWANDA AND BEYOND 333 (Phil Clark & Zachary D. Kaufman eds., 2009).

7. *See, e.g.*, WILLIAM SCHULZ, IN OUR OWN BEST INTEREST (2001).

8. *See, e.g.*, ATROCITIES AND INTERNATIONAL ACCOUNTABILITY: BEYOND TRANSITIONAL JUSTICE (Edel Hughes et al. eds., 2007); Payam Akhavan, *Beyond Impunity*, 95 AM. J. INT'L L. 7 (2001).

9. *See, e.g.*, Stephen Stedman, *Spoiler Problems in Peace Processes*, 22 INT'L SECURITY 5 (1997); Jack Snyder & Leslie Vinjamuri, *Trials and Errors*, 28 INT'L SECURITY 5, 14–15 (2003–2004).

10. Stephen Neff, *A Short History of International Law, in* INTERNATIONAL LAW 31, 38 (Malcolm D. Evans ed., 2003).

11. For more discussion of the relationship among justice, peace, security, and order, see, e.g., ORDER AND JUSTICE IN INTERNATIONAL RELATIONS (Rosemary Foot et al. eds., 2003).

12. NAT'L COMM'N ON TERRORIST ATTACKS UPON THE UNITED STATES, EXECUTIVE SUMMARY 16 (2004), *available at* http://www.9-11commission.gov/report/911Report_Exec.pdf.

13. Robert Axelrod & Robert Keohane, *Achieving Cooperation Under Anarchy*, 38 WORLD POL. 226, 226 (1985).

14. Arthur Stein, *Coordination and Collaboration*, 36 INT'L ORG. 299 (1982).

15. *See, e.g.*, MIKE HULME, WHY WE DISAGREE ABOUT CLIMATE CHANGE (2009).

16. *See, e.g.*, JOHN MEARSHEIMER, THE TRAGEDY OF GREAT POWER POLITICS (2001).

17. Zachary D. Kaufman, *Transitional Justice as Genocide Prevention: From a Culture of Impunity to a Culture of Accountability, in* CONFRONTING GENOCIDE IN RWANDA 363

(Jean-Damascène Gasanabo et al. eds., 2014) (arguing that four main transitional justice mechanisms have been pursued for Rwanda).

18. The "neo-neo debate" refers to the argument between two prominent international relations theories, neorealism (also sometimes called structural realism) and neoliberal institutionalism (NLI), about the possibility of and effort required for achieving cooperation in an anarchical international system. *See, e.g.*, NEOREALISM AND NEOLIBERALISM (David Baldwin ed., 1993).

19. For discussion of relative versus absolute gains, see *id.* at 170–233, 250–66.

20. John Mearsheimer, *The False Promise of International Institutions*, 19 INT'L SECURITY 5, 13 (1994–1995).

21. For a discussion of high versus low politics issues, see ROBERT KEOHANE & JOSEPH NYE, POWER AND INTERDEPENDENCE (4th ed. 2012).

22. For example, one estimate places the cost to the USG of the Iraq war alone at $3 trillion. Linda J. Bilmes & Joseph E. Stiglitz, *The Iraq War Will Cost US $3 Trillion, and Much More*, WASH. POST, Mar. 9, 2008, at B01. For a comparison of ICT costs to those of warfare, see DAVID SCHEFFER, ALL THE MISSING SOULS 27–29 (2012) (observing that "the total cost of the war crimes tribunals [(the ICTY, the ICTR, the SCSL, the ECCC, and the ICC)]—roughly $3.43 billion from 1993 through 2009—fell below the program costs of two Stealth bombers and equaled the two-week budget of American military operations in Iraq.").

23. Full data about the ICTY and ICTR budgetary apportionments is available at United Nations, Committee on Contributions—Tribunals, http://www.un.org/en/ga/contributions/tribunals.shtml (last visited July 26, 2015).

24. *See, e.g.*, Zachary Kaufman, *Sudan, the United States, and the International Criminal Court: A Tense Triumvirate in Transitional Justice for Darfur*, in THE CRIMINAL LAW OF GENOCIDE 49 (Ralph Henham & Paul Benhrens eds., 2007); Zachary Kaufman, *Justice in Jeopardy: Accountability for the Darfur Atrocities*, 16 CRIM. L.F. 343 (2006).

25. Examples include the SCSL, the ECCC, and the IST.

26. For a discussion of independent versus joint decision-making, see, e.g., Arthur Stein, *Coordination and Collaboration*, 36 INT'L ORG. 299 (1982).

27. *See, e.g.*, HUMAN RIGHTS WATCH, JUDGING DUJAIL (2006), *available at* http://hrw.org/reports/2006/iraq1106/.

28. A summary of the USG's arguments appear in Eric Ward & Matthew Heiman, Op-Ed., *Iraqi-Run Tribunal Is Major Progress Toward Democratic Rule of Law*, CHRISTIAN SCI. MONITOR, July 19, 2005, at 9.

29. *See, e.g.*, Robert Keohane & Lisa Martin, *The Promise of Institutionalist Theory*, 20 INT'L SECURITY 39, 42 (1995) (claiming that international institutions foster cooperation and can influence foreign policies because such institutions (1) facilitate the operation of reciprocity, (2) provide/share information/expertise, (3) reduce transaction costs, (4) promote burden-sharing, (5) establish focal points for coordination, (6) make commitments more credible, and (7) promote issue linkage).

30. Charles Kindelberger, *Dominance and Leadership in the International Economy*, 25 INT'L STUD. Q. 242 (1981).

31. Indeed, the ICC—established by the Rome Statute without ratification by the United States, China, or Russia—was created and operates without the official support of several of the most powerful states in the contemporary world.

32. *See, e.g.*, Michael Glennon, *Why the Security Council Failed*, Foreign Aff., May–June 2003, at 16.

33. Noah Feldman, *When Judges Make Foreign Policy*, N.Y. Times, Sept. 28, 2008, (Magazine), at MM50.

34. James Traub, *The War Presidents*, N.Y. Times, Jan. 30, 2011, (Magazine), at 20.

35. Andrew Revkin, *178 Nations Reach a Climate Accord; U.S. Only Looks On*, N.Y. Times, July 23, 2011, at A1.

36. Comm'n on Am.'s Nat'l Interests, America's National Interests 3–5 (2000), *available at* http://bcsia.ksg.harvard.edu/BCSIA_content/documents/AmerNatInter.PDF.

37. *Id.* at 6.

38. White House, National Security Strategy iii (2015), *available at* https://www.whitehouse.gov/sites/default/files/docs/2015_national_security_strategy.pdf [hereinafter 2015 National Security Strategy].

39. Of course, there are other theories of international relations that explain state behavior in world politics, such as constructivism. However, this chapter focuses on realism and liberalism because, as will be discussed, they are the most relevant theories to this book; prudentialism and legalism are subsets of each, respectively.

40. The Oxford Handbook of International Relations 131 (Christian Reus-Smit & Duncan Snidal eds., 2008) [hereinafter Oxford IR Handbook]. The seminal work on realism includes: Edward Carr, The Twenty Years' Crisis, 1919–1939 (2001); Thomas Hobbes, Leviathan (C.B. Macpherson ed., 1985); Niccolò Machiavelli, The Prince (Quentin Skinner & Russell Price eds., 1988); Hans Morgenthau, Politics Among Nations (5th ed. 1978); Thucydides, The Peloponnesian War (J.S. Rusten ed., 1988).

41. Classical realists, who share a pessimistic view of human nature, include Thucydides, Niccolò Machiavelli, Thomas Hobbes, and, more recently, E.H. Carr and Hans J. Morgenthau. This variant of realism contends that a drive for power is an inherent attribute of human nature that produces a constant threat of conflict.

42. Neorealism arose as a response to what some saw as flaws and limitations of classical realism. Developed by Kenneth Waltz, this variant contends that the anarchical structure of the international system, not human nature, is the force that drives state behavior. This anarchical condition causes a permanent permissive state of war among states and impedes international cooperation.

43. *See* Kenneth Waltz, Theory of International Politics (1979).

44. George Kennan, American Diplomacy 95 (1984).

45. Gary Bass, Stay the Hand of Vengeance 9 (2000) (citing Henry Kissinger, Diplomacy (1994)). Along with the IMT, the IMTFE and the ICTY were established by the publication date of 1994.

46. *Id.* at 285.

47. Snyder & Vinjamuri, *supra* note 9, at 5.

48. Moravcsik states that ideational liberal theories "link state behavior to varied conceptions of desirable forms of cultural, political, socioeconomic order"; commercial liberal theories "stress economic interdependence, including many variants of 'endogenous policy theory'"; and republican liberal theories "stress the role of domestic representative institutions, elites and leadership dynamics, and executive-legislative relations." Oxford IR Handbook, *supra* note 40, at 234–35.

49. Stanley Hoffmann, *Liberalism and International Affairs*, *in* JANUS AND MINERVA 394, 395 (1987).

50. *Id.* at 396.

51. *Id.* at 412–13.

52. KENNETH WALTZ, MAN, THE STATE, AND WAR (1959). The first image Waltz presents is the individual, and his third proposed image is the international system.

53. *See* IMMANUEL KANT, PERPETUAL PEACE (1939).

54. *See, e.g.*, Michael Doyle, *Liberalism and World Politics*, 80 AM. POL. SCI. REV. 1151 (1986).

55. *See, e.g.*, Bruce Russett & John Oneal, *The Classical Liberals Were Right*, 41 INT'L STUD. Q. 267 (1997).

56. *See, e.g.*, Andrew Moravcsik, *Taking Preferences Seriously*, 51 INT'L ORG. 513 (1997).

57. *See, e.g.*, Anne-Marie Burley, *Law Among Liberal States*, 92 COLUM. L. REV. 1907 (1992); Anne-Marie Slaughter, *A Liberal Theory of International Law*, 94 AM. SOC'Y INT'L L. PROC. 240 (2000).

58. *See* DEBATING THE DEMOCRATIC PEACE (Michael E. Brown et al. eds., 1996).

59. THOMAS FRIEDMAN, THE LEXUS AND THE OLIVE TREE ix (2000).

60. *See, e.g.*, Thomas Carothers, *Promoting Democracy and Fighting Terror*, FOREIGN AFF., Jan.–Feb. 2003, at 84; 2015 NATIONAL SECURITY STRATEGY, *supra* note 38.

61. *See* Mark Zacher & Richard Matthew, *Liberal International Theory*, *in* CONTROVERSIES IN INTERNATIONAL RELATIONS THEORY 108, 117 (Charles W. Kegley, Jr. ed., 1995).

62. G. John Ikenberry, *Why Export Democracy?*, 23 WILSON Q. 56 (1999).

63. BASS, *supra* note 45, at 286.

64. *Id.* at 286.

65. *Id.* at 7.

66. *Id.* at 7 ("that it is *right* for war criminals to be put on trial") (emphasis added).

67. *Id.* at 20 ("that war criminals *must* be put on trial") (emphasis added).

68. *Id.* at 18, 20.

69. *Id.* at 7–8.

70. *Id.* at 24 (emphasis in original).

71. *Id.* at 19 (both emphases in original).

72. *Id.* at 12.

73. *Id.* at 8–16.

74. *Id.* at 16.

75. *Id.* at 16–20.

76. *Id.* at 18.

77. *Id.* at 314 n.12 (citing JUDITH SHKLAR, LEGALISM (1986)).

78. *See, e.g., id.* at 3, 8, 12.

79. *Id.* at 6.

80. *See supra* Chapter I of this book, note 37.

81. Gideon Boas, *What Is International Criminal Justice?*, *in* INTERNATIONAL CRIMINAL JUSTICE: LEGITIMACY AND COHERENCE 1, 1 (Gideon Boas et al. eds., 2012).

82. BASS, *supra* note 45, at 16.

83. *Id.*

84. *Id.*

85. *See* Jack Donnelly, *The Ethics of Realism, in* OXFORD IR HANDBOOK, *supra* note 40, at 157.

86. *See generally* Alberto Coll, *Normative Prudence as a Tradition of Statecraft*, 5 ETHICS & INT'L AFF. 33 (1991) [hereinafter Coll (1991)]; Alberto Coll, *Prudent Statesmen*, 9 ETHICS & INT'L AFF. 193 (1995).

87. Coll (1991), *supra* note 86, at 35.

88. Martin Wight, *Western Values in International Relations*, *in* DIPLOMATIC INVESTIGATIONS 89, 128 (Herbert Butterfield & Martin Wight eds., 1966).

89. Coll (1991), *supra* note 86, at 34.

90. HANS MORGENTHAU, POLITICS AMONG NATIONS 12 (Kenneth W. Thompson rev., brief ed., 1993).

91. Max Weber, *The Profession and Vocation of Politics*, *in* WEBER: POLITICAL WRITINGS 354–55 (Peter Lassman & Ronald Speirs eds., 1994).

92. Andrew Hurrell, *Order and Justice in International Relations: What Is at Stake?*, *in* ORDER AND JUSTICE IN INTERNATIONAL RELATIONS 24, 29 (Rosemary Foot et al. eds., 2003).

93. CHRIS BROWN, INTERNATIONAL RELATIONS THEORY 97 (1992).

94. As Yale Law School Professor Oona Hathaway states:

In broad terms, "path dependence" means that an outcome or decision is shaped in specific and systematic ways by the historical path leading to it. It entails, in other words, a causal relationship between stages in a temporal sequence, with each stage strongly influencing the direction of the following stage. At the most basic level, therefore, path dependence implies that what happened at an earlier point in time will affect the possible outcomes of a sequence of events occurring at a later point in time.

Oona A. Hathaway, *Path Dependence in the Law: The Court and Pattern of Legal Change in a Common Law System*, 86 IOWA L. REV. 601, 604 (2001) (quotations and citations omitted).

95. BASS, *supra* note 45, at 28.

96. *Id.* at 20.

97. *Id.*

98. *Id.*

99. *Id.*

100. *Id.*

Chapter 4

1. *Wannsee Protocol*, Jan. 20, 1942, http://avalon.law.yale.edu/imt/wannsee.asp.

2. *Text of Resolution on German War Crimes Signed by Representatives of Nine Occupied Countries*, INTER-ALLIED REV. (Jan. 13, 1942), http://www.ibiblio.org/pha/policy/1942/420112a.html. China also signed this declaration.

3. ANN TUSA & JOHN TUSA, THE NUREMBERG TRIAL 22 (1995).

4. TELFORD TAYLOR, THE ANATOMY OF THE NUREMBERG TRIALS 26 (1993).

5. Franklin D. Roosevelt, President, Crimes Against Civilian Populations in Occupied Countries: Statement by the President (Aug. 21, 1942), *reprinted in* 10 DEP'T ST. BULL. 709, 710 (1942).

6. For related sources, see "Nazis/IMT" in the Bibliography.

7. *Ex parte* Quirin, 317 U.S. 1 (1942).

8. As the UNWCC predated the founding of the UN in 1945, "United Nations" referred in this sense to the Allied powers. TAYLOR, *supra* note 4, at 26.

9. *Political and Legal Organizations*, 1 INT'L ORG. 170, 173 (1947); WHITNEY HARRIS, TYRANNY ON TRIAL 4 (rev. ed. 1999); TAYLOR, *supra* note 4, at 26.

10. HARRIS, *supra* note 9, at 4; ROBERT CONOT, JUSTICE AT NUREMBERG 9 (1983).

11. Solis Horwitz, *The Tokyo Trial*, 28 INT'L CONCILIATION 473, 477–78 (1950).

12. *Annex, Memorandum to President Roosevelt from the Secretaries of State and War and the Attorney General, January 22, 1945*, Jan. 22, 1945, *available at* http://avalon.law.yale.edu/imt/jack01.asp.

13. Document 179.

14. HARRIS, *supra* note 9, at 4.

15. TAYLOR, *supra* note 4, at 28.

16. GARY BASS, STAY THE HAND OF VENGEANCE: THE POLITICS OF WAR CRIMES TRIBUNALS 13 (2000); TAYLOR, *supra* note 4, at 29.

17. RICHARD OVERY, INTERROGATIONS 6–8 (2001).

18. *The Moscow Conference; October 1943*, Oct. 30, 1943, http://avalon.law.yale.edu/wwii/moscow.asp.

19. CONOT, *supra* note 10, at 10; HARRIS, *supra* note 9, at 6–7.

20. *The Tehran Conference*, Nov. 28–Dec. 1, 1943, http://www.yale.edu/lawweb/avalon/wwii/tehran.htm.

21. For a discussion of this comment and the debate surrounding its seriousness, see HENRY KISSINGER, DIPLOMACY 411 (1994); TAYLOR, *supra* note 4, at 29–30. Some prominent USG officials also favored the execution of a large number of Nazis. For example, in July 1944, the Supreme Allied Commander of Europe (and later U.S. president) General Dwight Eisenhower stated that he wanted to "exterminate" several thousand Nazis. BASS, *supra* note 16, at 154; RAUL HILBERG, 3 THE DESTRUCTION OF THE EUROPEAN JEWS 1071 (1985).

22. *Document 12: From Henry Morgenthau Jr. to President Roosevelt (The Morgenthau Plan), September 5, 1944, in* BRADLEY SMITH, THE AMERICAN ROAD TO NUREMBERG 27–29 (1982) (emphases added).

23. *Id.; see also* Henry Morgenthau, *Suggested Post-Surrender Program for Germany* (Sept. 6, 1944), *available at* http://www.fdrlibrary.marist.edu/psf/box31/a297a01.html.

24. TAYLOR, *supra* note 4, at 42.

25. BASS, *supra* note 16, at 162.

26. *Id.* at 153.

27. *Document 14: Secretary of War (Stimson) to the President, September 9 1944, in* SMITH, *supra* note 22, at 30–31; *see also Document 13: From Henry L. Stimson to Henry Morgenthau, Jr., 5 September 1944, in id.* at 30.

28. Robert H. Jackson, *Introduction* to HARRIS, *supra* note 9, at xxixx, xxxiv (Feb. 1954) [hereinafter Jackson (Feb. 1954)].

29. *Document 15: Memorandum, "Major War Criminals," by the British Lord Chancellor Sir John Simon, 4 September 1944, in* SMITH, *supra* note 22, at 31–33.

30. TAYLOR, *supra* note 4, at 31, 33–34; SMITH, *supra* note 22, at 9–10.

31. TAYLOR, *supra* note 4, at 31.

32. *Id.*

33. Associated Press, *Morgenthau Plan on Germany Splits Cabinet Committee*, N.Y. TIMES, Sept. 24, 1944, at 1; Lansing Warren, *Own Aides Shaping Peace, Hull Says*, N.Y. TIMES, Sept. 26, 1944, at 11.

34. BASS, *supra* note 16, at 150–51, 168–69; TAYLOR, *supra* note 4, at 34.

35. TAYLOR, *supra* note 4, at 34–35; *Document 10: Telephone Conversations Between the Secretary of War (Henry Stimson) and the Judge Advocate General (Major General Myron C. Cramer), September 5, 1944, in* SMITH, *supra* note 22, at 30; BASS, *supra* note 16, at 164, 168.

36. *Document 16: Subject: Trial of European War Criminals (by Colonel Murray C. Bernays, G-1), September 15, 1944, in* SMITH, *supra* note 22, at 33–37.

37. *Document 17: Memorandum for Mr. McCloy from Colonel Ammi Cutter, Assistant Executive Officer, Office of the Assistant Secretary of War, October 1, 1944, in id.* at 37–38.

38. *Document 18: The Secretary of War (Stimson) to the Secretary of State (Hull), October 27, 1944, in id.* at 37–38.

39. *Document 19: Draft Memorandum for the President from the Secretaries of State, War and Navy, November 11, 1944, in id.* at 41–44.

40. JOHN BAUSERMAN, THE MALMEDY MASSACRE (2002).

41. SMITH, *supra* note 22, at 52.

42. *Document 35: Memorandum for the President, Subject: Trial and Punishment of Nazi War Criminals, January 22, 1945, in id.* at 117–22.

43. *Id.* (brackets in original); *see also id.* at 55–56.

44. *The Yalta (Crimea) Conference,* Feb. 4–11, 1945, http://avalon.law.yale.edu/wwii/yalta.asp.

45. TAYLOR, *supra* note 4, at 31.

46. HARRIS, *supra* note 9, at 10.

47. CONOT, *supra* note 10, at 13–14; TAYLOR, *supra* note 4, at 32; *Document 48: The Argument for Summary Process Against Hitler and Co., Prepared by the Lord Chancellor (Simon), April 16, 1945, in* SMITH, *supra* note 22, at 155–57.

48. SMITH, *supra* note 22, at 138; TAYLOR, *supra* note 4, at 32.

49. *Document 49: The Punishment of Those Guilty of War Crimes and Atrocities Is for Criminal Violation of International Law, Prepared in Assistant Secretary of War's Office, 20 April 1945, in* SMITH, *supra* note 22, at 158–61.

50. *Document 50: Memorandum of Proposals for the Prosecution and Punishment of Certain War Criminals and Other Offenders, 25–30 April 1945, in id.* at 158–61.

51. Exec. Order No. 9547, 10 Fed. Reg. 4961 (1945).

52. TAYLOR, *supra* note 4, at 32–33.

53. *Id.* at 40.

54. *Id.* at 58.

55. ROBERT H. JACKSON, REPORT TO THE PRESIDENT BY MR. JUSTICE JACKSON, JUNE 6, 1945 (1945), http://avalon.law.yale.edu/imt/jack08.asp.

56. YVES BEIGBEDER, JUDGING WAR CRIMINALS: THE POLITICS OF INTERNATIONAL JUSTICE 34 (1999); HARRIS, *supra* note 9, at 15–16; TAYLOR, *supra* note 4, at 59, 63–64; Jackson (Feb. 1954), *supra* note 28, at xxxv; Robert H. Jackson, *The Nuremberg Trial: An Example of Procedural Machinery for Development of International Substantive Law, in* DAVID DUDLEY FIELD: CENTENARY ESSAYS 314, 319–24 (Alison Reppy ed., 1949).

57. CONOT, *supra* note 10, at 18–19; TAYLOR, *supra* note 4, at 59; HARRIS, *supra* note 9, at 16–18.

58. TAYLOR, *supra* note 4, at 65–67; CONOT, *supra* note 10, at 21–24; HARRIS, *supra* note 9, at 18–21.

59. CONOT, *supra* note 10, at 19, 21; HARRIS, *supra* note 9, at 17–18.

60. TAYLOR, *supra* note 4, at 59; *see also id.* at 76–77, 633.

61. *Id.* at 60.

62. *Minutes of Conference Session of July 25, 1945*, Proceedings of International Conference on Military Trials, London, 1945, http://avalon.law.yale.edu/imt/jack51.asp.

63. TAYLOR, *supra* note 4, at 72.

64. *Id.* at 72.

65. *Id.* at 639.

66. *Id.* at 67–70.

67. CONOT, *supra* note 10, at 17; *see also* HARRIS, *supra* note 9, at 14.

68. *London Agreement of August 8th 1945*, Aug. 8, 1945, http://avalon.law.yale.edu/imt/imtchart.asp.

69. *Id.* art. 4.

70. *Id.* art. 6.

71. *Charter of the International Military Tribunal*, Aug. 8, 1945, art. 6, http://avalon.law.yale.edu/imt/imtconst.asp.

72. *Id.* art. 27.

73. *Indictment*, Oct. 6, 1945, http://avalon.law.yale.edu/imt/count.asp.

74. However, when the IMT granted the motion, filed by Gustav Krupp's defense counsel on November 4, 1945, to defer the proceedings against Krupp on medical grounds, the tribunal's acquiescence eliminated any representation from the German armament industry, a critical component of the alleged Nazi conspiracy. HARRIS, *supra* note 9, at 32.

75. CONOT, *supra* note 10, at 26–28; HARRIS, *supra* note 9, at 28–30.

76. ROBERT JACKSON, THE CASE AGAINST THE NAZI WAR CRIMINALS 3 (1946).

77. *Judgment of the International Military Tribunal for the Trial of German Major War Criminals*, Sept. 30–Oct. 1, 1946, http://avalon.law.yale.edu/subject_menus/judcont.asp.

78. Zachary D. Kaufman, *The Nuremberg Tribunal v. The Tokyo Tribunal: Designs, Staffs, and Operations*, 43 J. MARSHALL L. REV. 753, 762–63 (2010).

79. TAYLOR, *supra* note 4, at 53–54.

80. *Id.* at 54.

81. *Revised Draft of Agreement and Memorandum Submitted by American Delegation*, June 30, 1945, http://avalon.law.yale.edu/imt/jack18.asp.

82. *Id.*

83. *Id.*

84. The UN had not yet been created so prosecution through that forum was not a possibility. The UN was officially established on October 24, 1945, two-and-a-half months *after* the London Agreement, which included the IMT Charter, had been signed.

85. *Control Council Law No. 10*, Dec. 20, 1945, http://avalon.law.yale.edu/imt/imt10.asp; *see also Allied Control Councils and Commissions*, 1 INT'L ORG. 162, 167–68 (1947); *Allied Control Councils and Commissions*, 2 INT'L ORG. 146, 150–51 (1948).

86. *Ordinance No. 7*, Oct. 18, 1946, http://avalon.law.yale.edu/imt/imt07.asp [hereinafter *Ordinance No. 7*]. Ordinance No. 7 was amended by Ordinance No. 11, which became effective on February 17, 1947. *Ordinance No. 11*, Feb. 17, 1947, http://avalon.law.yale.edu/imt/imtor11.asp.

87. *Ordinance No. 7, supra* note 86, art. II(c).

88. CONOT, *supra* note 10, at 516.

89. HARRIS, *supra* note 9, at 559.

90. For more information on the twelve trials of the NMT, see, e.g., CONOT, *supra* note 10, at 516–17; HARRIS, *supra* note 9, at 546–58. The atrocities documented in the first trial, the Doctors (or Medical) case, have been the subject of much research. *See, e.g.*, ROBERT LIFTON, THE NAZI DOCTORS (2000); GERALD POSNER & JOHN WARE, MENGELE (2000); VIVIEN SPITZ, DOCTORS FROM HELL (2005). The third trial, the Justice (or Judges) case, served as the inspiration for JUDGMENT AT NUREMBERG (United Artists 1961).

91. HARRIS, *supra* note 9, at 548–49.

92. BASS, *supra* note 16, at 203.

93. *Id.* at 203; JON ELSTER, CLOSING THE BOOKS 54 (2004); MICHAEL BAZYLER & FRANK TUERKHEIMER, FORGOTTEN TRIALS OF THE HOLOCAUST (2014).

94. CONOT, *supra* note 10, at 518.

95. U.S. president John F. Kennedy felt that Taft's political courage in vocally opposing the IMT was so significant that it merited inclusion in Kennedy's Pulitzer Prize-winning profile of eight U.S. senators who adhered to their principles at great risk to their careers and reputations. JOHN KENNEDY, PROFILES IN COURAGE 231–44 (memorial ed. 1964).

96. CONOT, *supra* note 10, at 517; Jackson (Feb. 1954), *supra* note 28, at xxxiii; KENNEDY, *supra* note 95, at 236; JOSEPH PERSICO, NUREMBERG 437–38 (1995).

97. CONOT, *supra* note 10, at 517–18.

98. *See, e.g.*, HANNAH ARENDT, EICHMANN IN JERUSALEM 253 (rev. ed. 1964); HARRIS, *supra* note 9, at 559–63; Jack Ewing & Alan Cowell, *Ex-guard at Nazi Death Camp Is Found Guilty by German Court*, N.Y. TIMES, May 13, 2011, at A4.

99. TOM BOWER, THE PAPERCLIP CONSPIRACY (1987); ANNIE JACOBSEN, OPERATION PAPERCLIP (2014); CLARENCE LASBY, PROJECT PAPERCLIP (1971); ERIC LICHTBLAU, THE NAZIS NEXT DOOR: HOW AMERICA BECAME A SAFE HAVEN FOR HITLER'S MEN (2014); JOHN LOFTUS & MARK AARONS, THE SECRET WAR AGAINST THE JEWS 290 (1994).

100. Len Ackland, *Official Secrecy Fostered Coverup*, BULL. ATOMIC SCIENTISTS, Apr. 1985, at 2; Linda Hunt, *U.S. Coverup of Nazi Scientists*, BULL. ATOMIC SCIENTISTS, Apr. 1985, at 16, 16, 20.

101. ANDREW DUNAR & STEPHEN WARING, POWER TO EXPLORE (1999); DENNIS PISZKIERWICZ, WERNER VON BRAUN (1998); BOB WARD, DR. SPACE (2005).

102. Hunt, *supra* note 100, at 16–19; *see also* Peter Bond, *Obituary: Faith & Reason: Arthur Rudolph*, INDEPENDENT (United Kingdom), Jan. 6, 1996, http://www.independent.co.uk/news/people/obituary-faith-reason-arthur-rudolph-1322619.html; David Johnston, *Scientist Accused as Ex-Nazi is Denied Citizenship*, N.Y. TIMES, Feb. 20, 1993, http://www.nytimes.com/1993/02/20/us/scientist-accused-as-ex-nazi is-denied-citizenship.html.

103. Hunt, *supra* note 100, at 20–23.

104. Eric Lichtblau, *In Cold War, U.S. Spy Agencies Used 1,000 Nazis*, N.Y. TIMES, Oct. 27, 2014, at A1; Deborah Lipstadt, *Safe House*, N.Y. TIMES, Nov. 2, 2014, at BR20 (reviewing ERIC LICHTBLAU, THE NAZIS NEXT DOOR).

105. ALLAN RYAN, JR., KLAUS BARBIE AND THE UNITED STATES GOVERNMENT 16 (1984).

106. TOM BOWER, KLAUS BARBIE (1984); BRENDAN MURPHY, THE BUTCHER OF LYON (1983); RYAN, *supra* note 105; CHRISTOPHER STIMPSON, BLOWBACK (1983).

107. RYAN, *supra* note 105, at xviii.

108. Associated Press, *Documents: CIA Concealed Nazi War Criminals*, MSNBC.COM, June 7, 2006, http://www.msnbc.msn.com/id/13171278/; Pam Benson, *CIA Papers: U.S.*

Failed to Pursue Nazi, CNN.com, June 7, 2006, http://www.cnn.com/2006/US/06/06/ nazi.crimes/index.html; Shmuel Rosner, *Documents Show Post-war CIA Covered Up Nazi Crimes*, Haaretz, June 6, 2006, http://www.haaretz.com/news/documents-show-post-war-cia-covered-up-nazi-war-crimes-1.189490; Scott Shane, *C.I.A. Knew Where Eichmann Was Hiding, Documents Show*, N.Y. Times, June 6, 2007, at A3.

109. For related sources, see "Adolf Eichmann" in the Bibliography.

110. *Potsdam Conference*, July 26, 1945, art. II.A.6, http://avalon.law.yale.edu/20th_century/decade17.asp.

111. Constantine FitzGibbon, Denazification (1969); James Tent, Mission on the Rhine (1982); Timothy Vogt, Denazification in Soviet-Occupied Germany (2000).

112. Jackson (Feb. 1954), *supra* note 28, at xxxii.

113. Taylor, *supra* note 4, at 53.

114. István Deák, Letter to the Editor, *The Nuremberg Precedent*, N.Y. Rev. Books, Nov. 4, 1993, at 32; István Deák, Letter to the Editor, *Judgment at Nuremberg: An Exchange*, N.Y. Rev. Books, Jan. 13, 1994, at 52, 52; István Deák, *Misjudgment at Nuremberg*, N.Y. Rev. Books, Oct. 7, 1993, at 45, 48 (1993).

115. Jackson (Feb. 1954), *supra* note 28, at xxxi–ii.

116. Harris, *supra* note 9, at 501.

117. John Dippel, Letter to the Editor, *Judgment at Nuremberg: An Exchange*, N.Y. Rev. Books, Jan. 13, 1994, at 51; Renate Bridenthal & Marion Kaplan, Letter to the Editor, *Judgment at Nuremberg: An Exchange*, N.Y. Rev. Books, Jan. 13, 1994, at 52.

118. Arendt, *supra* note 98, at 274–75.

119. Jackson (Feb. 1954), *supra* note 28, at xxxii.

120. Robert Jackson, Assoc. Justice, U.S. Supreme Court, Address to the Am. Soc'y of Int'l Law (Apr. 13, 1945).

121. Taylor, *supra* note 4, at 53.

122. Gary Bass, *Atrocity & Legalism*, Daedalus, Winter 2003, at 73, 78.

123. Bass, *supra* note 16, at 169.

124. After years of denial, Russian leaders recently have become more forthcoming about their country's role in Katyn. *See, e.g.*, Anne Applebaum, Op-Ed., *Is Russia Finally Ditching Its Revisionist History on Katyn?*, Wash. Post, Apr. 6, 2010, at A13.

125. Taylor, *supra* note 4, at 77.

126. *Id.* at 74.

127. Benjamin Rhodes, United States Foreign Policy in the Interwar Period, 1918–1941 (2001).

128. Stephen Skowronek, The Politics Presidents Make (1997).

129. James Lindsay, Congress and the Politics of U.S. Foreign Policy 81 (1994).

Chapter 5

1. For an example of this expansive definition of "Tokyo," see Tim Maga, Judgment at Tokyo: The Japanese War Crimes Trials xi (2001).

2. Charter of the International Military Tribunal for the Far East art. 1, Jan. 19, 1946, T.I.A.S. No. 1589, 4 Bevans 20 (as amended Apr. 26, 1946, 4 Bevans 27), *reprinted in* Documents on the Tokyo International Military Tribunal: Charter,

INDICTMENT AND JUDGMENTS 7–11 (Neil Boister & Robert Cryer eds., 2008) [hereinafter IMTFE Charter].

3. JOHN W. DOWER, EMBRACING DEFEAT: JAPAN IN THE WAKE OF WORLD WAR II 444 (1999) ("It was by no means inevitable that major war-crimes trials, let alone precedent-breaking ones, would follow the war.").

4. *Three-Power Pact Between Germany, Italy, and Japan*, Sept. 17, 1940, *available at* http://avalon.law.yale.edu/wwii/triparti.asp.

5. *See, e.g.,* LAURENCE REES, HORROR IN THE EAST: JAPAN AND THE ATROCITIES OF WORLD WAR II (2002).

6. *See, e.g.,* GEORGE MORGENSTERN, PEARL HARBOR: THE STORY OF THE SECRET WAR (1947); GORDON W. PRANGE WITH DONALD M. GOLDSTEIN & KATHERINE V. DILLON, AT DAWN WE SLEPT: THE UNTOLD STORY OF PEARL HARBOR (1981); GORDON PRANGE WITH DONALD M. GOLDSTEIN & KATHERINE V. DILLON, PEARL HARBOR: THE VERDICT OF HISTORY (1986); ROBERT STINNETT, DAY OF DECEIT: THE TRUTH ABOUT FDR AND PEARL HARBOR (2000); ROBERTA WOHLSTETTER, PEARL HARBOR: WARNING AND DECISION (1962).

7. *See, e.g.,* JOHN COSTELLO, THE PACIFIC WAR (1981); JOHN W. DOWER, WAR WITHOUT MERCY: RACE AND POWER IN THE PACIFIC WAR (1986); HARRY A. GAILEY, THE WAR IN THE PACIFIC: FROM PEARL HARBOR TO TOKYO BAY (1996); RONALD SPECTOR, EAGLE AGAINST THE SUN: THE AMERICAN WAR WITH JAPAN (1985).

8. *See, e.g.,* YVES BEIGBEDER, JUDGING WAR CRIMINALS: THE POLITICS OF INTERNATIONAL JUSTICE 52–54 (1999); THE BURMA-THAILAND RAILWAY: MEMORY AND HISTORY (Gavan McCormack & Hank Nelson eds., 1993); IRIS CHANG, THE RAPE OF NANKING: THE FORGOTTEN HOLOCAUST OF WORLD WAR II (1997); GAVAN DAWS, PRISONERS OF THE JAPANESE: POWs OF WORLD WAR II IN THE PACIFIC (1994); GEORGE HICKS, THE COMFORT WOMEN: JAPAN'S BRUTAL REGIME OF ENFORCED PROSTITUTION IN THE SECOND WORLD WAR (1994); JAPANESE WAR CRIMES: THE SEARCH FOR JUSTICE (Peter Li ed., 2003); DONALD KNOX, DEATH MARCH: THE SURVIVORS OF BATAAN (1981); REES, *supra* note 5; YUKI TANAKA, HIDDEN HORRORS: JAPANESE WAR CRIMES IN WORLD WAR II (1996); WITH ONLY THE WILL TO LIVE: ACCOUNTS OF AMERICANS IN JAPANESE PRISON CAMPS 1941–1945 (Robert La Forte et al. eds., 1994).

9. HOWARD BALL, PROSECUTING WAR CRIMES AND GENOCIDE: THE TWENTIETH-CENTURY EXPERIENCE 67 (1999) (citing Kevin Uhrich, *The Other Holocaust*, L.A. READER, July 1, 1994).

10. *Id.* at 69; CHANG, *supra* note 8, at 52.

11. Franklin D. Roosevelt, President, Crimes Against Civilian Populations in Occupied Countries: Statement by the President (Aug. 21, 1942), *reprinted in* 10 DEP'T ST. BULL. 709, 709 (1942) [hereinafter 1942 FDR Statement].

12. Franklin D. Roosevelt, President, War Refugees: Statement by the President (Mar. 24, 1944), *reprinted in* 10 DEP'T ST. BULL. 277, 277 (1944).

13. 1942 FDR Statement, *supra* note 11.

14. Solis Horwitz, *Tokyo Trial*, 28 INT'L CONCILIATION 473, 477–78 (1950) (citing Wallace's address of December 28, 1942, on "America's Part in World Reconstruction").

15. *Cairo Conference 1943*, Nov. 1943, http://avalon.law.yale.edu/wwii/cairo.asp.

16. *Id.*

17. MAGA, *supra* note 1, at 27.

18. 1942 FDR Statement, *supra* note 11.

19. RICHARD LAEL, THE YAMASHITA PRECEDENT: WAR CRIMES AND COMMAND RESPONSIBILITY 40 (1982).

20. PHILIP R. PICCIGALLO, THE JAPANESE ON TRIAL: ALLIED WAR CRIMES OPERATIONS IN THE EAST, 1945–1951, at 4 (1979).

21. DOWER, *supra* note 3, at 444–45.

22. Horwitz, *supra* note 14, at 479 n.9.

23. MAGA, *supra* note 1, at 28.

24. Special Far E. & Pac. Comm., Draft Summary of Recommendations Concerning Japanese War Crimes and Atrocities (Aug. 28, 1945), *reprinted in* Donald Cameron Watt, *Historical Introduction* to 1 THE TOKYO MAJOR WAR CRIMES TRIAL xi (R. John Pritchard & Sonia Magbauna Zaide eds., 1981).

25. *Id.* at xii.

26. *Id.*

27. *Id.* at xiii.

28. Agreement for the Prosecution and Punishment of the Major War Criminals of the European Axis, Aug. 8, 1945, 59 Stat. 1544, 82 U.N.T.S 280, *reprinted in* 1 TRIAL OF THE MAJOR WAR CRIMINALS BEFORE THE INTERNATIONAL MILITARY TRIBUNAL: NUREMBERG, 14 NOVEMBER 1945–1 OCTOBER 1946, at 8, 8 (1947) [hereinafter London Agreement].

29. Watt, *supra* note 24, at xiv.

30. The Berlin (Potsdam) Conference, July 17–Aug. 2, 1945, *available at* http://avalon.law.yale.edu/20th_century/decade17.asp; *see also* DOCUMENTS ON THE TOKYO INTERNATIONAL MILITARY TRIBUNAL, *supra* note 2, at 1–2.

31. DOWER, *supra* note 3, at 445.

32. *See, e.g.,* GAR ALPEROVITZ, THE DECISION TO USE THE ATOMIC BOMB (1996); THE ATOMIC BOMB: VOICES FROM HIROSHIMA AND NAGASAKI (Kyoko Seldon & Mark Selden eds., 1989); ROBERT J. C. BUTOW, JAPAN'S DECISION TO SURRENDER (1954); JOHN HERSEY, HIROSHIMA (1989); RONALD TAKAKI, HIROSHIMA: WHY AMERICA DROPPED THE ATOMIC BOMB (1995); J. SAMUEL WALKER, PROMPT AND UTTER DESTRUCTION: TRUMAN AND THE USE OF ATOMIC BOMBS AGAINST JAPAN (1997).

33. ARNOLD C. BRACKMAN, THE OTHER NUREMBERG: THE UNTOLD STORY OF THE TOKYO WAR CRIMES TRIALS 40–42, 57, 60 (1987).

34. WILLIAM MANCHESTER, AMERICAN CAESAR: DOUGLAS MACARTHUR 1880–1964 (1983).

35. For more biographical information on MacArthur, see, e.g., JOHN GUNTHER, THE RIDDLE OF MACARTHUR: JAPAN, KOREA AND THE FAR EAST (1975); MACARTHUR AND THE AMERICAN CENTURY: A READER (William M. Leary ed., 2001); DOUGLAS MACARTHUR, REMINISCENCES (1964); GEOFFREY PERRET, OLD SOLDIERS NEVER DIE: THE LIFE OF DOUGLAS MACARTHUR (1996); RICHARD H. ROVERE & ARTHUR SCHLESINGER, Jr., GENERAL MACARTHUR AND PRESIDENT TRUMAN: THE STRUGGLE FOR CONTROL OF AMERICAN FOREIGN POLICY (1992); STANLEY WEINTRAUB, MACARTHUR'S WAR: KOREA AND THE UNDOING OF AN AMERICAN HERO (2000); *Commander of Armies That Turned Back Japan Led a Brigade in World War I*, N.Y. TIMES, Apr. 6, 1964, at 26.

36. *See infra* Part I.A.6 & Part I.B.

37. *See, e.g.,* DOWER, *supra* note 3; TAKEMAE EIJI, INSIDE GHQ: THE ALLIED OCCUPATION OF JAPAN AND ITS LEGACY (Robert Ricketts & Sebastian Swann trans., 2002); MICHAEL SCHALLER, THE AMERICAN OCCUPATION OF JAPAN: THE ORIGINS OF THE COLD WAR IN ASIA (1985).

38. BALL, *supra* note 9, at 71–73; BRACKMAN, *supra* note 33, at 43–44.

39. BUTOW, *supra* note 32, at 249–50.

40. U.S. Initial Post-Surrender Policy for Japan (Sept. 22, 1945), *reprinted in* 13 DEP'T ST. BULL. 423, 425 (1945).

41. BALL, *supra* note 9, at 73.

42. *Id.*; Horwitz, *supra* note 14, at 480; TANAKA, *supra* note 8, at 1.

43. Policy of the United States in Regard to the Apprehension and Punishment of War Criminals in the Far East (Oct. 25, 1945) *reprinted in* 1 THE TOKYO MAJOR WAR CRIMES TRIAL, *supra* note 24, at xiv–vi.

44. Horwitz, *supra* note 14, at 481.

45. Executive Order No. 9660, 10 Fed. Reg. 14591 (Nov. 30, 1945). According to one historian, Tim Maga, MacArthur personally lobbied for Keenan's appointment. MAGA, *supra* note 1, at 31.

46. Keenan, who was nicknamed "Joe the Key" because of his effectiveness in political circles, was educated at Brown University and Harvard Law School before serving in the U.S. military during WWI. Prior to his IMTFE appointment, Keenan had served as an assistant to the U.S. Attorney General and director of the U.S./DoJ's Criminal Division. During that time, Keenan developed a reputation as a tough, successful prosecutor from his personal experience trying some of the most notorious organized criminals of the era, including George "Machine Gun" Kelly, and as an effective White House and U.S./DoJ liaison to Congress on legislation and political appointments. *See, e.g.,* BRACKMAN, *supra* note 33, at 54–56; MAGA, *supra* note 1, at 29–31; RICHARD MINEAR: VICTORS' JUSTICE: THE TOKYO WAR CRIMES TRIAL 40 (1971); *Joseph B. Keenan, Prosecutor, Dies,* N.Y. TIMES, Dec. 9, 1954, at A33.

47. BALL, *supra* note 9, at 76; DOWER, *supra* note 3, at 319; Horwitz, *supra* note 14, at 482.

48. The ten states were: Australia, Canada, China, France, India, the Netherlands, New Zealand, the Philippine Commonwealth, the Soviet Union, and the United Kingdom. *War and Transitional Organizations: Allied Control Councils and Commissions,* 1 INT'L ORG. 162, 176–77 (1947) (regarding "The Far Eastern Commission").

49. IMTFE Charter, *supra* note 2, art. 8(b).

50. BALL, *supra* note 9, at 76.

51. *Interim Meeting of Foreign Ministers of the United States, the United Kingdom, and the Union of Soviet Socialist Republics, Moscow,* § II.A (Dec. 16–26, 1945), *available at* http://avalon.law.yale.edu/20th_century/decade19.asp [hereinafter *Interim Meeting*].

52. Horwitz, *supra* note 14, at 481; *War and Transitional Organizations, supra* note 48, at 169 (regarding the "Allied Control Council for Japan").

53. *Interim Meeting, supra* note 51, at § II.A; Horwitz, *supra* note 14, at 481; *see also Far Eastern Commission,* 3 INT'L ORG. 180, 180–82 (1949); *War and Transitional Organizations, supra* note 48, at 176–78; *War and Transitional Organizations: Political and Legal Organizations,* 2 INT'L ORG. 156, 156–57 (1948) (regarding the "Far Eastern Commission"); Samuel S. Stratton, *The Far Eastern Commission,* 2 INT'L ORG. 1, 1–18 (1948).

54. *Interim Meeting, supra* note 51, at § II.B.

55. *Id.* § II.B.2; *see also War and Transitional Organizations, supra* note 48, at 169 (regarding the "Allied Control Council for Japan"); *War and Transitional Organizations: Allied Control Councils and Commissions*, 2 INT'L ORG. 151, 151–52 (1948) (regarding the "Allied Council for Japan").

56. *Interim Meeting, supra* note 51, at §§ II.A.II.C, II.A.III, II.B.5.

57. *Id.* at §§ II.A.V.2, II.A.VII, and II.B.2.

58. James F. Byrnes, U.S. Sec'y of State, Report by the Secretary of State on the Meeting of Foreign Ministers (Dec. 30, 1945), *reprinted in* 13 DEP'T ST. BULL. 1033, 1033 (1945) [hereinafter *Byrnes Report*].

59. When established in 1945, the permanent members of the UNSC were China, France, the Soviet Union, the United Kingdom, and the United States. In 1991, the Russian Federation replaced the Soviet Union. UNITED NATIONS, DIVIDED WORLD: THE UN'S ROLE IN INTERNATIONAL RELATIONS 534 (Adam Roberts & Benedict Kingsbury eds., 2d ed. 1993).

60. *Byrnes Report, supra* note 58. Byrnes stated:

> The agreement at Moscow meets our insistence that all states which took an active part in the war should participate in the peace. It also frankly recognizes the responsible role of the larger powers in the making of peace. Our agreement is that the terms of peace in the first instance should be drawn by the principal powers which were signers of the respective armistices. But it was decided that as soon as these terms were drawn up, they should be submitted to a peace conference called by the five states—the United States, the Soviet Union, Great Britain, France, and China who constitute the Council of Foreign Ministers and are the permanent members of the [UNSC] . . . . While the United States sustained the major burden in crushing the military power of Japan, we have always considered the war against Japan a part of the war against the Axis. From the outset we have planned to make the control of Japan an Allied responsibility.

Id. at 1033–35.

61. IMTFE Charter, *supra* note 2.

62. MINEAR, *supra* note 46, at 20; PICCIGALLO, *supra* note 20, at 11; B.V.A. RÖLING, THE TOKYO TRIAL AND BEYOND: REFLECTIONS OF A PEACEMONGER 2 (Antonio Cassese ed., 1993).

63. Rules of Procedure for the International Military Tribunal of the Far East, Apr. 25, 1946, *reprinted in* DOCUMENTS ON THE TOKYO INTERNATIONAL MILITARY TRIBUNAL, *supra* note 2, at 12–15.

64. Horwitz, *supra* note 14, at 482–83; *see also* DOWER, *supra* note 3, at 455.

65. Horwitz, *supra* note 14, at 483. The amended Charter featured, for example, that the bench was expanded to include the nominated members of India and the Philippines, that six members were sufficient to convene the IMTFE, and that a quorum could be constituted by a majority of all members. *See* NEIL BOISTER & ROBERT CRYER, THE TOKYO INTERNATIONAL MILITARY TRIBUNAL 27 (2008).

66. BRACKMAN, *supra* note 33, at 18.

67. Horwitz, *supra* note 14, at 483, 488.

68. The nine states were: Australia, Canada, China, France, the Netherlands, New Zealand, the Soviet Union, the United Kingdom, and the United States. *Id.* at 488–89.

244 Notes to Pages 100–101

69. IMTFE Charter, *supra* note 2, art. 2.

70. BRACKMAN, *supra* note 33, at 63.

71. Horwitz, *supra* note 14, at 489.

72. DOWER, *supra* note 3, at 465.

73. Horwitz, *supra* note 14, at 489.

74. IMTFE Charter, *supra* note 2, art. 3(a).

75. BRACKMAN, *supra* note 33, at 19 (noting that Webb was absent for over two months during the defense presentation).

76. BALL, *supra* note 9, at 76–77.

77. BRACKMAN, *supra* note 33, at 74–75; Horwitz, *supra* note 14, at 492; PICCIGALLO, *supra* note 20, at 13–14; RÖLING, *supra* note 62, at 36–37.

78. Watt, *supra* note 24, at xxi–xxii.

79. Prosecutor v. Araki et al., IMTFE, Indictment (Apr. 29, 1946), *reprinted in* 2 THE TOKYO MAJOR WAR CRIMES TRIAL, *supra* note 24.

80. The twenty-eight indicted individuals were: Sadao Araki, Kenji Doihara, Kingoro Hashimoto, Shunroku Hata, Kiichirō Hiranuma, Kōki Hirota, Naoki Hoshino, Seishiro Itagaki, Okinori Kaya, Kōichi Kido, Heitaro Kimura, Kuniaki Koiso, Iwane Matsui, Yōsuke Matsuoka, Jirō Minami, Akira Mutō, Osami Nagano, Takasumi Oka, Shūmei Ōkawa, Hiroshi Ōshima, Kenryo Sato, Mamoru Shigemitsu, Shigetarō Shimada, Toshio Shiratori, Teiichi Suzuki, Shigenori Tōgō, Hideki Tōjō, and Yoshijiro Umezu. *Id.*

81. For definitions of these crimes, see IMTFE Charter, *supra* note 2, art. 5.

82. *See* DOCUMENTS ON THE TOKYO INTERNATIONAL MILITARY TRIBUNAL, *supra* note 2, at 18–33.

83. WHITNEY R. HARRIS, TYRANNY ON TRIAL: THE TRIAL OF THE MAJOR GERMAN WAR CRIMINALS AT THE END OF WORLD WAR II AT NUREMBERG, GERMANY, 1945–1946, at 543 (1999) (The IMTFE "conducted a trial of major Japanese war criminals in which the Nuremberg pattern was closely followed."); Whitney R. Harris, *A World of Peace and Justice Under the Rule of Law: From Nuremberg to the International Criminal Court*, 6 WASH. U. GLOBAL STUD. L. REV. 689, 696 (2007) (same).

84. The Transcripts of the Proceedings, May 3, 1946, *reprinted in* 2 THE TOKYO MAJOR WAR CRIMES TRIAL, *supra* note 24, at 21 [hereinafter The Transcripts of the IMTFE Proceedings].

85. BRACKMAN, *supra* note 33, at 18.

86. The Transcripts of the IMTFE Proceedings, *supra* note 84.

87. Prosecutor v. Araki et al., IMTFE, Judgment (Nov. 4-12, 1948), *reprinted in* DOCUMENTS ON THE TOKYO INTERNATIONAL MILITARY TRIBUNAL, *supra* note 2, at 71 *passim* (including the majority judgment and other opinions).

88. *See Judgment, Monday, September 30, 1946, in* 22 TRIAL OF THE MAJOR WAR CRIMINALS BEFORE THE INTERNATIONAL MILITARY TRIBUNAL 411–589 (1948) (containing the IMT's judgment and pronouncement of sentences as read on Sept. 30–Oct. 1, 1946); *see also Judgment of the International Military Tribunal for the Trial of German Major War Criminals, in* 1 INTERNATIONAL MILITARY TRIBUNAL AT NUREMBERG, GERMANY COMMENCING 20 NOV. 1945 (1946), *available at* http://avalon.law.yale.edu/imt/judgen.asp.

89. JOHN L. GINN, SUGAMO PRISON, TOKYO: AN ACCOUNT OF THE TRIAL AND SENTENCING OF JAPANESE WAR CRIMINALS IN 1948, BY A U.S. PARTICIPANT 37 (1992).

90. R. John Pritchard, *The International Military Tribunal for the Far East and Its Contemporary Resonances*, 149 MIL. L. REV. 25, 26 (1995).

91. Those sentenced to death by hanging were Doihara, Hirota, Itagaki, Kimura, Matsui, Mutō, and Tōjō. *See* Documents on the Tokyo International Military Tribunal, *supra* note 2, at 627–28 (Webb's pronouncement of the sentences).

92. Those sentenced to life imprisonment were Araki, Hashimoto, Hata, Hiranuma, Hoshino, Kaya, Kido, Koiso, Minami, Oka, Ōshima, Sato, Shimada, Shiratori, Suzuki, and Umezu. *Id.*

93. The individual sentenced to twenty years imprisonment was Tōgō. *Id.* at 628.

94. The individual sentenced to seven years imprisonment was Shigemitsu. *Id.*

95. *Id.* at 227–28.

96. Matsuoka and Nagano died during the trial in 1946 and 1947, respectively. *See* Brackman, *supra* note 33, at 101, 268.

97. Ōkawa had been judged medically unfit for trial. *See id.* at 104.

98. For the text of MacArthur's explanation for not commuting the sentences delivered by the IMTFE, see Documents on the Tokyo International Military Tribunal, *supra* note 2, at 70.

99. *See* Ginn, *supra* note 89, at 123.

100. Hirota v. MacArthur, 335 U.S. 876 (1948).

101. *Id.* at 876–81.

102. Hirota v. MacArthur, 338 U.S. 197 (1948).

103. *Id.* at 197–98.

104. *Id.* at 198.

105. For a description of Sugamo Prison, see Ginn, *supra* note 89, at 1–13.

106. During WWII, however, the USG instituted an additional mechanism for confronting people of Japanese descent residing in the United States: indefinite detention. On February 19, 1942, two months after the Japanese attack on Pearl Harbor, FDR signed Executive Order 9066, which empowered the USG to intern Japanese and Japanese-Americans. 7 Fed. Reg. 1407 (1942). It was not until President Gerald Ford's proclamation exactly thirty-four years later that this executive order officially terminated. *President Gerald R. Ford's Proclamation 4417, Confirming the Termination of the Executive Order Authorizing Japanese-American Internment During World War II* (Feb. 19, 1976), *available at* http://www.fordlibrarymuseum.gov/library/speeches/760111p.htm (noting that "[o]ver one hundred thousand persons of Japanese ancestry were removed from their homes, detained in special camps, and eventually relocated"); *see also* Korematsu v. United States, 323 U.S. 214 (1944) (finding constitutional exclusion orders based on Executive Order 9066).

107. The UN Charter was signed on June 26, 1945, and ratified on October 24, 1945. *See* U.N. Charter; United Nations, Divided World, *supra* note 59, at 6, 529.

108. As discussed in Chapters II, VI, and VII of this book, the ICTY and the ICTR share an appeals chamber and, until 2003, also shared a chief prosecutor.

109. *See infra* Part II.C.4, Part IV.D.

110. *See infra* Part IV.D.

111. Brackman, *supra* note 33, at 47; Watt, *supra* note 24, at vii, xxi.

112. Dower, *supra* note 3, at 323.

113. *Id.* at 467.

114. Historian Tim Maga claims, incorrectly, that, "Classified as Class A war criminal suspects, the eighty [indicted men] were tried between May 3, 1946, and November 12, 1948, in Yokohama, near Tokyo." Maga, *supra* note 1, at 2. Only twenty-eight of the Class A war criminals were indicted by the IMTFE's prosecutors. John Ginn, who worked as a

guard at Sugamo Prison during the trials, claims that there were originally eighty-four Class A war criminals held at the prison, from which the twenty-eight eventually tried were chosen. *See* GINN, *supra* note 89, at 44.

115. BALL, *supra* note 9, at 78; BRACKMAN, *supra* note 33, at 405; GINN, *supra* note 89, at 242; MINEAR, *supra* note 46, at 39.

116. DOWER, *supra* note 3, at 627, n.19.

117. 103 THE TOKYO MAJOR WAR CRIMES TRIAL, *supra* note 24 (transcript of Webb's pronouncement of the judgment).

118. BRACKMAN, *supra* note 33, at 411.

119. *Id.* at 385.

120. DOWER, *supra* note 3, at 474.

121. *Id.*

122. *In re* Yamashita, 327 U.S. 1, 10–11 (1946).

123. PICCIGALLO, *supra* note 20, at 95 tbl. For a description and analysis of some of these trials, see BALL, *supra* note 9, at 74; GINN, *supra* note 89, at 56–119; MAGA, *supra* note 1, at 1–33, 93–119.

124. PICCIGALLO, *supra* note 20, at 6.

125. *See, e.g.,* BRACKMAN, *supra* note 33, at 53.

126. DOWER, *supra* note 3, at 443–44.

127. PICCIGALLO, *supra* note 20, at 32.

128. *In re* Yamashita, 327 U.S. 1, 5, 14 (1946).

129. *Id.* at 25–26.

130. A. FRANK REEL, THE CASE OF GENERAL YAMASHITA 234, 239 (1949).

131. *Id.* at 1; LAEL, *supra* note 19, at xi.

132. MAGA, *supra* note 1, at 18.

133. TANAKA, *supra* note 8, at 2.

134. 984 were sentenced to death (920 of whom were actually executed), 475 were sentenced to life imprisonment, and 2944 were sentenced to more limited prison terms. *Id.*; DOWER, *supra* note 3, at 447.

135. DOWER, *supra* note 3, at 447; TANAKA, *supra* note 8, at 2. For a description of some of these Allied trials, see, e.g., PICCIGALLO, *supra* note 20. Some of the Classes B and C war criminals faced multiple trials. MINEAR, *supra* note 46, at 6 n.3.

136. DOWER, *supra* note 3, at 447.

137. Horwitz, *supra* note 14, at 521.

138. DOWER, *supra* note 3, at 449.

139. Robert Barr Smith, *Japanese War Crime Trials*, WORLD WAR II MAG., Sept. 1996, *available at* http://www.historynet.com/japanese-war-crime-trials.htm.

140. Zachary D. Kaufman, *Transitional Justice Delayed Is Not Transitional Justice Denied: Contemporary Confrontation of Japanese Human Experimentation During World War II Through a People's Tribunal*, 26 YALE L. & POL'Y REV. 645, 646–48 (2008) [hereinafter Kaufman, *Transitional Justice Delayed Is Not Transitional Justice Denied*]. For related sources, see also "Japanese/IMTFE" in the Bibliography.

141. *See, e.g.,* HANS BAERWALD, THE PURGE OF JAPANESE LEADERS UNDER THE OCCUPATION 99 (1959).

142. *Interim Meeting, supra* note 51, at §§ II.A.III, II.A.VI.

143. MINEAR, *supra* note 46, at 20–21; PICCIGALLO, *supra* note 20, at 11.

144. BEIGBEDER, *supra* note 8, at 55.

145. *See, e.g.*, Horwitz, *supra* note 14, at 485, 565.

146. *Id.* at 480–81.

147. *Id.* at 490; BALL, *supra* note 9, at 76.

148. Horwitz, *supra* note 14, at 494.

149. *Id.* at 509, 517–18.

150. *Id.* at 541; Pritchard, *supra* note 90, at 31; Smith, *supra* note 139.

151. RÖLING, *supra* note 62, at 37.

152. GINN, *supra* note 89, at 16.

153. BRACKMAN, *supra* note 33, at 44.

154. *Id.* at 365–66.

155. PICCIGALLO, *supra* note 20, at 6.

156. *See* IMTFE Charter, *supra* note 2, art. 2.

157. *See id.* art. 3(a).

158. *See id.* art. 3(b)(1).

159. *See id.* art. 8(a).

160. BRACKMAN, *supra* note 33, at 72.

161. IMTFE Charter, *supra* note 2, art. 2, 3(a), 3(b)(1), 8(a), 17.

162. MINEAR, *supra* note 46, at 164–65.

163. Awaya Kentarō, *In the Shadows of the Tokyo Tribunal, in* THE TOKYO WAR CRIMES TRIAL: AN INTERNATIONAL SYMPOSIUM 79, 83–84 (C. Hosoya et al. eds., 1986).

164. BALL, *supra* note 9, at 76.

165. DOWER, *supra* note 3, at 458.

166. RÖLING, *supra* note 62, at 31.

167. Hirota v. MacArthur, 338 U.S. 197, 207 (1948) (Douglas, J., concurring).

168. Far E. Comm'n, Apprehension, Trial, and Punishment of War Criminals in the Far East (Apr. 3, 1946), *reprinted in* 16 DEP'T ST. BULL. 804, 804 (1946).

169. DOWER, *supra* note 3, at 74.

170. Wu Tianwei, *The Failure of the Tokyo Trial*, Century of China, 1995, *available at* http://www.centurychina.com/wiihist/japdeny/tokyo_trial.html.

171. MAGA, *supra* note 1, at 63 (quoting Blakeney).

172. *Id.* at 29 (quoting French and Dutch officials).

173. BOISTER & CRYER, *supra* note 65, at 50–54.

174. MAGA, *supra* note 1, at 35.

175. Horwitz, *supra* note 14, at 498.

176. GINN, *supra* note 89, at 43–44. For a description of the selection of the accused, see, e.g., BOISTER & CRYER, *supra* note 65, at 50–54; BRACKMAN, *supra* note 33, at 72–82; MINEAR, *supra* note 46, at 93–117; PICCIGALLO, *supra* note 20, at 14–16; Horwitz, *supra* note 14, at 495–98.

177. Of a total of 16,354,000 Americans who served in WWII, 405,400 were killed or went missing, 670,800 were wounded, and 139,700 were POWs. During campaigns in Northwest Europe, Tunisia, and Italy, a total of 143,000 Americans were killed or went missing and 448,090 were wounded, as compared to a total of 58,710 Americans who were killed or went missing and 164,830 who were wounded during campaigns in Southeast Asia and the Pacific. JOHN ELLIS, WORLD WAR II: A STATISTICAL SURVEY: THE ESSENTIAL FACTS AND FIGURES FOR ALL THE COMBATANTS 254–56 (1993).

178. Brackman, *supra* note 33, at 23.

179. Watt, *supra* note 24, at x.

180. Tanaka, *supra* note 8, at 3; *see also* Ball, *supra* note 9, at 84.

181. Dower, *supra* note 3, at 446.

182. Antonio Cassese, *Introduction* to Röling, *supra* note 62, at 5.

183. Beigbeder, *supra* note 8, at 61.

184. *See, e.g.*, Gar Alperovitz, Atomic Diplomacy: Hiroshima and Potsdam 234–35 (1994); Alperovitz, *supra* note 32, at 127–29.

185. Dower, *supra* note 3, at 419.

186. Antonio Cassese, *Introduction* to Röling, *supra* note 62, at 5.

187. Dower, *supra* note 3, at 469.

188. Chang, *supra* note 8, at 199–214, 216–17.

189. *See, e.g.*, Piccigallo, *supra* note 20, at 6–7.

190. Horwitz, *supra* note 14, at 486–87.

191. Watt, *supra* note 24, at ix.

192. Tianwei, *supra* note 170.

193. Piccigallo, *supra* note 20, at 6–7.

194. IMTFE Charter, *supra* note 2, art. 4(b).

195. 1 Int'l Military Tribunal, Trial of the Major War Criminals Before the International Military Tribunal, Nuremberg, 14 November 1945–1 October 1946, at 1 (1947).

196. Brackman, *supra* note 33, at 63–64.

197. *World War II War Crimes—Fact Sheet 61*, Nat'l Archives Austl., http://www.naa.gov.au/collection/fact-sheets/fs61.aspx (last visited July 26, 2015).

198. Maga, *supra* note 1, at 29, 65.

199. Horwitz, *supra* note 14, at 489.

200. Mark Osiel, Mass Atrocity, Collective Memory, and the Law 138 (1997); *see also* Ball, *supra* note 9, at 73–74; *see also* Brackman, *supra* note 33, at 77–78; MacArthur, *supra* note 35, at 287–88; Piccigallo, *supra* note 20, at 16–17.

201. Dower, *supra* note 3, at 323.

202. *Id.* at 324.

203. Horwitz, *supra* note 14, at 497.

204. Henri Bernard, *Dissenting Judgment of the Member from France of the International Military Tribunal for the Far East*, Nov. 1, 1948, *in* Documents on the Tokyo International Military Tribunal, *supra* note 2, at 661, 677; William Flood Webb, *Separate Opinion of the President*, Nov. 1, 1948, *in* Documents on the Tokyo International Military Tribunal, *supra*, at 629, 638–39.

205. *See, e.g.*, Herbert P. Bix, Hirohito and the Making of Modern Japan 336–39, 447–48 (2000).

206. For further discussion of U.S. encouragement of Japanese postwar remilitarization, see Zachary D. Kaufman, *No Right to Fight: The Modern Implications of Japan's Pacifist Postwar Constitution*, 33 Yale J. Int'l L. 266 (2008).

207. James Bowen, *How the United States Protected Japanese War Criminals and Facilitated Japan's Denial of War Guilt and War Crimes*, Pac. War Historical Soc'y, 2000, *available at* http://www.pacificwar.org.au/JapWarCrimes/USWarCrime_Coverup.html; *see also* Tianwei, *supra* note 170.

208. Dower, *supra* note 3, at 454.

209. Although no consensus exists about whether American POWs were among the human guinea pigs of Unit 731 specifically, they certainly were victims of Japanese human experiments elsewhere. *See, e.g.*, DANIEL BARENBLATT, A PLAGUE UPON HUMANITY: THE HIDDEN HISTORY OF JAPAN'S BIOLOGICAL WARFARE PROGRAM XX (2004) (claiming that American POWs were experimented on and killed as part of Japanese biological warfare research during WWII); MARK FELTON, THE DEVIL'S DOCTORS: JAPANESE HUMAN EXPERIMENTS ON ALLIED PRISONERS OF WAR 7 (2012) ("[T]here is little direct evidence that has survived that definitively answers the question of whether Unit 731 conducted tests on American … POWs … But there is incontrovertible evidence that Japanese physicians conducted tests on American … POWs in other parts of Asia …."); HAL GOLD, UNIT 731 TESTIMONY 9 (1997) (stating that Americans were among the three thousand individuals Unit 731 victimized); SHELDON H. HARRIS, FACTORIES OF DEATH 171 (rev. ed. 2002) ("although American POWs may have been victims of [biological warfare] tests, there is no substantive evidence currently available to prove that the experiments took place at Camp Mukden" under Ishii's direction); Ralph Blumenthal, *Comparing the Unspeakable to the Unthinkable*, N.Y. TIMES, Mar. 7, 1999, at WK4 (stating that "perhaps some American prisoners of war" were among the 10,000 or more individuals killed in Japanese human experimentation during WWII); Michael Daly, *Japan Dissected My Granddad Alive in World War II*, DAILY BEAST, Apr. 18, 2015, http://www.thedailybeast.com/articles/2015/04/08/world-war-ii-japan-dissected-my-granddad-alive.html (describing vivisections conducted at Kyushu University by Japanese on eight American POWs); Thomas Easton, *A Quiet Honesty Records a World War II Atrocity*, BALT. SUN, May 28, 1995, http://articles.baltimoresun.com/1995-05-28/news/1995148003_1_japan-kyushu-university-fukuoka ("Kyushu University stands out as the only site where Americans were incontrovertibly used in dissections" by Japanese.); Arthur Kleinman et al., *Introduction, in* JAPAN'S WARTIME MEDICAL ATROCITIES: COMPARATIVE INQUIRIES IN SCIENCE, HISTORY, AND ETHICS 1, 8 (Jing-Bao Nie et al. eds., 2010) (stating that the victims of Unit 731 were Chinese, Russians, and Koreans); Nicholas D. Kristof, *Unmasking Horror—A Special Report; Japan Confronting Gruesome War Atrocity*, N.Y. TIMES, Mar. 17, 1995, http://www.nytimes.com/1995/03/17/world/unmasking-horror-a-special-report-japan-confronting-gruesome-war-atrocity.html ("There is no evidence that Americans were among the victims in the Unit 731 compound, although there have been persistent but unproven accusations that American prisoners of war in Mukden (now Shenyang) were subject to medical experimentation."); Elaine O'Flynn, *US Bomber Crew Shot Down over Japan Were Dissected While Alive in Horrific WW2 Experiments*, DAILY MAIL (United Kingdom), Apr. 7, 2015, http://www.dailymail.co.uk/news/article-3028694/U-S-POWs-shot-Japan-70-years-ago-dissected-ALIVE-macabre-experiments-controversial-new-exhibition-shows.html (describing medical experiments performed on American POWs at Kyushu University); Didi Kirsten Tatlow, *Q. and A.: Gao Yubao on Documenting Unit 731's Brutal Human Experiments*, N.Y. TIMES, Oct. 21, 2015, http://sinosphere.blogs.nytimes.com/2015/10/21/china-unit-731-japan-war-crimes/ (claiming that the Ishii-led Unit 731 conducted some of its experiments on American prisoners); Suzy Wang, *Medicine-Related War Crimes Trials and Post-War Politics and Ethics, in* JAPAN'S WARTIME MEDICAL ATROCITIES, *supra*, at 33, 50, n.7 (noting that "some testimonies have also claimed that U.S. prisoners of war were subjects of such human experimentation" by Japan generally but that a declassified USG document from 1995 states that "no documentary evidence could be found to support the claims that American POWs were used for" experiments conducted by Unit 731 specifically).

210. *See supra* Chapter IV of this book, notes 90, 99–103 and accompanying text.

211. C.A. WILLOUGHBY, REPORT ON BACTERIOLOGICAL WARFARE (1947) (on file with the author); Letter from C.A. Willoughby, U.S. Army Forces, Pac., Military Intelligence Section, Gen. Staff, to Major Gen. S.J. Chamberlin, Dir. of Intelligence, War Dep't Gen. Staff (July 22, 1947) (on file with the author).

212. JOHN LOFTUS & MARK AARONS, THE SECRET WAR AGAINST THE JEWS: HOW WESTERN ESPIONAGE BETRAYED THE JEWISH PEOPLE 290 (1994).

213. Kaufman, *Transitional Justice Delayed Is Not Transitional Justice Denied, supra* note 140, at 646–48.

214. In the immediate aftermath of WWII, the USG itself deliberately infected humans with disease. From 1946 to 1948, USG-funded American researchers—using prostitutes, injections, and other methods—intentionally exposed approximately 1300 Guatemalan prisoners, soldiers, and mental patients to syphilis, gonorrhea, and chancroid. One stated purpose of the experiments was to determine if penicillin could prevent infection after exposure to disease. Donald G. McNeil, Jr., *Panel Hears Grim Details of V.D. Test on Inmates*, N.Y. TIMES, Aug. 30, 2011, at A4.

215. GINN, *supra* note 89, at 245.

216. BEIGBEDER, *supra* note 8, at 73–74.

Chapter 6

1. STEVEN EMERSON & BRIAN Duffy, THE FALL OF PAN AM 103 (1990); Victims of Pan Am Flight 103, Inc., https://www.victimsofpanamflight103.org (last visited July 26, 2015).

2. Elaine Sciolino, *U.S. Is Said to Withhold Evidence of War Crimes Committed by Iraq*, N.Y. TIMES, July 6, 1992, at A6 [hereinafter Sciolino, *U.S. Is Said to Withhold Evidence*].

3. WHITNEY HARRIS, TYRANNY ON TRIAL 572–73 (rev. ed. 1999).

4. G.A. Res. 260 (III), part B (Dec. 9, 1948).

5. HARRIS, *supra* note 3, at 573.

6. Michael Scharf, *Swapping Amnesty for Peace*, 31 TEX. INT'L L.J. 1 (1996); Robert Quinn, *Will the Rule of Law End?*, 62 FORDHAM L. REV. 905 (1993).

7. Benjamin Ferencz, *Introduction* to 1 AN INSIDER'S GUIDE TO THE INTERNATIONAL CRIMINAL TRIBUNAL FOR THE FORMER YUGOSLAVIA xxi (Virginia Morris & Michael Scharf eds., 1995).

8. James Robbins, Op-Ed., *Iraqi War Criminals Face Hanging*, WALL ST. J., Jan. 23, 1991, at A12.

9. Paul Lewis, *U.N. Sets Up War-Crimes Panel on Charges of Balkan Atrocities*, N.Y. TIMES, Oct. 7, 1992, at A1.

10. Press Release, Statement by Secretary-General, U.N. Doc. L/2870 (June 15, 1998).

11. G.A. Res. 260 (III) (Dec. 9, 1948); *see also* William Schabas, *Origins of the Genocide Convention: From Nuremberg to Paris*, 40 CASE W. RES. J. INT'L L. 35 (2008).

12. LAWRENCE LeBLANC, THE UNITED STATES AND THE GENOCIDE CONVENTION (1991).

13. Convention on the Prevention and Punishment of the Crime of Genocide art. II, Dec. 9, 1948, 102 Stat. 3045, 78 U.N.T.S. 277, 280.

14. *Id.* art. I.

15. *Id.* art. VI.

16. Document 179.

17. *See, e.g.*, Michael Belknap, The Vietnam War on Trial (2002).

18. Document 171.

19. For related sources, see "The Balkans" in the Bibliography.

20. Theodor Meron, *The Case for War Crimes Trials in Yugoslavia*, 72 Foreign Aff., Summer 1993, at 122.

21. *Id.* at 125.

22. S.C. Res. 749 (Apr. 7, 1992).

23. S.C. Res. 764 (July 13, 1992).

24. Gerald Seib, *U.S. Calls for U.N. Diplomatic Actions to Shut Any Serbian-Run Death Camps*, Wall St. J., Aug. 6, 1992, at A14 [hereinafter Seib, *U.S. Calls for U.N. Diplomatic Actions*].

25. S.C. Res. 771 (Aug. 13, 1992).

26. Seib, *U.S. Calls for U.N. Diplomatic Actions, supra* note 24.

27. *World-Wide*, Wall St. J., Aug. 27, 1992, at A1.

28. *London Conference documents—London Conference on Yugoslavia—Transcript*, U.S. Dep't of State Dispatch, Sept. 1992.

29. Michael Scharf, Balkan Justice 32 (1997).

30. U.N. Doc. E/CN.4/1992/S-1/1 (Aug. 28, 1992).

31. S.C. Res. 776 (Sept. 14, 1992).

32. Document 178.

33. *Id.*

34. Document 181.

35. *Id.*

36. Document 180.

37. Document 182.

38. S.C. Res. 780 (Oct. 6, 1992).

39. Lewis, *supra* note 9.

40. *Id.*

41. *Id.*

42. *Id.; see also* Chapter IV of this book.

43. Document 183. This "United Nations War Crimes Commission" is a different body than the same-named UNWCC that operated at the end of WWII. *See* Chapters IV and V of this book.

44. Document 181.

45. S.C. Res. 787 (Nov. 16, 1992).

46. Chuck Sudetic, *U.N. Investigating Croats' Grave Site*, N.Y. Times, Nov. 29, 1992, at A1.

47. *Id.*

48. Scharf, *supra* note 29, at 43.

49. Elaine Sciolino, *U.S. Names Figures It Wants Charged with War Crimes*, N.Y. Times, Dec. 17, 1992, at A1 [hereinafter Sciolino, *U.S. Names Figures*].

50. *Id.*

51. Document 184.

52. G.A. Res. 47/133 (Dec. 18, 1992).

53. G.A. Res. 47/135 (Dec. 18, 1992).

54. Elaine Sciolino, *U.S. Moves Ahead on War-Crimes Tribunal*, N.Y. Times, Jan. 27, 1993, at A3 [hereinafter Sciolino, *U.S. Moves Ahead*].

55. *Id.*

56. Roy Gutman, *War Crime Unit Hasn't a Clue; UN Setup Seems Designed to Fail*, NEWSDAY, Mar. 4, 1993, at 8.

57. U.N. Doc. S/25307 (Feb. 18, 1993).

58. U.N. Doc. S/25274 (Feb. 10, 1993).

59. *Id.* at 20.

60. Paul Lewis, *U.N. Council Moves to Create Balkan War-Crimes Tribunal*, N.Y. TIMES, Feb. 19, 1993, at A3.

61. S.C. Res. 808 (Feb. 22, 1993).

62. *UN Security Council Adopts Resolution 808 on War Crimes Tribunal*, U.S. DEP'T OF STATE DISPATCH, Mar. 22, 1993.

63. U.N. Doc. S/25575 (Apr. 12, 1993).

64. *Id.*

65. *Id.*

66. *Id.*

67. *Id.*

68. *Id.*

69. *Id.*

70. Document 188.

71. *See* Chapter VII of this book.

72. Document 188.

73. SCHARF, *supra* note 29, at 56.

74. *Id.* at 58–60.

75. *Id.* at 60–61.

76. U.N. Doc. S/25829 (May 24, 1993).

77. UNSC Res. 827, para. 2 (May 25, 1993). For related sources, see "ICTY" in the Bibliography.

78. Documents 175, 176.

79. Documents 175, 176.

80. Documents 175, 176.

81. Documents 175, 176.

82. Document 175.

83. Sciolino, *U.S. Moves Ahead, supra* note 54. For more discussion of Iraq, see infra Part III.B.2.

84. *Confirmation Hearing for Warren Christopher as Secretary of State*, 103rd Cong. (1993) (statement of Warren Christopher).

85. *Id.*

86. Sciolino, *U.S. Moves Ahead, supra* note 54.

87. *Id.*

88. SCHARF, *supra* note 29, at xv, 32–33.

89. Ferencz, *supra* note 7, at xix.

90. Gutman, *supra* note 56.

91. *Id.*

92. *Id.*

93. *Id.*

94. *Id.*

95. *Id.*

96. Document 181.

97. *Id.*

98. *Id.*

99. *Id.*

100. *Id.* For more discussion of Libya, including UNSC Resolution 748, see infra Part III.B.2.

101. Document 181.

102. *Id.*

103. *Id.*

104. Document 185.

105. *Id.*

106. ICTY, Case Information Sheet, http://www.icty.org/action/cases/4 (last visited July 26, 2015) [hereinafter ICTY Cases].

107. Olga Kavran, *Bosnian Serb Leader Radovan Karadzic Arrested: What Lies Ahead*, WASH. POST, July 23, 2008, http://www.washingtonpost.com/wp-dyn/content/discussion/2008/07/22/DI2008072201921.html.

108. CONFRONTING THE YUGOSLAV CONTROVERSIES 187 (Charles Ingrao & Thomas Emmert eds., 2009); Nick Hawton, *Hague Probes Karadzic "Deal" Claim*, BBC NEWS, Oct. 26, 2007, http://news.bbc.co.uk/2/hi/europe/7062288.stm; Marlise Simons, *Envoy Denies Immunity Offer to Leader of Bosnian Serbs*, N.Y. TIMES, Mar. 26, 2009, at A12; Marlise Simons, *Study Backs Bosnian Serb's Claim That U.S. Envoy Promised Immunity*, N.Y. TIMES, Mar. 22, 2009, at A6 [hereinafter Simons, *Study Backs Claim*]; Jon Swaine, *Radovan Karadzic "Was Under US Protection Until 2000,"* TELEGRAPH (United Kingdom), Aug. 4, 2008, http://www.telegraph.co.uk/news/worldnews/europe/serbia/2496948/Karadzic-was-under-US-protection.html. For discussion by two senior USG officials at the time of how, during the previous year, the "Bosnia Contact Group" of France, Germany, Russia, the United Kingdom, and the United States considered offering amnesty to Karadžić, Milošević, and Mladić, see DAVID SCHEFFER, ALL THE MISSING SOULS 19 (2012); JOHN SHATTUCK, FREEDOM ON FIRE 141–42 (2003).

109. SCHEFFER, *supra* note 108, at 129–37.

110. Carl Bildt, Op-Ed., *Now, NATO Troops Should Catch the Big Fish*, N.Y. TIMES, July 12, 1997, at A21; *see also* Steven Myers, *Rights Group Says Bosnian Suspects Flaunt Freedom*, N.Y. TIMES, Nov. 26, 1996, at A11.

111. *See, e.g.*, RICHARD HOLBROOKE, TO END A WAR 339 (1998); Jack Snyder & Leslie Vinjamuri, *Trials and Errors*, 28 INT'L SECURITY 5, 42 (2003–2004); *see also* SCHEFFER, *supra* note 108, at 124–59, 412.

112. R. W. Apple, Jr., *Milosevic Remains, Souring a Victory*, N.Y. TIMES, June 5, 1999, at A5; Editorial, *A Mixed Message on War Crimes*, N.Y. TIMES, Feb. 13, 1996, at A20; Philip Shenon, *From the U.S., Mixed Signals on Bosnia War Crime Issue*, N.Y. TIMES, June 4, 1996, at A1 [hereinafter Shenon, *Mixed Signals*]; Philip Shenon, *G.I.'s in Bosnia Shun Hunt for War-Crime Suspects*, N.Y. TIMES, Mar. 2, 1996, at A3 [hereinafter Shenon, *G.I.'s Shun Hunt*].

113. Reuters, *Embattled Bosnian Serb Leader Orders Parliament Dissolved*, N.Y. TIMES, July 4, 1997, at A1.

114. Raymond Bonner, *Allies Weigh Raid to Seize Bosnian Serb Leaders*, N.Y. TIMES, July 6, 1996, at A1.

115. Shenon, *G.I.'s Shun Hunt, supra* note 112; Shenon, *Mixed Signals, supra* note 112; Simons, *Study Backs Claim, supra* note 108.

116. Document 178.

117. Matheson interview 3.

118. Shattuck interview 3.

119. GARY BASS, STAY THE HAND OF VENGEANCE 207 (2000) (emphasis in original.)

120. Walker interview.

121. Steven Holmes, *State Dept. Expert on Croatia Resigns to Protest Policy in Balkans,* N.Y. TIMES, Aug. 24, 1993, at A6.

122. Seib, *U.S. Calls for U.N. Diplomatic Actions, supra* note 24.

123. Shattuck interview 3.

124. SCHEFFER, *supra* note 108, at 19.

125. Document 171.

126. Document 178.

127. Documents 186, 190.

128. Documents 186, 190.

129. Documents 186, 190.

130. *Bosnia in Light of the Holocaust,* U.S. DEP'T OF STATE DISPATCH, Apr. 18, 1994.

131. Document 171.

132. Document 189.

133. Walker interview.

134. SCHEFFER, *supra* note 108, at 18, 26.

135. Document 186.

136. Shattuck interview 3.

137. Document 171.

138. Document 186.

139. Document 179.

140. *Id.*

141. *Id.*

142. Document 187.

143. Walker interview.

144. *Id.*

145. Shattuck interview 3.

146. Document 186.

147. Document 190.

148. *Id.*

149. U.N. Charter art. 49.

150. Document 185.

151. Document 186.

152. SCHEFFER, *supra* note 108, at 20.

153. Jerome Shestack, Op-Ed, *Rule of Law,* WALL ST. J., Feb. 10, 1993, at A15.

154. Ferencz, *supra* note 7, at xxii.

155. Walker interview.

156. Shattuck interview 3.

157. Document 171 (emphasis added.)

158. *See supra* note 80 and accompanying text.

159. ICTY Cases, *supra* note 106. For an account of the case, see WILLIAM SCHABAS & MICHAEL SCHARF, SLOBODAN MILOSEVIC ON TRIAL (2002).

160. BASS, *supra* note 119, at 207.

161. Matheson interview 3.

162. Scharf interview.

163. BASS, *supra* note 119, at 222.

164. Document 176.

165. S.C. Res. 748 (Mar. 31, 1992).

166. Document 175.

167. *Id.*

168. Document 176.

169. Document 175.

170. Document 179.

171. S.C. Res. 731 (Jan. 21, 1992).

172. Document 179.

173. Matheson interview 3.

174. Scharf interview.

175. *Id.*

176. Shattuck interview 3.

177. For example, on September 12, 2001, in response to the previous day's terrorism that was perpetrated solely on U.S. soil, the UNSC, including the USG, condemned such attacks as "international" offenses that constituted "a threat to international peace and security." S.C. Res. 1368 (Sept. 12, 2001).

178. Paul Barrett, *U.S. Backs Off Iraqi War Crimes Trials Due to Logistic, Political Considerations*, WALL ST. J., Jan. 22, 1991, at B4; James Robbins, Op-Ed., *Iraqi War Criminals Face Hanging*, WALL ST. J., Jan. 23, 1991, at A12; Gerald Seib, *Bush Hints U.S. to Seek War-Crime Trial of Iraq's Leaders for Actions in Kuwait*, WALL ST. J., Oct. 16, 1990, at A8 [hereinafter Seib, *Bush Hints*]; Gerald Seib & Bruce Ingersoll, *Military Details of Progress in Gulf Sobering*, WALL ST. J., Jan. 22, 1991, at A3.

179. Seib, *Bush Hints, supra* note 178.

180. Seib & Ingersoll, *supra* note 178; Robbins, *supra* note 178.

181. S.C. Res. 674 (Oct. 29, 1990).

182. Sciolino, *U.S. Is Said to Withhold Evidence, supra* note 2.

183. *See supra* note 83 and accompanying text.

184. MICHAEL NEWTON & MICHAEL SCHARF, ENEMY OF THE STATE (2008).

185. Meron, *supra* note 20, at 124.

186. SCHARF, *supra* note 29, at 38.

187. *Id.* at 39.

188. Document 177.

189. Document 175.

190. Document 177.

191. Barrett, *supra* note 178; Laurie Mylroie, Op-Ed., *Planning Saddam's Ouster*, WALL ST. J., July 27, 1992, at A10.

192. Richard Gardner, Op-Ed., *Trying Saddam Might Be a Bad Idea*, WALL ST. J., March 1, 1991, at A8.

193. Matheson interview 3.

194. Meron, *supra* note 20, at 124.

195. *See* Chapter VII of this book.

196. Meron, *supra* note 20, at 124.

197. S.C. Res. 687 (Apr. 3, 1991).

198. Meron, *supra* note 20, at 124.

199. Matheson interview 3.

200. Document 177.

201. *Id.*

202. *Id.*

203. Document 175.

204. Document 177.

205. *Id.*

206. *Id.*

207. *Id.*

208. *Id.*

209. *Id.*

210. Document 179.

211. *Former Yugoslavia—US Military Operations*, GLOBALSECURITY.ORG, http://www.globalsecurity.org/military/ops/yugo-ops.htm (last visited July 26, 2015).

212. Document 179.

213. *Id.*

214. *Id.*

215. *Id.*

216. *Id.*

217. *Id.*

218. Shattuck interview 3.

219. Document 176.

220. Document 177.

221. Document 171.

222. Documents 175, 176.

223. Document 177.

224. Document 179.

225. *Id.*

226. *Id.*

227. *Id.*

228. *Id.*

229. *Id.*

230. *Id.*

231. Document 171.

232. Sciolino, *U.S. Names Figures, supra* note 49.

233. Document 171.

234. Document 178.

235. Document 179.

236. SCHARF, *supra* note 29, at 41.

237. *See supra* note 229 and accompanying text.

238. For a discussion of analogical reasoning in U.S. foreign-policy decision-making, see Yuen Foong Khong, Analogies at War (1992).

239. Matheson interview 3.

240. G.A. Res. 95(I) (Dec. 11, 1946).

241. Scharf interview.

242. Shattuck interview 3; Walker interview.

243. *See* Chapter IV of this book.

244. Matheson interview 3 ("The individuals who proposed and implemented this policy [of supporting the ICTY creation] were largely non-political and worked in both administrations.").

245. Ferencz, *supra* note 7, at xxii.

246. Seib, *U.S. Calls for U.N. Diplomatic Actions, supra* note 24.

247. Roger Thurow, *War Criminal or Patriot?*, N.Y. Times, Dec. 18, 1992, at A7.

248. Document 189.

249. Tamar Lewin, *The Balkans Rapes*, N.Y. Times, Oct. 7, 1992, at B16.

Chapter 7

1. *See generally* Phil Clark & Zachary D. Kaufman, *Rwanda: Recent History, in* Africa South of the Sahara 2016, 969 (Iain Frame ed., 2015); Zachary D. Kaufman & Pierre-Richard St. Hilaire, *The Rwandan Experience, in* Rwanda and South Africa in Dialogue: Addressing the Legacies of Genocide and a Crime Against Humanity 41 (Charles Villa-Vicencio & Tyrone Savage eds., 2001). For related sources, see also "Rwanda" in the Bibliography.

2. Philip Gourevitch, We Wish to Inform You That Tomorrow We Will Be Killed with Our Families 180, 244–45 (1998).

3. Org. of African Unity, Rwanda: The Preventable Genocide xiii–xiv, 73–74 (2000). In 2013, Clinton stated that, had the USG intervened in Rwanda sooner, at least 300,000 lives could have been saved. *Bill Clinton: We Could Have Saved 300,000 Lives in Rwanda*, CNBC, Mar. 13, 2013, http://www.cnbc.com/id/100546207.

4. Because it had such a limited mandate and such hopelessly insufficient capacity, the author does not consider the UN Assistant Mission for Rwanda (UNAMIR) to have served as a meaningful intervention. In addition, because it was so controversial and similarly limited and ineffective, the author does not consider the French-initiated *Opération Turquoise* to have served as a meaningful intervention either. For discussion of documents declassified from the Clinton White House about UNAMIR, see National Security Archive, *1994 Rwanda Pullout Driven by Clinton White House, U.N. Equivocation* (Apr. 16, 2015), http://nsarchive.gwu.edu/NSAEBB/NSAEBB511/. For discussion by a senior USG official at the time about UNAMIR and *Opération Turquoise*, see David Scheffer, All the Missing Souls 45–68 (2012).

5. Lake interview.

6. Shattuck interview 1.

7. Scheffer interview 1.

8. *Id.*

9. Pub. Broad. Serv., 100 Days of Slaughter, 1999, http://www.pbs.org/wgbh/pages/frontline/shows/evil/etc/slaughter.html [hereinafter 100 Days of Slaughter].

10. *Id.*

11. UN Doc. S/PRST/1994/16 (Apr. 7, 1994).

12. White House, Statement by the Press Secretary (Apr. 22, 1994).

13. ALISON DES FORGES, LEAVE NONE TO TELL THE STORY 284 (1999).

14. Document 27.

15. *Id.*

16. Bushnell interview 2.

17. SAMANTHA POWER, "A PROBLEM FROM HELL": AMERICA AND THE AGE OF GENOCIDE 370 (2002).

18. U.S./DoS, cable number 113672 (Apr. 29, 1994), *available at* http://www.gwu.edu/~nsarchiv/NSAEBB/NSAEBB53/rw042994.pdf.

19. Document 45.

20. SCHEFFER, *supra* note 4, at 61.

21. UN Doc. S/1999/1257 (Dec. 16, 1999).

22. UN Doc. S/PV.3453 14, 16 (Nov. 8, 1994).

23. UN Doc. S/PRST/1994/21 (Apr. 30, 1994).

24. *Id.*

25. *Id.*

26. ELIZABETH NEUFFER, THE KEY TO MY NEIGHBOR'S HOUSE 129 (2001).

27. 100 Days of Slaughter, *supra* note 9.

28. U.S./DoD, Discussion Paper (May 1, 1994), *available at* http://www.gwu.edu/~nsarchiv/NSAEBB/NSAEBB53/rw050194.pdf.

29. U.S./DoS, Draft Legal Analysis (May 16, 1994), *available at* http://www.gwu.edu/~nsarchiv/NSAEBB/NSAEBB53/rw051694.pdf.

30. U.S./DoS, "Rwanda—Genocide Convention Violations" (circa May 18, 1994), *available at* http://www.gwu.edu/~nsarchiv/NSAEBB/NSAEBB53/rw051894.pdf.

31. Document 109.

32. *See also* POWER, *supra* note 17, at 362.

33. Document 109.

34. U.S./NSC, "Donald Steinberg to Anthony Lake; re: Situation in Rwanda" (May 27, 1994), *available at* http://www.clintonlibrary.gov/assets/storage/Research-Digital-Library/formerlywithheld/batch7/2006-0218-F.pdf.

35. Jared Cohen & Zachary Kaufman, Op-Ed., *A Genocide by Any Other Name*, BROWARD TIMES, July 15, 2005, at 6. Scheffer, however, argues against "[t]he popular theory . . . that Washington refused to use the term ["genocide"] for fear of being compelled to act with military force in Rwanda." SCHEFFER, *supra* note 4, at 65.

36. Documents 1, 2.

37. Documents 1, 2.

38. Holly Burkhalter, *The Question of Genocide*, 11 WORLD POL'Y J. 44, 52 (1994–1995).

39. UN/HCHR, E/CN.4/S-3/3 (May 19, 1994), Annex Paras. 10, 20, 32; S.C. Res 918 (1994).

40. Document 28.

41. Document 29.

42. Documents 62, 96, 97.

43. SCHEFFER, *supra* note 4, at 69.

44. Document 31.

45. *Id.*

46. Document 32.

47. UN/HCHR, S/1994/867 (July 25, 1994), Intro., Annex Para. 26.

48. UN/ICER, S/1994/1125. (Oct. 4, 1994), Art. II, Sec. B, Para. 27; *see also* Document 8.

49. Documents 3, 4, 5.

50. Document 4.

51. S.C. Res 935 (July 1, 1994), Preamble, Para. 3; Scheffer interview 1.

52. William Ferroggiaro, The US and the Genocide in Rwanda 1994, Aug, 20, 2001, http://www.gwu.edu/~nsarchiv/NSAEBB/NSAEBB53/press.html.

53. *Christopher Urges Trial over Genocide in Rwanda*, WASH. POST, July 1, 1994, at A29.

54. *Id.*

55. UN Doc. S/PV.3400 (July 1, 1994), 4.

56. Scheffer interview 1.

57. White House, Statement by the White House on Rwanda (July 15, 1994).

58. Document 31.

59. Documents 33, 35, 36.

60. Document 39.

61. JOHN SHATTUCK, FREEDOM ON FIRE 325 (2003).

62. S.C. Res. 936 (July 8, 1994).

63. RICHARD GOLDSTONE, FOR HUMANITY 74, 81 (2000).

64. LINDA MELVERN, A PEOPLE BETRAYED 60 n.20 (2000).

65. Documents 9, 46, 47.

66. Document 15.

67. Document 11.

68. Document 10.

69. Scheffer interview 1.

70. Document 12; *see also* SCHEFFER, *supra* note 4, at 71.

71. Matheson interview 1; Stanton interview 1.

72. Documents 42, 44.

73. Document 48.

74. SCHEFFER, *supra* note 4, at 72.

75. The governments included those of France, Spain, the UK, China, Ireland, Belgium, the Netherlands, Tanzania, South Africa, Kenya, and Uganda. *See* Documents 13, 14, 17, 22, 23, 38, 40, 43, 50–55, 61, 63, 65, 68, 72-74, 78, 79, 82–84, 90, 91, 100, 106, 113, 116, 119, 120, 122.

76. Document 37.

77. Document 122.

78. Document 90.

79. *Id.*

80. Documents 58, 64.

81. Documents 58, 64.

82. Document 90.

83. Those states included Burundi, Djibouti, DRC, Ethiopia, Kenya, Nigeria, Tanzania, and Uganda. *See* Document 78.

84. Matheson interview 1; Blewitt interview.

85. Document 115.

86. Document 69.

87. Document 77.

88. *Id.*

89. Document 81.

90. Document 85.

91. Document 59.

92. Document 60.

93. Document 71.

94. Document 66.

95. SHATTUCK, *supra* note 61, at 59–66; Document 68.

96. Documents 67, 78, 118.

97. Document 70.

98. Document 86.

99. *Try Rwandan War Cases in Hague, Says U.S.*, RECORD, Sept. 21, 1994, at A17.

100. Matheson interview 1.

101. John Shattuck, Op-Ed., *War Crimes First*, WASH. POST, Aug. 23, 1994, at A19.

102. Documents 75, 80, 89; SCHEFFER, *supra* note 4, at 75.

103. Document 76.

104. *Id.*

105. Document 88.

106. S. Frederick Starr, Op-Ed., *It's Up to Us to Defuse the Rwandan Time Bomb*, WASH. POST, Sept. 6, 1994, at A17.

107. Document 87.

108. Des Forges interview; Scheffer interview 1; Scheffer interview 2; Shattuck interview 1; Documents 18, 112.

109. UN/ICER, S/1994/1405 (Dec. 9, 1994), Art. II, Sec. A, Para. 35.

110. Documents 93–95, 98.

111. UNSG, S/1994/1125 (Oct. 4, 1994), Annex, paras. 133–45, 149–52.

112. *Id.*, at Annex, para. 140.

113. UN Doc. S/1994/1115 (Sept. 29, 1994).

114. Farhan Haq, *Rwanda*, INTER PRESS SERV., Oct. 4, 1994; *see also* SCHEFFER, *supra* note 4, at 80–84.

115. UN Doc. A/49/PV.21 (1994). 5.

116. SCHEFFER, *supra* note 4, at 78.

117. Documents 12, 19, 49, 110. Neither China nor the United Kingdom expressed a preference.

118. Document 111; SCHEFFER, *supra* note 4, at 74, 77.

119. Matheson interview 1; Scheffer interview 1; SCHEFFER, *supra* note 4, at 78.

120. Document 123.

121. Document 20.

122. Document 123.

123. Document 99; *see also* Document 123.

124. Document 124.

125. Document 100.

126. Documents 123, 125.

127. Document 22.

128. Documents 101, 125.

129. Document 21.

130. Matheson interview 1; Documents 24, 25, 100–104, 107, 125.

131. 1 Virginia Morris & Michael Scharf, The International Criminal Tribunal for Rwanda 67 (1998).

132. Documents 101–104, 107, 108; Scheffer, *supra* note 4, at 80–84.

133. Scheffer interview 1.

134. Document 104.

135. Argentina would join later as a co-sponsor.

136. Document 24.

137. Document 25.

138. Scheffer interview 2.

139. S.C. Res 955 (Nov. 8, 1994); *see generally* Zachary D. Kaufman, *International Criminal Tribunal for Rwanda, in* The Encyclopedia of Transitional Justice 233 (Lavinia Stan & Nadya Nedelsky eds., 2012). For related sources, see also "ICTR" in the Bibliography.

140. UN Doc. S/PV.3453 (Nov. 8, 1994).

141. *Id.* at 11.

142. *See infra* Part III.5.C.

143. S.C. Res. 977 (Feb. 22, 1995).

144. Roy Lee, *The Rwanda Tribunal*, 9 Leiden J. Int'l. L. 37 (1996) (emphasis added).

145. For details and discussion of these four options, see Nicola Palmer, Courts in Conflict: Interpreting the Layers of Justice in Post-genocide Rwanda (2015); Zachary D. Kaufman, *Transitional Justice as Genocide Prevention: From a Culture of Impunity to a Culture of Accountability, in* Confronting Genocide in Rwanda: Dehumanization, Denial, and Strategies for Prevention 363 (Jean-Damascène Gasanabo et al. eds., 2014) [hereinafter Kaufman, *Transitional Justice as Genocide Prevention*]; William Schabas, *Post-genocide Justice in Rwanda: A Spectrum of Options, in* After Genocide: Transitional Justice, Post-conflict Reconstruction, and Reconciliation in Rwanda and Beyond 207 (Phil Clark & Zachary D. Kaufman eds., 2009) [hereinafter Schabas, *Post-genocide Justice in Rwanda*].

146. Schabas, *Post-genocide Justice in Rwanda, supra* note 145, at 207.

147. Amnesty Int'l, Rwanda 1–5 (2000).

148. African Rights, Gacaca Justice 2 (2003); William Schabas, *Genocide Trials and Gacaca Courts*, 3 J. Int'l Crim. Just. 879 (2005).

149. For related sources, see "Gacaca" in the Bibliography.

150. Phil Clark, The Gacaca Courts, Post-genocide Justice and Reconciliation in Rwanda 3 (2010).

151. Kaufman, *Transitional Justice as Genocide Prevention, supra* note 145, at 368–70; William Schabas, *Anti-complementarity: Referral to National Jurisdictions by the UN International Criminal Tribunal for Rwanda*, 13 Max Planck Y.B. of United Nations L. 29 (2009); William Schabas, *National Courts Finally Begin to Prosecute Genocide, the "Crime of Crimes,"* 1 J. Int'l Crim. Just. 39, 45–53 (2003).

152. Chris McGreal, *Rwandan Woman Stripped of US Citizenship After Lying about Genocide*, Guardian (United Kingdom), Feb. 22, 2013, http://www.guardian.co.uk/world/2013/feb/22/rwandan-woman-stripped-citizenship-genocide.

153. St. Hilaire interview; Silverwood interview.

154. St. Hilaire interview.

155. POWER, *supra* note 17.

156. *Id.* at 373; UN Doc. S/1994/470 (Apr. 20, 1994); S.C. Res 912 (Apr. 21, 1994); SCHEFFER, *supra* note 4, at 45–68.

157. Ferroggiaro, *supra* note 52.

158. Document 11.

159. Symposium, *Identifying and Prosecuting War Crimes*, 12 N.Y.L. SCH. J. HUM. RTS. 631, 650 (1995) (remarks of Rwandan UN/PR Ambassador Manzi Bakuramutsa).

160. Des Forges interview.

161. NEUFFER, *supra* note 26, at 128.

162. Stanton interview 1.

163. *Id.*

164. James Bennett, *Clinton Declares U.S. and the World Failed Rwandans*, N.Y. TIMES, Mar. 26, 1998, at A1.

165. Shattuck interview 1.

166. MADELEINE ALBRIGHT, MADAM SECRETARY 147 (2003).

167. Scheffer interview 1.

168. SCHEFFER, *supra* note 4, at 46, 68.

169. *Id.* at 57.

170. Matheson interview 1.

171. Dana Hughes, *Rwanda, and What Bill Clinton Left Out When He Criticized Obama on Syria*, ABCNEWS.COM, June 13, 2013, http://abcnews.go.com/blogs/politics/2013/06/rwanda-and-what-bill-clinton-left-out-of-criticism-of-obama-on-syria/.

172. Kate Snow, *Bill Clinton's "Lifetime Responsibility" to Rwanda*, ABCNEWS.COM, Aug. 2, 2008, http://abcnews.go.com/GMA/story?id=5502860.

173. Lake interview; Matheson interview 1; Stanton interview 1.

174. Neil Lewis, *Papers Show U.S. Knew of Genocide in Rwanda*, N.Y. TIMES, Aug. 22, 2001, at A5; Timothy Longman, *What Did the Clinton Administration Know About Rwanda*, WASH. POST, Apr. 6, 2015, http://www.washingtonpost.com/blogs/monkey-cage/wp/2015/04/06/what-did-the-clinton-administration-know-about-rwanda/; Colum Lynch, *Exclusive: Rwanda Revisited*, FOREIGN POL'Y, Apr. 5, 2015, https://foreignpolicy.com/2015/04/05/rwanda-revisited-genocide-united-states-state-department/; Samantha Power, *Bystanders to Genocide*, ATL. MONTHLY, Sept. 2001, at 84.

175. MARK BOWDEN, BLACK HAWK DOWN (2000).

176. Stanton interview 1; Scheffer interview 2; Document 31. While acknowledging the role the failed Somalia intervention played in "shap[ing] the context for failing to intervene to end Rwanda's genocide," Scheffer argues that "more contemporary issues that required immediate decisions for effective action . . . instead triggered a multitude of excuses and devastating delays." SCHEFFER, *supra* note 4, at 47. *See also id.* at 58.

177. Shattuck interview 1.

178. Matheson interview 1.

179. Scheffer interview 2; *see also* Stanton interview 1; Matheson interview 2.

180. Document 31.

181. Document 39 (stating that, "[a]s the crisis in Rwanda has unfolded, the United States has taken a leading role in efforts to protect the Rwandan people and ensure humanitarian assistance," including providing more than $95 million in relief supplies, airlifting relief supplies, and supporting the UN peacekeeping mission).

182. Station interview 1.

183. Shattuck interview 2.

184. Stanton interview 1.

185. Matheson interview 1.

186. SCHEFFER, *supra* note 4, at 69.

187. Shattuck interview 1.

188. Matheson interview 1; Lake interview; Stanton interview 1; Documents 12, 48, 78.

189. SHATTUCK, *supra* note 61, at 75.

190. Scheffer interview 1; Matheson interview 1; Lake interview; Stanton interview 1.

191. Documents 12, 48.

192. Stanton interview 1; Scheffer interview 1; Matheson interview 1.

193. Matheson interview 1.

194. Stanton interview 1; Michael Scharf, *Responding to Rwanda*, 52 J. INT'L AFF. 621, 624 (1999).

195. *See* Convention on the Prevention and Punishment of the Crime of Genocide art. VI, Dec. 9, 1948, 102 Stat. 3045, 78 U.N.T.S. 277, 280.

196. Matheson interview 1.

197. Bushnell interview 1; Stanton interview 1; Bennet interview.

198. Shattuck interview 1.

199. Matheson interview 1.

200. Bushnell interview 1.

201. Shattuck interview 1; Scheffer interview 1.

202. Document 51.

203. Document 71.

204. Neil Kritz, *The Dilemmas of Transitional Justice, in* 1 TRANSITIONAL JUSTICE xxix (1995).

205. Shattuck interview 1.

206. Stanton interview 1.

207. Shattuck interview 1.

208. Lake interview; Matheson interview 1; Shattuck interview 1; Stanton interview 1.

209. Document 106.

210. Documents 72, 114, 119.

211. Bennet interview.

212. Lake interview; Matheson interview 1; Stanton interview 1.

213. Stanton interview 1.

214. Document 15.

215. Matheson interview 1.

216. Documents 12, 48, 60, 68, 78, 86, 90.

217. Matheson interview 1; SCHEFFER, *supra* note 4, at 73–74, 78, 112.

218. Matheson interview 1.

219. Documents 93–95, 98.

220. GARY BASS, STAY THE HAND OF VENGEANCE: THE POLITICS OF WAR CRIMES TRIBUNALS 11 (2000).

221. Stanton interview 1.

222. Scheffer interview 1.

223. Matheson interview 1; Shattuck interview 1; Stanton interview 1; Bushnell interview 1.

224. Bennet interview.

225. UN Doc. S/PV.3453 (Nov. 8, 1994), 18; Scheffer interview 1; Stanton interview 1.

226. Document 60; *see also* Documents 71, 73, 123, 124.

227. Shattuck interview 1; Documents 12, 48, 78, 86.

228. Matheson interview 1; *see also* Lee, *supra* note 144, at 61; Daphna Shraga & Ralph Zacklin, *The International Criminal Tribunal for Rwanda*, 7 Eur. J. Int'l L. 501, 505 (1996); Jelena Pejic, *The Tribunal and the ICC*, 60 Alb. L. Rev. 841, 853 (1997); S.C. Res. 955 (Nov. 8, 1994); Document 77.

229. Lake interview.

230. Bushnell interview 1.

231. Scheffer interview 1.

232. Shattuck interview 1.

233. Blewitt interview.

234. Scheffer interview 1.

235. Matheson interview 1.

236. Bushnell interview 1; Documents 31, 106, 119.

237. Matheson interview 1; Document 31; Shattuck, *supra* note 61, at 19.

238. Bushnell interview 1; Stanton interview 1.

239. Matheson interview 1; Documents 12, 31, 71, 110.

240. Documents 71, 110; Scheffer, *supra* note 4, at 79.

241. Scheffer interview 1; Matheson interview 1; Documents 12, 48, 72, 78, 86, 90; Scheffer, *supra* note 4, at 79–80.

242. Matheson interview 1.

243. Stanton interview 1; Documents 31, 90, 121.

244. *See, e.g.*, William A. Schabas, *United States Hostility to the International Criminal Court: It's All About the Security Council*, 15 Eur. J. Int'l L. 701 (2004).

245. Stanton interview 1; Shattuck interview 1; Document 31.

246. Documents 12, 54, 86.

247. Document 72.

248. Matheson interview 1.

249. Scheffer interview 1; Document 31.

250. Scheffer interview 1.

251. Lake interview; Bushnell interview 2; Document 31.

252. Document 84.

253. Stanton interview 1.

254. Stanton interview 1; Document 90.

255. The UNSC authorized economic sanctions and military force against the Cedras-led coalition that had staged a coup in Haiti in 1991. *See* S.C. Res 940 (July 31, 1994); S.C. Res 944 (Sept. 29, 1994).

256. Scheffer interview 1.

257. Matheson interview 1; Bushnell interview 1.

258. M. Cherif Bassiouni, *Appraising UN Justice-Related Fact-Finding Missions*, 5 Wash. U. J.L. & Pol'y 35, 42–43 (2001).

259. Scheffer interview 1.

260. Bassiouni, *supra* note 258, at 44.

261. Bushnell interview.

262. *See, e.g.,* ANDREW WALLIS, SILENT ACCOMPLICE: THE UNTOLD STORY OF FRANCE'S ROLE IN THE RWANDAN GENOCIDE (rev. ed. 2014).

263. UN Doc. S/PV.3453 (Nov. 8, 1994), 13-16. For a discussion of some misconceptions about the GoR's objection to the ICTR, see Zachary D. Kaufman, *Steven D. Roper & Lilian A. Barria's Designing Criminal Tribunals: Sovereignty and International Concerns in the Protection of Human Rights,* 10 Yale Hum. Rts. & Dev. L.J. 209, 213 (2007) (book review).

264. Stanton interview; SCHEFFER, *supra* note 4, at 83–84.

265. Document 104.

266. SHATTUCK, *supra* note 61, at 59.

267. Des Forges interview.

268. Scheffer interview 2; *see also* SCHEFFER, *supra* note 4, at 84.

269. Document 118; *see also* SCHEFFER, *supra* note 4, at 80–84.

270. Scheffer interview 1; *see also* SCHEFFER, *supra* note 4, at 80–84.

271. Scheffer interview 1.

272. *Id.*

273. Matheson interview 1.

274. Shattuck interview 1. Scheffer similarly notes that the GoR shouldered "liability" for offenses committed after the Rwandan genocide formally ended in July 1994. *See* SCHEFFER, *supra* note 4, at 81.

275. Scheffer interview 1; Stanton interview; Shattuck interview 1; *see also* GOLDSTONE, *supra* note 63, at 109.

276. Scheffer interview 1.

277. *Id.*

278. MORRIS & SCHARF, *supra* note 131, at 72.

279. SCHEFFER, *supra* note 4, at 84.

280. UN Doc. S/PV.3453 (Nov. 8, 1994), 17.

281. Lake interview.

282. Scheffer interview 1.

283. Stanton interview 1.

284. Lake interview; Scheffer interview 1.

285. S.C. Res. 877 (Oct. 21, 1993). For discussion of various candidates to become the first ICTY chief prosecutor, see SCHEFFER, *supra* note 4, at 30–33.

286. M. Cherif Bassiouni, *From Versailles to Rwanda in Seventy-Five Years,* 10 HARV. HUM. RTS. J. 11, 44 (1997).

287. *Id.* at 43.

288. Luisa Vierucci, *The First Steps of the International Criminal Tribunal for the Former Yugoslavia,* 6 EUR. J. INT'L L. 134, 140 (1995).

289. HOWARD BALL, PROSECUTING WAR CRIMES AND GENOCIDE 142 (1999).

290. S.C. Res. 936 (July 8, 1994); *see also* GOLDSTONE, *supra* note 63, at 74, 81.

291. Vierucci, *supra* note 288, at 136.

292. ALBRIGHT, *supra* note 166, at 183.

293. SHATTUCK, *supra* note 61, at 68.

294. Scheffer interview 1.

295. Matheson interview 1.

296. Stanton interview 1.

297. BALL, *supra* note 289, at 141.

298. Scheffer interview 1; Shattuck interview 1.

299. Schrag interview.

300. Matheson interview 1.

301. Scheffer interview 1.

302. Bushnell interview 1; Shattuck interview; Stanton interview 1.

303. Peter Burns, *An International Criminal Tribunal*, 5 CRIM. L.F. 341, 380 (1994).

304. S.C. Res. 780 (Oct. 6, 1992); S.C. Res. 827 (May 25, 1993).

305. Matheson interview.

306. Shattuck interview.

307. Shraga & Zacklin, *supra* note 228, at 501.

308. Payam Akhavan, *The International Criminal Tribunal for Rwanda*, 90 AM. J. INT'L L. 501, 501 (1996).

Chapter 8

1. As discussed in Chapter III of this book, Democratic Peace Theory primarily contends that democratic states are unlikely to go to war against one another. Political scientist Jack Levy believes this theory to be "as close as anything we have to an empirical law in international relations." Jack Levy, *Domestic Politics and War*, 18 J. INTERDISC. HIST. 653, 662 (1988). Other scholars agree, with Russett arguing that the absence of war among democracies is "one of the strongest nontrivial and nontautological generalizations that can be made about international relations." BRUCE RUSSETT, CONTROLLING THE SWORD 123 (1990). Democratic Peace Theory also argues that democratic states are likely to ally with each other, while also acknowledging that these states are as likely as any other to enter into conflict with undemocratic states. Democratic Peace Theory argues that these phenomena are caused by the inherent attributes of democratic states, including cultural factors, such as a shared norm of peaceful conflict resolution, and structural or institutional factors, such as checks and balances, separation of powers, and the need for public discussion of foreign policy. For related sources, see "Democratic Peace Theory" in the Bibliography.

2. GARY BASS, STAY THE HAND OF VENGEANCE: THE POLITICS OF WAR CRIMES TRIBUNALS 18 (2000).

3. Similarly, political scientists Henry Farber, Joanne Gowa, Christopher Layne, Ido Oren, and David Spiro cite instances in which democratic states have, in fact, gone to war against each other, thus undermining Democratic Peace Theory. Henry Farber & Joanne Gowa, *Polities and Peace*, 20 INT'L SECURITY 123 (1995); Christopher Layne, *Kant or Cant*, 19 INT'L SECURITY 5 (1994); Ido Oren, *The Subjectivity of the "Democratic" Peace*, 20 INT'L SECURITY 147 (1995); David Spiro, *The Insignificance of the Liberal Peace*, 19 INT'L SECURITY 50 (1994).

4. BASS, *supra* note 2, at 12.

5. *Id.* at 173.

6. *Id.* at 281 (both emphases added).

7. *Id.* (emphasis added).

8. *Id.*

9. *Id.* at 195.

10. *Id.*

11. *Id.*

12. Bass does not define what he means by "overwhelmingly," and he contradicts himself elsewhere by noting that only "sometimes" do liberal states "pursue war crimes tribunals" (*id.* at 8) or "leave[] the fate of war criminals up to the courts" (*id.* at 26).

13. Annie R. Bird, US Foreign Policy on Transitional Justice 3 (2015) (claiming that the USG "promotes a retributive model of transitional justice" because of "[t]he American tradition of punishment through law" and "a US foreign policy bureaucracy that has dedicated significant resources to supporting criminal prosecutions").

14. For example, in contexts such as the Armenian and Cambodian genocides, liberal states did not attempt—or at least, in the case of Cambodia, did not attempt for decades—to prosecute either the main perpetrators or their foot soldiers.

15. Bass, *supra* note 2, at 8 (emphasis added).

16. *Id.* at 28.

17. *Id.* at 330 (emphasis added).

18. *Id.* at 18 (emphasis added).

19. By no means is Bass alone in making these claims, in part because Bass's book has led others astray. See, for example, the following reviews of Bass's book: Susan K. Arnold, *Stay the Hand of Vengeance: The Politics of War Crimes Tribunals*, 172 Mil. L. Rev. 195, 197 (2002) (book review) (arguing that Bass "easily supports [the claim that only liberal states support bona fide war crimes tribunals] with all of the cited historical examples"); Arthur W. Blaser, *Gary Jonathan Bass's Stay the Hand of Vengeance*, 96 Am. Pol. Sci. Rev. 255, 256 (2002) (book review) (Bass "convincingly argues that [liberal states] are the only ones to have created war crimes tribunals."); Antonio Cassese, *Gary Jonathan Bass's Stay the Hand of Vengeance*, 24 Int'l Hist. Rev. 238, 238 (2002) (book review) ("[I]lliberal or totalitarian states do not promote or pursue international criminal justice.").

20. Bass, *supra* note 2, at 203.

21. John Gaddis, *Order Versus Justice: An American Foreign Policy Dilemma*, *in* Order and Justice in International Relations 160 (Rosemary Foot et al. eds., 2003); *see also* The Black Book of Communism: Crimes, Terror, Repression (Stéphane Courtois et al. eds., Jonathan Murphy & Mark Kramer trans., 1999) (documenting Soviet atrocities).

22. The "Polity IV" database measures historical trends in regime types across countries and regions of the world. One indicator, "POLITY," is determined by subtracting the assigned autocracy value from the assigned democracy value, resulting in a single regime score ranging from +10 (full democracy) to -10 (full autocracy). Monty Marshall et al., Polity IV Project 14 (2010), *available at* http://www.systemicpeace.org/inscr/ p4manualv2013.pdf. The states noted in this paragraph as "liberal" are those adjudged by the Polity IV database as having POLITY scores of or close to +10, whereas those noted as "illiberal" are those adjudged by the Polity IV database as having POLITY scores of or close to -10. In both 1945 and 1946, the Polity IV database deemed both the United Kingdom and the United States as having POLITY scores of +10, indicating strongly democratic (and thus liberal) regimes. In both 1945 and 1946, the database calculated a POLITY score of -9 for the Soviet Union, indicating a strongly authoritarian (and thus

illiberal) regime. In 1946, the database assigned China a POLITY score of -5, indicating a fairly strong authoritarian (and thus illiberal) regime. POLITY IV PROJECT, http://www. systemicpeace.org/polityproject.html (last visited July 26, 2015).

23. UN, MEMBERS OF THE SECURITY COUNCIL IN 1993, http://www.un.org/en/sc/inc/ searchres_sc_year_english.asp?year=1993.

24. The "Freedom in the World" database assesses global political rights and civil liberties. The states noted in this paragraph as "liberal" are those adjudged by Freedom House as "free" during the years under consideration, whereas those noted as "illiberal" are those considered by Freedom House to be "not free" during the years under consideration. FREEDOM HOUSE, FREEDOM IN THE WORLD COMPARATIVE AND HISTORICAL DATA, https://freedomhouse.org/report-types/freedom-world#.VZL9FmBXq5N (last visited July 26, 2015).

25. Some of the most liberal states in the world—including the Bahamas, El Salvador, India, Indonesia, Israel, Jamaica, Micronesia, Monaco, Palau, Sao Tome and Principe, Tuvalu, and the United States—have not ratified or acceded to the Rome Statute, whereas some of the most illiberal states in the world—including Afghanistan, Cambodia, Chad, Congo (Brazzaville), the DRC, Djibouti, Gabon, Jordan, Tajikistan, and Tunisia—have done so. (For a list of the Rome Statute signatories and parties, see Rome Statute of the International Criminal Court, United Nations Treaty Collection, https://treaties.un.org/ Pages/ViewDetails.aspx?src=TREATY&mtdsg_no=XVIII-10&chapter=18&lang=en (last visited July 26, 2015).) Moreover, the ECCC, the IST, and the STL were established (in 2001, 2003, and 2007, respectively) with the support and involvement of their respective home states—Cambodia, Iraq, and Lebanon—which had either illiberal or somewhat illiberal regimes at those times. (For the methodology used in this footnote to determine whether a country was "liberal" or "illiberal" during the years under consideration, see *supra* note 24. The "Freedom in the World" database adjudged Cambodia and Iraq "not free" during 2001 and 2003, respectively, and Lebanon only "partly free" during 2007.)

26. Layne makes a similar argument concerning the weakness of Democratic Peace Theory's causal logic. Layne, *supra* note 3.

27. BASS, *supra* note 2, at 173.

28. YVES BEIGBEDER, JUDGING WAR CRIMINALS: THE POLITICS OF INTERNATIONAL JUSTICE 40 (1999).

29. BASS, *supra* note 2, at 6.

30. *Id.* at 26 (emphasis added).

31. *See supra* note 12 and accompanying text.

32. BASS, *supra* note 2, at 5.

33. *Id.* at 8.

34. *Id.*

35. *See* SAMANTHA POWER, "A PROBLEM FROM HELL": AMERICA AND THE AGE OF GENOCIDE 329–89 (2002).

36. Such individuals include Bagasora, bin Laden, Luis Echeverría, Gaddafi, Hissène Habré, Saddam, Karadžić, Milošević, Mladić, Augusto Pinochet, and Taylor. The atrocities to which I refer as having been committed in the United States were the terrorist attacks on September 11, 2001.

37. BASS, *supra* note 2, at 280.

38. Layne argues that Russett's acknowledgment that, in certain cases, "power and strategic considerations are predominant" in accounting for the absence of war among democracies not only "give[s] the game away" to realist explanations but "ends the game decisively" in the latter's favor. Christopher Layne, *On the Democratic Peace*, 19 INT'L SECURITY 175, 175–76 (1995).

39. BASS, *supra* note 2, at 8.

{ BIBLIOGRAPHY }

I. Primary Sources
  A. Personal Interviews
  B. Documents Obtained Through Freedom of Information Act Requests

II. Secondary Sources[1]
  A. Transitional Justice and Related Human Rights Issues
  B. Multiple Atrocities
  C. Multiple War Crimes Tribunals
  D. Multiple Hybrid Tribunals
  E. Military Commissions/Tribunals
  F. Universal Jurisdiction
  G. Armenian Genocide
  H. Nazis/IMT
  I. Adolf Eichmann
  J. Japanese/IMTFE
  K. Pol Pot/Khmer Rouge/ECCC
  L. The Balkans
  M. ICTY
  N. Rwanda
  O. ICTR
  P. *Gacaca*
  Q. ICC
  R. International Citizens' War Crimes Tribunals
  S. Truth Commissions
  T. Exile
  U. Lustration
  V. Amnesty
  W. Lethal Force
  X. Indefinite Detention
  Y. Democratic Peace Theory
  Z. Foreign Policy Analysis/U.S. Foreign Policy

---

1. For the sake of brevity, secondary sources appear in only one of these categories even though some of these sources could properly be listed in multiple such categories. These lists of secondary sources are not meant to be exhaustive.

I. Primary Sources

A. PERSONAL INTERVIEWS[2]

I conducted a total of twenty-eight interviews with twenty people. Below is a chart outlining the interviews conducted and formatted as follows:

(1) *Number*: This column provides a unique number for each interview I conducted. The order is not chronological by interview date; it is simply the order in which the interviews were entered into this database. Note that I interviewed some people multiple times. Each interview is listed separately.

(2) *Interviewee*: This column provides the name of the interviewee. The interviewee's name format is: surname, first name, and then any initials or other identifiers (e.g., Jr., II).

(3) *Type*: This column provides the interviewee's profession during the time frame for which I interviewed the person. Three types of professions are indicated in the chart: USG Official, UN Official, and Scholar. Of course, many of these individuals have held different types of professions at other times. Each individual within a particular type is grouped together in alphabetical order by surname.

(4) *Title*: This column provides the interviewee's title during the time frame about which I interviewed the person. If the person was a USG or UN official, the chart indicates the years during which the person held that particular title. Of course, many of these individuals have held different titles at other times.

(5) *Date*: This column provides the date on which I conducted the interview. The date format is year, month, and day (YYYY.MM.DD).

(6) *Method*: This column provides the method by which I conducted the interview. I employed two methods: "Oral" and "Written." Where the interview was oral, I conducted it either in person or over the phone. Where the interview was written, I conducted it via email, and the date corresponds to that on which I received the interviewee's response, not the date on which I sent my questions.

(7) *Interview—Shorthand*: This column provides a unique abbreviation for each interview. I employ this shorthand to refer to these interviews in this book.

(1) Number	(2) Interviewee	(3) Type	(4) Title	(5) Date	(6) Method	(7) Interview— Shorthand
1	Bennet, Douglas J.	USG Official	*1993–1995*: U.S. Assistant Secretary of State for International Organization Affairs	2003.08.29	Oral	Bennet interview
2	Bushnell, Prudence	USG Official	*1993–1996*: Principal U.S. Deputy Assistant Secretary of State for African Affairs	2003.09.02	Oral	Bushnell interview 1
3	Bushnell, Prudence	USG Official	*1993–1996*: Principal U.S. Deputy Assistant Secretary of State for African Affairs	2004.01.02	Written	Bushnell interview 2

---

2. Transcripts of personal interviews are on file with the author.

(1) Number	(2) Interviewee	(3) Type	(4) Title	(5) Date	(6) Method	(7) Interview— Shorthand
4	Johnston, Harry A., II	USG Official	*1992–1994*: Chairman, Subcommittee on Africa, House Committee on International Relations, U.S. Congress	2003.03.12	Oral	Johnston interview
5	Kimble, Melinda L.	USG Official	*1991–1997*: U.S. Deputy Assistant Secretary of State for International Organization Affairs	2003.10.08	Oral	Kimble interview 1
6	Kimble, Melinda L.	USG Official	*1991–1997*: U.S. Deputy Assistant Secretary of State for International Organization Affairs	2003.10.21	Oral	Kimble interview 2
7	Lake, Anthony	USG Official	*1993–1997*: U.S. National Security Adviser	2003.09.09	Oral	Lake interview
8	Matheson, Michael J.	USG Official	*1990–2000*: Principal Deputy Legal Adviser, U.S. Department of State	2003.08.26	Oral	Matheson interview 1
9	Matheson, Michael J.	USG Official	*1990–2000*: Principal Deputy Legal Adviser, U.S. Department of State	2005.11.11	Written	Matheson interview 2
10	Matheson, Michael J.	USG Official	*1990–2000*: Principal Deputy Legal Adviser, U.S. Department of State	2008.07.29	Written	Matheson interview 3
11	Rice, Susan	USG Official	*1993–1995*: Director for International Organizations and Peacekeeping, U.S. National Security Council	2003.10.13	Oral	Rice interview
12	Scharf, Michael P.	USG Official	*1991–1993*: Attorney-Adviser, United Nations Affairs, U.S. Department of State	2008.07.30	Oral	Scharf interview
13	Scheffer, David J.	USG Official	*1993–1996*: Senior Advisor and Counsel to Ambassador Albright, U.S. Mission to the United Nations	2003.06.24	Oral	Scheffer interview 1
14	Scheffer, David J.	USG Official	*1993–1996*: Senior Advisor and Counsel to Ambassador Albright, U.S. Mission to the United Nations	2005.11.18	Written	Scheffer interview 2
15	Shattuck, John	USG Official	*1993–1998*: U.S. Assistant Secretary of State for Democracy, Human Rights, and Labor	2003.10.09	Oral	Shattuck interview 1
16	Shattuck, John	USG Official	*1993–1998*: U.S. Assistant Secretary of State for Democracy, Human Rights, and Labor	2005.11.21	Oral	Shattuck interview 2
17	Shattuck, John	USG Official	*1993–1998*: U.S. Assistant Secretary of State for Democracy, Human Rights, and Labor	2008.08.06	Written	Shattuck interview 3
18	Silverwood, James	USG Official	*1998–2012*: Regional Director, Africa and the Middle East, Office of Overseas Prosecutorial Development, Assistance, and Training, U.S. Department of Justice	2004.01.03	Written	Silverwood interview
19	St. Hilaire, Pierre	USG Official	*2000–2002*: U.S. Resident Legal Advisor to Rwanda, Office of Overseas Prosecutorial Development Assistance and Training, U.S. Department of Justice	2004.01.05	Written	St. Hilaire interview

(Continued)

(1) Number	(2) Interviewee	(3) Type	(4) Title	(5) Date	(6) Method	(7) Interview— Shorthand
20	Stanton, Gregory	USG Official	*1992–1999*: Political Officer, Office for United Nations Political Affairs, Bureau of International Organization Affairs, U.S. Department of State	2003.06.26	Oral	Stanton interview 1
21	Stanton, Gregory	USG Official	*1992–1999*: Political Officer, Office for United Nations Political Affairs, Bureau of International Organization Affairs, U.S. Department of State	2003.08.25	Oral	Stanton interview 2
22	Walker, Stephen W.	USG Official	*1993*: Desk Officer, Croatia, U.S. Department of State	2008.08.28	Written	Walker interview
23	Ward, George F., Jr.	USG Official	*1992–1994*: Principal Deputy Assistant Secretary of State for International Organization Affairs	2003.10.09	Oral	Ward interview
24	Blewitt, Graham	UN Official	*1993–2003*: Deputy Prosecutor, ICTY	2003.06.11	Oral	Blewitt interview
25	Johnson, Michael	UN Official	*2002*: Acting Deputy Prosecutor, ICTR	2003.08.05	Oral	Johnson interview
26	Schrag, Minna	UN Official	*1994–1995*: Senior Trial Attorney, ICTY	2003.09.04	Oral	Schrag interview
27	Des Forges, Alison	Scholar	Author, *Leave None to Tell the Story*; *1990–2009*: Senior Advisor, Africa Division, Human Rights Watch	2003.05.24	Oral	Des Forges interview
28	Melvern, Linda	Scholar	Author, *A People Betrayed: The Role of the West in Rwanda's Genocide*; Author, *Conspiracy to Murder: The Rwanda Genocide and the International Community*	2003.06.16	Oral	Melvern interview

B. DOCUMENTS OBTAINED THROUGH FREEDOM OF INFORMATION ACT REQUESTS[3]

I received a total of 194 declassified documents from the U.S./DoS, 163 released in full and 31 released in part. The U.S./DoS indicated it withheld in full 40 documents it found to be responsive to my FOIA requests. Details of the individual packages of released documents are as follows:

- In a package dated April 21, 2004, the U.S./DoS indicated that it had retrieved 101 documents responsive to one of my FOIA requests, but released only 96 of them (82 fully declassified and 14 partially declassified), thus withholding 5 in full.
- In a package dated April 27, 2005, the U.S./DoS indicated that it had retrieved 33 documents responsive to one of my FOIA requests, but released only 29 of them (25 fully declassified and 4 partially declassified), thus withholding 4 in full.

---

3. Documents are on file with the author.

- In a package dated March 29, 2007, the U.S./DoS indicated that it had retrieved 75 documents responsive to one of my FOIA requests, but released only 44 of them (33 fully declassified and 11 partially declassified), thus withholding 31 in full.
- In a package dated July 13, 2007, the U.S./DoS indicated that it had retrieved 25 documents responsive to one of my FOIA requests and released all 25 of them (23 fully declassified and 2 partially declassified).

According to the U.S./DoS, some documents or portions of documents were withheld during these declassification episodes either because they (1) are "in the interest of national defense or foreign relations," (2) "contain[] exchanges between attorney and client and/or litigation materials prepared by an attorney," (3) "[are] of such a nature that [their] release would constitute a clearly unwarranted invasion of personal privacy," or (4) "consist[] of pre-decisional deliberative process material."

I also submitted FOIA requests to the U.S./DoD and the U.S./DoJ. Both departments claimed that they possessed no documents responsive to my FOIA requests.

Below is a chart of the declassified documents I received organized as follows:

(1) *Title/Description*: This column indicates the subject of each document. The exact title, if drawn directly from the document, is indicated verbatim within quotation marks. Where the document lacks a title, a general description is provided without quotation marks and in brackets. Note that some documents have general and/or identical subject lines.

(2) *Title/Description—Shorthand*: This column provides a unique number for each document. The order is not chronological by date or topic; it is simply the order in which the documents were entered into this database. I employ this shorthand to refer to documents in this book.

(3) *Date*: This column provides, where it appeared on the document, the date. The date format is year, month, and day (YYYY.MM.DD). In some cases the exact date was not included in a document. In such instances, this column reads "Undated" with either the YYYY.MM in brackets, if known, or nothing appended, if the date is completely unknown.

(4) *Cable Number*: For documents representing cable communications, if the cable number is identifiable, this column provides that number. For all other documents, this column indicates "N/A," for "not applicable."

(5) *Number of Pages*: This column indicates the number of pages in each document.

(6) *Alphanumeric Code*: This column indicates the alphanumeric code assigned by the U.S./DoS to each document corresponding to the batches of documents released to me. For example, all documents with an alphanumeric code beginning with "E" were released in a separate grouping from those documents with alphanumeric codes beginning with "L" or "U." Note that documents pertaining to more than one of the transitional justice episodes may be grouped together with the same letter (E, L, or U) at the beginning of the alphanumeric code.

(7) *Released in Full/Part*: This column indicates the amount of each document the U.S./DoS released to me. If the document was not redacted at all before being released, this column indicates that it was released in "Full." If, however, the U.S./DoS decided to redact portions of a document before releasing it, this column indicates "Part" and then provides alphanumeric codes (e.g., B5, 1.4D) the U.S./DoS offered as an explanation in the process of declassification.

(1) Title/Description	(2) Title/ Description— Shorthand	(3) Date	(4) Cable Number	(5) Number of Pages	(6) Alphanumeric Code	(7) Released in Full/ Part
[U.S. Department of State Office of the Spokesman—Q&A]	Document 1	1994.05.26	N/A	2	L4	Full
"White House Press Guidance: Rwanda"	Document 2	1994.06.13	N/A	1	L5	Full
"L Press Guidance"	Document 3	1994.06.13	N/A	2	L6	Full
"L Press Guidance"	Document 4	1994.06.14	N/A	2	L7	Full
"To Pru Bushnell for Hill Briefing"	Document 5	1994.06.16	N/A	1	L8	Full
[Secretary Christopher's Appearance before U.S./SCFR]	Document 6	1994.06.30	N/A	2	L10	Full
[UNSC Resolution—Draft]	Document 7	1994.07.07	N/A	2	L12a	Full
"Human Rights Commission: Special Rapporteur Concludes Genocide Has Occurred in Rwanda"	Document 8	1994.07.15	Geneva 05974	4	L12b	Full
"Rwanda: 19 July Security Council— Rwanda Absent; French Intent on Leaving by August"	Document 9	1995.07.20	USUN New York 002972	1	L15	Full
[State Department Response to Rep. Tony Hall's 1994.07.01 Letter]	Document 10	1994.07.27	N/A	2	L17	Full
[1994.07.01 Letter from Rep. Tony Hall to Secretary Christopher]	Document 11	1994.07.01	N/A	2	L17b	Full
"Rwanda War Crimes"	Document 12	1994.07.28	State 202027	3	L18	Full
"Human Rights Tribunal—Rwanda"	Document 13	1994.08.01	State 205480	1	L19	Full
"Human Rights Tribunal—Rwanda"	Document 14	1994.08.02	Brussels 08559	1	L20	Full
"Rwanda War Crimes: Tanzania's Position"	Document 15	1994.08.03	Dar es Salaam 004940	1	L21	Full
[Intra-State Department Memo on Detaining Suspects in Rwanda/ Burundi]	Document 16	1994.08.24	N/A	7	L28	Full
"Rwanda War Crimes Tribunal Demarche to GoT"	Document 17	1994.08.31	Dar es Salaam 005510	1	L33	Full
"USG Interview Trip to Rwanda"	Document 18	1994.09.12	State 246554	1	L35	Full

(1) Title/Description	(2) Title/ Description— Shorthand	(3) Date	(4) Cable Number	(5) Number of Pages	(6) Alphanumeric Code	(7) Released in Full/ Part
"Rwanda War Crimes"	Document 19	1994.09.23	USUN New York 004014	1	L41	Full
"Resolution Establishing War Crimes Tribunal for Rwanda"	Document 20	1994.09.28	State 262739	1	L42	Full
"Rwanda War Crimes Tribunal—Japanese Views"	Document 21	1994.10.21	USUN New York 004514	1	L45	Full
"Tanzanian Views on War Crimes Tribunal"	Document 22	1994.10.24	Dar es Salaam 006900	1	L49	Full
"Rwanda War Crimes Tribunal"	Document 23	1994.10.27	Kampala 008705	1	L50	Full
"Rwanda War Crimes Tribunal—Meeting of Co-Sponsors"	Document 24	1994.11.04	USUN New York 004749	1	L52	Full
"Rwanda War Crimes Tribunal"	Document 25	1994.11.05	USUN New York 004783	1	L53	Full
"Secretary General Shares Concerns About War Crimes Tribunal, Burundi, Relations with USG"	Document 26	1994.04.29	USUN New York 001794	2	E1	Full
"Daily Press Briefing of Thursday, April 28, 1994"	Document 27	1994.04.28	State 112290	30	E2	Full
"International Jurist Comments on Human Rights Inquiry in Rwanda"	Document 28	1994.05.16	Brussels 05416	2	E4	Full
"Under Secretary for Global Affairs Wirth's Meeting with Director of Operations for ICRC, Jean de Courten, May 17, 1994"	Document 29	1994.05.24	State 137577	4	E5	Full
"Uganda Not Supporting RPF Museveni Tells Danes"	Document 30	1994.06.09	Copenhagen 003075	6	E6	Full
"Rwanda: Bringing the Guilty to Justice"	Document 31	1994.06.15	USUN New York 002491	6	E7	Full
"Press Guidance— Friday, July 1, 1994"	Document 32	1994.07.01	State 177024	6	E8	Full
"Human Rights Violations: Detention of Gatete and Associates"	Document 33	1994.07.07	State 180972	2	E9	Full

(Continued)

(1) Title/Description	(2) Title/ Description— Shorthand	(3) Date	(4) Cable Number	(5) Number of Pages	(6) Alphanumeric Code	(7) Released in Full/ Part
"Africa Bureau Friday Report, 07/8/94"	Document 34	1994.07.09	State 182529	22	E10	Full
"Gatete Departure from Benaco"	Document 35	1994.07.09	State 183627	5	E11	Full
"Gatete"	Document 36	1994.07.11	State 184429	5	E12	Full
"Consultations with France and Others on Rwanda"	Document 37	1994.07.12	State 184612	3	E13	Full
"Next Steps in Addressing War Crimes in Rwanda"	Document 38	1994.07.15	State 188919	2	E16	Full
"Non-Recognition of Interim Government of Rwanda"	Document 39	1994.07.15	State 190358	5	E17	Full
"Rwanda: War Crimes, Non-Recognition, and APC's"	Document 40	1994.07.18	Madrid 007615	2	E18	Full
"Rwanda: 18 Jul 94 Security Council Meeting"	Document 41	1994.07.19	USUN New York 02952	3	E19	Full
"Leopoldo Torres Boursault for Rwanda War Crime Tribunal"	Document 42	1994.07.19	Madrid 007697	2	E20	Full
"British Response Muted in Considering Next Steps in Addressing War Crimes in Rwanda"	Document 43	1994.07.19	London 011339	2	E21	Full
"Rwanda War Crimes Tribunal"	Document 44	1994.07.19	State 192051	2	E22	Full
"Press Guidance— Wednesday, July 20, 1994"	Document 45	1994.07.20	State 194391	8	E23	Full
"Rwanda: 22 July Security Council Meeting"	Document 46	1994.07.23	State 197812	3	E24	Full
"Rwanda: 22 July Security Council Meeting"	Document 47	1994.07.23	USUN New York 03046	5	E25	Full
"Rwanda War Crimes"	Document 48	1994.07.26	State 198848	5	E27	Full
"Rwanda War Crimes Tribunal—Russian Demarche"	Document 49	1994.07.27	USUN New York 003089	3	E28	Full
"Human Rights Tribunal—Rwanda"	Document 50	1994.07.27	Brussels 08330	2	E29	Full
"Rwanda War Crimes Demarche: Minister of Home Affairs Reaction and Pitch for Financial Aid"	Document 51	1994.07.28	Dar es Salaam 004815	5	E30	Full

(1) Title/Description	(2) Title/ Description— Shorthand	(3) Date	(4) Cable Number	(5) Number of Pages	(6) Alphanumeric Code	(7) Released in Full/ Part
"MGRW02: Irish Reaction to President Clinton's and Aid Administrator Atwood's Letters on Rwanda"	Document 52	1994.07.29	Dublin 04148	6	E31	Full
"Human Rights Tribunal—Rwanda"	Document 53	1994.07.29	Brussels 08418	2	E32	Full
"South Africa: Goldstone Involvement in Yugoslavia War Crimes Tribunal Should Insure South African Support for Concept"	Document 54	1994.07.29	Pretor 10774	3	E33	Full
"Human Rights Tribunal—Rwanda"	Document 55	1994.07.29	State 202705	2	E34	Full
"MGRWO2: Additional Field Monitors for Rwanda"	Document 56	1994.08.02	Geneva 06703	5	E35	Full
"Press Guidance— August 3, 1994"	Document 57	1994.08.03	State 207687	7	E36	Full
"Rwanda War Crimes"	Document 58	1994.08.03	State 206761	3	E37	Full
"Travel of A/S Shattuck to Uganda, Rwanda, Burundi, Zaire and France"	Document 59	1994.08.04	State 207893	4	E38	Full
"A/S Shattuck Visit to Rwanda: Objectives"	Document 60	1994.08.05	State 209882	4	E41	Full
"Visit of A/S John Shattuck"	Document 61	1994.08.05	State 210227	3	E42	Full
"Meeting with High Commissioner for Human Rights: Rwanda, Cuba, China, and Other Issues"	Document 62	1994.08.05	Geneva 06844	10	E43	Full
"Talking Points for A/S Moose's Use with GOF and GOB Officials"	Document 63	1994.08.06	State 211528	5	E45	Full
"AF A/S Moose's Talking Points for his Meeting with President Mandela"	Document 64	1994.08.06	State 211529	4	E46	Full
"Visit to Kenya of A/S Shattuck"	Document 65	1994.08.08	Nairob 14073	2	E47	Full
"Press Guidance— August 8, 1994"	Document 66	1994.08.08	State 212243	8	E50	Full
"Press Guidance— August 9, 1994"	Document 67	1994.08.09	State 213680	4	E52	Full
"Interim Trip Report— Kigali and Goma"	Document 68	1994.08.09	Kampala 006337	5	E54	Full
"Official—Informal"	Document 69	1994.08.10	State 215074	3	E58	Full

(*Continued*)

(1) Title/Description	(2) Title/ Description— Shorthand	(3) Date	(4) Cable Number	(5) Number of Pages	(6) Alphanumeric Code	(7) Released in Full/ Part
"Rwanda: SC Statement Issued August 10"	Document 70	1994.08.11	USUN New York 003310	6	E62	Full
"A/S Shattuck Urges Support for War Crimes Tribunal"	Document 71	1994.08.11	Kampala 006441	6	E63	Full
"A/S Shattuck's Meeting with French on Rwanda War Crimes Tribunal and Burundi"	Document 72	1994.08.12	Paris 22245	10	E64	Full
"DRL/MLA Director Rosenblatt's Meeting with Belgian Official on Rwanda Tribunal and Monitors"	Document 73	1994.08.13	Paris 22398	4	E66	Full
"Demarche to Russian MFA on UN War Crimes Tribunal for Rwanda"	Document 74	1994.08.15	Moscow 023223	1	E69	Full
"Rwanda: Pending Meetings in Geneva with Ayala Lasso and the Commission of Experts"	Document 75	1994.08.17	State 221084	5	E70	Full
"Rwanda: Initial Meeting with Commission of High Experts"	Document 76	1994.08.18	Geneva 07233	4	E71	Full
"Rwanda—Crimes Tribunal—Meeting with UN Legal Counsel"	Document 77	1994.08.19	USUN New York 003437	4	E72	Full
"Establishment of UN War Crimes Tribunal for Rwanda"	Document 78	1994.08.20	State 224856	7	E74	Full
"Establishment of UN War Crimes Tribunal for Rwanda"	Document 79	1994.08.20	State 224672	2	E75	Full
"Demarche for International Tribunal in Rwanda"	Document 80	1994.08.24	State 228408	4	E77	Full
"Rwanda War Crimes Tribunal UN Sect. Views"	Document 81	1994.08.24	USUN New York 003495	2	E78	Full
"UN War Crimes Tribunal for Rwanda: Russia Position"	Document 82	1994.08.25	Moscow 24407	4	E79	Full
"Assistant Secretary Moose's Discussions with Belgian Foreign Minister on Rwanda, Burundi, Zaire"	Document 83	1994.08.25	Brussels 09371	18	E80	Full

(1) Title/Description	(2) Title/ Description— Shorthand	(3) Date	(4) Cable Number	(5) Number of Pages	(6) Alphanumeric Code	(7) Released in Full/ Part
"Establishment of a War Crimes Tribunal for Rwanda: Dutch Views"	Document 84	1994.08.30	State 234040	3	E82	Full
"War Crimes Tribunal for Rwanda"	Document 85	1994.08.30	USUN New York 003594	1	E83	Full
"Resolution Establishing War Crimes Tribunal for Rwanda"	Document 86	1994.09.12	State 237220	11	E86	Full
"Visit by UN Commission of Experts; Recommendation for U.S. Assistance"	Document 87	1994.09.07	Kigali 001509	3	E88	Full
"Presidential Mission Returns from Central Africa; Recommendations Track Closely with U.S.G. Policy"	Document 88	1994.09.09	State 243592	6	E90	Full
"Official—Informal"	Document 89	1994.09.12	State 245815	4	E92	Full
"UN War Crimes Prosecutions for Rwanda"	Document 90	1994.09.16	State 251046	5	E93	Full
"French Perspective on Rwanda War Crimes Tribunal"	Document 91	1994.09.19	Paris 25531	3	E95	Full
"UN Human Rights Program in Rwanda"	Document 92	1994.09.21	State 256438	4	E98	Full
"Official—Informal"	Document 93	1994.09.23	State 259321	5	E100	Full
"Press Guidance— September 23, 1994"	Document 94	1994.09.24	State 259570	9	E101	Full
"Press Guidance— September 26, 1994"	Document 95	1994.09.26	State 260743	6	E102	Full
"Meeting with High Commissioner for Human Rights: Burma, Rwanda, Cuba"	Document 96	1994.09.27	Geneva 008272	6	E104	Full
"Meeting with High Commissioner for Human Rights: Burma, Rwanda, Cuba"	Document 97	1994.09.27	Geneva 008273	6	E105	Full
"Press Guidance— September 27, 1994"	Document 98	1994.09.27	State 261704	6	E106	Full
"French Confirm Concurrence on Rwanda War Crimes Tribunal"	Document 99	1994.09.29	Paris 26809	1	E107	Full

(Continued)

(1) Title/Description	(2) Title/ Description— Shorthand	(3) Date	(4) Cable Number	(5) Number of Pages	(6) Alphanumeric Code	(7) Released in Full/ Part
"Resolution Establishing War Crimes Tribunal for Rwanda"	Document 100	1994.10.15	State 280506	3	E121	Full
"Rwanda War Crimes"	Document 101	1994.10.19	State 283000	4	E122	Full
"Rwandan Position on Rwanda War Crimes Tribunal"	Document 102	1994.10.19	Kigali 001872	3	E125	Full
"Rwandan Views on War Crimes Tribunal"	Document 103	1994.10.20	USUN New York 004459	8	E126	Full
"Follow-Up Demarches on Rwanda War Crimes Tribunal Resolution: Prime Minister and Justice Minister"	Document 104	1994.10.20	Kigali 001883	5	E127	Full
"Points on Rwanda for UNSYG"	Document 105	1994.10.21	State 285608	2	E128	Full
"Rwanda War Crimes"	Document 106	1994.10.21	State 286662	3	E130	Full
"Rwanda War Crimes"	Document 107	1994.10.22	Kinshasa 06331	1	E131	Full
"Rwanda War Crimes Tribunal: Zero Hour"	Document 108	1994.10.22	State 286781	2	E133	Full
"Has Genocide Occurred in Rwanda?"	Document 109	1994.05.21	N/A	4	L3	Part B1, 1.4D, B5
"Establishment of UN War Crimes Tribunal for Rwanda"	Document 110	1994.08.14	State 218325	1	L25	Part B1, 1.4B, 1.4D, B6
"War Crines [sic] Tribunal For Rwanda"	Document 111	1994.08.30	USUN New York 003604	1	L32	Part B1, 1.4B, 1.4D
"UN Human Rights Program in Rwanda— Getting It All Together"	Document 112	1994.09.17	Geneva 008006	4	L37	Part B6
"Consultations with France on Rwanda War Crimes Issue"	Document 113	1994.07.13	Paris 19216	4	E14	Part B1, 1.4D
"SC Discussion of Rwanda, 4 Aug 94"	Document 114	1994.08.04	USUN New York 03228	5	E39	Part B1, 1.4D
"Rwanda War Crimes"	Document 115	1994.08.05	USUN New York 03237	5	E44	Part B1, 1.4D
"MGRW02: A/S Moose Briefs Quai on Rwanda Trip"	Document 116	1994.08.08	Paris 21685	13	E48	Part B1, 1.4D
"Rwanda War Crimes"	Document 117	1994.08.09	USUN New York 003281	5	E51	Part B1, 1.4B, 1.4D

(1) Title/Description	(2) Title/ Description— Shorthand	(3) Date	(4) Cable Number	(5) Number of Pages	(6) Alphanumeric Code	(7) Released in Full/ Part
"International Tribunal on Rwanda: Further Thoughts"	Document 118	1994.08.09	Bujumb 02676	10	E53	Part B5, B1, 1.4D
"Official—Informal"	Document 119	1994.08.11	London 12721	6	E61	Part B1, 1.4B, 1.4D
"A/S Shattuck's Discussion on the Proposed Rwanda War Crimes Tribunal with HMG"	Document 120	1994.08.15	London 012901	6	E68	Part B1, 1.4B, 1.4D
"Official—Informal"	Document 121	1994.09.03	State 238830	6	E87	Part B1, 1.4D
"UN War Crimes Prosecutions for Rwanda"	Document 122	1994.09.19	Moscow 026935	3	E94	Part B1, 1.4D
"A/S Shattuck Discussions with Secretariat, ICRC, and Missions Regarding Haiti, Rwanda, Burundi, China, Turkey, and Funding for UN Human Rights Activities"	Document 123	1994.09.29	USUN New York 004101	13	E108	Part B1, 1.4D
"Resolution and Statute Establishing War Crimes Tribunal for Rwanda"	Document 124	1994.09.30	USUN New York 004112	2	E110	Part B1, 1.4B, 1.4D
"Official—Informal"	Document 125	1994.10.19	State 282985	7	E124	Part B5, B1, 1.4D
"Arria Style Meeting with President of Sierra Leone"	Document 126	1996.10.07	N/A	2	U1	Part B5
"Sierra Leone: Security Council Informals October 30"	Document 127	1996.10.29	N/A	2	U2	Part B5, B1, 1.4D
"Sierra Leone: Security Council Consultations, July 8, 5:00 p.m."	Document 128	1999.07.08	N/A	2	U18	Full
"U.S. Position Paper on Sierra Leone Amnesty"	Document 129	1999.07.16	N/A	2	U19	Full
"Sierra Leone: Security Council Consultations, August 4, 10:30 a.m."	Document 130	1999.08.03	N/A	3	U20	Full
"Trip Report—Sierra Leone"	Document 131	1999.08.04	N/A	6	U21	Full
"Sierra Leone: Steps to Reinvigorate the Peace Process"	Document 132	Undated	N/A	6	U23a	Full

(*Continued*)

(1) Title/Description	(2) Title/ Description— Shorthand	(3) Date	(4) Cable Number	(5) Number of Pages	(6) Alphanumeric Code	(7) Released in Full/ Part
"Sierra Leone: What Is to be Done"	Document 133	Undated	N/A	3	U24a	Full
"Sierra Leone Tribunal"	Document 134	2000.06.08	N/A	3	U28	Part B5, B6
[UNSC Resolution—Draft]	Document 135	Undated	N/A	2	U28a	Full
"Sierra Leone Tribunal"	Document 136	2000.06.09	N/A	1	U29	Part B5
"FW: The Lockerbie Trial—For Possible Consideration in the Sierra Leone Context"	Document 137	2000.06.12	N/A	1	U33	Part B5
"Sierra Leone Accountability Latest Version"	Document 138	2000.06.19	N/A	1	U33	Part B5, B6
[UNSC Role in SCSL]	Document 139	Undated	N/A	5	U33a	B5, B6
"Sierra Leone: Security Council Private Meetings with ECOWAS Foreign Ministers, UNSC Formal Chamber, June 21, 10:00 a.m."	Document 140	2000.06.20	N/A	3	U34	Full
"A Special Court for Sierra Leone: the Facts on the Ground"	Document 141	2000.06.26	N/A	8	U35	Part B1, 1.4B, 1.4D. B5
"Sierra Leone Resolution"	Document 142	2000.06.29	N/A	2	U38	B5, B6
"Other Matters/ Sierra Leone: Security Council Consultations, July 5, 4:30 p.m."	Document 143	2000.07.05	N/A	3	U40	Full
"U.N. Security Council Resolution for a Special Court for Sierra Leone"	Document 144	2000.06.29	N/A	3	U40a	Full
"Terms of Reference"	Document 145	2000.06.29	N/A	1	U40b	Full
[Dan Feldman— Pierre Prosper Correspondence]	Document 146	2000.07.13	N/A	1	U42	Full
"Sierra Leone Special Court"	Document 147	2000.07.13	N/A	2	U43	Part B5
"U.N. Security Council Resolution for a Special Court for Sierra Leone"	Document 148	2000.06.29	N/A	3	U43a	Full
"Terms of Reference"	Document 149	2000.06.29	N/A	1	U43b	Full
"U.N. Security Council Resolution for a Special Court for Sierra Leone"	Document 150	2000.07.12	N/A	2	U43c	Full

(1) Title/Description	(2) Title/ Description— Shorthand	(3) Date	(4) Cable Number	(5) Number of Pages	(6) Alphanumeric Code	(7) Released in Full/ Part
"[Terms of Reference]"	Document 151	2000.07.12	N/A	2	U43d	Full
"Concept Paper on a Special Court for Sierra Leone"	Document 152	2000.07.20	N/A	3	U48	Full
"Sierra Leone: Security Council Consultations, July 27, 9:45 a.m."	Document 153	2000.07.26	N/A	4	U51	Full
"Draft Resolution on a Special Court for Sierra Leone"	Document 154	2000.07.25	N/A	3	U51a	Full
"Sierra Leone: Security Council Consultations, August 10, 10:00 a.m."	Document 155	2000.08.09	N/A	4	U54	Full
"UN Security Council Resolution for a special court for Sierra Leone"	Document 156	2000.08.09	N/A	3	U54a	Full
"OP3, option 1 (preferred language)"	Document 157	Undated	N/A	1	U54b	Full
"Sierra Leone Special Court"	Document 158	2000.10.04	N/A	1	U59	Full
"Talking Points"	Document 159	Undated	N/A	1	U59a	Full
"Financing of Sierra Leone Court"	Document 160	2000.10.27	N/A	1	U62	Full
"Instructions on U.S. Negotiation of Sierra Leone Independent Special Court"	Document 161	Undated	N/A	2	U69a	Full
"Letter to the SYG"	Document 162	2000.11.13	N/A	1	U71b	Full
"Sierra Leone Tribunal"	Document 163	2000.11.16	N/A	1	U73	Full
"Talking Points"	Document 164	Undated	N/A	1	U73a	Full
"Financing of Sierra Leone Court"	Document 165	2000.11.17	N/A	2	U74	Part B5, B6
"Your Scheduled 11/29 Telephone Discussion with Ken Roth, Human Rights Watch, 9:00 am"	Document 166	2000.11.28	N/A	4	U75	Full
[HRW Letter to Greenstock]	Document 167	2000.10.04	N/A	5	U75a	Full
[HRW Letter to UNSC]	Document 168	2000.10.31	N/A	2	U75b	Full
"Sierra Leone Special Court in the Security Council, November 8, 10:30 a.m., Informal Chamber"	Document 169	2001.11.07	N/A	4	U84	Full
"Sierra Leone: The US/ GOSL Special Court Concept"	Document 170	Undated	N/A	3	L01	Full

(Continued)

(1) Title/Description	(2) Title/ Description— Shorthand	(3) Date	(4) Cable Number	(5) Number of Pages	(6) Alphanumeric Code	(7) Released in Full/ Part
[U.S. Investigation and Prosecution in the FRY]	Document 171	Undated	N/A	19	L02	Full
"Letter Dated March 1993 from the Permanent Representative of the Untied States to the United Nations Addressed to the Secretary General"	Document 172	Undated [March 1993]	N/A	1	L03	Full
"Creation of an International Tribunal for Violations of International Humanitarian Law in the Former Yugoslavia"	Document 173	Undated	N/A	2	L03a	Full
"Draft Charter of the International Tribunal for Violations of International Humanitarian Law in the Former Yugoslavia"	Document 174	1993.03.02	N/A	12	L03b	Part B3, CIA-PO
"Establishment of a War Crimes Commission for the Former Yugoslavia"	Document 175	1992.08.31	N/A	6	L04	Full
"Supporting the Establishment of a War Crimes Commission for Yugoslavia"	Document 176	1992.08.31	N/A	4	L05	Full
"War Crimes: Distinction Between Yugoslavia and Iraq"	Document 177	1992.09.08	N/A	2	L06	Full
[Presidential Announcement on the FRY]	Document 178	1992.09.15	N/A	1	L07	Full
"Background: 1943 UN War Crime Commission"	Document 179	Undated	N/A	14	L07a	Full
"Abrams Testimony to Helsinki Commission"	Document 180	1992.09.21	N/A	1	L07b	Full
"Update on War Crimes Commission and International Criminal Court Issues"	Document 181	1992.09.25	N/A	4	L08	Full
"Testimony of Warren Zimmerman"	Document 182	1992.10.22	N/A	4	L09	Full
"War Crimes Commission—Next Steps"	Document 183	1992.11.02	N/A	2	L09a	Full

(1) Title/Description	(2) Title/ Description— Shorthand	(3) Date	(4) Cable Number	(5) Number of Pages	(6) Alphanumeric Code	(7) Released in Full/ Part
"ICFY Ministerial: Accusing Individuals as War Criminals"	Document 184	1992.12.11	N/A	18	L10	Full
"Establishment of an International Criminal Court"	Document 185	1993.01.12	N/A	3	L11	Full
"International Tribunal for the Former Yugoslavia"	Document 186	1993.04.22	N/A	9	L12	Full
"War Crimes"	Document 187	1993.04.23	N/A	1	L12a	Full
"War Crimes: Yugoslavia"	Document 188	1993.04.23	N/A	1	L12b	Full
"Background Paper: War Crimes Tribunal for the Former Yugoslavia"	Document 189	1993.05.04	N/A	3	L13	Full
"Q and As: International Tribunal for the Former Yugoslavia"	Document 190	Undated	N/A	5	L13a	Full
"U.S. Response to Secretary General's War Crimes Reports"	Document 191	1993.05.07	N/A	1	L14	Full
"Letter Dated May 1993 from the Permanent Representative of the United States of America to the United Nations Addressed to the Secretary General"	Document 192	Undated [1993.05]	N/A	9	L14a	Full
"Special Court for Sierra Leone"	Document 193	2000.11.30	N/A	2	L19	Full
"Sierra Leone: The US/GOSL Special Court"	Document 194	2001.02.08	N/A	2	L20	Full

II. Secondary Sources

A. TRANSITIONAL JUSTICE AND RELATED HUMAN RIGHTS ISSUES[4]

- ACCOUNTABILITY FOR COLLECTIVE WRONGDOING (Tracy Isaacs & Richard Vernon eds., 2011).
- Kenneth Anderson, *Who Owns the Rules of War?*, N.Y. TIMES MAG., Apr. 13, 2003, at 38.
- TIMOTHY GARTON ASH, THE FILE: A PERSONAL HISTORY (1997).

---

4. An extensive bibliography on transitional justice is available at: Transitional Justice Bibliography, http://sites.google.com/site/transitionaljusticedatabase/transitional-justice-bibliography (last visited July 26, 2015).

- Timothy Garton Ash, *The Truth about Dictatorship*, N.Y. Rev. Books, Feb .19, 1998, at 35 (reviewing Transitional Justice: How Emerging Democracies Reckon with Former Regimes: Volume II: Country Studies (Neil J. Kritz ed., 1995), Transitional Justice: How Emerging Democracies Reckon with Former Regimes: Volume III: Laws, Rulings, and Reports (Neil J. Kritz ed., 1995), Gesine Schwan, Politik und Schuld: Die zerstörerische Macht des Schweigens [Politics and Guilt: The Destructive Power of Staying Silent] (1997), Die Engquete-Kommission "Aufarbeitung von Geschichte und Folgen der SED-Diktatur in Deutschland" im Deutschen Bundestag [Inquiry commission in the German Bundestag (for the) "Treatment of the Past and Consequences of the SED-Dictatorship in Germany"], Spór o PRL [The Controversy about the Polish People's Republic]).
- Atrocities and International Accountability: Beyond Transitional Justice (Edel Huges et al. eds., 2007).
- Elazar Barkan, The Guilt of Nations: Restitution and Negotiating Historical Injustices (2000).
- M. Cherif Bassiouni, *Appraising UN Justice-Related Fact-Finding Missions*, 5 Wash. U. J.L. & Pol'y 35 (2001).
- M. Cherif Bassiouni, Crimes Against Humanity in International Criminal Law (1992).
- Lynn Berat & Yossi Shain, *Retribution or Truth-Telling in South Africa? Legacies of the Transitional Phase*, 20 Law & Soc. Inquiry 163 (1995).
- Bill Berkeley, The Graves Are Not Yet Full: Race, Tribe, and Power in the Heart of Africa (2001).
- Annie R. Bird, US Foreign Policy on Transitional Justice (2015).
- Alison Bisset, Truth Commissions and Criminal Courts (2012).
- Reed Brody, *Justice: The First Casualty of Truth?*, Nation, Apr. 30, 2001, at 25 (reviewing Truth v. Justice: The Morality of Truth Commissions (Robert I. Rothberg & Dennis Thompson eds., 2000), Priscilla B. Hayner, Unspeakable Truths: Confronting State Terror and Atrocity (1st ed. 2000), Ruti G. Teitel, Transitional Justice (2000), Richard J. Goldstone, For Humanity: Reflections of a War Crimes Investigator (2000)).
- Jonathan I. Charney, *International Criminal Law and the Role of Domestic Courts*, 95 Am. J. Int'l L. 197 (2001).
- Phil Clark, Zachary D. Kaufman & Kalypso Nicolaïdis, *Tensions in Transitional Justice, in* After Genocide: Transitional Justice, Post-conflict Reconstruction, and Reconciliation in Rwanda and Beyond 381 (Phil Clark & Zachary D. Kaufman eds., 2009).
- Stanley Cohen, *State Crimes of Previous Regimes: Knowledge, Accountability, and the Policing of the Past*, 20 Law & Soc. Inquiry 7 (1995).
- Robert F. Drinan, The Mobilization of Shame: A World View of Human Rights (2001).
- Jon Elster, Closing the Books: Transitional Justice in Historical Perspective (2004).
- Evaluating Transitional Justice: Accountability and Peacebuilding in Post-conflict Sierra Leone (Kirsten Ainley et al. eds., 2015).
- Globalizing Transitional Justice (Ruti Teitel ed., 2014).

- Luc Huyse, *Justice After Transition: On the Choices Successor Elites Make in Dealing with the Past*, 20 LAW & SOC. INQUIRY 51 (1995).
- IMPUNITY AND HUMAN RIGHTS IN INTERNATIONAL LAW AND PRACTICE (Naomi Roht-Arriaza ed., 1995).
- Zachary D. Kaufman, *The Future of Transitional Justice*, 1 ST. ANTONY'S INT'L REV. 58 (2005).
- BRONWYN LEEBAW, JUDGING STATE-SPONSORED VIOLENCE, IMAGINING POLITICAL CHANGE (2011)
- RAPHAEL LEMKIN, AXIS RULE IN OCCUPIED EUROPE: LAWS OF OCCUPATION, ANALYSIS OF GOVERNMENT, PROPOSALS FOR REDRESS (1944).
- JAIME MALAMUD-GOT, GAME WITHOUT END: STATE TERROR AND THE POLITICS OF JUSTICE (1996).
- MAHMOOD MAMDANI, WHEN VICTIMS BECOME KILLERS: COLONIALISM, NATIVISM, AND THE GENOCIDE IN RWANDA (2001).
- MARTHA MINOW, BETWEEN VENGEANCE AND FORGIVENESS: FACING HISTORY AFTER GENOCIDE AND MASS VIOLENCE (1998).
- MARTHA MINOW, BREAKING THE CYCLES OF HATRED: MEMORY, LAW, AND REPAIR (Nancy L. Rosenbaum ed., 2002).
- Madeleine H. Morris, *The Trial of Concurrent Jurisdiction: The Case of Rwanda*, 7 DUKE J. COMP. & INT'L L. 349 (1997).
- Daryl A. Mundis, *New Mechanisms for the Enforcement of International Humanitarian Law*, 95 AM. J. INT'L L. 934 (2001).
- MY NEIGHBOR, MY ENEMY: JUSTICE AND COMMUNITY IN THE AFTERMATH OF MASS ATROCITY (Eric Stover & Harvey Weinstein eds., 2004).
- Aryeh Neier, *The Quest for Justice*, N.Y. REV. BOOKS, Mar. 8, 2001, at 31 (reviewing ALEX BORAINE, A COUNTRY UNMASKED (2000), PRISCILLA B. HAYNER, UNSPEAKABLE TRUTHS: CONFRONTING STATE TERROR AND ATROCITY (2000), GARY JONATHAN BASS, STAY THE HAND OF VENGEANCE: THE POLITICS OF WAR CRIMES TRIBUNALS (2000), GEOFFREY ROBERTSON, CRIMES AGAINST HUMANITY: THE STRUGGLE FOR GLOBAL JUSTICE (2000), INDEPENDENT INTERNATIONAL COMMISSION ON KOSOVO, KOSOVO REPORT: CONFLICT, INTERNATIONAL RESPONSE, LESSONS LEARNED (2000), RICHARD J. GOLDSTONE, FOR HUMANITY: REFLECTIONS OF A WAR CRIMES INVESTIGATOR (2000)).
- ARYEH NEIER, WAR CRIMES: BRUTALITY, GENOCIDE, TERROR, AND THE STRUGGLE FOR JUSTICE (1998).
- ELIZABETH NEUFFER, THE KEY TO MY NEIGHBOR'S HOUSE: SEEKING JUSTICE IN BOSNIA AND RWANDA (2001).
- CAROL OFF, THE LION, THE FOX AND THE EAGLE: A STORY OF GENERALS AND JUSTICE IN YUGOSLAVIA AND RWANDA (2000).
- Diane F. Orentlicher, *Settling Accounts: The Duty to Prosecute Human Rights Violations of a Prior Regime*, 100 YALE L.J. 2537 (1991).
- Michelle Parlevliet, *Considering Truth: Dealing with a Legacy of Gross Human Rights Violations*, 16 NETH. Q. HUM. RTS. 141 (1998).
- Jelena Pejic, *The Tribunal and the ICC: Do Precedents Matter?*, 60 ALB. L. REV. 841 (1997).
- Chris Maina Peter, *The International Criminal Tribunal: Bringing the Killers to Book*, 1997 INT'L REV. RED CROSS 695.
- RESPONDING TO GENOCIDE: THE POLITICS OF INTERNATIONAL ACTION (Adam Lupel & Ernesto Verdeja eds., 2013).

- RESTORATIVE JUSTICE, RECONCILIATION, AND PEACEBUILDING (Jennifer J. Llewellyn & Daniel Philpott eds., 2014).
- ANDREW RIGBY, JUSTICE AND RECONCILIATION: AFTER THE VIOLENCE (2001).
- GEOFFREY ROBERTSON, CRIMES AGAINST HUMANITY: THE STRUGGLE FOR GLOBAL JUSTICE (rev. ed. 2006).
- RWANDA AND SOUTH AFRICA IN DIALOGUE: ADDRESSING THE LEGACIES OF GENOCIDE AND A CRIME AGAINST HUMANITY (Charles Villa-Vicencio & Tyrone Savage eds., 2001).
- William A. Schabas, *Conjoined Twins of Transitional Justice? The Sierra Leone Truth and Reconciliation Commission and the Special Court*, 2 J. INT'L CRIM. JUST. 1082 (2004).
- William A. Schabas, *National Courts Finally Begin to Prosecute Genocide, the "Crime of Crimes,"* 1 J. INT'L CRIM. JUST. 39 (2003).
- William A. Schabas, *The Relationship Between Truth Commissions and International Courts: The Case of Sierra Leone*, 25 HUM. RTS. Q. 1035 (2003).
- David J. Scheffer, *The Future of Atrocity Law*, 25 SUFFOLK TRANSNAT'L L. REV. 389 (2002).
- David J. Scheffer, *International Judicial Intervention*, FOREIGN POL'Y, Spring 1996, at 34.
- WILLIAM SHAWCROSS, JUSTICE AND THE ENEMY: NUREMBERG, 9/11, AND THE TRIAL OF KHALID SHEIKH MOHAMMED (2011).
- Richard Lewis Siegel, *Transitional Justice: A Decade of Debate and Experience*, 20 HUM. RTS. Q. 431 (1998) (reviewing TIMOTHY GARTON ASH, THE FILE: A PERSONAL HISTORY (1998), ALISON BRYSK, THE POLITICS OF HUMAN RIGHTS IN ARGENTINA: PROTEST, CHANGE, AND DEMOCRATIZATION (1994), TRANSITIONAL JUSTICE: HOW EMERGING DEMOCRACIES RECKON WITH FORMER REGIMES: VOLUME II: COUNTRY STUDIES (Neil J. Kritz ed., 1995), TRANSITIONAL JUSTICE: HOW EMERGING DEMOCRACIES RECKON WITH FORMER REGIMES: VOLUME III: LAWS, RULINGS, AND REPORTS (Neil J. Kritz ed., 1995), JAIME MALAMUD-GOTI, GAME WITHOUT END: STATE TERROR AND THE POLITICS OF JUSTICE (1996), TINA ROSENBERG, THE HAUNTED LAND: FACING EUROPE'S GHOSTS AFTER COMMUNISM (1995), TRANSITION TO DEMOCRACY IN LATIN AMERICA: THE ROLE OF THE JUDICIARY (Irwin P. Stotzky ed., 1993), LAWRENCE WESCHLER, A MIRACLE, A UNIVERSE: SETTLING ACCOUNTS WITH TORTURERS (1990)).
- KATHRYN SIKKINK, THE JUSTICE CASCADE: HOW HUMAN RIGHTS PROSECUTIONS ARE CHANGING WORLD POLITICS (2011).
- Jack Snyder & Leslie Vinjamuri, *Trials and Errors: Principles and Pragmatism in Strategies of International Justice*, INT'L SEC., Winter 2003/2004, at 5.
- Symposium, *Accountability for International Crimes and Serious Violations of Fundamental Human Rights*, 59 LAW & CONTEMP. PROBS. (1996).
- Symposium, *Justice in Cataclysm*, DUKE J. COMP. & INT'L L. 319 (1997).
- Ruti G. Teitel, *The Law and Politics of Contemporary Transitional Justice*, 38 CORNELL INT'L L.J. 837 (2005).
- RUTI G. TEITEL, TRANSITIONAL JUSTICE (2000).
- Ruti G. Teitel, *Transitional Justice Genealogy*, 16 HARV. HUM. RTS. J. 69 (2003).
- Ruti G. Teitel, *Transitional Justice: The Role of Law in Political Transformations*, 106 YALE L.J. 2009 (1997).

- TRANSITION TO DEMOCRACY IN LATIN AMERICA: THE ROLE OF THE JUDICIARY (Irwin P. Stotzky ed., 1993).
- TRANSITIONAL JUSTICE: HOW EMERGING DEMOCRACIES RECKON WITH FORMER REGIMES. VOLUME I: GENERAL CONSIDERATIONS (Neil Kritz ed., 1995).
- TRANSITIONAL JUSTICE: HOW EMERGING DEMOCRACIES RECKON WITH FORMER REGIMES. VOLUME II: COUNTRY STUDIES (Neil Kritz ed., 1995).
- TRANSITIONAL JUSTICE: HOW EMERGING DEMOCRACIES RECKON WITH FORMER REGIMES. VOLUME III: LAWS, RULINGS, AND REPORTS (Neil Kritz ed., 1995).
- TRANSITIONAL JUSTICE AND THE RULE OF LAW IN NEW DEMOCRACIES (James A. McAdams ed., 1997).
- TRANSITIONAL JUSTICE IN THE TWENTY-FIRST CENTURY: BEYOND TRUTH VERSUS JUSTICE (Naomi Roht-Arriaza & Javier Mariezcurrena eds., 2006).
- TRUTH COMMISSIONS AND COURTS: THE TENSION BETWEEN CRIMINAL JUSTICE AND THE SEARCH FOR TRUTH (William A. Schabas & Shane Darcy eds., 2005).
- LAWRENCE WESCHLER, A MIRACLE, A UNIVERSE: SETTLING ACCOUNTS WITH TORTURERS (1990).
- Leila Sadat Wexler, *Reflections on the Trial of Vichy Collaborator Paul Touvier for Crimes Against Humanity in France*, 20 LAW & SOC. INQUIRY 191 (1995).
- WHEN SORRY ISN'T ENOUGH: THE CONTROVERSY OVER APOLOGIES AND REPARATIONS FOR HUMAN INJUSTICE (Roy L. Brooks ed., 1999).
- José Zalaquett, *Balancing Ethical Imperatives and Political Constraints: The Dilemma of New Democracies Confronting Past Human Rights Violations*, 43 HASTINGS L.J. 1425 (1992).

B. MULTIPLE ATROCITIES

- ALEX J. BELLAMY, MASSACRES AND MORALITY: MASS ATROCITIES IN AN AGE OF CIVILIAN IMMUNITY (2012).
- CENTURY OF GENOCIDE: CRITICAL ESSAYS AND EYEWITNESS ACCOUNTS (Samuel Totten et al. eds., 4th ed. 2012).
- DON CHEADLE & JOHN PRENDERGAST, NOT ON OUR WATCH: THE MISSION TO END GENOCIDE IN DARFUR AND BEYOND (2007).
- Jared Cohen & Zachary D. Kaufman, Op-Ed., *A Genocide by Any Other Name: Debating Genocide in Rwanda and Sudan*, BROWARD TIMES, July 15, 2006, at 6.
- CRIMES OF WAR 2.0: WHAT THE PUBLIC SHOULD KNOW (Roy Gutman et al. eds., 2d ed. 2007).
- PETER DU PREEZ, GENOCIDE: THE PSYCHOLOGY OF MASS MURDER (1994).
- ENCYCLOPEDIA OF GENOCIDE AND CRIMES AGAINST HUMANITY (Dinah L. Shelton ed., 2005).
- GENOCIDE: CONCEPTUAL AND HISTORICAL DIMENSIONS (George J. Andreopoulos ed., 1994).
- DANIEL JONAH GOLDHAGEN, WORSE THAN WAR: GENOCIDE, ELIMINATIONISM, AND THE ONGOING ASSAULT ON HUMANITY (2009).
- DONALD L. HOROWITZ, ETHNIC GROUPS IN CONFLICT (1985).
- ADAM LEBOR, "COMPLICITY WITH EVIL": THE UNITED NATIONS IN THE AGE OF MODERN GENOCIDE (2006).
- THE NEW KILLING FIELDS: MASSACRE AND THE POLITICS OF INTERVENTION (Nicolaus Mills & Kira Brunner eds., 2002).

- WILLIAM A. SCHABAS, GENOCIDE IN INTERNATIONAL LAW: THE CRIME OF CRIMES (2d ed. 2009).
- WILLIAM A. SCHABAS, WAR CRIMES AND HUMAN RIGHTS: ESSAYS ON THE DEATH PENALTY, JUSTICE, AND ACCOUNTABILITY (2008).
- SOCIAL ENTREPRENEURSHIP IN THE AGE OF ATROCITIES: CHANGING OUR WORLD (Zachary D. Kaufman ed., 2012).
- ERVIN STRAUB, THE ROOTS OF EVIL: THE ORIGINS OF GENOCIDE AND OTHER GROUP VIOLENCE (1989).
- BENJAMIN A. VALENTINO, FINAL SOLUTIONS: MASS KILLING AND GENOCIDE IN THE 20TH CENTURY (2004).

C. MULTIPLE WAR CRIMES TRIBUNALS

- Payam Akhavan, *Beyond Impunity: Can International Criminal Justice Prevent Future Atrocities?*, 95 AM. J. INT'L L. 7 (2001).
- Payam Akhavan, *Book Reviews and Notes*, 93 AM. J. INT'L L. 253 (1999) (reviewing STEVEN R. RATNER & JASON S. ABRAMS, ACCOUNTABILITY FOR HUMAN RIGHTS ATROCITIES IN INTERNATIONAL LAW: BEYOND THE NUREMBERG LEGACY (1st ed. 1997)).
- ATROCITIES ON TRIAL: HISTORICAL PERSPECTIVES ON THE POLITICS OF PROSECUTING WAR CRIMES (Patricia Heberer & Jürgen Matthäus eds., 2008).
- HOWARD BALL, PROSECUTING WAR CRIMES AND GENOCIDE: THE TWENTIETH CENTURY EXPERIENCE (1999).
- Gary Jonathan Bass, *Atrocity & Legalism*, DAEDALUS 73 (2003).
- GARY JONATHAN BASS, STAY THE HAND OF VENGEANCE: THE POLITICS OF WAR CRIMES TRIBUNALS (2000).
- YVES BEIGBEDER, JUDGING WAR CRIMINALS: THE POLITICS OF INTERNATIONAL JUSTICE (1999).
- Graham T. Blewitt, *Ad Hoc Tribunals Half a Century After Nuremberg*, 149 MIL. L. REV. 101 (1995).
- John R. Bolton, *The Global Prosecutors: Hunting War Criminals in the Name of Utopia*, FOREIGN AFF., Jan.–Feb. 1999, at 157 (reviewing ARYEH NEIER, WAR CRIMES: BRUTALITY, GENOCIDE, TERROR AND THE STRUGGLE FOR JUSTICE (1998), MARTHA MINOW, BETWEEN VENGEANCE AND FORGIVENESS: FACING HISTORY AFTER GENOCIDE AND MASS VIOLENCE (1998)).
- Thomas Burgenthal, *Proliferation of International Courts and Tribunals: Is It Good or Bad?*, 14 LEIDEN J. IN'L L. 267 (2001).
- Jonathan G. Cedarbaum, *Restrictions on U.S. Attorneys, Practicing before International Criminal Tribunals*, 98 AM. J. INT'L L. 141 (2004).
- Jonathan I. Charney, *Is International Law Threatened by Multiple International Tribunals?*, RECUEIL DES COURS, 1998, at 101.
- Helena Cobban, *International Courts*, FOREIGN POL'Y, Mar.–Apr. 2006, at 22.
- Robert Cryer, *Human Rights and the Question of International Criminal Courts and Tribunals, in* INTERNATIONAL INTERVENTION IN THE POST-COLD WAR WORLD: MORAL RESPONSIBILITY AND POWER POLITICS (Michael C. Davis et al. eds., 2004).
- RICHARD J. GOLDSTONE, FOR HUMANITY: REFLECTIONS OF A WAR CRIMES INVESTIGATOR (2000).

- Gilbert Guillaume, *Advantages and Risks of Proliferation: A Blueprint for Action*, 2 J. INT'L CRIM. JUST. 300 (2004).
- THE HIDDEN HISTORIES OF WAR CRIMES TRIALS (Kevin Jon Heller & Gerry Simpson eds., 2013).
- Zachary D. Kaufman, *The Nuremberg Tribunal v. The Tokyo Tribunal: Designs, Staffs, and Operations*, 43 J. MARSHALL L. REV. 753 (2010).
- Zachary D. Kaufman, *Steven D. Roper & Lilian A. Barria's Designing Criminal Tribunals: Sovereignty and International Concerns in the Protection of Human Rights*, 10 YALE HUM. RTS. & DEV. L.J. 209, 213 (2007) (book review).
- Joanne Lee & Richard Price, *International Tribunals and the Criminalization of International Violence*, in THE UNITED NATIONS AND GLOBAL SECURITY (Richard M. Price & Mark W. Zacher eds., 2004).
- Juan E. Méndez, *Accountability for Past Abuses*, 19 HUM. RTS. Q. 255 (1997).
- Theodor Meron, *From Nuremberg to the Hague*, 149 MIL. L. REV. 107 (1995).
- Theodor Meron, *International Criminalization of Internal Atrocities*, 89 AM. J. INT'L L. 554 (1995).
- KINGSLEY CHIEDU MOGHALU, GLOBAL JUSTICE: THE POLITICS OF WAR CRIMES TRIALS (2008).
- Alan Nissel, *Yuval Shany's The Competing Jurisdictions of International Courts and Tribunals*, 3 J. INT'L CRIM. JUST. 525 (book review).
- W. Hays Parks, *A Few Tools in the Prosecution of War Crimes*, MIL. L. REV., Summer 1995, at 73.
- Victor Peskin, *Beyond Victor's Justice? The Challenge of Prosecuting the Victors at the International Criminal Tribunals for the Former Yugoslavia and Rwanda*, 4 J. HUM. RTS. 213 (2005).
- VICTOR PESKIN, INTERNATIONAL JUSTICE IN RWANDA AND THE BALKANS: VIRTUAL TRIALS AND THE STRUGGLE FOR STATE COOPERATION (2008).
- Fausto Pocar, *The Proliferation of International Criminal Courts and Tribunals: A Necessity in the Current International Community*, 2 J. INT'L CRIM. JUST. 304 (2004).
- Amy Powell, *Three Angry Men: Juries in International Criminal Adjudication*, 79 N.Y.U. L. REV 2341 (2004).
- STEVEN R. RATNER ET AL., ACCOUNTABILITY FOR HUMAN RIGHTS ATROCITIES IN INTERNATIONAL LAW: BEYOND THE NUREMBERG LEGACY (3d ed. 2009).
- STEVEN D. ROPER & LILIAN A. BARRIA, DESIGNING CRIMINAL TRIBUNALS: SOVEREIGNTY AND INTERNATIONAL CONCERNS IN THE PROTECTION OF HUMAN RIGHTS (2006).
- Christopher Rudolph, *Constructing an Atrocities Regime: The Politics of War Crimes Tribunals*, 55 INT'L ORG. 655 (2001).
- WILLIAM SCHABAS, THE UN INTERNATIONAL CRIMINAL TRIBUNALS: THE FORMER YUGOSLAVIA, RWANDA, AND SIERRA LEONE (2006).
- WILLIAM SCHABAS, UNIMAGINABLE ATROCITIES: JUSTICE, POLITICS, AND RIGHTS AT THE WAR CRIMES TRIBUNALS (2014).
- DAVID SCHEFFER, ALL THE MISSING SOULS: A PERSONAL HISTORY OF THE WAR CRIMES TRIBUNALS (2012).
- YUVAL SHANY, THE COMPETING JURISDICTIONS OF INTERNATIONAL COURTS AND TRIBUNALS (2003).

- CHARLES ANTHONY SMITH, THE RISE AND FALL OF WAR CRIMES TRIALS: FROM CHARLES I TO BUSH II (2012).
- Symposium, *The Fifth Annual Ernst C. Steifel Symposium: 1945–1995: Critical Perspectives on the Nuremberg Trials and State Accountability: Panel III: Identifying and Prosecuting War Crimes: Two Case Studies: The Former Yugoslavia and Rwanda*, 12 N.Y.L. SCH. J. HUM. RTS. 631 (1995).
- Colin Warbrick, *The United Nations System: A Place for Criminal Courts?*, 5 TRANSNAT'L L. & CONTEMP. PROBS. 237 (1995).
- Ruth Wedgwood, *Prosecuting War Crimes*, 149 MIL. L. REV. 217 (1995).
- RICHARD ASHBY WILSON, WRITING HISTORY IN INTERNATIONAL CRIMINAL TRIALS (2011).
- John Yoo, *Prosecuting the Peace*, WALL ST. J., Jan. 6, 2012, http://www.wsj.com/articles/SB10001424052970204720204577128610335846568 (reviewing DAVID SCHEFFER, ALL THE MISSING SOULS (2012)).
- Ralph Zacklin, *The Failings of Ad Hoc International Tribunals*, 2 J. INT'L CRIM. JUST. 541 (2004).

D. MULTIPLE HYBRID TRIBUNALS

- Laura Dickinson, *The Promise of Hybrid Courts*, 97 AM. J. INT'L L. 295 (2003).
- Laura Dickinson, *Transitional Justice in Afghanistan: The Promise of Mixed Tribunals*, 31 DENV. J. INT'L L. & POL'Y 23 (2002).
- Etelle R. Higonnet, *Restructuring Hybrid Courts: Local Empowerment and National Criminal Justice Reform*, 23 ARIZ. J. INT'L & COMP. L. 347 (2006).
- INTERNATIONALIZED CRIMINAL COURTS: SIERRA LEONE, EAST TIMOR, KOSOVO, AND CAMBODIA (Cesare P.R. Romano et al. eds., 2004).
- Susanne Katzenstein, *Hybrid Tribunals: The Search for Justice in East Timor*, 16 HARV. HUM. RTS. J. 245 (2003).
- William A. Schabas, *The Special Tribunal for Lebanon: Is a "Tribunal of an International Character" Equivalent to an "International Criminal Court"?*, 21 LEIDEN J. INT'L L. 513 (2008).

E. MILITARY COMMISSIONS/TRIBUNALS

- Editorial, *Let There Be Law*, WASH. POST, July 2, 2006, at B06.
- Editorial, *Sins of Commissions*, WASH. POST, Mar. 27, 2006, at A14.
- Editorial, *A Victory for Law*, WASH. POST, June 30, 2006, at A26.
- LOUIS FISHER, MILITARY TRIBUNALS: HISTORICAL PATTERNS AND LESSONS (2004), *available at* http://www.loufisher.org/docs/mt/RL32458.pdf.
- LOUIS FISHER, MILITARY TRIBUNALS: THE QUIRIN PRECEDENT (2002), *available at* http://www.loufisher.org/docs/mt/RL31340.pdf.
- Joan Fitzpatrick, *Jurisdiction of Military Commissions and the Ambiguous War on Terrorism*, 96 AM. J. INT'L L. 345 (2002).
- HUMAN RIGHTS WATCH, BRIEFING PAPER ON U.S. MILITARY COMMISSIONS (2004), http://www.hrw.org/legacy/backgrounder/usa/2004/1.htm.
- HUMAN RIGHTS WATCH, MAKING SENSE OF THE GUANTANAMO BAY TRIBUNALS (2004), http://www.hrw.org/legacy/english/docs/2004/08/16/usdom9235.htm.

- HUMAN RIGHTS WATCH, U.S. COMMISSION MEETS SOME, NOT ALL, RIGHTS CONCERNS (2002), http://www.hrw.org/news/2002/03/20/us-commission-rules-meet-some-not-all-rights-concerns.
- HUMAN RIGHTS WATCH, U.S.: MILITARY COMMISSIONS LACK FAIR TRIAL PROTECTIONS (2004), http://www.hrw.org/news/2004/08/18/us-military-commissions-lack-fair-trial-protections.
- Neal Katyal, *Sins of Commissions: Why Aren't We Using the Courts-Martial System at Guantanamo?*, SLATE (Sept. 8, 2004), http://www.slate.com/articles/news_and_politics/jurisprudence/2004/09/sins_of_commissions.html.
- Harold Hongju Koh, *The Case Against Military Commissions*, 96 AM. J. INT'L L. 337 (2002).
- Harold Hongju Koh, Op-Ed., *We Have the Right Courts for Bin Laden*, N.Y. TIMES, Nov. 23, 2001, at A39.
- Charles Krauthammer, Op-Ed., *The Trouble with Trials*, WASH. POST, Mar. 9, 2001, at A27.
- Jonathan Lurie, *Military Justice 50 Years After Nuremberg: Some Reflections on Appearance v. Reality*, 149 MIL. L. REV. 189 (1995).
- Michael J. Matheson, *U.S. Military Commissions: One of Several Options*, 96 AM. J. INT'L L. 354 (2002).
- Daryl A. Mundis, *The Use of Military Commissions to Prosecute Individuals Accused of Terrorist Acts*, 96 AM. J. INT'L L. 320 (2002).
- Aryeh Neier, *The Military Tribunals on Trial*, N.Y. REV. BOOKS, Feb. 14, 2002, at 11.
- PETER JUDSON RICHARDS, EXTRAORDINARY JUSTICE: MILITARY TRIBUNALS IN HISTORICAL AND INTERNATIONAL CONTEXT (2007).
- David J. Scheffer, Op-Ed., *Reality Check on Military Commissions*, CHRISTIAN SCI. MONITOR, Dec. 10, 2001, at 11.
- Ruth Wedgwood, *Al Qaeda, Terrorism, and Military Commissions*, 96 AM. J. INT'L L. 328 (2002).
- Josh White, *U.S. Officials Scramble to Find Options*, WASH. POST, June 30, 2006, at A6.

F. UNIVERSAL JURISDICTION

- Georges Abi-Saab, *The Proper Role of Universal Jurisdiction*, 1 J. INT'L CRIM. JUST. 596 (2003).
- Louise Arbour, *Will the ICC Have an Impact on Universal Jurisdiction?*, 1 J. INT'L CRIM. JUST. 585 (2003).
- Richard Bernstein, *Belgium Rethinks Its Prosecutorial Zeal*, N.Y. TIMES, Apr. 1, 2003, at A8.
- Antonio Cassese, *Is the Bell Tolling for Universality? A Plea for a Sensible Notion of Universal Jurisdiction*, 1 J. INT'L CRIM. JUST. 589 (2003).
- George P. Fletcher, *Against Universal Jurisdiction*, 1 J. INT'L CRIM. JUST. 580 (2003).
- Christopher C. Joyner, *Arresting Impunity: The Case for Universal Jurisdiction in Bringing War Criminals to Accountability*, 59 LAW & CONTEMP. PROBS. 153 (1996).
- Zachary D. Kaufman, *Naomi Roht-Arriaza's The Pinochet Effect: Transnational Justice in the Age of Human Rights*, 32 YALE J. INT'L L. 297 (2006) (book review).
- Henry A. Kissinger, *The Pitfalls of Universal Jurisdiction: Risking Judicial Tyranny*, FOREIGN AFF., July–Aug. 2001, at 86.

- STEPHEN MACEDO, UNIVERSAL JURISDICTION: NATIONAL COURTS AND THE PROSECUTION OF SERIOUS CRIMES UNDER INTERNATIONAL LAW (2004).
- PRINCETON PRINCIPLES ON UNIVERSAL JURISDICTION (2001), http://lapa.princeton.edu/hosteddocs/unive_jur.pdf.
- Roger O'Keefe, *Universal Jurisdiction: Clarifying the Basic Concept*, 2 J. INT'L CRIM. JUST. 735 (2004).
- Kenneth C. Randall, *Universal Jurisdiction Under International Law*, 66 TEX. L. REV. 785 (1988).
- Luc Reydams, *Belgium Reneges on Universality: The 5 August 2003 Act on Grave Breaches of International Humanitarian Law*, 1 J. INT'L CRIM. JUST. 679 (2003).
- Luc Reydams, *Belgium's First Application of Universal Jurisdiction: The Butare Four Case*, 1 J. INT'L CRIM. JUST. 428 (2003).
- LUC REYDAMS, UNIVERSAL JURISDICTION: INTERNATIONAL AND MUNICIPAL PERSPECTIVES (2003).
- Luc Reydams, *Universal Jurisdiction over Atrocities in Rwanda: Theory and Practice*, 1 EUR. J. CRIME CRIM. L. & CRIM. JUST. 18 (1996).
- NAOMI ROHT-ARRIAZA, THE PINOCHET EFFECT: TRANSNATIONAL JUSTICE IN THE AGE OF HUMAN RIGHTS (2005).
- Kenneth Roth, *The Case for Universal Jurisdiction*, FOREIGN AFF., Sept.–Oct. 2001, at 150.
- David J. Scheffer, *Opening Address*, 35 NEW ENG. L. REV. 233 (2001).

G. ARMENIAN GENOCIDE

- TANER AKCAM, FROM EMPIRE TO REPUBLIC: TURKISH NATIONALISM AND THE ARMENIAN GENOCIDE (2004).
- PETER BALAKIAN, THE BURNING TIGRIS: THE ARMENIAN GENOCIDE AND AMERICA'S RESPONSE (2003).
- KEVORK BARDAKJIAN, HITLER AND THE ARMENIAN GENOCIDE (1985).
- DONALD BLOXHAM, THE GREAT GAME OF GENOCIDE: IMPERIALISM, NATIONALISM, AND THE DESTRUCTION OF THE OTTOMAN ARMENIANS (2005).
- VAHAKN N. DADRIAN, THE HISTORY OF THE ARMENIAN GENOCIDE: ETHNIC CONFLICT FROM THE BALKANS TO ANATOLIA TO THE CAUCUS (1995).
- A CRIME OF SILENCE, THE ARMENIAN GENOCIDE: THE PERMANENT PEOPLES' TRIBUNAL (Gerard Libaridian ed., 1985).
- AMERICA AND THE ARMENIAN GENOCIDE OF 1915 (Jay Winter ed., 2003).

H. NAZIS/IMT

- MICHAEL BAZYLER & FRANK TUERKHEIMER, FORGOTTEN TRIALS OF THE HOLOCAUST (2014).
- TOM BOWER, THE PAPERCLIP CONSPIRACY (1987).
- John T. Burton, *"War Crimes" During Operations Other than War: Military Doctrine and Law 50 Years After Nuremberg and Beyond*, 149 MIL. L. REV. 199 (1995).
- RANDALL L. BYTWERK, JULIUS STREICHER: NAZI EDITOR OF THE NOTORIOUS ANTI-SEMITIC NEWSPAPER DER STÜRMER (2001).
- ROBERT E. CONOT, JUSTICE AT NUREMBERG (1983).
- Hans Corell, *Nuremberg and the Development of an International Criminal Court*, 149 MIL. L. REV. 87 (1995).

- István Deák, *Misjudgement at Nuremberg*, N.Y. REV. BOOKS, Oct. 7, 1993, at 46 (reviewing TELFORD TAYLOR, THE ANATOMY OF THE NUREMBERG TRIALS: A PERSONAL MEMOIR (1st ed. 1992), EDWARD ALEXANDER, A CRIME OF VENGEANCE: AN ARMENIAN STRUGGLE FOR JUSTICE (1991), STEPHEN A. GARRETT, ETHICS AND AIRPOWER IN WORLD WAR II: THE BRITISH BOMBING OF GERMAN CITIES (1993), ALAIN FINKIELKRAUT, REMEBERING IN VAIN: THE KLAUS BARBIE TRIAL AND CRIMES AGAINST HUMANITY (Roxanne Lapidus & Sima Godfrey trans., 1992)).
- István Deák, *Post World War II Political Justice in a Historical Perspective*, 149 MIL. L. REV. 137 (1995).
- STUART E. EIZENSTAT, IMPERFECT JUSTICE: LOOTED ASSETS, SLAVE LABOR, AND THE UNFINISHED BUSINESS OF WORLD WAR II (2003).
- Robinson O. Everett, *Opening Comments*, 149 MIL. L. REV. 13 (1995).
- ALAIN FINKIELKRAUT, REMEMBERING IN VAIN: THE KLAUS BARBIE TRIAL AND CRIMES AGAINST HUMANITY (Roxanne Lapidus & Sima Godfrey trans., 1992).
- WILLI FRISCHAUER, THE RISE AND FALL OF HERMANN GOERING (1951).
- DANIEL JONAH GOLDHAGEN, HITLER'S WILLING EXECUTIONERS: ORDINARY GERMANS AND THE HOLOCAUST (1996).
- Joseph L. Graves Jr. & David E. Graham, *Introduction*, 149 MIL. L. REV. v (1995).
- WHITNEY R. HARRIS, TYRANNY ON TRIAL: THE TRIAL OF THE MAJOR GERMAN WAR CRIMINALS AT THE END OF THE WORLD WAR II AT NUREMBERG GERMANY 1945–46 (rev. ed. 1999).
- PETER HEIGL, NUREMBERG TRIALS (2001).
- Linda Hunt, *U.S. Coverup of Nazi Scientists*, BULL. ATOMIC SCIENTISTS, Apr. 1985, at 16.
- DAVID IRVING, GÖRING: A BIOGRAPHY (1989).
- ROBERT H. JACKSON, THE CASE AGAINST THE NAZI WAR CRIMINALS: OPENING STATEMENT FOR THE UNITED STATES OF AMERICA BY ROBERT H. JACKSON AND OTHER DOCUMENTS (1946).
- Robert H. Jackson, *Introduction* to WHITNEY R. HARRIS, TYRANNY ON TRIAL: THE TRIAL OF THE MAJOR GERMAN WAR CRIMINALS AT THE END OF THE WORLD WAR II AT NUREMBERG GERMANY 1945–46 at xxix (rev. ed. 1999).
- Robert H. Jackson, *Report to the President from Justice Robert H. Jackson, Chief of Counsel for the United States in the Prosecution of the Axis War Criminals*, June 7, 1945, 39 AM. J. INT'L L. 178 (1945).
- ROBERT H. JACKSON, REPORT OF ROBERT H. JACKSON: UNITED STATES REPRESENTATIVE TO THE INTERNATIONAL CONFERENCE ON MILITARY TRIALS (1949).
- ANNIE JACOBSEN, OPERATION PAPERCLIP: THE SECRET INTELLIGENCE PROGRAM TO BRING NAZI SCIENTISTS TO AMERICA (2014).
- Douglas Jehl, *C.I.A. Defers to Congress, Agreeing to Disclose Nazi Records*, N.Y. TIMES, Feb. 7, 2005, at A4.
- Hans-Heinrich Jesheck, *The General Principles of International Criminal Law Set Out in Nuremberg, as Mirrored in the ICC Statute*, 2 J. INT'L CRIM. JUST. 38 (2004).
- Henry T. King, Jr., *The Nuremberg Context from the Eyes of a Participant*, 149 MIL. L. REV. 37 (1995).
- Thomas F. Lambert, Jr., *Recalling the War Crimes Trials of World War II*, 149 MIL. L. REV. 15 (1995).
- CLARENCE LASBY, PROJECT PAPERCLIP (1971).

- Eric Lichtblau, The Nazis Next Door: How America Became a Safe Haven for Hitler's Men (2014).
- Roger Manvell & Heinrich Fraenkel, Goering: The Rise and Fall of the Notorious Nazi Leader (2011).
- Mark S. Martins, *"War Crimes" During Operations Other than War: Military Doctrine and Law Fifty Years After Nuremberg—and Beyond*, 149 Mil. L. Rev. 145 (1995).
- John Norton Moore, *Opening Comments*, 149 Mil. L. Rev. 7 (1995).
- Fred L. Morrison, *The Significance of Nuremberg for Modern International Law*, 149 Mil. L. Rev. 207 (1995).
- Airey Neave, On Trial at Nuremberg (1979).
- Edward J. O'Brien, *The Nuremberg Principles, Command Responsibility, and the Defense of Captain Rockwood*, 149 Mil. L. Rev. 275 (1995).
- Richard J. Overy, Goering (2000).
- Richard J. Overy, Goering: The "Iron Man" (1984).
- Richard J. Overy, Interrogations: The Nazi Elite in Allied Hands, 1945 (2001).
- Joseph E. Persico, Nuremberg: Infamy on Trial (1994).
- Michael P. Scharf, *Have We Really Learned the Lessons of Nuremberg?*, 149 Mil. L. Rev. 65 (1995).
- Bradley F. Smith, The American Road to Nuremberg: The Documentary Record, 1944–45 (1982).
- Bradley F. Smith, Reaching Judgment at Nuremberg (1977).
- Timothy Snyder, Black Earth: The Holocaust as History and Warning (2015).
- Telford Taylor, The Anatomy of the Nuremberg Trials: A Personal Memoir (1992).
- Ann Tusa & John Tusa, The Nuremberg Trial (1995).

I. ADOLF EICHMANN

- Hannah Arendt, Eichmann in Jerusalem: A Report on the Banality of Evil (rev. ed. 1964).
- Associated Press, *Documents: CIA Concealed Nazi War Criminals*, MSNBC, June 7, 2006, http://www.nbcnews.com/id/13171278/.
- Hans W. Baade, *The Eichmann Trial: Some Legal Aspects*, 1961 Duke L.J. 400 (1961).
- Pam Benson, *CIA Papers: U.S. Failed to Pursue Nazi*, CNN, June 7, 2006, http://www.cnn.com/2006/US/06/06/nazi.crimes/index.html.
- David Cesarani, Becoming Eichmann: Rethinking the Life, Crimes, and Trial of a "Desk Murderer" (2007).
- Barry Gewen, *The Everyman of Genocide*, N.Y. Times, May 14, 2006, at 10 (reviewing David Cesarani, Becoming Eichmann: Rethinking the Life, Crimes, and Trial of a "Desk Murderer" (2007)).
- Lord Russell of Liverpool, The Trial of Adolph Eichmann (1962).
- Peter Papadatos, The Eichmann Trial (1964).
- Moshe Pearlman, The Capture and Trial of Adolph Eichmann (1963).
- Shmuel Rosner, *Documents Show Post-war CIA Covered Up Nazi Crimes*, Haaretz, June 7, 2006, http://www.haaretz.com/beta/documents-show-post-war-cia-covered-up-nazi-war-crimes-1.189490.

- Scott Shane, *C.I.A. Knew Where Eichmann Was Hiding, Documents Show*, N.Y. Times, June 7, 2006, at A3.

J. JAPANESE/IMTFE

- Daniel Barenblatt, A Plague upon Humanity: The Hidden History of Japan's Biological Warfare Program (2004).
- Gary Jonathan Bass, Op-Ed., *A Shrine to Japan's Tainted Past*, N.Y. Times, Aug. 5, 2006, at A13.
- Ralph Blumenthal, *Comparing the Unspeakable to the Unthinkable*, N.Y. Times, Mar. 7, 1999, at WK4.
- Arnold C. Brackman, The Other Nuremberg: The Untold Story of the Tokyo War Crimes Trials (1987).
- The Burma-Thailand Railway: Memory and History (Gavan McCormack & Hank Nelson eds., 1993).
- Iris Chang, The Rape of Nanking: The Forgotten Holocaust of World War II (1997).
- Michael Daly, *Japan Dissected My Granddad Live in World War II*, Daily Beast, Apr. 8, 2015, http://www.thedailybeast.com/articles/2015/04/08/world-war-ii-japan-dissected-my-granddad-alive.html.
- Roger Daniels, The Japanese American Cases: The Rule of Law in Time of War (2013).
- Gavan Daws, Prisoners of the Japanese: POWs of World War II in the Pacific (1994).
- Thomas Easton, *A Quiet Honesty Records a World War II Atrocity*, Balt. Sun, May 28, 1995, http://articles.baltimoresun.com/1995-05-28/news/1995148003_1_japan-kyushu-university-fukuoka.
- Mark Felton, The Devil's Doctors: Japanese Human Experiments on Allied Prisoners of War (2012).
- Madoka Futamura, War Crimes Tribunals and Transitional Justice: The Tokyo Trial and the Nuremberg Legacy (2007).
- Hal Gold, Unit 731 Testimony (1997).
- Shane Green, *The Asian Auschwitz of Unit 731*, Age (Australia), Aug. 29, 2002, http://www.theage.com.au/articles/2002/08/28/1030508070534.html.
- Sheldon H. Harris, Factories of Death: Japanese Biological Warfare, 1932–45, and the American Coverup (2002).
- George L. Hicks, The Comfort Women: Japan's Brutal Regime of Enforced Prostitution in the Second World War (1995).
- Solis Horwitz, *The Tokyo Trial*, Int'l Conciliation, Nov. 1950, at 473.
- Japan's Wartime Medical Atrocities: Comparative Inquiries in Science, History, and Ethics (Jing-Bao Nie et al. eds., 2010).
- Japanese War Crimes: The Search for Justice (Peter Li ed., 2003).
- *Joseph B. Keenan, Prosecutor, Dies*, N.Y. Times, Dec. 9, 1954, at 33.
- Zachary D. Kaufman, *No Right to Fight: The Modern Implications of Japan's Pacifist Postwar Constitution*, 33 Yale J. Int'l L. 266 (2008).
- Zachary D. Kaufman, *Transitional Justice for Tōjō's Japan: The United States Role in the Establishment of the International Military Tribunal for the Far East and Other*

Transitional Justice Mechanisms for Japan After World War II, 27 EMORY INT'L L. REV. 755 (2013).
- DONALD KNOX, DEATH MARCH: THE SURVIVORS OF BATAAN (1981).
- Nicholas D. Kristof, *Unmasking Horror—A Special Report; Japan Confronting Gruesome War Atrocity*, N.Y. TIMES, Mar. 17, 1995, http://www.nytimes.com/1995/03/17/world/unmasking-horror-a-special-report-japan-confronting-gruesome-war-atrocity.html.
- Kyodo, *US Paid for Japanese Human Germ Warfare Data*, AUSTL. BROADCASTING CORP., Aug. 15, 2005, http://www.abc.net.au/news/2005-08-15/us-paid-for-japanese-human-germ-warfare-data/2080618.
- Bruce D. Landrum, *The Yamashita War Crimes Trials: Command Responsibility Then and Now*, 149 MIL. L. REV. 293 (1995).
- TIM MAGA, JUDGMENT AT TOKYO: THE JAPANESE WAR CRIMES TRIALS (2001).
- Justin McCurry, *Japan's Sins of the Past*, GUARDIAN UNLIMITED, Oct. 28, 2004, http://www.theguardian.com/world/2004/oct/28/worlddispatch.justinmccurry.
- RICHARD H. MINEAR, VICTORS' JUSTICE: THE TOKYO WAR CRIMES TRIAL (1971).
- Elaine O'Flynn, *US Bomber Crew Shot Down over Japan Were Dissected While Alive in Horrific WW2 Experiments*, DAILY MAIL (United Kingdom), Apr. 7, 2015, http://www.dailymail.co.uk/news/article-3028694/U-S-POWs-shot-Japan-70-years-ago-dissected-ALIVE-macabre-experiments-controversial-new-exhibition-shows.html.
- R. John Pritchard, *The International Military Tribunal for the Far East and Its Contemporary Resonance*, 149 MIL. L. REV. 25 (1995).
- LAURENCE REES, HORROR IN THE EAST: JAPAN AND THE ATROCITIES OF WORLD WAR II (2002).
- BERNARD VICTOR A. RÖLING, THE TOKYO TRIAL AND BEYOND: REFLECTIONS OF A PEACEMONGER (Antonio Cassese ed., 1993).
- YUKI TANAKA, HIDDEN HORRORS: JAPANESE WAR CRIMES IN WORLD WAR II (1996).
- Didi Kirsten Tatlow, *Q. and A.: Gao Yubao on Documenting Unit 731's Brutal Human Experiments*, N.Y. TIMES, Oct. 21, 2015, http://sinosphere.blogs.nytimes.com/2015/10/21/china-unit-731-japan-war-crimes/.
- THE TOKYO WAR CRIMES TRIAL: AN INTERNATIONAL SYMPOSIUM (C. Hosoya et al. eds., 1986).
- PETER WILLIAMS & DAVID WALLACE, UNIT 731: JAPAN'S SECRET BIOLOGICAL WARFARE IN WORLD WAR II (1989).
- WITH ONLY THE WILL TO LIVE: ACCOUNTS OF AMERICANS IN JAPANESE PRISON CAMPS, 1941–45 (Robert La Forte et al. eds., 1994).

K. POL POT/KHMER ROUGE/ECCC

- Mann (Mac) Bunyanunda, *The Khmer Rouge on Trial: Whither the Defense?*, 74 S. CAL. L. REV 1581 (2001).
- DAVID CHANDLER, VOICE FROM S-21: TERROR AND HISTORY IN POL POT'S SECRET PRISON (1999).
- JOHN D. CIORCIARI & ANN HEINDEL, HYBRID JUSTICE: THE EXTRAORDINARY CHAMBERS IN THE COURTS OF CAMBODIA (2014).
- BENEDICT F. KIERNAN, THE POL POT REGIME: RACE, POWER, AND GENOCIDE IN CAMBODIA UNDER THE KHMER ROUGE, 1975–79 (3d ed. 2008).
- GENOCIDE AND DEMOCRACY IN CAMBODIA: THE KHMER ROUGE, THE UNITED NATIONS AND THE INTERNATIONAL COMMUNITY (Benedict F. Kiernan ed., 1993).

- Benedict F. Kiernan, Cambodia: The Eastern Zone Massacres (1986).
- Benedict F. Kiernan, How Pol Pot Came to Power: A History of Communism in Kampuchea, 1930–75 (1985).
- Scott Luftglass, *Crossroad in Cambodia: The United Nations' Responsibility to Withdraw Involvement from the Establishment of a Cambodian Tribunal to Prosecute the Khmer Rouge*, 90 Va. L. Rev. 893 (2004).
- Seth Mydans, *Pol Pot, Brutal Dictator Who Forced Cambodians to Killing Fields, Dies at 73*, N.Y. Times, Apr. 17, 1998, at A14.
- David J. Scheffer, Op-Ed., *Justice for Cambodia*, N.Y. Times, Dec. 21, 2002, at A21.
- Philip Short, Pol Pot: Anatomy of a Nightmare (2005).

L. THE BALKANS

- Ivo Andrić, The Bridge of the Drina (Lovett F. Edwards trans., 1994).
- Wesley K. Clark, Waging Modern War: Bosnia, Kosovo, and the Future of Combat (2002).
- Ivo H. Daalder, Getting to Dayton: The Making of America's Bosnia Policy (2000).
- Aleksa Djilas, The Contested Country: Yugoslav Unity and Communist Revolution, 1919–53 (1996).
- Aleksa Djilas, Yugoslavia: Dictatorship and Disintegration (1999).
- Misha Glenny, The Balkans: Nationalism, War, and the Great Powers, 1804–1999 (2000).
- Misha Glenny, The Fall of Yugoslavia: The Third Balkan War (3d rev. ed. 1996).
- Christine Gray, *Bosnia and Herzegovina: Civil War or Inter-state Conflict? Characterization and Consequences*, Brit. Y.B. Int'l L., 1996, at 155.
- Chris Hedges, *Kosovo's Next Masters?*, Foreign Aff., May–June 1999, at 24.
- Richard Holbrooke, To End a War (1998).
- Timothy Judah, The Serbs: History, Myth and the Destruction of Yugoslavia (1997).
- Robert D. Kaplan, Balkan Ghosts: A Journey Through History (1996).
- Noel Malcolm, Bosnia: A Short History (1996).
- Noel Malcolm, Kosovo: A Short History (1999).
- David Rohde, Endgame: The Betrayal and Fall of Srebrenica: Europe's Worst Massacre Since World War II (1997).
- Laura Silber & Allan Little, Yugoslavia: Death of a Nation (1997).
- Rebecca West, Black Lamb and Grey Falcon: A Journey Through Yugoslavia (1994).

M. ICTY

- Payam Akhavan, *Enforcement of the Genocide Convention: A Challenge to Civilization*, 8 Harv. Hum. Rts. J. 229 (1995).
- Payam Akhavan, *Justice in The Hague, Peace in the Former Yugoslavia? A Commentary on the United Nations War Crimes Tribunal*, 20 Hum. Rts. Q. 737 (1998).
- Payam Akhavan, *Punishing War Crimes in the Former Yugoslavia: A Critical Juncture for the New World Order*, 15 Hum. Rts. Q. 262 (1993).

- Payam Akhavan, *The Yugoslav Tribunal at a Crossroads: The Dayton Peace Agreement and Beyond*, 18 HUM. RTS. Q. 259 (1996).
- Louise Arbour, *The Crucial Years*, 2 J. INT'L CRIM. JUST. 396 (2004).
- Gary Jonathan Bass, *Milosevic in the Hague*, FOREIGN AFF., May–June 2003, at 82.
- M. Cherif Bassiouni, *The United Nations Commission of Experts Established Pursuant to Security Council Resolution 780* (1992), 88 AM. J. INT'L L. 784 (1994).
- Andrew Bell-Fialkoff, *A Brief History of Ethnic Cleansing*, FOREIGN AFF., Summer 1993, at 110.
- MICHAEL BROWN, THE TRIAL OF SLOBODAN MILOSEVIC (2004).
- Antonio Cassese, *The ICTY: A Living and Vital Reality*, 2 J. INT'L CRIM. JUST. 585 (2004).
- NORMAN CIGAR & PAUL WILLIAMS, INDICTMENT AT THE HAGUE: THE MILOŠEVIĆ REGIME AND CRIMES OF THE BALKAN WARS (2002).
- HANS CORELL, PROPOSAL FOR AN INTERNATIONAL WAR CRIMES TRIBUNAL FOR THE FORMER YUGOSLAVIA (1993).
- Anthony D'Amato, *Peace vs. Accountability in Bosnia*, 88 AM. J. INT'L L. 500 (1994).
- SLAVENKA DRAKULIC, THEY WOULD NEVER HURT A FLY: WAR CRIMINALS ON TRIAL IN THE HAGUE (2004).
- ALEKSANDER FATIĆ, RECONCILIATION VIA THE WAR CRIMES TRIBUNAL? (2000).
- Richard Goldstone, *A View from the Prosecution*, 2 J. INT'L CRIM. JUST. 380 (2004).
- JOHN HAGAN, JUSTICE IN THE BALKANS: PROSECUTING WAR CRIMES IN THE HAGUE TRIBUNAL (2003).
- PIERRE HAZAN, JUSTICE IN A TIME OF WAR: THE TRUE STORY BEHIND THE INTERNATIONAL CRIMINAL TRIBUNAL FOR THE FORMER YUGOSLAVIA (James Thomas Snyder trans., 2004).
- Larry D. Johnson, *Ten Years Later: Reflections on the Drafting*, 2 J. INT'L CRIM. JUST. 368 (2004).
- RACHEL KERR, THE INTERNATIONAL CRIMINAL TRIBUNAL FOR THE FORMER YUGOSLAVIA: AN EXERCISE IN LAW, POLITICS, AND DIPLOMACY (2004).
- ADAM LeBOR, MILOSEVIC: A BIOGRAPHY (2004).
- KARINE LESCURE, INTERNATIONAL JUSTICE FOR FORMER YUGOSLAVIA: THE WORKINGS OF THE INTERNATIONAL CRIMINAL TRIBUNAL OF THE HAGUE (1996).
- Gabrielle Kirk McDonald, *Problems, Obstacles and Achievements of the ICTY*, 2 J. INT'L CRIM. JUST. 558 (2004).
- Theodor Meron, *Answering for War Crimes: Lessons from the Balkans*, FOREIGN AFF., Jan.–Feb. 2001, at 2.
- Theodor Meron, *The Case for War Crimes Trials in Yugoslavia*, FOREIGN AFF., Summer 1993, at 122.
- Theodor Meron, *War Crimes in Yugoslavia and the Development of International Law*, 88 AM. J. INT'L L. 78 (1994).
- THE MILOŠEVIĆ TRIAL: AN AUTOPSY (Timothy William Waters ed., 2014).
- VIRGINIA MORRIS & MICHAEL P. SCHARF, AN INSIDER'S GUIDE TO THE INTERNATIONAL CRIMINAL TRIBUNAL FOR THE FORMER YUGOSLAVIA (1995).
- James C. O'Brien, *The International Tribunal for Violations of International Humanitarian Law in the Former Yugoslavia*, 87 AM. J. INT'L L. 639 (1993).

- Victor Peskin & Mieczysław P. Boduszyński, *International Justice and Domestic Politics: Post-Tudjman Croatia and the International Criminal Tribunal for the Former Yugoslavia*, 55 Eur.–Asia Stud. 1117 (2003).
- Michael P. Scharf, Balkan Justice: The Story Behind the First International War Crimes Trial Since Nuremberg (1997).
- Michael P. Scharf & William A. Schabas, Slobodan Milosevic on Trial: A Companion (2002).
- David J. Scheffer, *Three Memories from the Year of Origin, 1993*, 2 J. Int'l Crim. Just. 353 (2004).
- Minna Schrag, *Lessons Learned from ICTY Experience*, 2 J. Int'l Crim. Just. 427 (2004).
- Daphna Shraga & Ralph Zacklin, *The International Criminal Tribunal for the Former Yugoslavia*, 5 Eur. J. Int'l L. 360 (1994).
- Chris Stephen, Judgement Day: The Trial of Slobodan Milošević (2004).
- Ninian Stephen, *A Viable International Mechanism*, 2 J. Int'l Crim. Just. 385 (2004).
- Eric Stover, The Witnesses: War Crimes and the Promise of Justice in The Hague (2005).
- Paul C. Szasz, *The Proposed War Crimes Tribunal for Ex-Yugoslavia*, 25 N.Y.U. J. Int'l L. & Pol. 405 (1993).
- United Nations, ICTY, The Path to the Hague: Selected Documents on the Origins of the ICTY (1996).
- United States Congress, Commission on Security and Cooperation in Europe, The War Crimes Trials for the Former Yugoslavia: Prospects and Problems (1996).
- Luisa Vierucci, *The First Steps of the International Criminal Tribunal for the Former Yugoslavia*, 6 Eur. J. Int'l L. 134 (1995).
- L.C. Vohrah, *Some Insights into the Early Years*, 2 J. Int'l Crim. Just. 388 (2004).
- Patricia M. Wald, *ICTY Judicial Proceedings: An Appraisal from Within*, 2 J. Int'l Crim. Just. 466 (2004).
- Paul R. Williams & Michael P. Scharf, Peace with Justice?: War Crimes and Accountability in the Former Yugoslavia (2002).
- The "Yugoslav" Crisis in International Law (Daniel Bethlehem & Marc Weller eds., 1997).
- Ralph Zacklin, *Some Major Problems in the Drafting of the ICTY Statute*, 2 J. Int'l Crim. Just. 361 (2004).

N. RWANDA

- African Rights, Rwanda: Death, Despair, and Defiance (rev. ed. 1995).
- African Rights, Rwanda: Killing the Evidence: Murder, Attacks, Arrests, and Intimidation of Survivors and Witnesses (1996).
- African Rights, Rwanda: Not so Innocent: When Women Become Killers (1995).
- After Genocide: Transitional Justice, Post-conflict Reconstruction, and Reconciliation in Rwanda and Beyond (Phil Clark & Zachary D. Kaufman eds., 2009) (republished 2013 by Oxford University Press).

- José E. Alvarez, *Crimes of State/Crimes of Hate: Lessons from Rwanda*, 24 YALE J. INT'L L. 365 (1999).
- MICHAEL BARNETT, EYEWITNESS TO A GENOCIDE: THE UNITED NATIONS AND RWANDA (2002).
- James Bennett, *Clinton Declares U.S. and the World Failed Rwandans*, N.Y. TIMES, Mar. 26, 1998, at A1.
- JOHN A. BERRY & CAROL POTT BERRY, GENOCIDE IN RWANDA: A COLLECTIVE MEMORY (1999).
- Boutros Boutros-Ghali, *Introduction* to UNITED NATIONS DEP'T OF PUB. INFORMATION, THE UNITED NATIONS AND RWANDA, 1993–96, at 3 (1996).
- Phil Clark & Zachary D. Kaufman, *After Genocide*, *in* AFTER GENOCIDE: TRANSITIONAL JUSTICE, POST-CONFLICT RECONSTRUCTION, AND RECONCILIATION IN RWANDA AND BEYOND 1, 1–19 (Phil Clark & Zachary D. Kaufman eds., 2009).
- Phil Clark & Zachary D. Kaufman, *Rwanda: Recent History*, *in* AFRICA SOUTH OF THE SAHARA 2016, 969 (Iain Frame ed., 2015).
- Phil Clark & Zachary D. Kaufman, *Rwanda: Recent History*, *in* AFRICA SOUTH OF THE SAHARA 2015, 971 (Iain Frame ed., 2014).
- Phil Clark & Zachary D. Kaufman, *Rwanda: Recent History*, *in* AFRICA SOUTH OF THE SAHARA 2014, 980 (Iain Frame ed., 2013).
- Phil Clark & Zachary D. Kaufman, *Rwanda: Recent History*, *in* AFRICA SOUTH OF THE SAHARA 2013, 984 (Iain Frame ed., 2012).
- Phil Clark & Zachary D. Kaufman, *Rwanda: Recent History*, *in* AFRICA SOUTH OF THE SAHARA 2012, 993 (Iain Frame ed., 2011).
- Phil Clark & Zachary D. Kaufman, *Rwanda: Recent History*, *in* AFRICA SOUTH OF THE SAHARA 2011, 977 (Iain Frame ed., 2010).
- Phil Clark & Zachary D. Kaufman, *Rwanda: Recent History*, *in* AFRICA SOUTH OF THE SAHARA 2010, 968 (Iain Frame ed., 2009).
- Phil Clark & Zachary D. Kaufman, *Rwanda: Recent History*, *in* AFRICA SOUTH OF THE SAHARA 2009, 924 (Iain Frame ed., 2008).
- Phil Clark & Zachary D. Kaufman, *Rwanda: Recent History*, *in* AFRICA SOUTH OF THE SAHARA 2008, 927 (Iain Frame ed., 2007).
- Phil Clark & Zachary D. Kaufman, *Rwanda: Recent History*, *in* AFRICA SOUTH OF THE SAHARA 2007, 935 (Iain Frame ed., 2006).
- ROMÉO DALLAIRE, SHAKE HANDS WITH THE DEVIL: THE FAILURE OF HUMANITY IN RWANDA (2003).
- Roméo Dallaire et al., *The Major Powers on Trial*, 3 J. INT'L CRIM. JUST. 861 (2005).
- ALISON DES FORGES, LEAVE NONE TO TELL THE STORY: GENOCIDE IN RWANDA (1999).
- ALAIN DESTEXHE, RWANDA AND GENOCIDE IN THE TWENTIETH CENTURY (Alison Marschner trans., 1995).
- Mark Drumbl, *Sclerosis: Retributive Justice and the Rwandan Genocide*, 2 PUNISHMENT & SOC'Y 287 (2000).
- NIGEL ELTRINGHAM, ACCOUNTING FOR HORROR: POST-GENOCIDE DEBATES IN RWANDA (2004).
- JOHN ERIKSSON, THE INTERNATIONAL RESPONSE TO CONFLICT AND GENOCIDE: LESSONS FROM THE RWANDA EXPERIENCE (1996), *available at* http://pdf.usaid.gov/pdf_docs/PNACG921.pdf.

- Scott R. Feil, Preventing Genocide: How the Early Use of Force Might Have Succeeded in Rwanda (1998).
- Lee Ann Fujii, Killing Neighbors: Webs of Violence in Rwanda (2009).
- Philip Gourevitch, We Wish to Inform You That Tomorrow We Will Be Killed with Our Families: Stories from Rwanda (1998).
- Fred Grünfeld & Anke Huijboom, The Failure to Prevent Genocide in Rwanda: The Role of Bystanders (2007).
- Jean Hatzfeld, The Antelope's Strategy: Living in Rwanda After the Genocide (Linda Coverdale trans., 2009).
- Jean Hatzfeld, Into the Quick of Life: The Rwandan Genocide: The Survivors Speak (Gerry Feehily trans., 2005).
- Jean Hatzfeld, Machete Season: The Killers in Rwanda Speak (Linda Coverdale trans., 2005).
- Immaculée Ilibagiza, Left to Tell: Discovering God Amidst the Rwandan Holocaust (2006).
- Joshua James Kassner, Rwanda and the Moral Obligation of Humanitarian Intervention (2012).
- Zachary D. Kaufman, *Transitional Justice as Genocide Prevention: From a Culture of Impunity to a Culture of Accountability, in* Confronting Genocide in Rwanda: Dehumanization, Denial, and Strategies for Prevention 363 (Jean-Damascène Gasanabo et al. eds., 2014).
- Zachary D. Kaufman & Pierre-Richard St. Hilaire, *The Rwandan Experience, in* Rwanda and South Africa in Dialogue: Addressing the Legacies of Genocide and a Crime Against Humanity 41 (Charles Villa-Vicencio & Tyrone Savage eds., 2001).
- Fergal Keane, Season of Blood: A Rwandan Journey (1995).
- Arthur Jay Klinghoffer, The International Dimension of Genocide in Rwanda (1998).
- Alan J. Kuperman, The Limits of Humanitarian Intervention: Genocide in Rwanda (2001).
- Alan J. Kuperman, *Rwanda in Retrospect*, Foreign Aff., Jan.–Feb. 2000, at 94.
- Neil A. Lewis, *Papers Show U.S. Knew of Genocide in Rwanda*, N.Y. Times, Aug. 22, 2001, at A5.
- Paul J. Magnarella, *The Background and Causes of the Genocide in Rwanda*, 3 J. Int'l Crim. Just. 801 (2005).
- Linda Melvern, Conspiracy to Murder: The Rwandan Genocide and the International Community (rev. ed. 2006).
- Linda Melvern, A People Betrayed: The Role of the West in Rwanda's Genocide (2d ed. 2009).
- Jamie Frederic Metzl, *Rwandan Genocide and the International Law of Radio Jamming*, 91 Am. J. Int'l L. 628 (1997).
- Larry Minear & Philippe Guillot, Soldiers to the Rescue: Humanitarian Lessons from Rwanda (1996).
- Jean Mukimbiri, *The Seven Stages of the Rwandan Genocide*, 3 J. Int'l Crim. Just. 823 (2005).
- Louise Mushikiwabo & Jack Kramer, Rwanda Means the Universe: A Native's Memoir of Blood and Bloodlines (2006).

- ORGANIZATION OF AFRICAN UNITY, RWANDA: THE PREVENTABLE GENOCIDE (2000), *available at* http://www.refworld.org/pdfid/4d1da8752.pdf.
- NICOLA PALMER, COURTS IN CONFLICT: INTERPRETING THE LAYERS OF JUSTICE IN POST-GENOCIDE RWANDA (2015).
- THE PATH OF A GENOCIDE: THE RWANDA CRISIS FROM UGANDA TO ZAIRE (Howard Adelman & Astri Suhrke eds., 1999).
- GÉRARD PRUNIER, AFRICA'S WORLD WAR: CONGO, THE RWANDAN GENOCIDE, AND THE MAKING OF A CONTINENTAL CATASTROPHE (2009).
- GÉRARD PRUNIER, THE RWANDA CRISIS, 1959–94: HISTORY OF A GENOCIDE (2d ed. 1998).
- REMAKING RWANDA: STATE BUILDING AND HUMAN RIGHTS AFTER MASS VIOLENCE (Scott Straus & Lars Waldorf eds., 2011).
- David J. Scheffer, *Lessons from the Rwandan Genocide*, GEO. J. INT'L AFF., Summer–Fall 2004, at 125.
- SCOTT STRAUS, THE ORDER OF GENOCIDE: RACE, POWER, AND WAR IN RWANDA (2006).
- UNITED NATIONS, THE UNITED NATIONS AND RWANDA: 1993–96 (1996).
- THE US AND THE GENOCIDE IN RWANDA 1994: EVIDENCE OF INACTION (William Ferroggiaro ed., 2001), *available at* http://nsarchive.gwu.edu/NSAEBB/NSAEBB53/press.html.
- U.S. INST. PEACE, RWANDA: ACCOUNTABILITY FOR WAR CRIMES AND GENOCIDE (1995), *available at* http://www.usip.org/publications/rwanda-accountability-war-crimes-and-genocide.
- PETER UVIN, AIDING VIOLENCE: THE DEVELOPMENT ENTERPRISE IN RWANDA (1998).
- Peter Uvin, *Prejudice, Crisis, and Genocide in Rwanda*, AFR. STUD. REV., Sept. 1997, at 91.
- ANDREW WALLIS, SILENT ACCOMPLICE: THE UNTOLD STORY OF FRANCE'S ROLE IN THE RWANDAN GENOCIDE (rev. ed. 2014).

O. ICTR

- Payam Akhavan, *The International Criminal Tribunal for Rwanda: The Politics and Pragmatics of Punishment*, 90 AM. J. INT'L L. 501 (1996).
- Payam Akhavan, *Justice and Reconciliation in the Great Lakes Region: The Contribution of the International Criminal Tribunal for Rwanda*, 7 DUKE J. COMP. & INT'L L. 325 (1997).
- Cécile Aptel, *The International Criminal Tribunal for Rwanda*, 1997 INT'L REV. RED CROSS 605.
- Olivier Dubois, *Rwanda's National Criminal Courts and the International Tribunal*, 1997 INT'L REV. RED CROSS 717.
- Gerhard Erasmus & Nadine Fourie, *The International Criminal Tribunal for Rwanda: Are All Issues Addressed? How Does It Compare to South Africa's Truth and Reconciliation Commission?*, 1997 INT'L REV. RED CROSS 705.
- Frederik Harhoff, *The Rwanda Tribunal: A Representation of Some Legal Aspects*, 1997 INT'L REV. RED CROSS 665.
- Jaana Karhilo, *The Establishment of the International Tribunal for Rwanda*, 64 NORDIC J. INT'L L. 683 (1995).

- Zachary D. Kaufman, *International Criminal Tribunal for Rwanda, in* THE ENCYCLOPEDIA OF TRANSITIONAL JUSTICE ;233 (Lavinia Stan & Nadya Nedelsky eds., 2012).
- Zachary D. Kaufman, *The United States Role in the Establishment of the United Nations International Criminal Tribunal for Rwanda, in* AFTER GENOCIDE: TRANSITIONAL JUSTICE, POST-CONFLICT RECONSTRUCTION, AND RECONCILIATION IN RWANDA AND BEYOND 229 (Phil Clark & Zachary D. Kaufman eds., 2009).
- Roy S. Lee, *The Rwanda Tribunal,* 9 LEIDEN J. INT'L L. 37 (1996).
- PAUL J. MAGNARELLA, JUSTICE IN AFRICA: RWANDA'S GENOCIDE, ITS COURTS, AND THE UN CRIMINAL TRIBUNAL (2000).
- KINGLSEY MOGHALU, RWANDA'S GENOCIDE: THE POLITICS OF GLOBAL JUSTICE (2005).
- VIRGINIA MORRIS & MICHAEL P. SCHARF, THE INTERNATIONAL CRIMINAL TRIBUNAL FOR RWANDA (1998).
- Erik Møse, *Main Achievements of the ICTR,* 3 J. INT'L CRIM. JUST. 920 (2005).
- Victor Peskin, *Conflicts of Justice—An Analysis of the Role of the International Criminal Tribunal for Rwanda,* INT'L PEACEKEEPING, July–Dec. 2000, at 128.
- Victor Peskin, *Courting Rwanda: The Promises and Pitfalls of the ICTR Outreach Programme,* 3 J. INT'L CRIM. JUST. 950 (2005).
- Victor Peskin, *Rwandan Ghosts,* LEGAL AFF., Sept.–Oct. 2002, at 21.
- William A. Schabas, *Anti-complementarity: Referral to National Jurisdictions by the UN International Criminal Tribunal for Rwanda,* MAX PLANCK Y.B. U.N. L., 2009, at 29.
- Michael P. Scharf, *Responding to Rwanda: Accountability Mechanisms in the Aftermath of Genocide,* 52 J. INT'L AFF. 621 (1999).
- Daphna Shraga & Ralph Zacklin, *The International Criminal Tribunal for Rwanda,* 7 EUR. J. INT'L L. 501 (1996).
- Lyal S. Sunga, *The Commission of Experts on Rwanda and the Creation of the International Criminal Tribunal for Rwanda,* 16 HUM. RTS. L.J. 121 (1995).
- DINA TEMPLE-RASTON, JUSTICE ON THE GRASS: THREE RWANDAN JOURNALISTS, THEIR TRIAL FOR WAR CRIMES, AND A NATION'S QUEST FOR REDEMPTION (2005).
- Brenda Sue Thornton, *The International Criminal Tribunal for Rwanda: A Report from the Field,* 52 J. INT'L AFF. 639 (1999).
- L. J. VAN DEN HERIK, THE CONTRIBUTION OF THE RWANDA TRIBUNAL TO THE DEVELOPMENT OF INTERNATIONAL LAW (2005).
- Mariann Meier Wang, *The International Criminal Tribunal for Rwanda: Opportunities for Clarification, Opportunities for Impact,* 27 COLUM. HUM. RTS. L. REV. 177 (1995).
- Djiena Wembou, *The International Criminal Tribunal for Rwanda: Its Role in the African Context,* 1997 INT'L REV. RED CROSS 685.

P. GACACA

- AFRICAN RIGHTS, GACACA JUSTICE: A SHARED RESPONSIBILITY (2003).
- AMNESTY INT'L, RWANDA: GACACA: A QUESTION OF JUSTICE (2002), *available at* http://www.amnesty.org/en/documents/AFR47/007/2002/en/.
- PHIL CLARK, THE GACACA COURTS, POST-GENOCIDE JUSTICE AND RECONCILIATION IN RWANDA: JUSTICE WITHOUT LAWYERS (2010).

- Phil Clark, *The Rules (and Politics) of Engagement: The Gacaca Courts and Post-Genocide Justice, Healing, and Reconciliation in Rwanda, in* AFTER GENOCIDE: TRANSITIONAL JUSTICE, POST-CONFLICT RECONSTRUCTION, AND RECONCILIATION IN RWANDA AND BEYOND 297 (Phil Clark & Zachary D. Kaufman eds., 2009).
- Phil Clark, *When the Killers Go Home: Local Justice in Rwanda*, DISSENT, Summer 2005, at 14.
- Helena Cobban, *The Legacies of Collective Violence: The Rwandan Genocide and the Limits of Law*, BOSTON REV. (Apr.–May 2002), *available at* http://new.bostonreview.net/BR27.2/cobban.html.
- Allison Corey & Sandra F. Joireman, *Retributive Justice: The* Gacaca *Courts in Rwanda*, 103 AFRICAN AFF. 73 (2004).
- Erin Daly, *Between Punitive Justice and Reconstructive Justice: The Gacaca Courts in Rwanda*, 34 N.Y.U. J. IN'TL L. & POL. 355 (2002).
- Alison Des Forges & Kenneth Roth, *Justice or Therapy*, BOSTON REV. (Summer 2002), available at http://new.bostonreview.net/BR27.3/rothdesForges.html (reviewing Helena Cobban, *The Legacies of Collective Violence: The Rwandan Genocide and the Limits of Law*, BOSTON REV. (Apr.–May 2002), *available at* http://new.bostonreview.net/BR27.2/cobban.html)).
- Jacques Fierens, Gacaca *Courts: Between Fantasy and Reality*, 3 J. INT'L CRIM. JUST. 896 (2005).
- PETER E. HARRELL, RWANDA'S GAMBLE: GACACA AND THE NEW MODEL OF TRANSITIONAL JUSTICE (2003).
- George Packer, *Justice on a Hill: Genocide Trials in Rwanda*, DISSENT, Spring 2002, at 59.
- William A. Schabas, *Genocide Trials and* Gacaca *Courts*, 3 J. INT'L CRIM. JUST. 879 (2005).
- Danielle L. Tully, *Human Rights Compliance and the Gacaca Jurisdictions in Rwanda*, 26 B.C. INT'L & COMP. L. REV. 385 (2003).
- Peter Uvin, *The Gacaca Tribunals in Rwanda (Case Study), in* RECONCILIATION AFTER VIOLENT CONFLICT: A HANDBOOK 116, 116–21 (D. Bloomfield et al. eds., 2003).
- Aneta Wierzynska, *Consolidating Democracy Through Transitional Justice: Rwanda's Gacaca Courts*, 79 N.Y.U. L. REV. 1934 (2004).

Q. ICC

- TIM ALLEN, TRIAL JUSTICE: THE INTERNATIONAL CRIMINAL COURT AND THE LORD'S RESISTANCE ARMY (2006).
- Mahnoush H. Arsanjani, *The Rome Statute of the International Criminal Court,* 93 AM. J. INT'L L. 22 (1999).
- M. Cherif Bassiouni, *Establishing an International Criminal Court: Historical Survey,* 149 MIL. L. REV. 49 (1995).
- M. Cherif Bassiouni, *From Versailles to Rwanda in Seventy-Five Years: The Need to Establish a Permanent International Criminal Court,* 10 HARV. HUM. RTS. J. 11 (1997).
- DAVID BOSCO, ROUGH JUSTICE: THE INTERNATIONAL CRIMINAL COURT IN A WORLD OF POWER POLITICS (2014).

- Bruce Broomhall, International Justice and the International Criminal Court: Between Sovereignty and the Rule of Law (2003).
- Matthew R. Brubacher, *Prosecutorial Discretion Within the International Criminal Court*, 2 J. Int'l Crim. Just. 71 (2004).
- Douglass Cassel, *Empowering United States Courts to Hear Crimes Within the Jurisdiction of the International Criminal Court*, 35 New Eng. L. Rev. 421 (2001).
- Commentary on the Rome Statute of the International Criminal Court (Otto Triffterer ed., 1999).
- Council on Foreign Relations, Toward an International Criminal Court? (1999).
- Courting Conflict? Justice, Peace and the ICC in Africa (Phil Clark & Nicholas Waddell eds., 2008).
- James Crawford, *The ILC Adopts a Statute for an International Criminal Court*, 89 Am. J. Int'l L. 404 (1995).
- Allison Marston Danner, *Enhancing the Legitimacy and Accountability of Prosecutorial Discretion at the International Criminal Court*, 97 Am. J. Int'l L. 510 (2003).
- Zsuzsanna Deen-Racsmany, *The Nationality of the Offender and the Jurisdiction of the International Criminal Court*, 95 Am. J. Int'l L. 606 (2001).
- Essays on the Rome Statute of the International Criminal Court (Flavia Lattanzi & William A. Schabas eds., 1999).
- Lee Feinstein & Tod Lindberg, Means to an End: U.S. Interest in the International Criminal Court (2009).
- Benjamin B. Ferencz, An International Criminal Court, a Step Toward World Peace: A Documentary History and Analysis (1980).
- George A. Finch, *Draft Statute for an International Criminal Court*, 46 Am. J. Int'l L. 89 (1952).
- Michael J. Gilligan, *Is Enforcement Necessary for Effectiveness? A Model of the International Criminal Regime*, 60 Int'l Org. 935 (2006).
- Jack Goldsmith, *The Self-Defeating International Criminal Court*, 70 U. Chi. L. Rev. 89 (2003).
- Manley O. Hudson, *The Proposed International Criminal Court*, 32 Am. J. Int'l L. 549 (1938).
- David Hunt, *The International Criminal Court*, 2 J. Int'l Crim. Just. 56 (2004).
- International Crimes, Peace, and Human Rights: The Role of the International Criminal Court (Dinah Shelton ed., 2000).
- The International Criminal Court: Elements of Crimes and Rules of Procedure and Evidence (Roy S. Lee ed., 2001).
- The International Criminal Court: The Making of the Rome Statute— Issues, Negotiations, Results (Roy S. Lee ed., 1999).
- Claude Jorda, *The Major Hurdles and Accomplishments of the ICC: What the ICC Can Learn from Them*, 2 J. Int'l Crim. Just. 572 (2004).
- Zachary D. Kaufman, *The United States, Syria, and the International Criminal Court: Implications of the Rome Statute's Aggression Amendment*, 55 Harv. Int'l L.J. Online 35 (2013).
- Zachary D. Kaufman, *Justice in Jeopardy: Accountability for the Darfur Atrocities*, 16 Crim. L.F. 343 (2006).

- Zachary D. Kaufman, *Sudan, the United States, and the International Criminal Court: A Tense Triumvirate in Transitional Justice for Darfur, in* THE CRIMINAL LAW OF GENOCIDE: INTERNATIONAL, COMPARATIVE AND CONTEXTUAL ASPECTS 49 (Ralph Henham & Paul Benhrens eds., 2007).
- Philippe Kirsch & John T. Holmes, *The Rome Conference on an International Criminal Court: The Negotiating Process*, 93 AM. J. INT'L L. 2 (1999).
- Monroe Leigh, *Evaluating Present Options for an International Criminal Court*, 149 MIL. L. REV. 113 (1995).
- Howard S. Levie, *Evaluating Present Options for an International Criminal Court*, 149 MIL. L. REV. 129 (1995).
- Daryl A. Mundis, *The Assembly of States Parties and the Institutional Framework of the International Criminal Court*, 97 AM. J. INT'L L. 132 (2003).
- Vespasian V. Pella, *Towards an International Criminal Court,* 44 AM. J. INT'L L. 37 (1950).
- THE ROME STATUTE OF THE INTERNATIONAL CRIMINAL COURT: A CHALLENGE TO IMPUNITY (Mauro Politi & Giuseppe Nesi eds., 2001).
- THE ROME STATUTE OF THE INTERNATIONAL CRIMINAL COURT: A COMMENTARY (Antonio Cassese et al. eds., 2002).
- LEILA NADYA SADAT, THE INTERNATIONAL CRIMINAL COURT AND THE TRANSFORMATION OF INTERNATIONAL LAW: JUSTICE FOR THE NEW MILLENNIUM (2002).
- William A. Schabas, *First Prosecutions at the International Criminal Court,* 25 HUM. RTS. L.J. 25 (2006).
- WILLIAM A. SCHABAS, THE INTERNATIONAL CRIMINAL COURT: A COMMENTARY ON THE ROME STATUTE (2010).
- WILLIAM A. SCHABAS, AN INTRODUCTION TO THE INTERNATIONAL CRIMINAL COURT (4th ed. 2011).
- William A. Schabas, *United States Hostility to the International Criminal Court: It's All About the Security Council*, 15 EUR. J. INT'L L. 701 (2004).
- Beth Simmons & Allison Danner, *Credible Commitments and the International Criminal Court*, 64 INT'L ORG. 225 (2010).
- Janice Simpson & Richard J. Goldstone, *Evaluating the Role of the International Criminal Court as a Legal Response to Terrorism*, 16 HARV. HUM. RTS. J. 13 (2003).
- Francisco Orrego Vicuña, *The International Criminal Court and the In and Out Club*, 2 J. INT'L CRIM. JUST. 35 (2004).
- Quincy Wright, *Proposal for an International Criminal Court*, 46 AM. J. INT'L L. 60 (1952).

R. INTERNATIONAL CITIZENS' WAR CRIMES TRIBUNALS

- Arthur S. Blaser, *How to Advance Human Rights Without Really Trying,* 14 HUM. RTS. Q. 339 (1992).
- Christine M. Chinkin, *Women's International Tribunal on Japanese Military Sexual Slavery,* 95 AM. J. INT'L L. 335 (2001).
- Zachary D. Kaufman, *Transitional Justice Delayed Is Not Transitional Justice Denied: Contemporary Confrontation of Japanese Human Experimentation During World War II Through a People's Tribunal*, 26 YALE L. & POL'Y REV. 645 (2008).
- Arthur Jay Klinghoffer, *International Citizens' Tribunals on Human Rights, in* GENOCIDE, WAR CRIMES AND THE WEST (Adam Jacobs ed., 2004).

- Arthur Jay Klinghoffer & Judith Klinghoffer, International Citizens' Tribunals: Mobilizing Public Opinion to Advance Human Rights (2002).

s. truth commissions

- Alex Boraine, A Country Unmasked: Inside South Africa's Truth and Reconciliation Commission (2000).
- Jamed Edward Beitler, Remaking Transitional Justice in the United States: The Rhetorical Authorization of the Greensboro Truth and Reconciliation Commission (2013).
- Mark Freeman, Truth Commissions and Procedural Fairness (2006).
- Priscilla B. Hayner, *International Guidelines for the Creation and Operation of Truth Commissions: A Preliminary Proposal*, 59 Law & Contemp. Probs. 173 (1996).
- Priscilla B. Hayner, Unspeakable Truths: Transitional Justice and the Challenge of Truth Commissions (2d ed. 2011).
- Spoma Jovanovic, Democracy, Dialogue, and Community Action: Truth and Reconciliation in Greensboro (2012).
- Lisa Magarrell & Joya Wesley, Learning from Greensboro: Truth and Reconciliation in the United States (2008).
- Maine Wabanaki–State Child Welfare Truth and Reconciliation Commission, http://www.mainewabanakitrc.org (last visited July 26, 2015).
- Nelson Rolihlahla Mandela, Long Walk to Freedom: The Autobiography of Nelson Mandela (1995).
- Margaret Popkin & Naomi Roht-Arriaza, *Truth as Justice: Investigatory Commissions in Latin America*, 20 L. & Soc. Inquiry 79 (1995).
- Michael P. Scharf, *The Case for a Permanent International Truth Commission*, 7 Duke J. Comp. & Int'l L. 375 (1997).
- Carsten Stahn, *Accommodating Individual Criminal Responsibility and National Reconciliation: The UN Truth Commission for East Timor*, 95 Am. J. Int'l L. 952 (2001).
- Jonathan D. Tepperman, *Truth and Consequences,* Foreign Aff., Mar.–Apr. 2002, at 128.
- Truth v. Justice: The Morality of Truth Commissions (Robert I. Rotberg & Dennis Thompson eds., 2000).
- Desmond Mpilo Tutu, No Future Without Forgiveness (1997).
- Desmond Mpilo Tutu, The Rainbow People of God: The Making of a Peaceful Revolution (1994).

t. exile

- Zachary D. Kaufman, *The Future of Transitional Justice,* 1 St. Antony's Int'l Rev. 58, 64–65, 69–71 (2005).
- Zachary D. Kaufman, Op-Ed., *Liberia: Charles Taylor's Exile, Disappearance, Arrest, and Transfer,* Liber. Times, May 20, 2006.
- *Mengistu Defends "Red Terror,"* BBC News (Dec. 28, 1999), http://news.bbc.co.uk/2/hi/africa/581098.stm.
- *U.S. Admits Helping Mengitsu Escape*, BBC News (Dec. 22, 1999), http://news.bbc.co.uk/2/hi/africa/575405.stm.
- Tim Weiner & Lydia Polgreen, *Under Pressure, Aristide Leaves Haiti,* N.Y. Times, Feb. 29, 2004, at A1.

U. LUSTRATION

- Jon Lee Anderson, *Out on the Street,* NEW YORKER, Nov. 15, 2004, at 72.
- Erhard Blankenburg, *The Purge of Lawyers After the Breakdown of the East German Communist Regime,* 20 L. & SOC. INQUIRY 223 (1995).
- Wolf Blitzer, *From "de-Baathification" to "re-Baathification"?,* CNN.COM (Apr. 22, 2004), http://www.cnn.com/2004/US/04/22/Iraq.rebaathification/.
- TOM BOWER, BLIND EYE TO MURDER: BRITAIN, AMERICA AND THE PURGING OF NAZI GERMANY—A PLEDGE BETRAYED (1981).
- Mark S. Ellis, *Purging the Past: The Current State of Lustration Laws in the Former Communist Bloc,* 59 LAW & CONTEMP. PROBS. 181 (1996).
- CONSTANTINE FITZGIBBON, DENAZIFICATION (1969).
- Zachary D. Kaufman, *The Future of Transitional Justice,* 1 ST. ANTONY'S INT'L REV. 58, 68–69 (2005).
- Maria Los, *Lustration and Truth Claims: Unfinished Revolutions in Central Europe,* 20 L. & SOC. INQUIRY 117 (1995).
- Eric Posner, Op-Ed., *Bring Back the Baathists,* N.Y. TIMES, Apr. 28, 2004, at A21.
- Eric Schmitt, *U.S. Generals Fault Ban on Hussein's Party,* N.Y. TIMES, Apr. 20, 2004, at A11.
- Herman Schwartz, *Lustration in Eastern Europe, in* TRANSITIONAL JUSTICE: HOW EMERGING DEMOCRACIES RECKON WITH FORMER REGIMES. VOLUME I: GENERAL CONSIDERATIONS 461 (Neil J. Kritz ed., 1995).
- Peter Siegelman, *The Problems of Lustration: Prosecution of Wrongdoers by Democratic Successor Regimes,* 20 L. & SOC. INQUIRY 1 (1995).
- Arthur L. Stinchcombe, *Lustration as a Problem of the Social Basis of Constitutionalism,* 20 L. & SOC. INQUIRY 245 (1995).

V. AMNESTY

- Roman Boed, *The Effect of a Domestic Amnesty on the Ability of Foreign States to Prosecute Alleged Perpetrators of Serious Human Rights Violations,* 33 CORNELL INT'L L.J. 297 (2000).
- Charles Krauthammer, Op-Ed., *Amnesty for Insurgents? Yes,* WASH. POST, June 30, 2006, at A27.
- Robert J. Quinn, *Will the Rule of Law End? Challenging Grants of Amnesty for the Human Rights Violations of a Prior Regime: Chile's New Model,* 62 FORDHAM L. REV. 905 (1993–1994).
- Naomi Roht-Arriaza & Lauren Gibson, *The Developing Jurisprudence on Amnesty,* 20 HUM. RTS. Q. 843 (1998).
- Michael P. Scharf, *Swapping Amnesty for Peace: Was There a Duty to Prosecute International Crimes in Haiti?,* 31 TEX. INT'L L.J. 1 (1996).

W. LETHAL FORCE

- ROBERT B. BAER, THE PERFECT KILL: 21 LAWS FOR ASSASSINS (2014).
- Orna Ben-Naftali & Keren R. Michaeli, *Justice-Ability: A Critique of the Alleged Non-justiciability of Israel's Policy of Targeted Killings,* 1 J. INT'L CRIM. JUST. 368 (2003).
- Louis René Beres, *On Assassination as Anticipatory Self-Defense: The Case of Israel,* 20 HOFSTRA L. REV. 321 (1991).

- *Bush Gives CIA License to Kill Terrorist Leaders*, Chi. Trib., Dec. 15, 2002, at 19.
- Daniel Byman, *Do Targeted Killings Work?*, Foreign Aff., Mar.–Apr. 2006, at 95.
- Vincent Cannistraro, *Assassination Is Wrong—And Dumb*, Wash. Post, Aug. 30, 2001, at A29.
- James W. Clarke, American Assassins: The Darker Side of Politics (1982).
- Letter from Jonathan Fanton and Kenneth Roth, Hum. Rts. Watch, to President George W. Bush, U.S. Policy on Assassinations (Sept. 20, 2001), *available at* http://www.hrw.org/press/2001/09/bushleto920.htm.
- Michael L. Gross, *Fighting by Other Means in the Mideast: A Critical Analysis of Israel's Assassination Policy*, 51 Pol. Stud. 350 (2003).
- Zachary D. Kaufman, *The Future of Transitional Justice,* 1 St. Antony's Int'l Rev. 58, 68–69 (2005).
- Joseph B. Kelly, *Assassination in Wartime*, 30 Mil. L. Rev. 101 (1965).
- Martin Kettle, *President "Ordered Murder" of Congo Leader*, Guardian (United Kingdom), Aug. 9, 2000, http://www.theguardian.com/world/2000/aug/10/martinkettle.
- James F. Kirkham et al., Assassination and Political Violence: A Report of the National Commission on the Causes and Prevention of Violence (2001).
- Linda Laucella, Assassination: The Politics of Murder (1999).
- Jonathan Masters, *Targeted Killings*, Council on Foreign Relations, May 23, 2013, http://www.cfr.org/counterterrorism/targeted-killings/p9627.
- Scott Shane, *Targeted Killing Comes to Define War on Terror*, N.Y. Times, Apr. 8, 2013, at A1.
- Daniel Statman, *The Morality of Assassination: A Response to Gross*, 51 Pol. Stud. 775 (2003).
- Targeted Killings: Law and Morality in an Asymmetrical World (Claire Finkelstein et al. eds., 2012).
- Michael Walzer, Arguing About War (2004).
- Michael Walzer, Just and Unjust Wars: A Moral Argument with Historical Illustrations (4th ed. 2006).
- Patricia Zengel, *Assassination and the Law of Armed Conflict*, 134 Mil. L. Rev. 123 (1991).
- Micah Zenko, *An Inconvenient Truth,* Foreign Pol'y (Apr. 10, 2013), http://foreign-policy.com/2013/04/10/an-inconvenient-truth/.

X. INDEFINITE DETENTION

- Karen Alonso, Korematsu v. United States: Japanese-American Internment Camps (1998).
- Roger Daniels et al., Japanese Americans, From Relocation to Redress (rev. ed. 1991).
- Fiona de Londras, Detention in the "War on Terror": Can Human Rights Fight Back? (2011).
- Peter Finn & Anne E. Kornblut, *Obama Allows Indefinite Detention*, Wash. Post, Mar. 8, 2011, at A1.
- Rachael Hanel, The Japanese American Internment (2008).

- COLLEEN E. HARDY, THE DETENTION OF UNLAWFUL ENEMY COMBATANTS DURING THE WAR ON TERROR (2009).
- BRIAN MASARU HAYASHI, DEMOCRATIZING THE ENEMY: THE JAPANESE AMERICAN INTERMENT (2004).
- PETER IRONS, JUSTICE AT WAR: THE STORY OF THE JAPANESE AMERICAN INTERNMENT CASES (1993).
- JUSTICE DELAYED: THE RECORD OF THE JAPANESE AMERICAN INTERNMENT CASES (Peter Irons ed., 1989).
- JOSEPH MARGULIES, GUANTÁNAMO AND THE ABUSE OF PRESIDENTIAL POWER (2006).
- WENDY L. NG, JAPANESE AMERICAN INTERNMENT DURING WORLD WAR II (2002).
- Vincent-Joel Proulx, *If That Hat Fits, Wear It, If That Turban Fits, Run for Your Life: Reflections on the Indefinite Detention and Targeted Killing of Suspected Terrorists*, 56 HASTINGS L.J. 801 (2005).
- GREG ROBINSON, BY ORDER OF THE PRESIDENT: FDR AND THE INTERMENT OF JAPANESE AMERICANS (2001).
- Carol Rosenberg, *Why Obama Can't Close Guantanamo*, FOREIGN AFF. (Dec. 14, 2011), https://www.foreignaffairs.com/articles/2011-12-14/why-obama-cant-close-guantanamo?cid=nlc-this_week_on_foreignaffairs_co-121511-why_obama_cant_close_guantanam_3-121511.
- ROBERT H. WAGSTAFF, TERROR DETENTIONS AND THE RULE OF LAW: US AND UK PERSPECTIVES (2013).
- MICHI WEGLYN, YEARS OF INFAMY: THE UNTOLD STORY OF AMERICA'S CONCENTRATION CAMPS (updated ed. 1996).
- BENJAMIN WITTES, DETENTION AND DENIAL: THE CASE FOR CANDOR AFTER GUANTANAMO (2011).
- Benjamin Wittes & Jack Goldsmith, *The Best Trial Option for KSM: Nothing*, WASH. POST, Mar. 19, 2010, at A23.

Y. DEMOCRATIC PEACE THEORY

- DEBATING THE DEMOCRATIC PEACE (Michael E. Brown et al. eds., 1996).
- Michael W. Doyle, *Kant, Liberal Legacies, and Foreign Affairs*, 12 PHIL. & PUB. AFF. 205 (1983).
- Michael W. Doyle, *Kant, Liberal Legacies, and Foreign Affairs, Part 2*, 16 PHIL. & PUB. AFF. 323 (1983).
- Michael W. Doyle, *Reflections on the Liberal Peace and Its Critics*, 19 INT'L SECURITY 180 (1995).
- GRASPING THE DEMOCRATIC PEACE: PRINCIPLES FOR A POST-COLD WAR WORLD (Bruce Russet ed., 1993).
- IMMANUEL KANT, PERPETUAL PEACE (1939).
- Christopher Layne, *Kant or Cant: The Myth of the Democratic Peace*, 19 INT'L SECURITY 5 (1994).
- Christopher Layne, *On the Democratic Peace*, 19 INT'L SECURITY 175 (1995).
- Edward D. Mansfield & Jack Snyder, *Democratization and the Danger of War*, 20 INT'L SECURITY 5 (1995).
- Ido Oren, *The Subjectivity of the "Democratic" Peace: Changing U.S. Perceptions of Imperial Germany*, 20 INT'L SECURITY 147 (1995).

- John M. Owen, *How Liberalism Produces Democratic Peace*, 19 INT'L SECURITY 87 (1994).
- David Spiro, *The Insignificance of the Liberal Peace*, 19 INT'L SECURITY 50 (1994).

Z. FOREIGN POLICY ANALYSIS/U.S. FOREIGN POLICY

- Kenneth W. Abbott & Duncan Snidal, *Why States Act Through Formal International Organizations*, 42 J. CONFLICT RES. 3 (1998).
- AMERICAN FOREIGN POLICY: THEORETICAL ESSAYS (G. John Ikenberry ed., 5th ed. 2004).
- W. BRIAN ARTHUR, INCREASING RETURNS AND PATH DEPENDENCE IN THE ECONOMY (1994).
- MARK BOWDEN, BLACK HAWK DOWN: A STORY OF MODERN WAR (2000).
- Holly J. Burkhalter, *The Question of Genocide: The Clinton Administration and Rwanda*, 11 WORLD POL'Y J. 44 (1994–1995).
- John P. Cerone, *Dynamic Equilibrium: The Evolution of US Attitudes Toward International Criminal Courts and Tribunals*, 18 EUR. J. INT'L L. 277 (2007).
- Chester A. Crocker, *The Lessons of Somalia*, FOREIGN AFF., May–June 1995, at 2.
- Mariano-Florentino Cuéllar, *The International Criminal Court and the Political Economy of Antitreaty Discourse*, 55 STAN. L. REV. 1597 (2003).
- MORTON HALPERIN ET AL., BUREAUCRATIC POLITICS AND FOREIGN POLICY (1974).
- Oona Hathaway, *Between Power and Principles: An Integrated Theory of International Law*, 72 U. CHI. L. REV. 469 (2005).
- ROBERT KAGAN, OF PARADISE AND POWER: AMERICA AND EUROPE IN THE NEW WORLD ORDER (2003).
- GEORGE F. KENNAN, AMERICAN DIPLOMACY (1984).
- YUEN FOONG KHONG, ANALOGIES AT WAR: KOREA, MUNICH, DIEN BIEN PHU, AND THE VIETNAM DECISIONS OF 1965 (1992).
- William Korey, *The United States and the Genocide Convention: Leading Advocate and Leading Obstacle*, 11 ETHICS & INT'L AFF. 271 (1997).
- Stanley J. Liebowitz & Stephen E. Marolis, *Path Dependence, Lock-In, and History*, 11 J.L. ECON. & ORG. 205 (1995).
- EDWARD C. LUCK, MIXED MESSAGES: AMERICAN POLITICS AND INTERNATIONAL ORGANIZATION, 1919–99 (1999).
- James Mahoney, *Path Dependence in Historical Sociology*, 29 THEORY & SOC'Y 507 (2000).
- MULTILATERALISM AND U.S. FOREIGN POLICY: AMBIVALENT ENGAGEMENT (Stewart Patrick & Shepard Forman eds., 2002).
- Daryl Mundis, *The United States of America and International Justice*, 2 J. INT'L CRIM. JUST. 2 (2004).
- Sean D. Murphy, *Contemporary Practice of the United States Relating to International Law*, 93 AM. J. INT'L L. 161 (1993).
- Ethan A. Nadelmann, *The Role of the United States in the International Enforcement of Criminal Law*, 31 HARV. INT'L L.J. 37 (1990).
- JOSEPH S. NYE, JR., THE PARADOX OF AMERICAN POWER: WHY THE WORLD'S ONLY SUPERPOWER CAN'T GO IT ALONE (2002).
- Paul Pierson, *Increasing Returns, Path Dependence, and the Study of Politics*, 94 AM. POL. SCI. REV. 251 (2000).

- Samantha Power, *Bystanders to Genocide: Why the United States Let the Rwandan Tragedy Happen*, ATL. MONTHLY, Sept. 2001, at 84.
- Samantha Power, Letter, ATL. MONTHLY, Dec. 2001, at 15.
- SAMANTHA POWER, "A PROBLEM FROM HELL": AMERICA AND THE AGE OF GENOCIDE (2002).
- W. Michael Reisman, *Learning to Deal with Rejection: The International Criminal Court and the United States*, 2 J. INT'L CRIM. JUST. 17 (2004).
- W. Michael Reisman, *The United States and International Institutions*, SURVIVAL, Winter 1999–2000, at 62.
- David J. Scheffer, *Court Order,* FOREIGN AFF., Nov.–Dec. 2001, at 201.
- David J. Scheffer, *How to Turn the Tide Using the Rome Statute's Temporal Jurisdiction*, 2 J. INT'L CRIM. JUST. 26 (2004).
- David J. Scheffer, Letter to the Editor, 95 AM. J. INT'L L. 624 (2001).
- David J. Scheffer, *A Negotiator's Perspective on the International Criminal Court*, 167 MIL. L. REV. 1 (2001).
- DAVID J. SCHEFFER, SPECIAL REPORT 78: OPTIONS FOR PROSECUTING INTERNATIONAL TERRORISTS (2001), *available at* http://www.usip.org/publications/options-prosecuting-international-terrorists.
- David J. Scheffer, *Staying the Course with the International Criminal Court*, 35 CORNELL INT'L L.J. 47 (2001–2002).
- David J. Scheffer, *The United States and the International Criminal Court*, 93 AM. J. INT'L L. 12 (1999).
- David J. Scheffer, *The U.S. Perspective on the ICC, in* THE UNITED STATES AND THE INTERNATIONAL CRIMINAL COURT: NATIONAL SECURITY AND INTERNATIONAL LAW 115 (Sarah B. Sewall & Carl Kaysen eds., 2000).
- JOHN SHATTUCK, FREEDOM ON FIRE: HUMAN RIGHTS WARS & AMERICA'S RESPONSE (2003).
- Natalie J. Sobchak, *The Aftermath of Nuremberg . . . The Problems of Suspected War Criminals in America*, 6 N.Y.L. SCH. J. HUM. RTS. 425 (1989).
- Paul Stephan, *US Constitutionalism and International Law: What the Multilateralist Move Leaves Out*, 2 J. INT'L CRIM. JUST. 11 (2004).
- THE SWORD AND THE SCALES: THE UNITED STATES AND INTERNATIONAL COURTS AND TRIBUNALS (Cesare P.R. Romano ed., 2009).
- UNILATERALISM AND U.S. FOREIGN POLICY: INTERNATIONAL PERSPECTIVES (Yuen Foong Khong & David M. Malone eds., 2003).
- THE UNITED STATES AND THE INTERNATIONAL CRIMINAL COURT: NATIONAL SECURITY AND INTERNATIONAL LAW (Sarah B. Sewall & Carl Kaysen eds., 2000).
- UNITED STATES HEGEMONY AND THE FOUNDATIONS OF INTERNATIONAL LAW (Michael Byers & Georg Nolte eds., 2003).
- US HEGEMONY AND INTERNATIONAL ORGANIZATIONS: THE UNITED STATES AND MULTILATERAL INSTITUTIONS (Rosemary Foot et al. eds., 2003).
- Patricia M. Wald, *Is the United States' Opposition to the ICC Intractable?*, 2 J. INT'L CRIM. JUST. 19 (2004).

- Ruth Wedgwood, *Fiddling in Rome: America and the International Criminal Court*, FOREIGN AFF., Nov.–Dec. 1998, at 20.
- Ruth Wedgwood, *The International Criminal Court: An American View*, 10 EUR. J. INT'L L. 93 (1999).
- Mark S. Zaid, *Will or Should the United States Ever Prosecute War Criminals?: A Need for Greater Expansion in the Areas of Both Criminal and Civil Liability*, 35 NEW ENG. L. REV. 447 (2001).

{ INDEX }